Language in the Media

Advances in Sociolinguistics

Series Editor: Professor Sally Johnson, University of Leeds

Since the emergence of sociolingustics as a new field of enquiry in the late 1960s, research into the relationship between language and society has advanced almost beyond recognition. In particular, the past decade has witnessed the considerable influence of theories drawn from outside of sociolingustics itself. Thus rather than see language as a mere reflection of society, recent work has been increasingly inspired by ideas drawn from social, cultural and political theory that have emphasized the constitutive role played by language/discourse in all areas of social life. The Advances in Sociolinguistics series seeks to provide a snapshot of the current diversity of the field of sociolinguistics and the blurring of the boundaries between sociolinguistics and other domains of study concerned with the role of language in society.

Discourses of Endangerment
Ideology and Interest in the Defence of Languages
Edited by Alexandre Duchêne and Monica Heller

Linguistic Minorities and Modernity
A Sociolinguistic Ethnography, 2nd edition
Monica Heller

Language, Culture and Identity
An Ethnolinguistic Perspective
Philip Riley

Language and Power
An Introduction to Institutional Discourse
Andrea Mayr, Bob Holland and Tony Bastow

Multilingualism
A Critical Perspective
Adrian Blackledge and Angela Creese

Media Sociolinguistics
Policy, Discourse, Practice
Helen Kelly-Holmes

Language in the Media

Representations, Identities, Ideologies

Edited by Sally Johnson and Astrid Ensslin

continuum

Continuum International Publishing Group
The Tower Building, 11 York Road, London SE1 7NX
80 Maiden Lane, Suite 704, New York, NY 10038

British Library Cataloguing-in-Publication Data
A catalogue record for this book is available from the British Library.

ISBN: HB: 0-8264-9548-6
      978-0-8264-9548-8
      0-8264-9549-4
      978-0-8264-9549-5

Library of Congress Cataloging-in-Publication Data
A catalog record for this book is available from the Library of Congress.

Typeset by Aarontype Limited, Easton, Bristol
Printed and bound in Great Britain by Antony Rowe Ltd, Chippenham, Wiltshire

Contents

Acknowledgements

The editors would like to thank a number of people for their support in the preparation of this book, not least, Siegfried Maser, Frank Finlay and Atik Baborie. We are also especially grateful to Jenny Lovel at Continuum for her consistent help and encouragement throughout the whole process of planning and production.

This volume has its origins in a conference of the same title that was held in September 2005 at the University of Leeds. We are particularly grateful to the British Academy for making funding available (ref: BCG-39950) to bring the four keynote speakers to Leeds, namely Jane Hill (Arizona), Alexandra Jaffe (California), Deborah Cameron (Oxford) and Elena Semino (Lancaster).

Finally, the editors and authors would like to express their gratitude to the following organizations and individuals for permission to reproduce various items in individual chapters:

- *Der Spiegel* for the front cover image contained in Chapter 6 by Sally Johnson;
- King Features for the ZITS cartoon and CartoonStock Ltd for the two cartoons on text messaging in Chapter 11 by Crispin Thurlow; and
- Ursula Hentschläger and Zelko Wiener (Zeitgenossen), Robert Kendall, Ursula Menzer and Urs Schreiber for extracts from the poems contained in Chapter 13 by Astrid Ensslin.

Notes on contributors

David Atkinson is Senior Lecturer in Spanish at the University of Limerick, Ireland. His previous publications include *Language and Power in the Modern World* (EUP and University of Alabama Press, 2003 – with Mary Talbot and Karen Atkinson) and articles on aspects of the politics of language in Catalonia in journals such as *International Journal of Iberian Studies, Current Issues in Language and Society, Journal of Multilingual and Multicultural Development, Journal of Language and Politics* and *Journal of Language Problems and Language Planning*. Email: david.atkinson@ul.ie.

Deborah Cameron is Rupert Murdoch Professor of Language and Communication at Oxford University, UK. Her research interests include language, gender and sexuality and language ideologies. Among her previous publications are *Verbal Hygiene* (Routledge, 1995), *Language and Sexuality* (Cambridge University Press, 2003 – with Don Kulick) and *On Language and Sexual Politics* (Routledge, 2006). Email: deborah.cameron@worc.ox.ac.uk.

Astrid Ensslin is Lecturer in New Media at the National Institute for Excellence in the Creative Industries at the University of Wales, Bangor. Her main research interests are in the areas of media stylistics and semiotics, discourse analysis, (historical) corpus linguistics and sociolinguistics (language attitudes, metalanguage and gender). Her publications include *Canonizing Hypertext: Explorations and Constructions* (Continuum, 2007), as well as articles in *Language and Literature, Journal of Literature and Aesthetics, Gender and Language, Journal of Gender Studies*, and *Corpora*. She is currently working on a co-edited special issue of *Dichtung Digital* for 2007 (with Alice Bell) and is founding editor of the *MHRA Working Papers in the Humanities*. Email: a.ensslin@bangor.ac.uk.

Simon Gieve is a Lecturer in Applied Linguistics and TESOL in the School of Education at the University of Leicester, UK. His main research interests are in classroom language learning, language teacher education, and interaction across linguistic difference. He has previously co-edited a book with Ines Miller on *Understanding the Language Classroom* (Palgrave Macmillan, 2006). Email: sng5@leicester.ac.uk.

John Heywood is a PhD student and part-time tutor in stylistics at Lancaster University, UK. His PhD is concerned with integrating discourse and stylistic analysis, focusing on how written style performs sexuality and gender and produces non-fiction. He has worked as a Research Associate with Mick Short, Elena Semino and Dan McIntyre on corpus investigations into 'Speech & Thought Presentation and Metaphor'. Email: j.heywood @lancaster.ac.uk.

Jane H. Hill is Regents' Professor of Anthropology and Linguistics at the University of Arizona, USA. She is a specialist on Native American languages, especially Uto-Aztecan. Her interests include the language of White racism in the USA and the role of language ideologies in racism. Professor Hill has served as President of the American Anthropological Association. She is a Fellow of the American Association for the Advancement of Science, a Member of the American Academy of Arts and Sciences, and holds the 2004 Viking Fund Medal in Anthropology. Email: jhill@email.arizona.edu.

Kristine Horner is Lecturer in German and Sociolinguistics in the Department of German, School of Modern Languages and Cultures at the University of Leeds, UK. Her research focuses on ethnic and national identities, language ideologies, and language, migration and globalization. She has published on linguistic purism (de Gruyter, 2005) and language and national identity in Luxembourg (de Gruyter, forthcoming), and is co-editor of *Life in Language: Studies in Honour of Wolfgang Kühlwein* (Wissenschaftlicher Verlag, Trier, 2005 – with Andreas J. Schuth and Jean Jacques Weber). She is presently preparing a monograph on language policy in Luxembourg. Email: gllkh @leeds.ac.uk.

Alexandra Jaffe is Professor of Linguistics at California State University, Long Beach, USA. She has done research on many dimensions of Corsican language use and ideologies, focusing on the media, orthography and education and the ideological dimensions of language planning. Recent publications include *Ideologies in Action: Language Politics on Corsica* (Mouton, 1999) and a special issue of the *Journal of Sociolinguistics* on Nonstandard Orthographies. She is currently working on a monograph on Corsican bilingual education and two edited volume projects: one on the *Sociolinguistics of Stance* and the other on orthography (with Sally Johnson, Mark Sebba and Jannis Androutsopoulos). Email: ajaffe@csulb.edu.

Adam Jaworski is Professor and Head at the Centre for Language and Communication Research, Cardiff University, Wales, UK. His research interests include multimodal approaches to the study of tourism, media discourse, linguistic landscapes and space, as well as the discursive production of élitism and social privilege (with Crispin Thurlow). Recent publications include:

Metalanguage: Social and Ideological Perspectives (Berlin, de Gruyter, 2004 – co-edited with Nikolas Coupland and Dariusz Galasiński). He also co-edits the book series Oxford Studies in Sociolinguistics (OUP, with Nikolas Coupland). Email: jaworski@cardiff.ac.uk.

Lesley Jeffries has worked at the University of Huddersfield since 1990, following research and teaching jobs at Reading and Leeds Universities in the UK. Her interests are in the contextual study of language through stylistics and critical discourse analysis of political (small 'p') texts and poetry. Her PhD (Leeds) was a corpus-based stylistic study of newspaper English. She now works on qualitative projects in news reporting and the construction of opposites in texts ranging from news to poems. She is editor of the *Perspectives on the English Language* series with Palgrave and recently completed a book, *Constructing the Female Body* (Palgrave, 2007). She is currently investigating the application of discourse analysis to conflict situations. Email: l.jeffries @hud.ac.uk.

Sally Johnson is Professor of Linguistics and Head of the Department of Linguistics and Phonetics in the School of Modern Languages and Cultures at the University of Leeds, UK. Her research interests are in sociolinguistics and language and gender, particularly in relation to the German language. Previous publications include *Gender, Group Identity and Variation in the Berlin Urban Vernacular* (Peter Lang, 1995), *Language and Masculinity* (Blackwell, 1997 – co-edited with Ulrike Hanna Meinhof), *Exploring the German Language* (Arnold, 1998) and *Spelling Trouble? Language, Ideology and the Reform of German Orthography* (Multilingual Matters, 2005). Email: s.a. johnson@leeds.ac.uk.

Helen Kelly-Holmes is a research scholar in the Department of Languages and Cultural Studies, University of Limerick, Ireland. Her main research interests concern the inter-relationship between media, markets and languages. Previous publications include *European Television Discourse in Transition* (ed., Multilingual Matters, 1999), *Minority Language Broadcasting: Breton and Irish* (ed., Multilingual Matters, 2001) and *Advertising as Multilingual Communication* (Palgrave Macmillan, 2005). Email: helen.kelly. holmes@ul.ie.

Tommaso M. Milani is a doctoral student at the Centre for Research on Bilingualism at the University of Stockholm, Sweden, researching how language policy and planning, language ideologies and national identity are intertwined in Swedish language debates. His areas of interest encompass Critical Discourse Analysis, language ideology and post-structuralism. He has also been involved, together with Kenneth Hyltenstam, in governmental commissions to assess the status of minority languages in Norway and Sweden. His publications include articles on language ideologies in Sweden and on performativity theory. Email: tommaso.milani@biling.su.se.

Julie Norton is a Lecturer in Education at CELTEAL, the School of Education, at the University of Leicester, UK. She teaches on MA courses and supervises doctoral students in applied linguistics and TESOL. Her research interests and areas of publication include: linguistic identity, intercultural pragmatics, discourse analysis and oral testing. Email: jen7@le.ac.uk.

Elena Semino is a Senior Lecturer in the Department of Linguistics and English Language at Lancaster University, UK. She works in the areas of stylistics, corpus linguistics and metaphor studies. She is author of *Language and World Creation in Poems and Other Texts* (Longman, 1997), co-editor (with Jonathan Culpeper) of *Cognitive Stylistics: Language and Cognition in Text Analysis* (John Benjamins, 2002) and co-author (with Mick Short) of *Corpus Stylistics: Speech, Writing and Thought Presentation in a Corpus of English Writing* (Routledge, 2004). She is currently working on a book entitled *Metaphor in Discourse*, to be published by Cambridge University Press. Email: e.semino @lancaster.ac.uk.

Crispin Thurlow is based in the Department of Communication at the University of Washington (Seattle, USA) where he also holds an adjunct appointment in Linguistics. His research on 'Discourse and Difference' examines the representation and production of interculturality and inequality/privilege in everyday social interaction, focusing on two main areas: young people, youth and intergenerational discourse; and tourism, global mobility and international discourse. His books include *Computer-Mediated Communication: Social Interaction and the Internet* (Sage, 2004), *Talking Adolescence: Perspectives on Communication in the Teenage Years* (Peter Lang, 2005) and *Tourism Discourse: The Language of Global Mobility* (Macmillan, 2006). Email: thurlow @u.washington.edu.

INTRODUCTION

1 Language in the media: theory and practice

Sally Johnson and Astrid Ensslin[1]

1.1 Issues and interests ...

The A* pupils who have only a basic grasp of grammar.
(Daily Mail, 18.07.06)

Internet culture spells doom for strait-laced orthographers.
(Guardian, 01.05.06)

Cows also have regional accents.
(BBC News, 23.08.06)

Along with the traditional poking of fun at mis-translations on menus in foreign restaurants, the above headlines might appear to be typical of what happens whenever the media turns its attention to *language*. For those of us who spend much of our professional lives researching and teaching in this area, it may well look as though all we can do is hold our heads in despair. Why does the media so often seem to get it wrong – either through its exaggerated focus on sheer linguistic trivia or the blatant *mis*-representation of what we, as language experts, know about the 'true' nature of language structure and usage?

This is not the first time that this question has been asked. Indeed the idea for this collection was originally inspired by an academic discussion in the *Journal of Sociolinguistics* that highlighted the media as a key site for potential mis-understandings and mis-representations of both language and linguistics (Wolfram 1998; Cyr 1999; Heller 1999a, 1999b; Laforest 1999; Rickford 1999; Aitchison 2001; Johnson 2001; Milroy 2001; Garrett 2001).[2] These essays raised a number of important issues that now form the point of departure for our present attempt to map out a fresh approach to questions around language in the media. Yes, it's undeniably the case that a lot of what the media has to say about language is either trivial or simply wrong. But equally unsatisfactory, we believe, is the commonplace assumption amongst language experts that linguists '*know*', the media *mis-represents* what linguists know and, as a direct consequence, the public *mis-understands* what there is to know about language. It is a problematic way of viewing

3

matters, not least since it is rooted in a concept of knowledge-making that itself draws on a so-called 'conduit metaphor' (Reddy 1993; see also Heywood and Semino, Chapter 2, this volume). The underlying, positivistic assumption is that knowledge is there to be discovered by experts, who in turn decide what can or should be communicated to the wider public. What then disrupts the flow of accurate information from sender to receiver is the *media*. Within this conduit metaphor, however, there is little sense of a meaning-making process that accords agency to either the producers or consumers of the media texts concerned. There is no real scope for understanding the motivations of the media, while the general public appears to have no tangible role beyond that of passive and uncritical receptacles for information that has been previously selected and potentially distorted. Finally, we are dealing with a view of the communication process that is itself predicated on the assumption that experts – in this case, linguists – have even tried to impart their specialist knowledge to a wider audience in the first place (which of course they frequently haven't). This is possibly because we have not recognized the value of doing so (and this is a collective 'we' that includes the institutions that help to frame and discipline our academic work). Alternatively – and herein lies the circularity – any attempt to communicate our individual and collective fascination with language is all too often thwarted prior to its very inception by our overwhelming fear of having our specialist knowledge somehow twisted by media hacks out for a quick and silly story.

Before we start to get too depressed about all of this, let us not forget that many experts do manage to successfully communicate language-related issues to an audience beyond academe – Jean Aitchison, David Crystal and Steven Pinker are three names that immediately come to mind. Moreover, for high-profile examples of sensible, indeed fascinating, interaction between linguists, the media and the general public, one need look no further than two recent multi-media projects in the English-speaking world – *BBC Voices* in the UK and *Do you speak American?* in the USA.[3] However, the new work to be presented in the present volume will take us beyond a mere exploration of the role of the media in relation to linguists' own success or otherwise at communicating with an audience outside of academe. Rather, it is our aim to open up a much broader debate on language in the media that allows us to embrace a wealth of language-related activity that, we believe, has a great deal to tell us about the nature of language, communication and meaning-making processes more generally. In other words, the contributors to this book are variously interested not only in how the media *represents* language-related issues but also how media policy and practice with respect to language are central to the very construction of what we all (experts or otherwise) think language is, could or ought to be like.

There is already a sizeable body of work that has begun to explore the representation and/or construction of language, discourse and communication in the context of media texts and practices. By far the most numerous are those analyses that draw on print media sources, such as the work by Susan DiGiacomo (1999) on debates over Castilian and Catalan in the run-up to the 1992 Barcelona Olympic Games, Wendy Bokhorst-Heng's (1999) study of the 'Speak Mandarin Campaign' in Singapore, Dimitris Koutsogiannis and Bessie Mitsikopoulou's (2003) analysis of press commentaries on 'Greeklish', a hybrid form of Greek and English used in online communication, Oliver Stenschke's (2005) study of newspaper responses to the recent reform of German spelling, or Adam Jaworski and Dariusz Galasiński's (2002) discussion of representations of non-verbal behaviour in press reactions to the video of President Clinton's Grand Jury testimony in 1998. Other work focuses on the theme of language on television such as Jaworski *et al*'s (2003) study of the representation and use of local languages on British holiday programmes, or in the cinema, for example, Rosina Lippi-Green's (1997: 79–103) analysis of foreign-accented speech in popular films such as *The Lion King* and *Schindler's List* (see also Lippi-Green on news media, ibid.: 133–51). Meanwhile, radio texts have also been drawn upon as a site for analysis as in Jaworski *et al*'s (2004a) study of 'leaks' in radio news broadcasts or Jacqueline Urla's (2001) work on the creation of 'alternative public spheres' on Basque free radio in northern Spain (see also Coupland 2001a; Busch 2005; Spitulnik 1998). Finally, many studies incorporate a range of media text types, for example, Alexandra Jaffe's work on Corsican, which draws on insights from both radio and print media (1999a, 1999b) or James Collins's (1999) study of the Ebonics controversy in the USA, which explores pronouncements garnered from a variety of mediated sources, but especially email and the World Wide Web (see also Ronkin and Karn 1999, on the use of Mock Ebonics on the internet).[4]

Although the relatively recent sample of work referred to above addresses a number of similar themes, it is fairly widely scattered across different types of books and journals. One purpose of this volume, therefore, is to try to bring together this emerging field and formulate a more coherent research agenda. That said, it is not our aim to narrow down the theoretical or methodological parameters within which this might occur. In fact, our project is inherently *inter*-disciplinary: the chapters' authors come from a range of academic backgrounds, including (in no particular order of importance) linguistics, modern languages, English, anthropology, education, communication studies and media/cultural theory. As a result, our contributors bring a wealth of approaches to the media texts and practices they are scrutinizing, drawing variously, for example, on conversational/text analysis, critical and multimodal discourse analysis, corpus linguistics, pragmatics, stylistics and speech act theory as well as historiographical and ethnographic techniques. Indeed, we see this *inter*-disciplinary premise as central to the more *trans*-disciplinary understanding for which we are ultimately aiming, that is to say, an appreciation of language in the media that is aspirationally greater than the sum of its individual disciplinary parts.

At this juncture, it is worth pointing out how this is *not* a book about media discourse in more general terms, a field of research that is already well established (see, *inter alia*, Aitchison and Lewis 2003; Bell 1991; Bell and Garrett 1998; Cotter 2001a; Fairclough 1995; Fowler 1991; Scollon 1998; van Dijk 1991). Our specific concern lies with those media texts and practices where language is itself more or less explicitly thematized. This compares to the somewhat broader focus of the analysis of media discourse generally, which tends to be interested in how language works in the representation and construction of *any* given topic. Of course, our work will still involve analyses of media discourse: the focus is simply narrower. We might therefore sum up our initial concerns by stating that we will be exploring both:

1. the language used to reflect on language within the media texts that are themselves the object of study, and
2. the language used by the producers and/or consumers of those texts when talking or writing about them.

As will become clear throughout the course of the book, however, our scope will ultimately extend beyond *language* – in the sense of speech and writing (see Kress and van Leeuwen 2006) – as the primary means of metalinguistic reflection so as to incorporate other semiotic modes – such as image, sound, and even touch – that can be employed in the medial construction of language. Moreover, what is particularly intriguing in this regard is the varying degree of *explicitness* with which such multimodal forms of linguistic reflexivity can be seen to occur, a central theoretical point to which we shall return below, not least in relation to the question of what counts as explicit and for whom.

The various contributors to this book draw on a wide range of media text types, including print media sources (both written and visual), radio and television broadcasts, as well as new media genres such as blogs, email and hyperpoetry. Before we take a closer look at the content and concerns of individual chapters, however, we will start by mapping out some key issues relating to the two main phenomena at the core of our overall project: language, on the one hand, and media, on the other.

1.2 Language

The study of language in the media as we have defined it so far is inextricably linked to a raft of broader concerns around the concept of *metalanguage*, in other words, the language that is used to talk about language.

It is commonplace in linguistics to argue that human language is unique in being able to represent itself, an insight that has traditionally underpinned much of the work undertaken by sociolinguists and social psychologists in the area of language attitudes and folk linguistics (e.g. Garrett *et al* 2003; Giles *et al* 1991; Giles and Powesland 1975; Niedzielski and Preston 1999; Ryan and Giles 1982). Recently however, the field of metalanguage more generally has been the subject of renewed interest, as exemplified not least by two key works, namely, Adam Jaworski, Nikolas Coupland and Dariusz Galasiński's edited collection *Metalanguage: Social and Ideological Perspectives* (2004b) and Ken Hyland's *Metadiscourse: Exploring Interaction in Writing* (2005). Before we explore the implications of these works for our study of language in the media, let us first consider some of the main ways in which metalanguage is currently defined.

A useful starting point is the tripartite model proposed by Dennis Preston (2004). According to Preston, Metalanguage 1 consists of *language about language*, i.e. those instances where people specifically comment on language, perhaps, for example, in a discussion over the correct pronunciation of a word (2004: 75). Metalanguage 2, by contrast, involves a presumably less explicit form of linguistic commentary where there is simply a *mention of talk* itself. This might include the use of expressions such as 'in other words', 'can you say that more clearly' or 'do you understand me?' (ibid.: 85) and is ultimately akin to Jakobson's (1960) notion of the phatic function of language. Finally, Metalanguage 3 consists of the more general body of shared beliefs and attitudes around language structure and use that obtain within a given speech community, thereby informing the kind of commentary typified by Metalanguage 1 and (though perhaps to a lesser extent) Metalanguage 2 (2004: 87).

In many ways, Preston's definition of Metalanguage 3 directly intersects with the concerns of scholars working in the field of language ideology studies (e.g. Blommaert 1999a, 2005; Gal and Woolard 2001; Joseph and Taylor, 1991; Kroskrity 2000; Lippi-Green 1997; Schieffelin *et al* 1998; Woolard 1992). Here a key impetus over the past decade or so has been the incorporation of theoretical insights from ideology studies more generally (e.g. Eagleton 1991; Thompson 1984) as a means of 'bridge-building' between hitherto more or less discrete areas of linguistic and social theory (see Woolard 1992, 1998a). This then involves an explicit focus on the questions of power and interest that cluster around, and are invested in, language structure and use. It is, moreover, an approach that seeks to gain a more holistic view of language by attending to the multiple contexts – discursive, cultural, social, technological, economic, political and historical – in which linguistic processes are variously embedded.

To a greater or lesser extent, all concerns around language ideology are simultaneously concerns about metalanguage. This is because much of what we can learn about the ideological underpinnings of linguistic activity will be derived from what people actually have to *say* about language in the sense of Preston's Metalanguage 1. Indeed, in Michael Silverstein's early definition of language ideologies as 'sets of beliefs about language articulated by users as a rationalization or justification of perceived language structure and use'

(1979: 193), we see a clear focus on the idea of *explicitly articulated* ideas about language. For others such as Kathryn Woolard, whilst the explicit metalinguistic dimension is certainly pervasive, theoretical concerns are framed in terms of a more general notion of language *representation*:

> populations around the world posit fundamental linkages among such apparently diverse cultural categories as language, spelling, grammar, and nation, gender, simplicity, intentionality, authenticity, knowledge, development, power, tradition. [Studies in language ideology] attempt to understand when and how these links are forged, whether by lay participants or by their expert analysts, through what semiotic and social processes, and with what consequences for linguistic and social life. (Woolard 1998a: 27)

It is worth pausing at this juncture to reflect on why questions of metalanguage, in particular, and language representation, in general, are central to our concerns around language in the media. The point here is not simply that the media self-evidently provide a channel for the articulation and transmission of language attitudes and ideologies. Rather we are interested in what Jaworski *et al* (2004b) and Hyland (2005) see as the universally *contextualizing* function of metalanguage together with the study of language representation as both constituted by and constitutive of linguistic reality. In other words, the ways in which language is represented (medially or otherwise) not only provide a discursive frame for language use in its own right: our very understanding of what language *is* depends to a greater or lesser extent on the constitutive role of that meta-dimension.

This idea of language as itself subject to a process of discursive construction is very much in tune with what Alastair Pennycook (2004) characterizes as a post-structuralist, anti-foundationalist approach to linguistic study, according to which the very moment of language use is itself seen as 'an act of identity that *calls language into being*' (2004: 17 – our emphasis). In this context, Pennycook draws on performativity theory (Butler 1990, 1997), with particular emphasis on language use as an instance of *performance* in its own right, in order to explore new ways of understanding 'how languages, identities and futures are *refashioned*' (2004: 17 – our emphasis). We shall return to the theme of performativity below. Suffice it to say for the time being, that what we want to explore in this book is the function of the *media* in relation to those kinds of performances whereby, following Pennycook, languages, identities and possible futures may be 'refashioned' in ways that contextualize and therefore help to constitute what counts as both linguistic and, ultimately, social reality.

The constitutive role accorded to metalanguage within the kind of antifoundationalist perspective described by Pennycook has also to be seen in relation to recent debates over linguistic reflexivity as central to the workings of late modernity, in general, and the new global economy, in particular (Chouliaraki and Fairclough 1999; Coupland 2003a; Fairclough 2006; Pennycook 2003; see also the contributions to this volume by Horner and Milani). It is something of a truism nowadays to note how the exponential increase in the speed and volume of information transfer that is characteristic of what Norman Fairclough (2003) calls the 'new capitalism' has utterly transformed the communicative landscape over the past decade or so. Technological innovations have revolutionized, for example, the whole concept of co-presence where language users are concerned, all of which have presupposed a significant re-ordering of the discursive contexts in which the production of meaning can occur – think web-conferencing, podcasting, internet relay chat (IRC) as well as the increased public participation and concomitant interactivity of what has come to be known as 'Web 2.0' typified by such virtual arenas as 'YouTube' and 'MySpace'. However, it is not only contexts of *production* that are affected by such developments, but also, and crucially for our purposes, contexts of *reception*. As has been widely argued, such technological shifts would appear to presuppose not only a heightened degree of linguistic reflexivity on the part of language users per se (alongside considerable potential for linguistic creativity) but also a host of fresh possibilities for the *policing* and *disciplining* of language, discourse and communication more widely (see Blommaert 2003; Cameron 2000; Chouliaraki and Fairclough 1999; Coupland and Jaworski 2004; see also Duchêne and Heller 2007 on discourses of language endangerment).

It will be clear by now that any attempt to explore the role of language in the media in relation to questions of language representation and linguistic reflexivity is going to require a fairly liberal conceptualization of metalanguage. Therefore, we are adopting, indeed embracing, a very broad view of what Jaworski *et al* (2004b: 5) refer to as the 'meta-zone', such that our field of interest extends to notions of metadiscourse, metapragmatics, metacommunication and metasemiotics (see especially Meinhof 2004 on representations of culture in television commercials, and Richardson 2004, on the historical symbolism of 'retro-shopping'). To this we will also be adding the concept of *metamediality*. We will not at this juncture enter into the complex, theoretical debate regarding the precise distinction between these different facets of the meta-zone (for a fuller treatment, see Jaworski *et al* 2004b; Richardson, 2006). Suffice it to say, however, that this certainly presupposes a somewhat wider definition of the meta-dimension than is afforded by Preston's tripartite model described above.

At this point, it will be useful to return to Kathryn Woolard, who summarizes the textual realizations, traces or 'sitings' of language ideologies as potentially observable in three main ways (including any combination thereof):

- *Linguistic/discursive practice* – what people actually *do* with language.
- *Metalinguistic/metadiscursive practice* – what people say/write about language/the views on language they explicitly express.
- *Implicit metapragmatics* – the regimentation of language use through implicit linguistic signalling (i.e. knowledge about language drawn upon in the use, and interpretation, of language acts). (Adapted from Woolard 1998a: 9)

The first component immediately highlights how the transactional, functional or referential dimensions of language and discourse remain central to any discussion of the meta-zone (see also Hyland 2005: 6). This would include, moreover, analyses of the language that is *itself* used to refer to language, for our purposes, in and around media texts (hence our overlapping concerns with the study of media discourse more generally). The second category of metalinguistic/metadiscursive practice is broadly similar to Preston's notion of Metalanguage 1. This, in turn, encompasses an analysis of the work of linguists themselves – linguistics as an academic discipline being the example *par excellence* of metalinguistic reflection (more on this below, but see especially Bauman and Briggs 2003). However, it is the third category, we believe, that raises some of the more challenging theoretical issues where the study of metalanguage in relation to our analyses of language in the media is concerned.

In his discussion of the role of metapragmatic awareness in language use, Jef Verschueren (2004) draws on the work of Roman Jakobson ([1955] 1985) to tease out some of the issues around a possible demarcation of the boundaries between explicit and implicit forms of metalanguage. It is not our aim here to recount the detailed and illuminating discussion provided by Verschueren, together with his efforts to provide a taxonomy of explicitness according to which, say, some kinds of contextualization cues (such as the use of reported speech) might be considered more explicit than others (such as codeswitching) (2004: 61). What is of particular interest for our purposes is how what might be deemed implicit or explicit is connected to questions of production and reception, not least in relation to audience awareness, perspective or expertise (see Hyland 2005). Thus it seems fairly uncontroversial to suggest that the language expert's own sensitivity to the instances of reported speech and codeswitching described by Verschueren is almost always likely to be more consciously perceived and/or explicitly articulated than that of the non-linguist. This is by very dint of the expert's own academic focus on language, in general, and notions of say contextualization cue, in particular – a view that can easily lead to a privileging of the analyst's own perspective. What ultimately counts, as emphasized by Verschueren himself (2004: 69), is that the function of all metalinguistic activity, whatever its degree of explicitness, is inextricably linked to questions of *context*. This insight is not, of course, new. But it does, in turn, bring us back to the issue of why we would want to separate out the meta-dimension for theoretical attention in the first place, a question that is central to the deliberations in Jaworski *et al* (2004b) and Hyland (2005).

Ironically, it seems that what actually presupposes, and hence justifies, the need for a more or less discrete focus on the meta-zone is its own historical exclusion from mainstream linguistic theory throughout the twentieth century, shored up by notions of what Coupland and Jaworski (2004: 15) refer to as 'linguistic innocence' (see also Horner, Chapter 7, this volume). Here, the dominant focus on language structure was, and still is, grounded in a relegation of both language use (at both the transactional and interactional level) to the margins of what is deemed to be relevant for linguistics as an academic discipline. And within such a model, the interactional, i.e. social, dimensions of the meta-zone have been further consigned to the peripheral status of the 'extra'-linguistic, a view that still underpins notions of 'soft' versus 'hard' linguistics, the former with its concerns, *inter alia*, for attitudes and beliefs about language as opposed to the latter's focus on language 'proper', i.e. language structure (see especially Bloomfield's, 1944, notion of secondary and tertiary responses to language). It is difficult to resist the temptation to point out how this is itself a prime example of what we mean by the notion of the meta-zone (here as posited by the academic discipline of linguistics) as not only constituted *by* but also constitutive *of* what counts as linguistic reality. In sum, our point is that the kind of alternative, more holistic context that is envisaged here is one which must nowadays, we believe, accord a key role to the *media* if we are to fully understand the contexts of production and reception of meaning in relation to the meta-zone, in general, and what this has to tell us about language, discourse and communication, in particular.

1.3 Media

In late- or post-modern western society, our daily lives are increasingly both characterized and determined by the production and consumption of diversely mediated meanings. Indeed, we are engaged in an almost constant process of encoding and decoding linguistic and non-linguistic messages. Consequently, we are subjected to, as well as in control of, a plethora of technological and medial information flows that both construct and transfer ideologies between ourselves, our information providers, and our target audiences.

The 'media' in their broadest sense encompass not only the classical communication channels they are commonly associated with, i.e. in chronological order of their evolution, newspapers/magazines, radio, cinema, television, and the new electronic media – the latter comprising per se a continuously expanding spectrum of digital technologies and communicative practices.[5] More widely, the term 'media' also covers any tools and techniques employable by intelligent mammals to carry out, consciously or unconsciously, an unlimited range of highly specific signifying practices. These

11

semiotic routines extend, at a personal, *micro*-cultural level, to clothes, hair-styles, gaits, and body language whereas, at a *macro*-cultural level, 'public' or 'collective' meanings are denoted and connoted by posters, road signs, architecture and advertising (Bignell 2002: 1). Finally, language itself may be subsumed under this wider notion of mediality (see McLuhan 1964), not least because it operates at both a micro- *and* macro-cultural level. Language thereby forms, along with the visual image, the most powerful communicative tool available to social actors.

In this book, we refer to 'the media' in the sense of communication or 'mass' media. As a collective noun derived from the Latin *medium* (means, method), the lexeme has adopted singular grammatical 'behaviour' despite the fact that, unlike any other member of its class, it embodies an increasing sense of plurality and diversity.[6] Indeed, as Ulrich Schmitz (2004: 12) notes, it is becoming extremely difficult to find a common denominator for what we typically refer to as 'mass media', not least because the degree of participation, co-authorship and indeed 'democracy' (Pugh 2005) is expanding so rapidly. Moreover, the media tend to embed, and thereby thematize or problematize, in multifarious ways, other media, looking both backwards and forwards in media history such that consumers and analysts alike are confronted with multiple levels of *intermediality* (Heibach 2003). This incorporates various types of language and metalanguage but also, in a no less ideologically charged way, *metamediality* (see Ensslin, Chapter 13, for a fuller discussion of this term as well as the contributions to this volume by Cameron, Hill, Jeffries and Thurlow for good examples of metamedial debates on language issues).

As linguists and editors of this book, our main concern is with media forms that use written and spoken language as their primary semiotic modes. In this respect, Johnson's chapter (Chapter 5) might be seen as something of an exception in that it provides a detailed analysis of how the visual (i.e. the pictographic *and* the graphemic) can be intertextually and intermedially exploited in media texts, thus offering an ample resource for multimodal discourse analysis (Kress and van Leeuwen 2006; O'Halloran 2004; Constantinou 2005) in relation to language ideological debates (Blommaert 1999a). At the same time, Jaffe's chapter on Corsican, and Gieve and Norton's discussion of foreign-language talk on British television, also offer insights into the role played by the visual in documentary film-making, while Ensslin's final chapter explores the delicate interplay between the written, spoken, visual and sensory in the fictional world of hyperpoetry.

Central to our understanding of the interface between technologies, meanings and social actors throughout this book are the notions of *mediation* and *mediatization*. The term 'mediation' is used to refer to the general processes of information encoding, transfer and decoding, which form an intricately interlinked interplay between sender, receiver and encoded message. Of arguably greater importance for a more socially oriented linguistics, however, is the notion of 'mediatization'. This refers to the organizational and orientational role performed by the media with respect to mutual perception, the allocation and adoption of diverse social roles, and human communication in general (Schmitz 2004: 14). From a system-theoretical point of view (Kittler [1985], 1990), the media are social systems interacting with other social systems, which make up their observable, salient environment. As a result, the media *mirror*, and hence implicitly *promote*, a dynamic set of ideological frameworks. Crucially, however, these are not necessarily restricted to dominant discourses but also enable marginal agencies to surface, and potentially alter, previous hierarchical relations or 'orders of discourse' (Foucault 1980). An illuminating instance of this is to be found in Jaffe's discussion in this volume of a television documentary filmed at a bilingual school on Corsica, where, somewhat paradoxically, bilingualism (an ability to speak both French *and* Corsican) is represented primarily in terms of monolingualism (i.e. an ability to speak Corsican). As Jaffe shows, while the film to some extent constitutes an *over*-representation of the actual use of Corsican within the school, processes of mediatization (including production and editorial interventions) facilitated in this instance the indexing of marginalized discourses, thereby offering a challenge (however fleeting) to hegemonic diglossic practices.

In their function as public agencies of observation, interpretation, performance, representation and dissemination, the media exhibit a variety of signifying practices, which are unconditionally purpose-driven. Depending upon their particular point of emphasis, media producers therefore combine *conative, emotive* and *conceptual* meanings so as to achieve a maximum effect on the target audience. By the same token, it is precisely the contextually contingent constellation of these three communicative parameters that informs the distinct stylistic choices of media producers with respect to text or media genre, semiotic modes, participants, foregrounding and backgrounding, and indeed textual discourse itself (Fairclough 1995: 4). Put differently, every media performance reflects the interpretations, perspectives and attitudes as well as, no less significantly, the constructions, 'inventions' (Schmitz 2004: 17) and thus the personal, institutional and corporate ideologies of media producers together with those of other social actors who are similarly authorized to stage themselves and their agendas medially. In other words, aesthetic production and linguistic expression are embedded in, and contingent upon, a range of conflicting arenas arising from the demanding and legitimating of power. At the same time, media producers have to meet and balance out diversely polarized interests and, simultaneously, satisfy the target perceivers' need for information as well as intellectual and spiritual *entertainment* (see Grewenig 1993; see also the contributions to this volume by Cameron, Kelly-Holmes and Atkinson, and Gieve and Norton).

All of the analyses presented in this book draw upon two general assumptions, shared by a wide range of contemporary media theorists

13

(e.g. Hayles 2000, 2002, 2004; Aarseth 1997; Ryan 2004; Goodman and O'Halloran 2006). First, the media as highly diversified 'organs of dissemination' (Jewitt 2004: 184) incorporate a range of distinctive material qualities that shape their particular practices of production and reception. On a more abstract level, the media constitute politically and ideologically governed institutions that necessarily represent their own concomitant infrastructures and social practices (Levinson 1984: 7). Second, there is a clear distinction to be made between *mediality* in the sense of abstract and material dissemination (as in the previous point) and *modality*. As a means of representation, *modes* are situated at the level of semiosis, which comprises, at the very least, writing, speech, image, sound and touch (Kress and van Leeuwen 2001, 2006; Constantinou 2005). Clearly, the choice of medium both enables and delimits the choice of modes. On the other hand, modes incorporate within themselves particular social traditions, environments, skills and practices, which again have a bearing on the availability and accessibility of certain media. Finally, the materiality of media technology influences sensual perception, and our cognitive and epistemological faculties respond sensitively to the culturally grounded semiotic practices performed by the media (Koch and Krämer 1997: 21). Crucially, for the purpose of the project we envisage in this book, discourse analysts need to take into account both that – and how – the modality and mediality of media texts *interact* so as to shape textual form and meaning.

Also significant for this book is the fact that we are not just dealing with meaning in general but, as already emphasized earlier, meaning in relation to the representation and construction of *language* itself. Following Pennycook (2004: 8), we need to consider language not as a fixed, pre-formed, autonomous organism (cf. de Saussure 1966). On the contrary, it is only in the process of reiterated discursive practice that language 'appears' as a 'substance' (see Butler 1990: 33). For essentially, language is a fluid, discursive construct – an 'emergent property of social interaction' (Pennycook 2004: 7) – that is itself contextually situated and thus reflects the specific ideological programme(s) of those social agents who engage with it discursively and performatively (see especially Thurlow's discussion, Chapter 11 in this volume, of adult constructions of young people's new-media practices). Evidently, therefore, the media offers the socially most powerful platform for such constructions, not least because of its ability to enact *local* concerns on a *global* scale. In fact, as becomes clear in a number of chapters in this volume (e.g. Ensslin; Gieve and Norton; Kelly-Holmes and Atkinson; Thurlow), one of the major attractions of the media is the distinct entertainment value that can arise from merging the 'marginal' with the 'dominant', the 'parochial' with the 'cosmopolitan', and the 'local' with the 'global' (Conboy 2003).

Of course, one of the predominant factors in relation to the changing meanings of language form and function at the present time is the rapid evolution and spread of the new global technologies, and indeed the role of globalization more generally (see Blommaert 2003; Coupland 2003a; Fairclough 2006; Heller 2003; House 2003; Machin and van Leeuwen 2003; Meyerhoff and Niedzielski 2003; Thurlow and Jaworski 2003; see also Horner, this volume). As cultural philosopher Ernst Cassirer puts it, human beings are inescapably enmeshed within a steadily expanding, medially constructed symbolic network that forms a 'new dimension of reality' (Cassirer [1944], 1990: 49 – our translation) and which supplements locality by a sense of seemingly all-comprehensive global reach. This idea of accessibility and geographic permeation allows, in turn, for new pragmatic and social functions of language, which may be used to mark social membership and belonging, as well as a subversive stance towards the familiar and the local (see Pennycook 2003, for an examination of rap/hip-hop language as an instance of global English in Japanese popular culture). At the same time, and perhaps more disturbingly, the voices of dominant ideological brokers are increasingly widely heard, read and indeed reproduced, by newly introduced methods of digital interaction (see e.g. Cameron Chapter 12 in this volume). It is in this particular context therefore that sociolinguists and discourse analysts need to step in so as 'to highlight the linguistic and discoursal nature of media power' (Fairclough 1995: 3) as these relate to the construction of not only *language* but also to the *people* who produce, consume and/or are represented by those media texts (see especially Milani and Horner, Chapters 6 and 7 in this volume). This is because such acts of language representation not only underpin the construction of particular language ideologies. Indeed, mediated and *mediatized* notions of language are central to the envisaging or 'imagining' (Anderson [1983] 1991) of possible *social* worlds across both time and space, *viz.* Pennycook's (2004) notion of 'futures' or Susan Gal and Kathryn Woolard's (2001) concept of 'publics', respectively. Put simply, what we think and say about *language* as shaped not least by the media is inextricably linked to what we may think and say about ourselves and the world(s) in which we live or, indeed, might like to live.

1.4 Overview of chapters

The remainder of this volume is divided into four sections as follows. In Part I *Metaphors and Meanings*, we begin with three chapters, each exploring the representation of language issues as these pertain to the print media in the UK and the USA. In Chapter 2, 'Metaphors for speaking and writing in the British press', John Heywood and Elena Semino deal with a key concept in any discussion of medial metalanguage, namely the use of metaphor to refer to acts of communication. Drawing on a large corpus of texts gathered from British newspapers, the authors show how, in their representations of spoken and written language, text producers typically draw on a fairly limited range of metaphors, most notably those relating to object manipulation, vision, movement and (physical) aggression. The authors then propose that while journalists' use of metaphor frequently facilitates the understanding of communicative processes on the part of readers, on the one hand, this may often lead to a degree of oversimplification, on the other. In Chapter 3, Lesley Jeffries similarly explores the extent to which journalists attempt to shape readers' understandings of language-related issues, albeit in the context of political disputes surrounding the US invasion of Iraq. In her chapter, 'Journalistic constructions of Blair's "apology" for the intelligence leading to the Iraq war', Jeffries draws on pragmatics and speech act theory to show how the very nature of what *counts* as an apology in this case is tied in to a complex metalinguistic and metamedial debate. Through close analysis of media commentaries on Blair's purported apology, the author shows how liberal journalists in the UK appear to have interpreted this speech act in relation to a 'cline of prototypicality', according to which Blair's choice of the performative ('I apologize') as opposed to the more conventionally British English expression of regret ('I'm sorry') was deemed inadequate. What Jeffries' analysis highlights is not only the key role played by journalists as ideological brokers in the shaping of readers' potential interpretation of what counts as a legitimately expressed form of regret, but also the implications of this debate for the classification of apologies within speech act theory more generally. In the final chapter in this section, Jane Hill continues on the theme of the medial contestation of meaning, here in the context of the US print media and the so-called blogosphere, a key new site for metamedial commentary. In her contribution 'Crises of meaning: personalist language ideology in US media discourse', Hill shows how the concept of 'personalism' emanates from a belief that speakers say what they believe and believe what is true, such that what is said is ultimately deemed to reflect reality. However, rather like the 'conduit metaphor' referred to above (see also Heywood and Semino in Chapter 2), this is a view of communication that affords little room for the co-construction of meaning that necessarily occurs as speakers' words are reproduced and recited by others or indeed themselves. Drawing on a range of examples, including (like Jeffries) debates over the war in Iraq, Hill describes how moral panics then typically occur in so-called 'media firestorms' when commentators hone in on the question of whether a given speaker, typically a politician or other public figure, really *meant* what they said. This in turn gives rise to extensive meta-reflection on the part of journalists and bloggers as to speakers' true intentions and, ultimately, their broader moral character. As Hill argues, the unpacking of personalist language ideology is crucial for the critical analysis of media discourse. This is partly due to its 'implicit metapragmatic' function in the shaping of such discourse in general terms but, more specifically, because the pervasive commitment to personalism in US media discourse (and almost certainly elsewhere in the western world) so often functions in ways that shore up hegemonic assumptions by giving a 'free pass' to, say, racists, whose true intentions are deemed 'personal' – hence ultimately beyond the ken of their apologists.

In Part II *National Identities, Citizenship and Globalization*, we continue to explore the role of the print media in processes of language representation and construction but shift the focus to three language ideological debates in non-English speaking, western European countries, namely Germany, Sweden and Luxembourg, respectively. In Chapter 5, Sally Johnson discusses the way in which the disputes surrounding the recent reform of German ortho-graphy were portrayed *visually* on the front cover of an influential German magazine. Her discussion 'The iconography of orthography: representing German spelling reform in the news magazine *Der Spiegel*', focuses not only on the broader context underpinning the production of this image, but also on the techniques of multimodal discourse analysis that can be employed in its examination. Drawing on Kress and van Leeuwen's (2006) *Reading Images: The Grammar of Visual Design*, Johnson shows how, through detailed attention to such concepts as the representation of social actors, positioning of viewer, modality and image composition, it is possible to achieve a more nuanced understanding of the ways in which the *Spiegel* image interdiscur-sively links the question of orthographic reform, on the one hand, and wider debates surrounding German history and national identity, on the other. The theme of language and national identity, albeit in more specific relation to the question of *citizenship*, is pursued further in Chapter 6 by Tommaso Milani. In his contribution 'A language ideology in print: the case of Sweden', Milani explores newspaper discourse as a potential site for the (re)produc-tion and dissemination of language ideologies, showing how through their writing and editorial practices journalists and other text producers may contribute to what Bourdieu (2000) refers to as the construction of 'tangible self-evidences'. The language ideological debate in question concerns the pos-sible introduction of language testing as a requirement for Swedish citizen-ship, and Milani shows how, through a subtle weaving of *inter alia* authorial account, indirect report and direct report, many of the texts under scrutiny embody a particular view of testing that mis-represents as self-evident the link between the need to test migrants' proficiency in Swedish, on the one hand, and their potential to find employment and thereby become 'proper' Swedish citizens, on the other. In the final chapter in this section, Kristine Horner similarly explores the relationship between language and citizenship, this time in the context of nationhood and *globalization*. In Chapter 7, 'Global challenges to nationalist ideologies: language and education in the Luxem-bourg press', Horner looks at the role of the print media in the (re)production of nationalist language ideologies in the context of a multilingual education system. Focusing on newspaper debates around the comparatively poor per-formance of Luxembourg pupils in the *Programme for International Student Assessment* (PISA), the results of which were published in 2001, and drawing on Irvine and Gal's (2000) notion of iconicity, fractal recursivity and erasure,

Horner shows how a number of texts contained in the conservative daily *Luxemburger Wort* presented the PISA results as a serious challenge to the model of trilingualism that is often idealized as being at the heart of Luxembourg's national self-image. Following the close analysis of a series of texts excerpts, Horner then shows how this trilingual ideal can in fact 'cut both ways', functioning, on the one hand, as a symbol of a collective national identity based on linguistic uniqueness and, on the other, as a symbol of moral division in so far as knowledge of three languages is what marks out 'good' Luxembourgers from 'others'.

The contributions to Part III, *Contact and Codeswitching in Multilingual Mediascapes*, continue to explore the theme of multilingualism albeit in relation to *broadcast media*, namely radio and television. In Chapter 8, 'Corsican on the airwaves: media discourse in a context of minority language shift', Alexandra Jaffe looks at both formal and informal news programming on Corsican radio as well as the making of a documentary film on a bilingual school. Through a combination of detailed textual and ethnographic analyses, Jaffe highlights the complex relationship between processes of mediation and mediatization in the construction of Corsican language practice, where French continues to dominate but Corsican has recently been the focus of sustained efforts towards revitalization. The author shows how the use of different modes such as spoken and written language, as well as the visual, variously shape the production and reception of Corsican, including not least its legitimation and/or marginalization. What is especially interesting here is the sheer unpredictability of the outcomes of mediatization processes, both in terms of their effects on the code itself as well as on broader sociolinguistic issues such as language shift. Much of Jaffe's chapter is given over to debates around the question of what counts as 'proper' usage in a minority language context and this is a theme that is also taken up in the next chapter, which looks at the situation in Ireland. In Chapter 9, ' "When Hector met Tom Cruise": attitudes to Irish in a radio satire', Helen Kelly-Holmes and David Atkinson begin by outlining the extent of Irish usage within the broadcast media in Ireland together with a discussion of the ways in which the language is itself medially represented. This is followed by an analysis of excerpts from an episode of a popular satirical radio show in which a character called Hector (based on the real-life entertainer and broadcaster, Hector Ó hEochagáin) supposedly meets the Hollywood actor Tom Cruise. The analysis is of interest on one level because, aside from Ensslin's chapter (see below), it is the only contribution in this collection to examine a *fictional* representation of language in the media. That said, the linguistic characterization of Hector can tell us much about attitudes towards Irish which, as the authors emphasize, span a continuum ranging from the extremes of superiority (Irish as the 'true' language of Ireland) to inferiority (a language of little or no relevance to the modern world). Through subtle analyses of the fictional dialogues in question, the authors then show how the character's imperfect use of Irish, typified by codeswitching/mixing and the extensive use of English loans (like that of his real-life counterpart) works to popularize Irish by giving airspace to a version of the language that is in reality closer to the competence of many L2 speakers. At the same time, the sketch's comedic effects are derived to some extent from the way in which the dialogues tap into both ends of the superiority/inferiority continuum that typifies attitudes to Irish more generally. In the final chapter in this section, we move away from multilingual broadcasting in the sense of the previous two chapters in order to look at the ways in which foreign-language interactions are handled in English-language television programming. In Chapter 10, 'Dealing with linguistic difference in encounters with Others on British television', Simon Gieve and Julie Norton begin by wondering why it is that, in so many represented encounters between English-speaking television presenters and their foreign interlocutors, complex attempts to communicate across linguistic difference are sidelined or even entirely erased. Based on the analysis of a corpus of travel, documentary and lifestyle programmes filmed on location outside the UK, the authors describe the multiple ways in which such processes of marginalization can occur. The chapter has real value for future researchers wishing to explore how representations of Others are both mediated – and mediatized – in a range of broadcast genres in so far as Gieve and Norton present a detailed taxonomy for the analysis of production/editorial practices, which simultaneously affords insights into their implicit metapragmatic consequences. Such consequences include, on the one hand, foreign subjects' own lack of opportunity for self-representation, which is frequently distorted by programme-makers' need to *entertain* a predominantly monolingual, English-speaking viewing audience. Moreover, production and editorial practices that all too often result in the ridiculing of those foreigners who *do* attempt to cross the linguistic divide are likely to do little to boost monolingual speakers' own desire to learn foreign languages, itself typically undermined by the hegemonic assumption that 'everyone speaks English anyway'.

In Part IV *Youth, Gender and Cyber-Identities*, we move away from discussions of multilingual mediascapes in order to look at a different set of identity constructs, this time in the context of new media. In Chapter 11, 'Fabricating youth: new-media discourse and the technologization of young people', Crispin Thurlow critiques the representations of young people's new-media practices, such as instant messaging, emailing and text-messaging, that are contained in an extensive and international corpus of English-language newspaper articles. Here the author identifies three recurrent themes: (1) the way in which the activities and identities of young people tend to be homogenized as either 'victims' or 'arch consumers' of new technologies; (2) how young people's new-media practices are often (mis-)represented as a threat to linguistic and moral standards generally; and (3) the exaggeration of inter-generational differences where new-media practices are concerned. In conclusion, Thurlow emphasizes the way in which this mediatized metadiscourse invokes a kind of 'triple whammy' involving adult moralizing about youth, fears with respect to declining language standards, and anxieties around the impact of new technologies more generally. He also shows how the conflation of these disparate social concerns places young people in an impossible double-bind, according to which they find themselves the focus of constant criticism from an adult-run media, whilst targeted by adult-driven commerce which simultaneously depends upon the commodification of young people's new-media practices for its own survival. In the next chapter, the focus shifts from the construction of 'youth' to that of 'gender', with a contribution by Deborah Cameron entitled 'Dreaming of Genie: language, gender difference and identity on the web'. In Chapter 12 Cameron explores a series of bloggers' responses to a piece of online interactive software known as the 'Gender Genie', which allows participants to submit a short text excerpt in order to ascertain whether its author is male or female. Given that the bloggers typically already know the author's gender, Cameron is primarily concerned with the broader implications of their commentaries for the mediation of knowledge about language and gender, on the one hand, and for popular understandings of science, on the other. What her analysis clearly demonstrates is that the use of new-media technologies per se by no means presupposes new content or even fresh ways of thinking about old issues – many of the bloggers' comments shore up (and only rarely question) some very well-established ideologies of both gender and language based on biological essentialism. In Cameron's view, one current challenge is therefore to see how new-media technologies can be harnessed in ways that enable audiences/users to encounter – and develop for themselves – more complex ways of thinking about the world and the (re-)production of knowledge more generally. One group of text producers who seem particularly well-positioned to take up this challenge are discussed in the final chapter in this section by Astrid Ensslin. In her contribution, 'Of chords, machines and bumble-bees: the metalinguistics of hyperpoetry', Ensslin examines a sample of work by a new generation of hyperpoets whose outputs are dependent upon the creative exploitation of computer programming codes in order to produce innovative forms of interactive digital verse. Ensslin's key theoretical purpose here is to stretch current sociolinguistic understandings of the more 'factual' or 'explicatory' dimensions of metalanguage by incorporating the notion of 'aesthetic metalanguage' that works instead on a largely *implicatory* basis in the context of a secondary, fictional reality. In doing so, the author shows how hyperpoets implicitly explore such issues as syntagmatic and paradigmatic relationships, grammatical and biological gender, hypermedia textuality and trans-semiotic signification. At the same time, their work contributes to deconstructionist debates about the decentralization of meaning and

20

authorship. This refers not least to the constantly changing interface between 'human operator' and the 'empowered (text) machine' that increasingly draws on the semiotic modes of not only writing, speech and the visual, but also touch and even human respiration. Ensslin's chapter provides a fitting conclusion to Part IV of this book, not least since it opens up to a socially oriented linguistics new ways of thinking about such fundamental issues as the relationship between medium, mode and message in the context of new-media technologies together with their relevance for linguistic-theoretical debates around the medial representation and construction of language, discourse and communication more widely.

In the final chapter, we bring the book to its conclusion with a commentary by Adam Jaworski entitled 'Language in the media: authenticity and othering'. Jaworski begins by re-visiting the potential ambiguity in the title of this volume, given that the very phrase 'language in the media' may refer to both the use of language/discourse in the media as well as metalinguistic issues around the representation and/or construction of language in the context of media texts and practices. Second, Jaworski reminds us how, as a substantial body of discourse analysis has already demonstrated, media discourse itself does not appear to differ so greatly from various forms of *un*-mediatized interaction (see Androutsopoulos 2006, for a similar point on computer-mediated communication). However, what sets mediatized communication apart as a key focus for work in sociolinguistics, (critical) discourse analysis and linguistic ethnography, is the media's ubiquity and typically élite status. For our purposes this means that media producers are exceptionally well positioned to influence a range of contemporary language practices and values, with an ever-increasing potential for global reach. Against this backdrop, what unites the various chapters, for Jaworski, is a focus on the ways in which such practices and values are metadiscursively ideologized in the context of media texts alongside an underlying concern with what Nikolas Coupland (2001b, 2004) refers to as the concept of 'sociolinguistic authenticities'. Thus, running through the chapters, in Jaworski's view, is the implicit theme of what counts as 'authentic' language practice and the ways in which the notion of authenticity is itself ideologized within the media texts and discourses under scrutiny. This is a process, moreover, that simultaneously serves as a crucial means of 'othering', potentially leading therefore to a marginalization of those linguistic practices that are rendered, by implication, 'inauthentic'. In sum, it is precisely the analysis of such discursive patterns of authentication and othering that lie at the heart of this book's project as a means of exploring not only the role of media discourse in the very construction of what it is that we understand by language, discourse and communication but also the possible social, political and economic implications thereof for language users in the real world.

Notes

1 We are grateful to Tommaso Milani at Stockholm University and Paul Baker at Lancaster University for their insightful comments on an earlier version of this chapter. Any remaining shortcomings are, of course, entirely our own.
2 Other works to have included discussions of media representations of language include Bauer and Trudgill (1998), Cameron (1995), Aitchison (1997) and Niedzielski and Preston (1999).
3 See www.bbc.co.uk/voices and www.pbs.org/speak, respectively.
4 See also many of the contributions to Duchêne and Heller (2007), which highlight the role of the media in relation to discourses of language endangerment. For discussions of media involvement in the revitalization of small and/or minority languages more generally, see Cotter (1999), Pietikänen and Dufva (2006) and Spitulnik (1998) as well as the chapters by Jaffe and Kelly-Holmes and Atkinson in this volume.
5 For an enlightening discussion of what counts as *new* media from a historical perspective, see Gitelman and Pingree (2001).
6 For this reason, the contributors to this book (including ourselves as editors) variously use 'the media' in the plural or singular, depending on whether they wish to emphasize medial plurality or refer to the word's unmarked (singular) meaning.

PART I
METAPHORS AND MEANINGS

2 Metaphors for speaking and writing in the British press[1]

John Heywood and Elena Semino

2.1 Introduction

In this chapter we present some of the results of a corpus-based study of metaphors for verbal communication in the British press. On the basis of an analysis of over 500 metaphorical references to speaking and writing, we show how verbal communication in our data is conventionally constructed metaphorically via source domains that are to do with physical, concrete experiences, such as manipulating objects, moving towards a destination or physically attacking someone. We argue that these source domains can be exploited to make complex and problematic aspects of communication more accessible and easier to express, but also to present a view of communication that is rather basic and simplistic. We also show how the authors of news reports tend to favour metaphorical expressions that dramatize and sensationalize the verbal behaviour of participants in news stories. We conclude the chapter by reflecting on the implications of our study for metaphor theory and analysis.

The study of metaphor has a long and venerable tradition, dating back at least to Greek and Roman antiquity. In the last few decades, however, the work of linguists, philosophers and cognitive scientists has led to new insights into the role of metaphor in language and thought. In particular, scholars working within 'cognitive' or 'conceptual' metaphor theory (hereafter CMT) have drawn attention to the existence of systematic patterns of conventional metaphorical expressions in everyday language (e.g. *She **shot down** every suggestion I made*, or *I successfully **defended** the new proposals*) and have claimed that these linguistic patterns reflect conventional patterns of metaphorical thought, known as conceptual metaphors (e.g. ARGUMENT IS WAR) (see Lakoff and Johnson 1980; Lakoff and Johnson 1999). Conceptual metaphors are defined as systematic sets of correspondences (or 'mappings') between a 'source' conceptual domain (e.g. WAR) and a 'target' conceptual domain (e.g. ARGUMENT). For example, the ARGUMENT IS WAR conceptual metaphor involves correspondences between interlocutors and opposing armies, criticisms and attacks, success in persuasion and military victory, and so on. Within this approach, metaphorical expressions such as *shot down* in the example above are seen as linguistic realizations of conceptual metaphors.

Metaphor scholars of all periods and persuasions have recognized, in different ways and with different emphases, that metaphors highlight some aspects of target domains (also known as 'topics' or 'tenors') and background others. Cognitive metaphor theorists, in particular, have argued that we systematically think and talk about relatively complex, abstract, poorly delineated areas of experience (such as time or emotions) in terms of more concrete, physical, better delineated areas of experience (such as movement in space or interactions with objects). These more concrete source domains structure the targets in particular ways, so that particular elements, relations and inference patterns are projected onto the targets. Communication, for example, is a relatively abstract and complex domain that, as we will show, is conventionally constructed metaphorically via several different source domains, including the WAR source domain in the conceptual metaphor ARGU-MENT IS WAR. Within this metaphor, the relationship between interlocutors is constructed as hostile and confrontational, and the goal of participants in an argument is constructed in terms of the prevalence of one's views and the defeat of the views of others. This particular metaphor therefore backgrounds the potentially collaborative aspect of arguments, and does not easily allow for the fact that the most desirable goal of arguments might be the joint formulation of mutually acceptable views.

CMT has inspired some important work on the ideological and political dimensions of metaphors. For example, George Lakoff has discussed the complex of metaphors that were used to justify the first Gulf War (Lakoff 1991), and explained the differences between the 'Liberal' and 'Conservative' ideologies in contemporary US politics in terms of different metaphorical systems (Lakoff 2002). Similarly, Paul Chilton has discussed the complex system of metaphors that dominated international relations in the west during the Cold War period, and Elena Semino and Michela Masci (1996) have shown how Silvio Berlusconi strategically used a small set of metaphors (e.g. football metaphors) in his first successful election campaign in Italy in 1994. A number of scholars have also considered the metaphors used to support anti-immigration and xenophobic views in different countries (e.g. El Refaie 2001; O'Brien 2003). What these studies have in common is that they do not simply investigate metaphor as a general linguistic and cognitive tool but explore the possible reasons and implications of the choice of particular metaphors within particular forms of communication at particular historical and political junctures.

In this chapter we consider the metaphors used in a corpus of British news reports to refer to communication, including both speaking and writing. We identify the main metaphorical patterns in our data and reflect on their implications for the ways in which communication is conventionally

26

constructed in the press (for an analysis of our data that focuses on its impli-cations for CMT, see Semino 2005). Our use of authentic corpus data and quantitative evidence is partly due to our awareness of some of the weak-nesses of CMT, which has been criticized for the use of artificially constructed examples and for the lack of an explicit methodology for the identification of metaphorical expressions and for the extrapolation of conceptual metaphors from linguistic evidence (e.g. Cameron 2003: 239–41; Low 2003; Ritchie 2003; see also Deignan 2005).

2.2 Corpus data and methodology

Our data is taken from a corpus of (late) twentieth-century written British English, which was constructed at Lancaster University in the mid-1990s as part of a project on speech, writing and thought presentation in fictional and non-fictional narratives (see Semino and Short 2004). The whole corpus contains 120 text samples of approximately 2,000 words each, amounting to a total of 258,348 words. It is equally divided into three sections contain-ing 40 text samples each from three main genres: prose fiction (87,709 words), newspaper news reports (83,603 words) and biography and autobio-graphy (87,036 words). Each genre was further subdivided into a 'serious' and 'popular' section (e.g. serious and popular novels, broadsheet and tabloid newspapers). In selecting our text samples, we restricted our focus both lin-guistically (by choosing texts written in British English) and temporally (by choosing texts published in the twentieth century, and ideally towards the end of the century). In the present chapter, we focus on the newspaper section of the corpus, which consists of news stories published in two 2-day periods in 1994 (4–5 December and 11–12 December), and two 2-day periods in 1996 (28–29 April and 12–13 May). The news stories were extracted in roughly equal proportions from six 'tabloid' and six 'broadsheet' newspapers.[2]

All the texts included in the corpus were systematically annotated for forms of speech, writing and thought presentation, such as direct speech, indirect writing, free indirect thought, and so on (see Wynne *et al* 1998). For example, the expression *Michael Howard, the Home Secretary, appealed for loyalty* was analysed as an instance of speech presentation (and, more pre-cisely, as an instance of 'Narrator's Representation of Speech acts', or NRSA, consisting of eight words). The analysis of the annotated corpus led to the development of an updated model of speech, writing and thought presenta-tion, as well as to a systematic account of the different ways in which the words and thoughts of participants in stories are presented in fictional and non-fictional narratives (see Semino and Short 2004). A quantitative analy-sis of the press section of the corpus in particular revealed that 47.15 per cent of this data involved the presentation of spoken communication, and 2.32 per cent involved the presentation of written communication, for a total of just under 50 per cent of the words in our news reports (Semino and Short

27

2004: 59). This combined figure is considerably higher than those for the two other genres included in the corpus: in the fiction section, 31.59 per cent of the words were analysed as speech presentation, and 0.63 per cent as writing presentation, for a total of just over 32 per cent; in the (auto)biography section, 22.52 per cent of the words were analysed as speech presentation, and 6.01 per cent as writing presentation, for a total of approximately 28.5 per cent.[3]

For the purposes of the present study, we used a concordancing programme (*Wordsmith Tools*, Scott 1999) to extract the previously classified instances of speech and writing presentation from the news section. These included: 'reporting clauses' of speech or writing (e.g. *she said, he wrote*); references to the speech act value of utterances or texts (e.g. *[S]enior Tory figures openly questioned the Prime Minister's judgement*), and minimal references to speech or writing taking place (e.g. *Each week Fergie would talk to fortune-teller Rita Rogers*).

We found a total of 2,238 such instances of references to verbal communication in the news data, of which 2,146 instances were speech presentation and 92 instances writing presentation. The examples were divided almost equally between the serious and popular news sections (the serious news examples accounting for 53 per cent of the instances of speech presentation and 52 per cent of writing presentation).

Within all these stretches of text, a particular linguistic expression referring to (a particular kind of) verbal communication was classified as metaphorical if:

- it has a more basic current sense that is not to do with (that particular kind of) verbal communication; and
- the (particular kind of) verbal communication sense of the relevant expression can be said to be motivated by the more basic sense via a cross-domain mapping where the target is (a particular type of) speaking/writing and the source is a different domain.[4]

As an example, consider the following extract from our tabloid data:

(1) Former Tory chairman Kenneth Baker **blasted** the Prime Minister for an act of 'crass stupidity'. (*Daily Star*, 05.12.94)

In this extract, the verb *blast* is used to refer to verbal communication, and particularly to the expression of strong criticism against someone. This metaphorical sense of the verb *blast*, which is of course highly lexicalized, contrasts with the more basic current sense of using weapons to cause physical damage to people or things, as in this other extract from our corpus data: *He crept along an alley beside Dr Meenaghan's home and blasted him through the kitchen window from about six feet* (*Daily Mirror*, 12.12.94). The sense of *blast* exemplified in

Example 1 can be explained in terms of a metaphorical mapping from the domain evoked by the basic sense (which we will call PHYSICAL AGGRESSION[5]) to the domain of verbal communication: the expression of strong criticism is metaphorically constructed in terms of a particularly devastating type of physical aggression. Indeed, within CMT, examples such as (1) would normally be seen as linguistic realizations of the conventional conceptual metaphor ARGUMENT IS WAR. We will discuss the analysis of such examples in more detail below.

Out of the 2,238 references to speaking (2,146) and writing (92) we extracted from our press data, 536 (i.e. 23.9 per cent) were analysed as involving metaphorical expressions. In the rest of this chapter, we discuss the main metaphorical patterns we identified in this set of expressions.

2.3 Metaphorical patterns and dominant source domains in our data

An important part of our analysis involved the identification of groups of metaphorical expressions within our data that could be related to particular metaphorical source domains. Within CMT, conceptual domains are fairly broad mental representations, that contain information about particular areas of experience, such as journeys, war, machines, and so on (see Grady 1997, for a version of CMT that focuses on a different kind of mental representation). Although, as we will show, more fine-grained explanations are often needed to account for specific meanings and uses, an analysis in terms of dominant source domains provides a useful summary of our findings, and an overview of the dominant ways in which verbal communication is conventionally metaphorized in our data. Table 2.1 lists the metaphorical source domains that account for the largest patterns of metaphorical expressions in our data. The right-hand columns indicate, respectively, the number of individual metaphorical references to speaking or writing that we have classified under each source domain, and the relevant percentages out of our 536 metaphorical expressions.

Table 2.1 shows that, in our data, verbal communication is primarily talked about via metaphorical expressions whose basic senses relate to a variety of domains to do with physical experience (e.g. object manipulation, movement, vision). This is consistent with the view that metaphor allows us to construct abstract and complex experiences in terms of more concrete and accessible ones. The fact that verbal communication is a complex and multifaceted domain, with many different aspects and dimensions (utterances, texts, speech acts, meanings, attitudes, social relations, etc.), explains why a number of different domains provide conventional metaphorical expressions for speaking and writing: as we will show, different source domains capture different aspects of verbal communication (see also Semino 2005). The source domains listed in Table 2.1, however, are not just conventionally

29

Table 2.1: Dominant metaphorical source domains in our data, and numbers of metaphorical expression classified under each source domain

Source domains	Instances of metaphorical expressions	% Total
Object manipulation	136	25.4%
'Discourse'[5]	103	19.2%
Visibility	89	16.6%
Physical aggression	62	11.6%
Movement	57	10.6%
Nature	20	3.7%
Physical contact	20	3.7%
Proximity	13	2.4%
Liquid	10	1.9%
Other	26	4.9%
Total	536	100%

involved in the metaphorical construction of communication, but, in most cases, have a wide metaphorical 'scope' (Kövecses 2002), namely they conventionally apply to a wide variety of target domains: for example, many different types of goal-directed behaviour are conventionally constructed in terms of movement (see Grady 1997 and Kövecses 2002, for versions of CMT that take this phenomenon into account).

In what follows, we will not consider the different source domains in order of frequency in our data, but in the sequence that best points out the relationships and connections between them.

2.3.1 Communication as object manipulation

It is well recognized in CMT that our experiences with objects are conventionally exploited in the metaphorical construction of a wide variety of abstract, non-physical experiences (see Lakoff and Johnson 1999: 240–1 for a discussion of the metaphorical construction of thinking in terms of object manipulation). Indeed, the largest group of metaphorical expressions we have identified in our data (136 instances) involves references to verbal communication via expressions that have basic senses to do with the manipulation of physical objects, broadly conceived (e.g. *give*, *hold* or *drop*). This large group of expressions, which accounts for just over 25 per cent of all our metaphorical examples, includes a number of more specific patterns that construct communication in terms of particular *types* of interactions with objects, including particularly the transfer of objects and the construction of objects.

2.3.1.1 Communication as transferring objects

In a classic study, Michael Reddy (1993) showed how, in English, communication is conventionally talked about in terms of the transfer of objects between participants. He argued that conventional expressions such as *Try to **get** your thoughts **across** better* and *You still haven't **given** me any idea of what you mean* (Reddy 1993: 166) construct language metaphorically as a 'conduit, transferring thoughts bodily from one person to another' (ibid.: 170). Reddy's data included many expressions that present speaking or writing as a process involving the insertion of thoughts or feelings into words, so that words are constructed as containers to be transferred to others, who then extract from them the original thoughts and feelings (see Grady 1998, for a re-analysis of Reddy's data in terms of 'primary metaphors'; see also Johnson and Ensslin in Chapter 1, who note how this metaphor is typically applied to public understandings of language/linguistics). Thirty-three of our OBJECT MANIPULATION examples fall within Reddy's 'conduit' metaphor, but involve a larger variety of expressions than those considered by Reddy:

> (2) Although he **delivered** a strong appeal for calm reflection and for a 'healing process', Mr Portillo markedly refused to back Mr Major's decision to withdraw the party whip from his rebels. (*Daily Telegraph*, 12.12.94)

> (3) Mr Delors, outgoing President of the European Commission, **gave** both personal and professional reasons as he read from a prepared statement during a television interview. (*Independent*, 12.12.94)

In (2) the verb *deliver* is used to refer to the performance of a particular speech act (*appeal*), while in (3) the verb *give* is similarly used to indicate the process of providing particular types of information (in this case, the reasons why Jacques Delors had decided not to run for the French presidency). Both verbs have basic senses to do with the transfer of objects, typically between people (e.g. *Letters were delivered twice a week only*, from the British National Corpus, hereafter the BNC), and both are conventionally used metaphorically in relation to communication. In expressions such as (2) and (3) speech acts and meanings/information are constructed as objects that are transferred from addresser to addressee in the process of spoken or written communication.

Our data shows that a wide range of aspects of communication are conventionally constructed as objects via the metaphorical use of verbs such as *give* and *deliver*. These include not just speech acts (e.g. *give advice*) and meanings/information (e.g. *give names, examples*), but also text-types or speech events (e.g. *give/deliver speeches, lectures*), types of turns (e.g. *give answers*) and ideas/opinions (e.g. *give views, assessments*). As Reddy also suggests, this particular metaphorical pattern provides a rather simplistic and distorted view of communication, in which speakers/writers pass (communicative) objects to addressees. On the one hand, this particular metaphorical view of communication emphasizes the active role of the speaker/writer, and the materiality of communication (which does involve physical sounds and objects such as paper). On the other hand, this pattern downplays the role of the addressee in constructing meaning and the inevitable differences between the intentions of speakers/writers and the interpretations of listeners/readers. Within the source domain, if someone gives or delivers an object to somebody else, prototypically the second person now has the original object. The use of expressions such as (2) and (3) implicitly constructs speech acts and meanings as similarly stable objects that can be straightforwardly transferred via language.

2.3.1.2   Communication as constructing objects

Another pattern, which accounts for about half of our OBJECT MANIPULATION examples (69 instances), involves the use of the verbs *make* and *add* to refer to a variety of communicative activities, as in the examples below:

> (4) In recent weeks Mr Balladur has **made** speeches opposing faster European integration. (*Daily Express*, 12.12.94)

> (5) A witness heard him **make** a remark about WASPS – White Anglo Saxon Protestants – seconds before the shootings. (*Daily Express*, 29.04.96)

> (6) He said a 999 call was received after the shooting and **added**: 'The emergency call was passed over to the police.' (*Independent*, 12.12.94)

The most basic sense of *make* is to do with the physical construction of objects (e.g. *The Aztecs did not [. . .] make objects to be contemplated for their beauty alone*, from the BNC). However, this verb has a wide variety of conventional metaphorical uses (e.g. *make an attempt, make a wish*, etc.), which have resulted in a high degree of delexicalization. Nonetheless, a potential contrast still exists between the basic sense of physical construction and the use of *make* in relation to various aspects of communication, in particular. In (4) and (5) above, the verb is used, respectively, in relation to a text-type/speech event (*speeches*) and to a particular speech act (*remark*). Our data includes a variety of similar examples, where *make* is used in relation to a range of speech acts (e.g. *make pleas, appeals, enquiries, complaints*) and types of texts or utterances (e.g. *make a joke, make a report*, etc.). All these expressions metaphorically present utterances, texts, speech acts, etc. as physical objects that are constructed by speakers. This metaphorical pattern is obviously consistent with the 'transfer of objects' pattern we discussed in the previous sub-section, and similarly foregrounds the role of speakers/writers in communication and the stability of the actions they perform and of the meanings they express.

In Example 6, the verb *add* is used to introduce a stretch of direct quotation. Like *make*, *add* has a basic sense to do with the construction of physical entities, and particularly with the process of putting objects or substances together with other objects or substances (e.g. *Some brewers add extra sugar at this stage to encourage the continuing fermentation*, from the BNC). This verb is also conventionally used to introduce what someone has said (or written) and indicate that this is related to something that has just been said (or written), as in Example 6. This use of *add* is frequent in our data (both with direct and indirect speech presentation), and metaphorically presents the unfolding of utterances or texts as the progressive accumulation of substances or (parts of) objects. Hence, words (and the meanings they express) are presented as physical entities that are sequentially amassed in the process of communication. This allows reporters, in particular, to present different parts of utterances or texts as both separate and related.

2.3.1.3   Other examples of communication as object manipulation

The examples from our data that we have classified under the broad source domain of OBJECT MANIPULATION contain many further individual cases and smaller-scale patterns that we cannot do justice to. We will, however, discuss two more instances, in order to provide a sense of the variety of experiences with objects that can be metaphorically used to construct different aspects of communication.

In the example below, the verb *drop* is used to indicate a particular communicative act within a process of industrial negotiations:

> (7)   Fed-up staff **dropped** their demand after the Government agreed to
> ... (*Daily Star*, 13.05.96)

The most basic sense of the verb *drop* is that of letting an object fall, whether deliberately or accidentally (e.g. *He dropped the pen and went on typing*, from the BNC). This verb also has a range of conventional metaphorical meanings, including that of not continuing something that had been previously undertaken (e.g. *Bass have **dropped** the plans*, from the BNC). In examples such as (7), *drop* is used more specifically to indicate the (expression of the) decision to stop performing a particular speech act within a particular communicative context.[6] As with the other verbs we have discussed in this section, this metaphorical use of *drop* implicitly constructs the particular speech act as an object. In the source scenario, when someone drops an object they are no longer in a position to act on it or use it to pursue a particular line of action. In examples such as (7) this scenario is applied to the performance of speech acts, which are constructed as physical objects that are dropped when the speaker/writer no longer intends to perform them, and to achieve the original perlocutionary effect.

The metaphorical references to speech/writing activity we have discussed so far involve highly conventional metaphorical expressions. However, our data also includes some less conventional uses of metaphor, such as the following:

(8) In the end this principle was agreed, but **wrapped up in** coded language, saying that there had to be 'equitable and balanced' arrangements for all parties. (*The Times*, 05.12.94)

The context of this extract is the 1994 crisis in the former Yugoslavia, and particularly the difficulty in reaching international agreement as to whether the Bosnian Serbs should be allowed, at least in principle, to form a confederation with Serbia. The way in which this principle was eventually formulated is metaphorically presented via the expression *wrapped up in coded language*. The expression *wrap up in*, which typically refers to the packaging of physical objects, metaphorically constructs language as a material that is used to cover, and partly disguise, the precise nature of the agreement. In context, this appears to relate particularly to the use of expressions that could be used to prevent the setting up of a confederation between Serbia and the Bosnian Serbs if this was not fully acceptable to the other ethnic and national groups in the region. Once again, the 'meanings' that were finally agreed are implicitly constructed as an object, which, within the metaphor, is separate from the language used to express it. This example can be seen as a creative use of an aspect of Reddy's 'conduit metaphor', which, he argues, presents words as containers for the 'content' of communication (see Johnson and Ensslin, Chapter 1, this volume). In this particular case, however, emphasis is placed on the fact that the process of wrapping something up not only partly disguises the precise nature of the object in question but can also make it more attractive.

As our discussion shows, a large variety of different metaphorical expressions were included under the general source domain of OBJECT MANIPULATION: all the examples we have discussed metaphorically present speaking or writing as a process that involves some form of interaction with physical objects, but there are differences in the kind of object manipulation that is involved, and the kind of metaphorical meanings that are conveyed. What brings together all the different examples is the fact that, on the one hand, the exploitation of some aspect of the domain of OBJECT MANIPULATION makes abstract and complex communicative processes more accessible and comprehensible. On the other hand, however, this tends to result in an oversimplified view of communication, where meanings, speech acts, etc. are straightforwardly transferred from addressers to addressees, and where language is separate from the meanings that it is used to express. As we will show, a similar view of communication is also conveyed by other metaphorical patterns in our data, including the one we will discuss next.

2.3.2 Communication as enabling vision

The third most frequent metaphorical pattern in our data consists of a range of expressions which have basic senses to do with visibility, and which are conventionally used to refer metaphorically to the process of providing information via speaking or writing. This pattern accounts for 89 examples, amounting to over 16 per cent of all our metaphorical references to communication. More specifically, 45 of these examples include expressions such as the following:

> (9) He **disclosed** that M Delors had presented papers to the summit that the only two countries who would be within the Maastricht single-currency criteria by 1996 were Germany and the United Kingdom. (*The Times*, 12.12.94)

> (10) after it was **revealed** that Labour plans to SACK half the Royal Family. (*Sun*, 05.12.94)

In these examples, acts of communication are referred to metaphorically via the verbs *disclose* and *reveal*. Both verbs have basic senses to do with exposing to view objects that were previously covered or not visible (e.g. *She laughed at him, the pretty mouth opening to reveal small, even teeth*, from the BNC; *The screen fell back [. . .] and disclosed a yawning opening in the sand*, from the Bank of English corpus). The metaphorical use of these verbs in relation to communication, which is highly conventional, once again constructs meanings or information as physical objects. In this case, however, verbal communication is presented as a process whereby something that was not previously accessible to the senses is made visible. In CMT, this particular metaphorical construct is explained with reference to the more general conceptual metaphor KNOWING IS SEEING (e.g. *Can you **see** the point I am trying to make?*, from the BNC), which involves the mapping of our experiences with vision onto our cognitive experiences of knowledge and understanding (Grady 1998; see also Reddy 1993: 193). This metaphor can also explain why verbs such as *disclose* and *reveal* are 'factive' when used in the way exemplified in (9) and (10), i.e. they presuppose the truth of the state of affairs described in the subordinate clause they introduce, unlike verbs such as *claim*, for example (Levinson 1983: 177ff.). In the metaphorical source scenario, the visibility of an object normally correlates with establishing that it exists (see Grady 1997); similarly, in the target scenario, information that is metaphorically presented as becoming visible is also presented as 'true'.

A closely related metaphorical pattern within our VISIBILITY examples (22 instances) includes expressions such as the following:

> (11) Mr Brookes-Baker warned of the dangers in adopting a Scandinavian style monarchy – and **pointed to** the example of Sweden. 'Other Scandinavian monarchs have some official duties, but

the King of Sweden does not even open Parliament,' he said. (*Daily Mirror*, 05.12.94)

(12) But ministers anxiously **point out** that Tuesday's division is on a procedural motion and can therefore not be seen as a vote of confidence. (*Independent on Sunday*, 04.12.94)

(13) Foreign Secretary Douglas Hurd has already **indicated** that he would back a referendum if necessary. (*Daily Star*, 12.12.94)

In all three cases the expression of particular meanings is metaphorically presented in terms of the process of pointing at an object. More specifically, the basic sense of *point to* is to do with drawing attention to an object that is potentially visible but which may not be or have been noticed otherwise (e.g. *She smiled and pointed to the wall to her right*, from the BNC). In the conventional metaphorical use exemplified in (11), *point to* refers to the process of verbally introducing something that has not yet been mentioned as relevant to the current topic. Similarly, *point out* has a basic sense to do with drawing attention to something that is potentially visible, but in this case the prepositional adverb *out* metaphorically suggests that the object to be observed is being distinguished from its visual context (e.g. *I pointed out the mountains*, from the BNC) (see Grady 1998). In its conventional metaphorical sense to do with communication, *point out* is used to refer to the process of mentioning some information that is relevant to the topic under discussion but that has not yet been taken into account, as in Example 12. Like *disclose* and *reveal*, *point out* is a factive expression, and its factivity can be explained in the same way: the inference that visible objects exist is mapped from the source scenario onto the truthfulness of the information that is presented as being *pointed out* in the target scenario. The metaphorical use of *indicate* exemplified in (13) can be explained in a similar way, even though this verb can be used more specifically to introduce a future plan or intention. This slight but significant difference in meaning and contexts of use cannot solely be explained in terms of conventional conceptual metaphors, but requires a broader consideration of patterns of use and collocations (see Deignan 2005).

Overall, the patterns we have examined in this section metaphorically construct meanings as visible objects, and the provision of reliable information as enabling vision. This is part of a more general metaphorical association between vision and knowledge. As with the OBJECT MANIPULATION source domain, the source domain that we have called VISIBILITY provides a convenient but rather oversimplified view of communication, where meanings are seen as stable entities that can easily become intersubjectively accessible.

2.4 Communication as movement

Since the early days of CMT, scholars have discussed the pervasiveness of metaphors involving MOVEMENT or JOURNEYS as source domains (e.g. LIFE IS A

JOURNEY and LOVE IS A JOURNEY in Lakoff and Johnson 1980). More recently, Joseph Grady (1997) has explained the ubiquity of movement metaphors in terms of a small set of more basic 'primary' metaphors, including PURPOSES ARE DESTINATIONS (e.g. *He'll ultimately be successful, but he's not **there** yet*) and ACTION IS SELF-PROPELLED motion (e.g. *I've got to start **moving** on this project* (Grady 1997: 286–7; see also Lakoff and Johnson 1999: 52–3). Our data shows how speaking and writing are also conventionally constructed in terms of movement. We have included 57 of our examples under the general MOVEMENT source domain, amounting to over 10 per cent of the total. As with other broad source domains, expressions indicating different types of movement are used in reference to different aspects of verbal communication.

The examples below involve expressions (*go on, back track*) whose basic senses are to do with movement along a path from a starting point to an end point. This is the most prototypical type of movement, which has received the most attention within CMT:

> (14) Prostitute Donna, 31, [...] **went on**: 'I got on his back and he galloped round the room. He had sex with a couple of girls that night.' (*News of the World*, 04.12.94)

> (15) Yesterday Mr Haigh [...] **back tracked** a little (*News of the World*, 11.12.94)

The verb *go on*, which has a basic sense to do with continued movement forward, is conventionally used to indicate the continuation of an action/ process in general (e.g. *The masons smiled at his fancy and **went on** with their work*, from the BNC). As Example 14 shows, this can also apply to communication: continuing to speak (or write) is metaphorically presented as continuing to move forward. More precisely, *go on* can be used in a similar way to *add* (see Example 6), namely to present an utterance or text as a sequence of separate but related parts, and to emphasize the utterance or text as a goal-directed, linear process in which the speaker or writer is engaged. This use of *go on* can be explained in terms of the primary metaphors we mentioned above: (communicative) action is metaphorically constructed as motion, and continued (communicative) action is constructed as continued movement forwards towards a destination.

The same metaphorical scenario can account for examples such as Example 15, where the verb *back track* is used to indicate a change of mind, or, more precisely, the expression of views that are partly different from previously expressed views. In other words, continuing to speak or write is constructed as movement forward, and expressing a change of mind is constructed as movement backwards. This may explain why the use of *back track* in examples such as (15) tends to suggest a negative evaluation of the speaker or writer, who, typically, is presented as first expressing controversial or extreme views, and then as being forced to express more moderate views as a result of others' reactions. Within the PURPOSES ARE DESTINATIONS metaphor, movement forward is positive, while movement backwards is negative. In conventional metaphorical uses of expressions to do with movement, moving forwards suggests success, positive change and innovation, while movement backwards suggests lack of success, negative change and lack of innovation (for example, the 2005 election slogan of the UK Labour Party was: 'Britain *forward* not back). The use of expressions such as *back track* in relation to communication therefore suggests that expressing a change of mind is a sign of failure, weakness and lack of conviction, rather than, for example, a sign of flexibility, thoughtfulness or receptiveness to others' views.

Some of the metaphorical expressions we have grouped under the general MOVEMENT source domain do not indicate movement along a path towards or away from an end point:

> (16) Friends started deserting her as word **spread** that Ariel had died of
> Aids. (*Today*, 05.12.94)

In its basic physical sense, the verb *spread* suggests movement outwards in all directions, typically involving substances such as liquids or gases (e.g. *Smoke wisped up from huts invisible among the bunched darkness of trees and spread in faint blue webs*, from the BNC). In examples such as Example 16, the verb is used metaphorically in relation to communication, and particularly to indicate the process whereby many people find out about something in the course of many different conversations. This conventional metaphorical use of *spread* emphasizes the overall outcome of many different instances of communication, rather than individual instances or the role of particular speakers/ writers. The communication of (particular items of) information is presented as movement in all directions: in Example 16, the grammatical subject of *spread* is *word that Ariel had died of Aids* (NB: the clause *that Ariel had died of Aids* is part of the noun phrase with *word* as head). Hence, expressions such as *spread* are typically used in cases where private information becomes widely known via rumour, rather than being deliberately revealed by the people involved. It is interesting to note that the metaphorical use of *spread* often has negative connotations even when it is not applied to communication: our experience of the movement of inanimate entities in all directions is metaphorically applied to our experience of uncontrollable and often threatening phenomena more generally, as in *Flu can **spread** very rapidly*, from the BNC.

2.4.1 Communication as causing *movement*

A notable specific pattern within our movement metaphors (32 instances) involves the use of the verbs *admit* and *dismiss* in expressions such as the following:

(17) One of the Queen's footmen 22-year-old Barry Mitford of Walsall confirmed Sylvia's drug revelations and **admitted** popping pills and smoking cannabis. (*News of the World*, 12.05.96)

(18) Reminded how he had **dismissed** the idea of a referendum, (*News of the World*, 11.12.94)

The verb *admit* has a basic sense to do with allowing someone or something to enter a physical space (e.g. *Do not even admit someone claiming to be a policeman or woman*, from the BNC), while *dismiss* has a basic sense to do with getting someone to leave a place (e.g. *She dismissed the video crew with the threat of terrible penalties if the video tape was not perfect*, from the BNC).[7] In the conventional metaphorical uses exemplified above, speakers/writers are presented as causing the movement of the particular meanings or information they talk about. More specifically, acknowledging the truth of something unpleasant or unfavourable is presented as allowing someone/something to enter a space (Example 17); conversely saying that something is untrue, mistaken, inadequate or inappropriate is presented as forcing someone/something to leave.[8] As with several of the patterns we have already discussed, communication is metaphorically constructed as a physical scenario, in which 'meanings' are physical entities that may either be allowed or forbidden to occupy a particular space. This space metaphorically corresponds to what the speaker or writer regards as valid and true.

2.5 Communication as physical aggression

In the previous sections, we have discussed metaphorical patterns that capture a number of related aspects of spoken or written communication, including particularly the production of utterances or texts, the performance of speech acts, and the expression of meaning or information. In this section we turn to metaphorical expressions that capture communicative behaviour in the context of arguments, debates or, more generally, disagreements between people, whether in face-to-face communication or otherwise. A typical example is given below:

(19) The Labour leader [...] **defended** Jack Straw, the Shadow Home Secretary, who **came under attack** for saying that Labour wanted to redefine the role of the monarchy. (*The Times*, 05.12.94)

In this extract, the expressions *defend* and *came under attack* refer to verbal processes and their consequences. More specifically, Jack Straw's *coming under attack* relates to the criticisms he received after outlining Labour's plans for reforming the monarchy (the Labour Party was in opposition at the time, and Straw was Shadow Foreign Secretary). The whole process whereby

Straw was strongly criticized by many different people is presented via an expression that has a basic sense to do with being physically hit, assaulted or invaded (e.g. *His first act was to seize possession of the Leonine City in Rome, which came under attack from rebellious Roman citizens based upon the Capitol,* from the BNC; NB: the use of *come* is metaphorical here). In particular, the noun *attack* has a basic sense to do with physical aggression (e.g. *Sussex police have warned other female students on the campus to be on their guard after the attack on Sunday,* from the BNC), but is conventionally used, especially in the media, to refer metaphorically to the expression of critical views. Similarly, the Labour leader's expression of agreement and solidarity with Straw is presented via a conventional metaphorical use of the verb *defend*, which has to do with protecting oneself or others from physical attack (e.g. *Michael told the Old Bailey he had tried to **defend** his brother Lee, 13, before his father turned on him,* from the BNC). The result is a metaphorical scenario in which those who express different views within a public political debate are engaged in a physical struggle of blows and counter-blows.

Within CMT, examples such as these have been traditionally seen as linguistic realizations of the conventional conceptual metaphor ARGUMENT IS WAR. More recently, however, it has been shown that there is linguistic evidence for a more general conceptual metaphor, in which the target domain of ANTAGONISTIC COMMUNICATION is constructed in terms of the source domain of PHYSICAL AGGRESSION, which includes war as the most large-scale manifestation of physical attack (see Ritchie 2003; Vanparys 1995; Semino 2005). This general conceptual metaphor provides a more adequate account for a pattern within our data that includes 62 individual instances, amounting to over 11 per cent of all our metaphorical expressions. Some representative examples are given below (see also Example 1 above):

(20) as she [Princess Diana] fled to Majorca following her **bust-up** with The Queen over divorce negotiations with Prince Charles. (*Sun*, 13.05.96)

(21) Crime victims **hit out** yesterday over plans to give thugs a five-star Christmas in jail. (*Sun*, 05.12.94)

(22) The Chancellor, Kenneth Clarke, yesterday stepped up his **guerrilla warfare** against the Tory right by insisting that [...]. (*Guardian*, 13.05.96)

(23) Mr Major [...] has warned his party's **warring** factions [...]. (*Daily Telegraph*, 05.12.94)

In each of these examples, expressions with basic senses to do with physical aggression are used to describe arguments and criticisms of others' views. In the case of (20) and (21), different types of antagonistic communication are metaphorically presented in terms of expressions (*bust-up* and *hit out*) whose basic senses relate to low-level, unarmed physical aggression (e.g. *ARDS man-ager Paul Malone fined himself a week's wages last night after a touchline bust-up with Linfield rival Trevor Anderson*, and *Very young babies show rage [...] but only when they become toddlers can they hit out at whoever is preventing them from doing what they want*, from the BNC). In Examples 22 and 23, political disagreements and debates are described in terms of different types of warfare (*guerrilla warfare*, *warring*).

As we suggested earlier, this metaphorical pattern foregrounds the con-frontational element in some kinds of communication, and the goal of prevail-ing over people who hold different views from one's own. More specifically, expressions such as the ones given above appear to be used in the press to emphasize and sensationalize conflict between newsworthy individuals or groups, and this often helps justify why those particular instances of commu-nication are reported in the first place. Indeed, the degree of violence and destructiveness suggested by the metaphorical expressions does not necessa-rily correlate with the intensity of the disagreements or negative attitudes that they refer to. For example, the expressions *Kenneth Baker blasted the Prime Minister* in Example 1 and *Crime victims hit out over plans* in Example 21 do not differ greatly in terms of the strength of the criticisms that they pre-sent. Rather, both seem to have a similar rhetorical function, namely that of exploiting a conventional conceptual metaphor in order to dramatize the ele-ments of conflict in particular instances of communication, thereby increas-ing their newsworthiness.

2.6 Metaphorical relations between different aspects or types of communication

So far we have treated 'communication' or 'speaking and writing' as a single broad domain, for the sake of expository clarity. Our discussion, however, has already shown how different metaphorical patterns relate to different aspects of verbal communication, such as the performance of speech acts or the expression of critical views. In the analysis of our data, we came across many expressions which constructed a particular aspect/type of communication in terms of a different aspect/type of communication, so that it was possible to analyse them in terms of mappings across different (sub-)domains within the general domain of verbal communication. Consider the examples below:

(24) Premier John Major dismissed **calls** last night to bring his Tory rebels back into the fold immediately. (*News of the World*, 11.12.94)

(25) Some Tories are **invoking the spectre** of the Labour leader, Tony Blair, getting in first by pledging to hold a referendum, so as to put pressure on Mr Major. (*Guardian*, 12.12.94)

The expressions we have put in bold in each extract have basic senses to do with communication. However, the particular acts of communication evoked in the extracts do not correspond to the basic senses of these expressions. The basic sense of *call* is to do with shouting loudly in order to be heard (e.g. *A passer-by heard his calls for help*, from the Bank of English corpus). In examples such as Example 24, the noun is used to indicate the intensity and urgency of particular requests, rather than their physical loudness. It could therefore be argued that a particular, relatively abstract aspect of communication (intensity, urgency) is conventionally constructed metaphorically in terms of a different, more concrete aspect (physical loudness). In the case of Example 25, the metaphoricity of the underlined expression is less controversial: a scenario in which someone tries to call up a spirit is used to indicate the way in which some Conservative MPs were raising the unwelcome prospect of the opposition leader promising to hold a referendum on the single currency before the then Conservative Prime Minister. In other words, an act of 'ordinary' communication is metaphorically constructed in terms of an attempt to summon up an infernal entity. The frightening, threatening nature of the source scenario is mapped onto the target scenario, in which an unwelcome future possibility is outlined so that action is taken to avoid it.

In Table 2.1, examples such as this are included under the general source domain of 'DISCOURSE', which we have used as a kind of shorthand to capture all those cases where one particular type/aspect of communication functions as metaphorical source domain for a different type/aspect of communication. In total, we have found 103 such examples, amounting to just over 19 per cent of all our metaphorical examples. However, this total figure includes many different patterns, which we do not have the space to do justice to here. The two examples we have quoted do, however, show two important tendencies that we have noted before. First, relatively more abstract aspects/types of communication are metaphorically presented in terms of relatively more concrete aspects/types of communication (note that the 'spectre' scenario provides a richer visual image than the target scenario, even though it is not part of physical, concrete experience, and would be regarded by most readers as outside the bounds of possibility). Second, the (conventional) metaphorical expressions favoured by the press often include an element of hyperbole that contributes to the dramatization and general newsworthiness of acts of communication within news stories: this applies to many of the expressions we analysed under PHYSICAL AGGRESSION and to many that were subsumed under the DISCOURSE source domain, as in the case of Example 25. The first tendency is to do with metaphor as a general linguistic and cognitive tool, as is of course well known in metaphor theory generally, and CMT in particular. The second tendency is to do with metaphor as a rhetorical tool in the particular genre we are considering: where a range of metaphorical and non-metaphorical expressions can be used, journalists often opt for expressions that sensationalize particular acts of communication and emphasize the antagonism and conflict between different participants in news stories.

2.7 Other patterns in our data

As shown in Table 2.1, each of the patterns considered so far accounts for more than 50 individual instances. In this section, we will briefly consider the other four source domains included in the table, which include between ten and 20 instances each. The remaining 26 examples (amounting to about 5 per cent of all cases) do not form sufficiently consistent patterns to be considered here.

In 20 cases (3.7 per cent of the total), verbal communication in our data is referred to via expressions which have basic senses to do with natural phenomena, and which we subsumed under the general source domain of NATURE. This includes, for example, references to rows *erupting* and the use of *thunder* as a speech reporting verb, as in *The Arsenal boss* **thundered***: '...'*. In such cases, the use of metaphorical expressions that literally refer to loud and/or threatening natural phenomena can be seen as part of the general tendency towards dramatization and hyperbole that we have already noted.[9] A more specific pattern involves the use of expressions that have basic senses to do with liquid substances, such as *pouring scorn* on somebody or *leaking* information. In such cases, meanings or attitudes are metaphorically constructed as liquids, and the process of communication as allowing liquids to flow. This particular pattern only accounts for ten instances in our data, but is consistent with the most frequent and conventional metaphorical expression used for speakers/writers in our data, namely *source* or *sources*, as in *a government* **source** *said* or *British* **sources** *say*. This use of *source* metaphorically constructs speakers and writers as the starting point of a flow of liquid, and is conventionally used in the media to refer to people who provide information without revealing their identity. Our data contains 29 such uses of *source(s)*, but these were not included in Table 2.1 as they constitute metaphorical references to *participants* in communication rather than to the *process* of communicating.

Another pattern in our data (13 instances, amounting to 2.4 per cent of the total) involves the use of expressions that have basic senses to do with physical proximity, such as the verb *back* and *stand by* in expressions such as *Mr Portillo [...]* **backed** *Mr Major's public positions* and *Mr Straw [...]* **stood by** *remarks about*. In these examples, communication is implicitly constructed as a physical scenario in which standing close to someone or something corresponds to the expression of agreement with and favour towards them. In CMT, similar metaphorical patterns have been captured by the conventional conceptual metaphors INTIMACY IS CLOSENESS and AGREEMENT IS BEING ON

THE SAME SIDE (Grady 1997; Lakoff and Johnson 1980; see Semino 2005, for a more detailed discussion).

Finally, 20 metaphorical expressions in our data (corresponding to 3.7 per cent of all cases) have basic senses to do with different kinds of physical contact. One of these expressions is *support* (either as a verb or noun), which is conventionally used to indicate help and assistance generally and, more specifically, the expression of a positive attitude towards someone or something, as in *he **supported** the very same regime in a letter to* ... (see Grady's 1997 discussion of the general conceptual metaphor ASSISTANCE IS SUPPORT). In contrast, the verb *press*, which involves physical pressure as well as contact, is used metaphorically to refer to the use of language to get others to do or say something they may not plan or wish to do, as in *the Mirror continued to **press** him over the stabbing of estranged wife Nicole*. The general metaphorical tendency to construct non-physical attempts to control other people's behaviour in terms of physical pressure has been captured by the conceptual metaphor COMPULSION IS A COMPELLING FORCE (Grady 1997; see Semino 2005, for more detail).

The last two patterns we have discussed are consistent with each other, in that they both construct the expression of attitudes and social relations in terms of a physical scenario in which physical closeness and physical support correspond to the expression of agreement and favour, while physical pressure corresponds to the use of language to modify others' behaviour. These patterns are also consistent with our PHYSICAL AGGRESSION metaphors, which construct antagonistic and critical communicative behaviour in terms of physical conflict.

2.8 Conclusions

We will begin our concluding remarks with some brief reflections on the implications of our discussion for metaphor studies, and CMT in particular. Readers will no doubt have noticed that the identification of conventional metaphorical expressions in texts is not a straightforward process. Even the application of the explicit criteria spelt out in 2.2 can lead to difficulties when, for example, the 'basic' sense of a particular expression is becoming archaic (as in the case of *disclose*), or when a verb is highly delexicalized (as in the case of *make*). The notion of conceptual 'domain' is also often problematic to operationalize. As we have suggested in 2.6, decisions about what count as separate domains may sometimes be controversial and, to some extent, arbitrary. In addition, the allocation of metaphorical expressions to conceptual domains can be done in different ways and at different levels of generality: for example, the metaphorical use of *thunder* we classified under the domain of NATURE (see 2.7) could be classified under the more specific source domain of WEATHER, or even under broader source domain of SOUND (cf. Vanparys 1995; see Croft 2002, for a discussion of the hierarchical nature of the domains within which concepts can be embedded; see also Cameron 2003, and Low 2003, for discussions of all these methodological issues). Nonetheless, a classification of metaphorical patterns in terms of fairly general source domains helps to provide an overview of dominant metaphorical constructs in particular sets of data or in language generally, as we hope to have shown. In order to explain the specific meanings and uses of individual expressions, however, it is often necessary to make reference to smaller and more specific mental representations, which, in our discussions, we have referred to as metaphorical 'scenarios' (see Musolff 2004; Heywood and Semino 2005; see also Grady's 1997 notion of 'scene'): for example, the metaphorical uses of *reveal* and *point at* can both be explained in terms of the general conceptual metaphor KNOWING IS SEEING, but the differences in their metaphorical uses can only be explained in terms of the different, more specific scenarios evoked by the basic senses of these verbs.

Even bearing these caveats in mind, a number of conclusions can be drawn from our study of metaphorical expressions for verbal communication in our press data. Just under a quarter of the references to speaking and writing we extracted from our news reports turned out to be metaphorical according to our criteria.[10] Although it is clearly possible to make references to communication that do not involve metaphor, it is in fact rather difficult to avoid the use of metaphorical expressions when talking about communication at any length. Indeed, in this chapter we have not been able to avoid using some of the metaphors that we have identified in our data (e.g. our expression *without **revealing** their identity* in 2.7).

The majority of the metaphorical references to communication in our data can be subsumed under a relatively small set of very general source domains, most of which are conventionally used to construct a variety of target domains (e.g. the source domains of MOVEMENT and PHYSICAL AGGRESSION). Each of these source domains contributes to the construction of particular aspects of communication, including for example the provision of information, the performance of speech acts, the expression of agreement or disagreement, and so on. Our analysis therefore confirms the general tendency noted in CMT and metaphor theory generally, whereby relatively abstract and complex domains, such as communication, are conventionally constructed in terms of relatively more concrete and simple domains. More specifically, we have shown that communication tends to be metaphorically constructed in terms of physical scenarios involving concrete objects and physical actions. In these physical scenarios, meanings, information, speech acts and utterances/texts are objects that can be constructed, added to, dropped, transferred to other people, and so on, while participants in communication can move in different directions, physically attack each other, and so on. On the one hand, this makes abstract and poorly delineated phenomena (e.g. the communication of meanings and attitudes) more

45

accessible and easier to express; on the other hand, this can also oversimplify the complexities and nuances of communication, and background important communicative phenomena, such as the way in which meanings are co-constructed in the process of communication, and the fact that attributing illocutionary force to utterances often involves inferences about speakers' unexpressed intentions.

While all of the patterns we have noted are conventional in English generally, we have also argued that many specific choices can be explained by the particular rhetorical goals of the writers of news stories, who often dramatize and sensationalize utterances and texts in order to emphasize their newsworthiness and keep the reader's attention. This is particularly important if we consider that many of the news stories in our data are either partly or exclusively about communicative acts (e.g. reports of reactions to the publication of a 'politically correct' version of the Bible, or of a debate over the future of the monarchy). Indeed, our press data (and particularly the tabloid section) contains most of the instances of PHYSICAL AGGRESSION metaphors in our corpus as a whole.

Overall, we hope to have shown that some awareness of metaphorical patterns is essential to our understanding of how communication is conventionally constructed, both in the media and in language generally.

Notes

1   We are grateful to the British Academy for funding the project of which this study is part (grant LGR-37225).
2   The broadsheet newspapers we sampled were: the *Daily Telegraph*, the *Guardian*, the *Independent*, the *Independent on Sunday*, the *Observer* and *The Times*. The tabloid newspapers we sampled were: the *Daily Express*, the *Daily Mirror*, the *News of the World*, the *Daily Star*, the *Sun* and *Today* (1994 samples only in the case of the latter, because it ceased publication before the 1996 sample was taken).
3   These figures do not take into account the parts of our data that we analysed as thought presentation, or as ambiguous between different modes of presentation (see Semino and Short 2004: 59). It should also be borne in mind that our annotation system captured only those stretches of text where it is signalled in some way that others' words are being presented, as opposed to those stretches of text where journalists report information that they gathered from spoken or written sources, but without any explicit attribution (see Thompson's 1996 notion of 'language reports').
4   As will become clear in the course of the discussion, our criterion for metaphoricity results in the inclusion of many highly conventional and lexicalized metaphorical expressions, such as the verb *give* in *give a speech* (as opposed to *give a present*). It is also worth noting that what we call the 'basic' senses of individual expressions are not necessarily more frequent than the metaphorical senses of these expressions. However, basic senses are normally more concrete and

more closely related to physical experiences. In many cases, they are also older than metaphorical senses (see Pragglejag Group, 2007, for a more detailed version of our identification procedure).

5   We classified under 'DISCOURSE' all those cases where a particular type or aspect of communication (e.g. intensity) is described in terms of a different type or aspect of communication (e.g. loudness). See 2.6 for more detail. We recognize that the physical aggression meaning of *blast* is itself derived from an older (and still current) meaning of violent movement of air that relates to natural phenomena.

6   In this context, both the original demand and the later indication that the demand was no longer being made may have involved written communication, or a combination of speech and writing.

7   In both cases, the same physical meanings are expressed by the Latin etymology of these verbs.

8   The basic sense of *dismiss* (i.e. telling someone to leave) is also to do with communication. The metaphoricity of examples such as Example 17 is due to the fact that here the uses of *dismiss* does not involve actual movement.

9   Expressions such as *erupt* and *thunder* can also be analysed more specifically in terms of metaphors for anger, such as ANGER IS A HOT FLUID IN A CONTAINER and ANGER IS A STORM (see Kövecses 2002).

10   The expressions we did not classify as metaphorical include 'literal' references to communication (e.g. *He said that . . .*), metonymies (e.g. the use of verbs such as *laugh* to report speech) and 'etymological' metaphorical expressions (e.g. *confirm*, whose Latin etymology is to do with strengthening an object).

3 Journalistic constructions of Blair's 'apology' for the intelligence leading to the Iraq war

Lesley Jeffries

3.1 Introduction

In October 2004 there was a rush of public apologies reported in the British media, including one by the Conservative Member of Parliament, Boris Johnson, editor of *The Spectator*, a right-wing weekly news magazine, for insulting the city of Liverpool:

> the colourful MP and *Spectator* editor ran an editorial in his magazine accusing Liverpudlians of wallowing in their "victim status" and over-reacting to the murder of Ken Bigley.[1] (Carter and Wintour, *Guardian*, 16.10.04)

Apologies also came from the then England football captain, David Beckham, for getting booked deliberately, and from the designer of the Princess Diana memorial fountain, for allegedly creating a safety hazard. The national newspapers were quick to pick up on the spate of apologies, particularly in the light of the most newsworthy of all the cases: Tony Blair's apology for the unreliability of the intelligence that led to the Iraq war. This apology was the subject of much discussion in the leader columns and by political commentators, partly because of its political significance (Blair had been repeatedly challenged to apologize in the months since the war) but also, and crucially, because many thought that this was not really an apology at all, or not an apology for the right offence.

This chapter focuses on the Blair 'apology' and in particular the analysis in the print media of its various components and effects. I aim to show the journalists' own construction of what an apology is, and is not, and to compare this with the view of researchers into speech acts. I will also consider the socio-political context of Blair's 'apology' and ask whether apologizing in political life – and, significantly for the purposes of this book, via the *media* – is a different kind of speech act to that performed in private conversations. This leads to a consideration of the speech act of apology in general and the extent to which this analysis contributes to some of the theoretical and descriptive apparatus of speech act theory.

The data upon which this analysis is based comes from the *Guardian* and the *Observer* from 1 October 2004 to 19 October 2004. All articles which explicitly discussed a public apology were collected, and those relating to Blair's 'apology' were analysed for all metadiscussion of what an apology is, whether he had performed such an apology, and the extent to which his words did or did not constitute an apology. The resulting analysis demonstrates the construction by a number of journalists of a set of features that are more or less essential to the apology speech act, and which are deemed to have been present to a greater or lesser extent in Blair's attempt at apology.

3.2 Apologies in English

The first question to be asked about speech acts is to what extent they are universal or culturally specific. The early discussion of speech acts, being philosophical in nature, was not directly concerned with these questions, but it makes sense to ask whether we are considering specific data as a realization of local social convention or something broader.

John Searle's use of the phrase 'necessary and sufficient conditions' (Searle 1969: 55) implies that he not only views speech acts as rule-governed, but that he assumes that speech acts are common to different languages, if not universal.[2] Such an approach, which was common as linguistics developed in the mid-twentieth century, often means that the resulting description will take some kind of 'prototypical' view of the data, and capture characteristics that are most typical of the phenomenon under consideration, whatever the local circumstances. Searle himself sums up this approach as follows:

> certain forms of analysis (. . .) are likely to involve (. . .) idealization of the concept analysed. In the present case, our analysis will be directed at the centre of the concept of promising. I am ignoring marginal, fringe, and partially defective promises. This approach has the consequence that counter-examples can be produced of ordinary uses of the word 'promise' which do not fit the analysis. [. . .] Their existence does not refute the analysis, rather they require an explanation of why and how they depart from the paradigm cases of promise making. (Searle 1969: 55)

Much recent research has at least implicitly questioned Searle's tacit assumption that the form of speech acts is universal, and has focused instead on

cross-cultural differences of realization rather than similarities. This is evident, for example, in the work of Anna Wierzbicka (1985, 1996) and Malgor-
zata Suszczynska (1999), who draw on a general model of the apology
developed by Andrew Cohen and Elite Olshtain (1981: 113–34) and Olshtain
and Cohen (1983: 22–3). This general model, considered below, summarizes
the range of practices observed in various cultural settings and does not
reduce these characteristics to a prototype. Such work reflects a general
reluctance in recent linguistic study to indulge in 'idealization' of data, perhaps arising as much from a reaction against introspective linguistics than
from any reasoned argument against prototype theory itself. Cohen and Olshtain's model concentrates upon the textual aspects of the apology, rather
than including cognitive and situational preconditions.

I will concern myself here largely with the realization of apologies *in
English*, noting, however, that the very existence of similar concepts and practices in other cultures raises the question of whether we are indeed looking at
the local version of a universal human interactive event. Cultural variation
across languages also raises the likelihood that there will be differences of
usage within a particular language, and that these may, like other sociolinguistic variables, vary with context. We will, therefore, consider to what
extent the public or political apology is considered by the journalists in question to have special features not typical of more private apologies.

Having established that we are considering the apology as a specifically
English speech act, we can now question what is meant by the label 'speech
act' itself. While Austin gave up on the distinction between performatives
and constatives, we might invoke the notion of performativity again here,
pointing out that what was 'special' about this subset was its explicit and
self-fulfilling nature. Thus, an apology would be rendered by *I apologize*, and a
promise by *I promise* respectively, whereas a simple statement would not
normally be flagged up in this way: *I state that I am tired.*

Jenny Thomas (1995: 44) outlines the unsustainability of the performative category as follows:

1. There is no formal (grammatical) way of distinguishing performative verbs from other sorts of verbs.
2. The presence of a performative verb does not guarantee that the
   specified action is performed.
3. There are ways of 'doing things with words' which do not involve
   using performative verbs.

She points out that, contrary to Austin's original claims, performatives are
not only spoken; they can be in the first person plural as well as singular;
indeed they may even be in the third person (*this court finds that* ...); they
are also not restricted to the present simple tense (*I am denying that* ...).
Performative verbs may also fail to perform, either through the failure of their

50

felicity conditions or through the indirect achieving of a different speech act, for example by apparently promising, though actually threatening (*I promise you, I will send you upstairs if you continue!*) The third reason for the failure of the performative hypothesis was that there are very many linguistic 'actions' which take place without the help of a performative verb, including flattery, discouragement and disparagement, for example.

Thomas questions whether speech acts are indeed rule-governed, as suggested by Searle. He tried to establish a set of conditions under which a speech act could be said to have occurred, and Thomas takes issue with this approach as inappropriate to language in use, though it may work for the abstract structures of grammar. She claims that the context of language use does not produce the kinds of regularity that can be captured by rules. We will see later that this reaction to the notion of rules is one that might be modified by the data under consideration here.

3.2.1 Apologies in context

We might ask what constitutes the nature of the evidence that we are using to identify speech acts, apart from our own intuitions and introspection. While there is some textual evidence of speech acts (e.g. the use of performative verbs), there are also aspects of the psycho-social context which are not amenable to observation. Thomas therefore suggests the use of other forms of evidence, and in particular the following:

- The perlocutionary effect of an utterance on the hearer
- Explicit commentary by the speaker
- Explicit commentary by someone other than the speaker
- Subsequent discourse (Thomas 1995: 204–5)

Most relevant here, and for the overall purposes of this book, is the third of these; a kind of 'metadiscussion' by journalists, which helps to shape the speech act concerned. These journalists are responsible for mediating between Blair and the public, and in this case are also consciously construct-ing the speech act in a particular way. For both of these reasons, journalists – as text producers and ideological brokers (Blommaert 1999a) – have a very great influence on the way in which Blair's words are received by their intended hearers, the electorate.

Thomas constructs a version of the apology, based on Searle's rules for the speech act of promising (S = speaker; H = hearer; A = act):

Propositional act:	S expresses regret for a past act of S.
Preparatory condition:	S believes that A was not in H's best interest.
Sincerity condition:	S regrets act A.
Essential condition:	Counts as an apology for act A. (Thomas 1995: 99)

In relation to the propositional act, the only *textual* part of the speech act, Suszczynska (1999) compares the textual components of apologies in English, Polish and Hungarian, and draws conclusions about the likely formal structure of the apology, including its immediate aftermath. Suszczynska draws upon the general model of the apology mentioned earlier (Cohen and Olshtain 1981: 113–34; Olshtain and Cohen 1983: 22–3 and included in Blum-Kulka *et al* 1989: 289). The version of this general model given in Suszczynska (1999: 1056) is summarized below:

1. Illocutionary Force Indicating Devices (IFIDs)
   a. An expression of regret
   b. An offer of apology
   c. A request for forgiveness
2. Explanation or Account
   Any external mitigating circumstances, 'objective' reasons for the violation
3. Taking on Responsibility
   a. Explicit self-blame
   b. Lack of intent
   c. Expression of self-deficiency
   d. Expression of embarrassment
   e. Self-dispraise
   f. Justify hearer
   g. Refusal to acknowledge guilt
      Denial of responsibility
      Blame the hearer
      Pretend to be offended
4. Concern for the hearer
5. Offer of repair
6. Promise of forbearance

Suszczynska's study finds that English speakers choose an expression of regret (e.g. *I'm sorry*) routinely as IFID, rather than the more clearly performative offer of apology (e.g. *I apologize*) or a request for forgiveness (e.g. *Please forgive me*). This choice may result from the English preference for social distance over face-threatening acts. Other languages seem less concerned to save the negative face of either participant and may prefer the performative, which threatens the speaker's positive face, or the request for forgiveness, which threatens the hearer's negative face. Both alternatives reduce social distance in a way that expressing regret does not. The remainder of the apology in English, according to Suszczynska's research, consists of an expression of concern (e.g. *are you OK?*) and an offer of help (e.g. *can I take you home?*). What is not usual in English apologies, according to this research, is any explicit acceptance of responsibility.

Our discussion of the Blair 'apology' and its construction by the media will be seen to uphold this model of the apology, and some of Suszczynska's findings about the subset used in English apologies. This model, together with Thomas's 'rules', may provide the basis of the description of prototypical apologies in English, and allow us to map out the more marginal members of that category. For example, some scholars have noted that there are occasions when the speaker may apologize for something that s/he didn't personally do:

> Holmes (1990: 163) points out that it is enough that s/he feels responsible in one way or another. Such examples include adults apologising for children or pets, or individuals apologising in the roles of representatives of organisations. (Deutschmann 2003: 36)

This consideration will be relevant to our discussion of Blair's 'apology', though it is important to note the inclusion of the word 'feels' in the quotation above. It is apparently not enough to claim responsibility: one has to also *feel* responsible.

The conditions of speech acts are less well researched than the form of the propositional act itself. The preparatory condition, in which the speaker believes that the act was not in the hearer's best interest, includes a number of assumptions. Thomas points out that we may sometimes apologize for something that we do not think is bad for the hearer. A dentist about to inject a patient may apologize, though only for the immediate pain, not for performing the action. The condition also assumes that the hearer is identical to the person to whom the apology is directed. A public apology brings into play many layers of implied addressee, but even ignoring the media commentators, the question remains who Blair is apologizing to: the House of Commons, the Labour Party, the British electorate or the Iraqi people?

Thomas's sincerity condition for the apology suggests that the speaker should actually regret a past act. This raises the question of whether an insincere apology is indeed an apology at all. Searle himself was of the opinion that the simple act of apologizing was a declaration of sincerity:

> Wherever there is a psychological state specified in the sincerity condition, the performance of the act counts as an *expression* of that psychological state. This law holds whether the act is sincere or insincere, that is whether the speaker actually has the specified psychological state or not. (Searle 1969: 65)[3]

Clearly, this is not the same as saying that an apology has to be sincere, though it does seem to suggest that the very enactment of a speech act asserts sincerity; the normal expectation of a hearer. Although we do not regularly and consistently question the cooperative motives of our interlocutors, we may question the sincerity of apologizers, particularly where there has been a prior demand for an apology, rather than one given freely and spontaneously. Children using certain intonation patterns when being forced to apologize for something are a case in point. We not only want people to say they're sorry; we also require them to *sound* sorry. In the case of the data under analysis here, the reader is supplied with this information (i.e. how Blair sounded) by the journalist, who is thereby responsible to a great extent for the final categorization of Blair's words as an apology or not an apology.

3.2.2   What counts as an apology?

Thomas's suggested essential condition is that an apology should *count* as an apology. While Searle may have understood this as some kind of conventional notion of what 'counts', we may take it as reflecting recent increasing interest in the recipient's contribution to meaning-making. Many researchers into speech acts since Searle, including Lionel Wee (2004), have commented on the need for a greater awareness of the hearer's role in speech acts:

> There have been recent calls for speech act theory to take into account the active role played by the hearer in the co-construction and negotiation of meaning, so that the hearer is not merely relegated to reconstructing as faithfully as possible the intentions of the actor (. . .). The key word here is that speech act theory needs to be more inter-subjective in orientation. (Wee 2004: 2163)

Thomas (1995) also suggests that all speech acts have a collaborative aspect, in differing degrees. At first sight, the successful performance of an apology seems to be entirely at the discretion of the speaker. However, there are occasions when the hearers' reluctance to accept an apology can be quite powerful. This question of power is one that is taken up by Michiel Leezenberg (2002), who argues that:

> power relations are at least in part constitutive of linguistic communication itself, and this claim is much more rarely made, let alone elaborated in theoretical or conceptual terms. (Leezenberg 2002: 894)

Leezenberg argues that a 'social contract' view of how language operates ignores the fact that in some cases (e.g. *I fire you; I sentence you to five years*) the hearer may not want to accede to the act, or to the principles behind it (e.g. taking excess sick leave is wrong; burglary is wrong), but has no power to negotiate the act away. As Leezenberg comments:

> Searle's analysis simply leaves no role for any such kind of struggle, competition, or negotiation concerning the powers involved in institutional facts. (Leezenberg 2002: 902)

Leezenberg's insistence on the speech act as a potential site of struggle is unwittingly prefigured by an article in the *Journal of Philosophy* from 1965 in which Alexander Sesonske makes a case for retaining the special category of performatives:

> The apparently clear and important distinction between performatives and constatives with which he started seemed to become ever more elusive the more persistent were his attempts at analysis. (. . .) Yet I believe that there is an important distinction here, which Austin turned up and buried again without ever really noticing it. (Sesonske 1965: 460)

Sesonske argues that Austin's original intention was to focus on the functions rather than the forms of utterances. However, he then tried to tie these functions to forms, and in doing so demonstrated that, as Sesonske says, there is indeed 'no strict correlation between grammatical form and function'. Sesonske suggests that we may find that in a primarily functional approach to speech acts, performatives still have a special role to play. He defines the primary function of performatives as being to alter formal relations between the interlocutors.

Leezenberg's view that negotiation may be one facet of speech acts that has been overlooked, together with Sesonske's functional approach to speech acts lead us to the viewpoint that I would like to take here, which would recognize a particular kind of communicative function as an 'apology', defined by its capacity to change the formal relations between the speaker and the hearer in certain ways. This communicative function has a range of possible forms, both cross-culturally Wierzbicka (1985, 1991, 1996) and within a given language across different communities of practice. Note that the case we are considering here is taking place in the community of practice which includes political journalists, who mediate between the producer (Blair) of the putative speech act, and the recipients, whose identity is less clear and will be discussed later.

What happens in practice if we take a functional view of the apology? What are the formal relations between people that are potentially altered by the uttering (or other 'performance') of an apology? Replacing the conditions of Thomas's set of rules would be an act of wrong doing, a wronged party, a wrong doer, who is also (prototypically) the apologizer. The act of apologizing, then, leaves the parties in a new and more positive formal relationship to each other. The question of whether the apology is accepted as such is covered by Thomas's essential condition and captured in Sesonske's terms by whether the new conditions prevail; whether the apology has been accepted as putting the formal relations between the parties onto a new, positive, footing. In the case in question, of course, the issue of whether the apology is accepted is partly mediated by the journalists who have the power of suggestion at least, as to whether the apology ought to be accepted as a 'good' exemplar of this category.

55

In addition to the success (or otherwise) of speech acts, there is also the question of their effect on face[4] (Goffman 1967; Brown and Levinson [1978] 1987), of both speaker and hearer. Apologies would normally harm the speaker's positive face (cf. Brown and Levinson 1987), by being an admission of wrong doing, and also acknowledge the harm to the hearer's face of the action which the apology refers to. Thus, the imposition by the speaker on the hearer of an accidental push in a supermarket queue is corrected by an apology that impinges on the speaker's positive face when s/he admits to having been at fault. Note that in the case of the Blair apology, we are not dealing with the face-to-face interaction that is often presumed to be typical by politeness theory and speech act theory. Rather, we have a situation where the participants are not only not co-present, but it is not even clear who the recipient is intended to be. The producers of the media reports, therefore, are responsible for shaping the conditions of acceptance (or otherwise) of the apology, most obviously on behalf of the public, though they also sometimes claim to act on behalf of other possible recipients, such as the Iraqi people.

Apologies in public tend to have a much greater proportional effect than those made in the supermarket or street, and in particular, they tend to be avoided by politicians whose loss of positive face would be seen as potentially disastrous in electoral terms. Thus, in the *New York Times Magazine*, Deborah Tannen (1996) comments on Hillary Clinton's high-profile apology as follows:

> The first part of this quote clearly indicates that the fault was not with her actions – 'the efforts on health care' – but rather with the way they were received and distorted by others. But because she went on to say the big, bad 'S' word, all hell broke loose.

In the same article, Tannen also comments on the attempted apology of Bill Clinton in his Grand Jury testimony during the Lewinsky affair. The press blamed him for not apologizing sufficiently because he used neither an expression of regret nor a performative verb. Mats Deutschmann (2003: 41) compares this with another very public apology discussed by Olshtain (1989), where Ariel Sharon, at the time a minister in the coalition government of Shimon Peres in Israel, was forced to apologize 'fully and unequivocally' after a number of rather half-hearted attempts.

What these examples imply is that it is considered dangerous for public figures to apologize, but also that apologies are not regarded by media commentators as clear all-or-nothing acts, representing instead points on a cline, with strong and prototypical apologies at one end and no apology at the other. Weak or less typical apologies seem to be constructed by the data in this study as belonging somewhere between these extremes.

3.3 Tony Blair's apology

The circumstances of the putative 'apology' of Tony Blair in 2004 are three-fold: he gave a speech to his party's conference on 28 September 2004; he was 'apologized for' by two ministers on broadcast media in the following days; and then returned to the topic in the House of Commons after questions from the then Conservative leader, Michael Howard. Blair's answer is reported by the journalist and political commentator, Simon Hoggart, as follows:

> 'I take full responsibility and apologize for any information given in good faith which has subsequently turned out to be wrong.'

> 'What I do not in any way accept is that there was any deception of anyone. I will not apologize for removing Saddam Hussein. I will not apologize for the conflict. I believe it was right then, is right now, and essential for the wider security of that region and the world.' (Hoggart, *Guardian*, 14.10.04)

Though the two Blair deliveries were in different venues and on different days, they share some features, and these will be treated together where relevant. We are concerned here with the news journalists' own analysis of Blair's words, and the extent to which this confirms or challenges current speech act accounts of apology. The situation in which this data occurred is one in which the journalists have the opportunity and responsibility to report what Tony Blair said in relation to the invasion of Iraq to an audience which is ostensibly the British public, though in fact can be considered to be much wider, and include the publics and diplomatic representatives of other coun-tries. The question of whether Blair's words constitute a speech act of apology, therefore, is one which readers can only easily answer with the aid of journalistic interpretation. From the perspective of speech act theory, the power to *mediate* the interpretation of a speech act is thus perhaps one of the under-recognized powers of the journalist and editor of newspapers (for a Bourdieuan perspective on the role of text producers, see Milani, Chapter 6, this volume).

The first point to note about Blair's words on both occasions is that he chooses to use the potentially performative verb *apologize*, rather than an expression of regret, such as *I'm sorry*, despite the latter being the more rou-tine choice in English apologies, as confirmed by Suszczynska's (1999) research. Paradoxically, this is universally interpreted in the data as effec-tively a refusal to perform the apology at all:

> But again he avoided the word sorry and, with it, any sense of personal shame. The word was reportedly dropped at the last minute from his party conference speech. (Wintour and Jones, *Guardian*, 14.10.04)

The view illustrated here, and echoed in other articles in the data, is that an expression of regret would have made it clear that the Prime Minister was sincere, whereas his use of *apologize* makes a performance of apologizing. This view may well reflect popular views of apologies, and places more emphasis on the sincerity condition than we might expect (thereby conforming to Hill's notion, this volume, of an ideology of 'personalism'). In this, it undermines Searle's notion of performance of speech acts so that, while we may utter the words of an apology, an apology is not always deemed to have taken place by the audience, unless sincerity can also be established. We see this view in an article headlined *It was wrong, I wasn't, Blair insists*, which emphasizes what the writer considers to be the logical conclusion from Blair's avoidance of the word *sorry*; that he does not consider himself in the wrong:

> For the umpteenth time since the post-war occupation began to go sour, Mr Blair avoided the word 'sorry'. (White, *Guardian*, 14.10.04)

This commentator thus believes – and states – that by using the performative rather than an expression of regret, Blair has avoided taking personal responsibility.

Again, the *Guardian* on 16 October draws attention to the difference between uttering the verb *apologize* and the adjective *sorry*:

> Tony Blair, despite constant demands that he should do so, hasn't actually apologized at all. He has created an aura of penitence around himself, said in his Labour party conference speech that he could apologize for the false intelligence about WMD, even claimed in a newspaper interview that he had apologized for it, but an apology itself has yet to issue from his lips.
>
> His reluctance to utter the word 'sorry' in this case might seem odd because Blair used to be notorious for his prodigal use of the apology. (Leader, *Guardian*, 16.10.04)

It couldn't be much clearer that the journalists represented here paradoxically do not consider the use of performative verb to be the same as apologizing. In particular, there is a view that personal responsibility is not being claimed, and sincerity is not clear, unless the word *sorry* is uttered.

3.3.1 Was it a real *apology*?

We will return to responsibility and sincerity shortly, but first, let us consider the framing of Blair's actual words and the bald question of whether, despite the commentators' views (above), he did actually apologize. In these two excerpts from Andrew Rawnsley's discussion of 17 October, we find that in an interview with *Observer* Tony Blair previews what he will say in the Commons:

58

Mr Blair told us [*Observer*]: 'I have been very happy to take full responsibility for information that has turned out to be wrong. It's absolutely
right that, as we've already done, we've *apologized* to people for the
information that was given being wrong.'

When we came away, we scratched our heads about his use of the past
tense. The Prime Minister had not previously *apologized* for the intelligence being wrong. He had expressed to us a (sort of) contrition, only
to diminish it by claiming not to be saying anything he hadn't said
before. I assume he could not bear the thought of the headline: Blair:
I Was Wrong. (Rawnsley, *Observer*, 17.10.04 – my italics)

Rawnsley, rightly, picks up on Blair's past tense (perfective) use of *apologize*,
and though he doesn't say it in so many words, recognizes that the performativity of the verb disappears when it is simply reporting something that happened in the past. Rawnsley then comments on the public version of the same
'apology' and makes this point more explicitly:

Mr Blair responded: 'I take full responsibility and, indeed, apologize for
any information given in good faith that has subsequently turned out to
be wrong. That is entirely proper; I have already done that.' He was
again using the past tense he deployed with us in the *Observer* interview. *He rendered his apology a non-apology by insisting it was an apology
he had already made.* He was regretting that the intelligence was wrong,
but still not apologizing for the way it was used to build his case for the
removal of Saddam. (Rawnsley, *Observer*, 17.10.04 – my italics)

So far, then, Blair is presented as having failed to use the conventional formula (an expression of regret) for an apology in English, and, having chosen a
more directly performative version (incorporating *apologize*), he invalidates it
as an apology by using the past tense. This is compounded, in the view of some
commentators, by the use of modal verbs in the earlier version of this apology,
as we can see in the following extracts:

So far at party conference the prime minister has said he 'could' apologize for the inaccurate information. He has also 'accepted full personal
responsibility for any errors made'. (Wintour and Jones, *Guardian*,
14.10.04)

Something similar happened at the conference itself. The word 'sorry'
was originally in the text of his conference speech, only to be excised
by the Prime Minister at the very last moment. 'I can apologize for the
information that turned out to be wrong,' he ended up saying to his
audience in Brighton, which is not quite the same as saying that he is
sorry. (Rawnsley, *Observer*, 17.10.04)

59

The epistemic modals *could* and *can* undermine the performativity of *apologize* in a slightly different way from the past tense that we saw earlier. In this case, the modal verbs entirely strip away the speech act itself, and instead give a view (the speaker's view) on whether such a speech act is possible.

Interestingly, in the terms of Cohen and Olshtain's universal model of apologies, Blair appears to deviate from the norms of English apologies not just in his choice of IFID, but also in his explicit taking of responsibility, which is reported by a number of commentators:

> Yesterday in the House of Commons he went a little further in reply to
> Michael Howard, saying that he took 'full responsibility and apologize
> for any information given in good faith that has subsequently turned
> out to be wrong'. (Leader, *Guardian*, 14.10.04)

Although this is not a normal part of apologizing in English generally, the use of explicit responsibility-taking may, if investigated further, turn out to be a more usual part of apologizing in mediated aspects of public life. The usual practice in English, of following the apology with some kind of expression of concern for those wronged, may simply be replaced by an explicit statement of responsibility in political routines. It is less clear, however, that some kind of offer of reparation is inappropriate. In public and press-mediated situations like the one under consideration, a penalty for those responsible would give the apology some credibility and effectively fulfil the sincerity pre-condition by a tangible outcome. Outcomes short of resignation might be the promise of a public inquiry, the offer of compensation, and so on.

The use of responsibility statements is also connected with the question of whether one can indeed apologize on behalf of someone else. There are two senses in which this question is relevant to the current case. On the one hand, there are two or three occasions when ministers apparently apologize on behalf of the prime minister, in their capacity as members of the government. This is quite understandable if we take cabinet government to be an example of joint responsibility, though the number of resignations from the cabinet following the Iraq war, and general concern among MPs about the erosion of cabinet government under Blair makes such joint responsibility statements look forced.

There is also the question of whether Tony Blair is within his (conversational) rights to apologize on behalf of whoever got the intelligence 'wrong'. There appear to be two things happening here. First, Tony Blair is behaving 'correctly' by 'apologizing' on behalf of someone (presumably officers of the British secret service agency, MI6), who had done something wrong in the name of his government. Secondly, Blair is distancing himself from 'real', i.e. personal, blame. Some of the commentators in the data seem to focus on the latter issue and Chancellor in particular picks over Blair's past apologies, including those for which current governments can't possibly be held responsible:

> it is precisely because they are clearly blameless that governments find it so easy to say sorry for ancient injustices. (Chancellor, *Guardian*, 16.10.04)

In relation to offences committed during his period of office there are fewer examples, though Blair did apologize for the Bernie Ecclestone scandal[5] when it was alleged that his government exempted Formula One motor racing from its ban on tobacco sponsorship of sport in return for a donation of £1m to the Labour Party:

> But that apology was accompanied by vehement denials of all the charges against him, so it wasn't clear what Blair thought he was apologizing for. This is, of course, the point, and it explains why an apology for the lack of WMD in Iraq has stuck in his gullet: Blair never says sorry for anything for which, in his estimation, he is actually to blame. (Chancellor, *Guardian*, 16.10.04)

The strong implication here is that in the current case, where Blair is apologizing for a nameless civil servant's mistake, he is likewise not really to blame, or at least is emphasizing his lack of personal involvement. Nevertheless, apologizing for things done in one's name is one of the things we might expect of a leader in politics, business, etc., unless the offence is clearly going to stick to the original perpetrator, which is not the case here. Robin Cook, a former member of Blair's government, picks up this point:

> At prime minister's questions, Tony Blair again pleaded the defence of good intentions – he acted in good faith but was misled by wrong information. This leaves a conundrum: why is he not more angry with those who misled him? (Cook, *Guardian*, 15.10.04)

Cook echoes a point made by Hoggart about Blair claiming to be acting for the greater good, but he also points out the problem with Blair taking responsibility. In public situations like the one under consideration, the person who takes responsibility is normally obliged to resign, even if s/he isn't directly responsible for the offence. In this case, we have neither Blair resigning nor the blame being allowed to rest on lower officials of his government. As Cook adds:

> Tony Blair is curiously indulgent to all those who led him into the most damaging episode of his premiership (. . .) A parade of the relevant officials down Whitehall in sackcloth and ashes would provide a more convincing demonstration that Downing Street is really sorry. (Cook, *Guardian*, 15.10.04)

In this context, media commentators mostly reflect the popular expectation that Blair should behave like a private individual in relation to the apology:

> The most basic reason why Tony Blair won't say sorry is that he isn't.
> (Rawnsley, *Observer*, 17.10.04)

> Another week when the prime minister didn't apologize. But then,
> what value is there in an apology from a man who believes he has
> done nothing wrong? (Leader, *Guardian*, 16.10.04)

In other words, these commentators are insisting on sincerity being the fundamental requirement of an apology in English. Note, incidentally, that neither of these commentators is under any illusion that Blair *has* apologized, presumably for all of the reasons we have discussed above. However, there is also some awareness that the performance of an apology is different, and has different consequences, for someone in Blair's position:

> there is no good reason to suppose that apologizing would rebuild trust
> in Mr Blair and plenty of reason to reckon that it would badly weaken
> him. Enemy would be delighted, and friend would despair. (Rawnsley,
> *Observer*, 17.10.04)

Rawnsley, then, reflects the situation of someone in the public eye who would weaken his positive face by a genuine apology for something he was actually responsible for. The conundrum is that increasingly, as the previous day's *Guardian* Leader observes, politicians are expected to behave publicly in the same way as private citizens:

> So when the plight of the victims of their ill-judged decisions is delivered
> by live television into every voter's home, the perception of individual
> responsibility and the demand for political contrition cannot be far
> behind. (Leader, *Guardian*, 16.10.04)

Perhaps the most consistent comment by all of the media analysts relates not to the *form* of the apology but to the *substance* of it. In effect, Blair's apology is not only undermined by being (1) about something he (claims he) didn't do, (2) a report (in the past tense) of something that didn't happen, and (3) a (modalized) assessment of the likelihood of the apology (the speech act) happening. In addition, this entire apologetic smokescreen is also centred on entirely the wrong question:

> Did Tony Blair apologize for the Iraq war? Of course not. Are you mad?
> (Hoggart, *Guardian*, 14.10.04)

> But he again denied misrepresenting the much-discredited intelligence
> he had received from M16, and refused to apologize for the war itself.
> (White, *Guardian*, 14.10.04)

This returns us, in a way, to the characteristic problem of Blair's situation. He is being urged to take personal responsibility for a war that is seen as unjust by many, and in order to deflect the criticism and baffle his opponents by obfuscation he is represented as finding and/or inventing a range of ways to not apologize for the wrong thing. As the *Irish Times* (quoted in the *Guardian* on 01.10.04) says:

> Mr Blair's skills of advocacy were much in evidence here, but they cannot conceal his vulnerability to criticism that he is basically wrong.

3.4 Discussion

We have seen in this chapter that the media commentators considered here have taken a fairly strong line on whether Blair did indeed apologize, and the consensus is that he didn't. The data, of course, can only be claimed to be typical of the liberal press, which was largely against the Iraq invasion, and the right-wing and tabloid press may take a different view of the same events. The journalists in the current data, nevertheless also seem to largely agree on the parameters that define a 'good' apology, and this clarity from users of the language, albeit with similar socio-political outlooks, seems to be at odds with comments such as the following:

> When we attempt to expand Searle's rules to reflect the way in which the speech act of apologizing operates in everyday life, the conditions become hopelessly complex, vague and unworkable. (Thomas 1995:102)

While recent work in pragmatics, which has often been qualitative in method, has wisely avoided the trap of over-generalizing its results, nevertheless, it seems to me that the evidence of media commentary on this incident confirms the popular understanding of apologies as relatively well defined contextually and prototypically performative. It is counter-intuitive to say that users of English have only a very general sense of a 'complex but vague' speech act popularly called an 'apology', when we have evidence here that at least one group of English speakers (liberal journalists) is very clear about what does not constitute an apology, and insistent upon what does. This demonstrates the strength of an approach which considers particular data in relation to specific events, and which by doing so also defines the context of production (by journalists on national newspapers) and reception (by readers). What would make a very interesting follow-up study to this analysis would be the testing of reader-responses to the data, to evaluate the extent to which they share the construction of the speech act of apology as presented here.

Having pointed out the possibilities for establishing consensus of practice in particular communities and for particular events, we may nevertheless agree that Thomas is right to point out that the kind of all-or-nothing rules proposed by Searle do not reflect the reality of language use. This, I would suggest, is not a question of pragmatics (Thomas's 'principles') versus grammar (rules), but rather more a question of the need to see all language structure and use in terms of 'points of reference', or prototypicality, rather than absolute categories. Teachers of English language will recognize the problem of teaching students about word classes, or clause structures, only to find that students come across very difficult counter-examples which don't fit neatly into the categories that have been so carefully described to them. This may incline them to lose faith in the whole project, instead of learning to critique the model that they are using, unless the teacher is able to show them a different way of seeing the descriptive tools that we use. Assuming that they have understood the principle of the vowel chart, or the abstract nature of the phoneme or the morpheme, these can be used as analogies to show that most language 'categories', across all the levels, are actually often unordered bundles of 'features' which may consist of binary terms (+ and −), but frequently represent a range of possible terms, or even a gradient between the two ends of the spectrum. These bundles of features represent the set of 'reference points' which speakers may be said to have available in assessing whether a particular text can be said to belong to one category (e.g. a speech act) or not. The decision, as in all such cases, may not be clear-cut. Let us consider how this might apply to the case of the apology as a speech act.

3.4.1 Apology and prototypicality

We may define the prototypical apology in English as a bundle of circumstances and textual features. Take away too many of them and the putative apology looks less and less like an apology that a speaker of English would recognize. Table 3.1 summarizes the features of a prototypical apology seen in this way.

Although we might assume that the first four, textual, features of the list in Table 3.1 would have priority, this is not obviously so. For example, a putative apology which fulfilled all of the other features, but had no expression of regret, might be expressed by body language (a shrug and suitable hang-dog expression) and still count as an apology. The final feature, the acceptance, is crucial here. Many of the other features may be lacking if the wronged person is willing to accept the communicative act as an apology. It is even possible that an apology may be construed where none is intended. It is not possible to say how many of these features are needed before we have a bona fide apology, because the hearer has a role in deciding, in any one instance, whether there are enough features for an apology or not. In the case of the Blair 'apology', only one of the prototypical features is fulfilled; the use of the first person pronoun, I, and this is clearly not enough for the media commentators, who roundly reject his half-hearted attempt at an apology.

Table 3.1: Prototypical features of apologies in English

Feature	Prototype apology
IFID	**expression of regret:** *I'm sorry*
tense/aspect	**simple present:** *I'm sorry*
person	**1st singular :** *I*
following text	**concern/reparation:** *Are you OK? Can I help?*
level of 'wrong'	**main:** the most significant wrong between speaker and wronged person
timing of 'wrong'	**recent past:** a prompt apology is the best
sincerity	**sincere:** sincerity is important, and needs to be accepted
addressee	**wronged:** ideally, an apology will be said directly to the wronged person
responsibility	**directly:** the apologizer is the one who acted wrongly
impetus	**unsolicited:** the apologizer does not have to be asked to do so
best interests	**agreed:** there is no dispute about the interests of the wronged person
equality	**equal:** ideally, the only difference in status or power is the wrong doing
intention	**intended:** the apologizer intends the communicative act as an apology
acceptable	**accepted:** the prototypical apology is one that is accepted by the wronged person

As we have already noted, these features of the prototypical apology are not all-or-nothing. There are lesser versions of many of them, and in some cases three, four or more levels of prototypicality. We can get an impression of how they work in Table 3.2.

Those features that are emboldened in Table 3.2 represent the level of each feature that Tony Blair achieves. While his 'apology' is not represented as prototypical by the media commentators here, neither is it clearly a complete 'non-apology', though it is, as we have seen, rejected by the commentators who attack his lack of grammatical performativity; his apologizing for a lesser wrong; his lack of sincerity (evidenced by use of the 'wrong' IFID); and his claim, rejected by them, to know better than his critics what is in the best interests of the Iraqi people.

Table 3.2: Features of the apology in English, represented as ranges

Feature	Prototype ... alternative (less central) ... least like an apology
IFID	expression of regret ... **performative** ... request for forgiveness ... other
tense/aspect	simple present .... present progressive ....**past**/future/**modal**
person	**1st singular** ..... 1st plural ..... 3rd deictic ..... 3rd other
following	concern/reparation ... explanation/**responsibility** ... nothing ... other
level of 'wrong'	main ..... **supplementary** ..... small, irrelevant
timing of 'wrong'	recent past ..... **distant past** ..... present ..... future
sincerity	sincere ..... **doing sincerity** ..... openly cynical
addressee	wronged ..... **symbolic of wronged** ..... **3rd party** ... no one/anyone
responsible	directly ..... **symbolically** ..... not responsible
impetus	unsolicited ..... solicited ..... **demanded**
interests of wronged	agreed .... **not agreed** ....
equality	equal .... **unequal** ....
intention	intended .... **ambivalent** .... unintended .... not intended
acceptable	accepted .... questioned .... **rejected**

The features in Table 3.2 are mostly self-explanatory, but two in particular warrant further comment. These are the ones labelled 'addressee' and 'responsible' in the table. These features invoke the possibility that the apology will not be given directly from the wrong-doer to the wronged in less than prototypical cases. Thus, Blair is not speaking to the people of Iraq, or indeed of Britain, when he gives a speech to parliament or the Labour Party conference. Nevertheless, there is an understanding that these are both channels by which the prime minister may promulgate his message. Similarly, with indirectness, as we have seen, it is possible for people to apologize for their children, animals or even 'their' weather. A potentially useful avenue of investigation to help us define the range of possible apologizers and recipients (on behalf of others) may be deixis. There is no space to develop this idea here, but it is worth noting that Thomas's example of a third person performative (*This court finds ...*) uses a proximal deictic determiner, and could not be spoken by just anybody.

Interestingly, the media coverage represented in this corpus does not attack Blair for the lack of spontaneity, or lateness, of his apology, though this is no doubt a factor in some of the discussions leading up to the week in question. Nor do they specifically question Blair's authority to assert, as he seems to be doing, that this apology is for the right thing, at the right time, to the right addressee. In support of the above set of features, though they stand to be modified by others using further data, is the discussion of other apologies in the same data. Boris Johnson, for example, is not entirely let off by the coverage, as his initial reaction was to try and explain what he 'really' meant:

> Mr Johnson hastily issued a statement to minimize the offence. 'The point of the leader was to criticize the slight culture of mawkishness and sentimentality in this country which one associates with the death of the Princess of Wales. We certainly did not mean to offend anybody in Liverpool. The *Spectator* loves Liverpool.' (Carter and Wintour, *Guardian*, 16.10.04)

The explanation, of course, features in Cohen and Olshtain's model of the apology, though not as a favoured part of the English version of that speech act. Possibly because he did not succeed in getting his apology unequivocally accepted, probably because of hostile media coverage, Johnson later went to Liverpool to apologize directly to the people of that city, demonstrating that an apology can take place over a period of time, and gradually work towards the centre of the prototype by adding more and more of the prototypical features, such as directness in this case, thus partly sidestepping the influence of the media whose role as mediator is thereby reduced.

In an article headlined 'Beckham Says Sorry', the evidence is that the writer in this case accepts Beckham's use of the performative verb rather than the expression of regret, probably because enough of the other features are near or at the prototypical end of the feature:

> 'I now know that was wrong and *apologize* to the FA, the England manager, my team-mates and all England fans for this. I have also apologized personally to my manager, Sven-Goran Eriksson.' (Kelso, *Guardian*, 14.10.04)

2.5 Concluding remarks

Returning to Blair's apology, we may wish to question whether the features given above are typical not of a *political* apology but of a *personal* one. Interestingly, the commentators themselves address the notion that the personal-style of apology is now much more required by the electorate, though the journalists themselves insist that it remains politically dangerous to expose your positive face in this way:

> the concept of saying sorry, in the manner in which individuals might, or the England captain, David Beckham, does after a particularly ill-advised burst of self-publicity, is still struggling to find a place in the political lexicon. (Leader, *Guardian*, 16.10.04)

Finally, we might ask, if Blair does not perform an apology on these occasions, does he perform some other speech act? Simon Hoggart sums up one view of what this might be:

> This is the Tony Blair school of abnegation. If he had a fault, he told us last Tuesday, it was that he wanted to get rid of bloodthirsty dictators. If he had a fault, he wanted us all to live in a safer, more peaceful world. It's not a new phenomenon, but he does it better than most – you might term it self-aggrandizing penitence. (Hoggart, *Guardian*, 14.10.04)

This view of Blair's failure to perform a clearly prototypical apology leaves the audience interpreting the speech act of Blair, presumably by reference to another, overlapping, set of features, not as an apology but as a boast.

Primary sources

Carter and Wintour, *Guardian*, 16.10.04.
Chancellor, *Guardian*, 16.10.04.
Cook, *Guardian*, 15.10.04.
Hoggart, *Guardian*, 14.10.04.
Irish Times quoted in the *Guardian* on 01.10.04.
Kelso *Guardian* 14.10.04.
Leader, *Guardian*, 14.10.04.
Leader, *Guardian*, 16.10.04.
Rawnsley, *Observer*, 17.10.04.
White, *Guardian*, 14.10.04.
Wintour and Jones, *Guardian*, 14.10.04.

Notes

1 Ken Bigley was one of many 'western' hostages taken captive during the after-math of the invasion of Iraq by US-led forces. He was beheaded in October 2004 and a video of his murder was shown on the internet.
2 Note that Searle's (1969) direct discussion of universals (mainly in Chapter 5 of his book) concerns philosophical (i.e. conceptual) universals and not the linguistic universals that linguists debate.

3   I am grateful to Dan McIntyre for this point, and the quotation, which supports a different argument in McIntyre (2004).

4   I am grateful to Derek Bousfield for his advice in relation to 'face'. All errors, of course, remain my own.

5   Bernie Ecclestone effectively controls Formula One motor racing and is one of the highest-salaried executives in the world. He owns Formula One Holdings, which controls almost every part of the motor sport.

4 Crises of meaning: personalist language ideology in US media discourse

Jane H. Hill

4.1 Introduction: on 'personalism' in language ideology

One of the most important ways that discourse works is to re-inscribe 'language ideologies', that is, understandings of the nature of language, and how it is linked to persons, that advance particular social interests (Woolard 1998a). This chapter looks at how media discourse in the United States serves élite interests by reproducing a language ideology that is often called 'personalism' (Duranti 1992).

Three dimensions of personalism are of special importance. The first is the idea of 'an inner self continuous through time, a self whose actions can be judged in terms of the sincerity, integrity, and commitment actually involved in his or her bygone pronouncements' (Rosaldo 1982: 218). The second is that the inner states associated with this self – its intentions, emotions and attitudes – are the most important sources of linguistic meaning. This commitment is obvious, for instance, in the theory of speech acts. Thus in John Searle's account of commissives, a 'promise' is not felicitous unless the speaker sincerely intends to do the act referred to, and unless the speaker believes that the hearer wants the speaker to do the act (Searle 1969). Third is the understanding that meanings that emanate from these psychological states of speakers will, in the default case, match the reality of the world. For instance, in H. Paul Grice's (1975) theory of conversation, interactors make appropriate conversational inferences by reasoning from a default assumption that speakers will produce utterances that correspond to reality in quantity, quality, relevance and clarity. Eve Sweetser (1987) uses this idea in her proposal for a cultural model of lying. She argues that people understand talk within a simplified model of the world in which 'beliefs are true' and speech emanates from beliefs. Reasoning from this position, people conclude that if a person uttered a false statement, that speaker must have intended to misinform and has therefore uttered a 'lie'.

Anthropologists have become very interested in personalism because they have found out that it is perfectly possible to get along without it. They have established that many people in the world care little about individual intention in assigning meaning to speech. For instance, Webb Keane (1997) notes that the Anakalang of the Indonesian island of Sumba do not ask of an utterance 'What does it mean?' They ask, 'Where does it strike?' Michelle Rosaldo (1982) pointed out that the Ilongot of the Philippines do not make promises and have much less interest in the truth of utterances than in their contribution to proper relations among kin. Alessandro Duranti (1992) showed that Samoans take a similar stance, giving little attention to speaker intention. They do not bother to try to figure out what little children mean when they babble, and they assign blame for an utterance not on the basis of intention, but on the basis of outcomes. Meanwhile Claudia Mitchell-Kernan (1972) showed that African American speech genres like 'marking' and 'signifying' derive their meaning from the interpretation of hearers, who are told 'If the shoe fits, wear it' – or, in my own favourite example, from a rapper defending his use of misogynist language in a television interview: 'If I say "bitch", you don't have to turn around.' Indeed, even thoroughly mainstream contexts provide occasions where meaning and personal intention are decoupled: 'The company's human relations policy requires me to inform you . . .' Children quickly learn that personalist focus on speaker intention permits a routine of deniability: 'I didn't *mean* it!' However, while personalist language ideology does offer loopholes, mainstream realizations of personalist ideology usually permit the faithful to give little attention to the impact of 'where words strike' as opposed to 'what the speaker means'. For instance, words from the vocabulary of racism 'strike' somewhere, bringing immense pain to their targets. But this is of little interest to those who utter these words, who often argue that such targets are simply 'oversensitive' because the speakers did not intend any pejorative racist meaning.

Keane (2002) has pointed out the roots of personalism in early Christianity and its insistence on the sincerity of belief as a precondition to salvation. One could 'render unto Caesar' and Caesar's gods merely as a public gesture of citizenship. But to be a Christian, one had to sincerely believe in the one God and his only son, the risen Christ. Keane has argued, however, that inherent in Christianity's prototypical speech act, the statement of belief or *Credo*, is a fundamental contradiction. 'Words that come from the heart', individualized expressions, are the clearest index of sincerity, yet the Credo is a formula. Belief is a matter between God and the individual, yet the Credo is recited publicly. Jacques Derrida's (1988) theory of 'iterability' raises another set of problems with personalism. Derrida points out that speech is by its very nature detachable from the original speaker, the site of belief, and repeatable for new purposes which can be increasingly remote from the original commitment or, indeed, entirely in opposition to it. On the other hand, as Mikhail Bakhtin (1981) pointed out, such repetition remains in struggle with earlier iterations: intentional meaning leaks among speakers, who cannot fully purge their words of the traces of history and the voices of others. Furthermore, important genres of contemporary discourse flout the match between words, beliefs and reality that personalism requires us to assume. Advertisements and solicitations are thought by most people to be insincere to the highest degree, intended only to manipulate and deceive. Political language is generally considered to be insincere; many people believe that 'Politicians will say anything to get elected.' In summary, personalist language ideology is in constant crisis. This crisis occurs not merely because we are surrounded with evident insincerity of all types. The crisis emanates as well from the fundamental nature of linguistic signs as conventional and public.

In spite of its contradictions and loopholes, personalist language ideology persists because of its dense links to other cultural dimensions and because it is extraordinarily useful in the workings of contemporary power. Personalism in language ideology resonates with other individualist understandings of fundamental human nature, such as the idea of *Homo economicus*, the rational calculator of gain-loss ratios centred on individual needs and desires. The interests and intentions of such individuals are understood in economic theory to constitute the basic dynamic of markets. Individualism is pervasive as well in political theory, where it shows up in the belief in the sacredness of the secret ballot, where individual intention is thought to be best protected from the pressure of the community. Keane (2002), following Max Weber, has suggested close links between the Protestant insistence on the origin of speech in intention and belief, the organization of the capitalist economy, and the validity claims of scientific discourse. Keane proposes that western élites share a 'representational economy' in which the universal exchangeability and openness of the world to transaction with money, and the source of the meaning of words within individual intentions, are inextricably connected. 'Referential language (as expressed in the values of transparency and truth) and the signifying practices that underlie abstract value (as expressed in money and commodities) . . . seek to abstract the subject from its material and social entanglements in the name of freedom and authenticity' (Keane 2002: 83).

In summary, much is at stake in defending personalism from the many challenges that confront it. To the degree that the mass media are controlled by those élites who operate fully within the representational economy suggested by Keane, and who benefit most from personalist ideology, we would expect media language to be a very important site for such defence, for the reproduction and reinscription of this ideology, and for the production of discourses that can only make sense if this ideology is thoroughly presupposed and forms the basis of 'common sense'. I do not wish to suggest that media discourse that reproduces personalist language ideology is somehow 'intended' to do so as a way of shoring up élite power. Media discourse does this job because personalist language ideology makes deep intuitive sense to those who produce it and those who consume it. And media discourse, with its privileged penetrating powers, is a crucial part of the representational economy in which we all live. Susan Philips (2004) has shown that different discourse situations may be sites for the expression of diverse and even opposing and contradictory language-ideological angles or standpoints. Indeed, I have argued that even in élite media discourse, discussions of political utterances can include alongside an explicitly personalist ideology that I have called 'the discourse of truth' a second discourse, 'the discourse of theatre', about questions such as the effective use of media by political figures (Hill 2000). Personalist ideology, however, is utterly pervasive in élite media in the United States. Deep presuppositions about the personalist sources of meaning are fundamental to the ways in which media seem to 'make sense' of our world.

My title, 'Crises of meaning', refers to the notion of moral panics (Cohen 1972) in which lies and misstatements by public figures create crises for personalist language ideology. Lies and misstatements are, of course, only one source of so-called moral panics. However, moral panics about utterances by public figures are an especially useful site for research on language ideology in media discourse. These play out in so-called 'media firestorms', where reportage and commentary on a single contested issue produce complex intertextual series that involve thousands of words over days or weeks. Thus there is a large corpus for testing hypotheses. Furthermore, I have found that discourse during these moral panics is especially likely to involve the explicit reproduction of personalist language ideology, permitting us to explore its terms across large samples of media text.

4.2 Implicit and explicit attention to personalist language ideology

Media discourse includes both *implicit* reproduction of personalist language ideology, where the ideology is part of a presuppositional sub-text, and *explicit* reproduction, where we find overt reference to the terms I have outlined in the introduction. Implicit reproduction is by far the more usual case. I illustrate these types here with one case of implicit reproduction, and one case of explicit reproduction.

4.2.1 An example of implicit reproduction

The lead story in the 27 August 2005 online edition of the *Washington Post* treated negotiations over the Iraqi draft constitution. Displaying the kind of 'balanced reportage' that is highly valued in American journalism, the *Post* quoted Sunnis, Shiites and Kurds. In the piece, six Iraqis are quoted by name. The quotes give their opinions on the state of negotiations. The last quotation in the piece is the following:

(1) 'I think for all intents and purposes we have a deal. We have a draft that cannot be improved upon,' said Planning Minister Barham Salih, a Kurd. 'No one could be entirely happy with what we have, but while some are opposed, many Sunnis expressed happiness.' (Finer and Fekeiki 2005)[1]

In order to find coherence in the *Washington Post* article, we must take the quotation from Planning Minister Salih to represent 'what he believes'. And furthermore, since personalist language ideology holds that speakers believe and say what is true, we personalists assume that Planning Minister Salih's statement is a truthful representation of a situation.

Of course there are other possible (and, I believe, better) interpretations. One is that the Planning Minister is taking a tough bargaining stance and is delighted to be able to use the influential *Washington Post* as the site for deploying his offensive. But the *Post* reportage certainly does not invite us to entertain that understanding.

Important in analysing this piece of reportage is a fact clearly evident to anyone who regularly reads the newspaper: that the *Post*, with its managerial, editorial and reportorial staff, who move in the highest social and political spheres in Washington DC, is basically a pro-administration newspaper. The *Post* has an agenda: to help the American government put the best possible light on the disaster produced by President Bush's invasion of Iraq. We know that the acceptance of an Iraqi constitution is essential to the credibility of the administration's 'spin' on the situation. So reportage in the *Post* almost always advances the line that Iraqis are successfully moving towards a constitutional government.

Any critical discourse analyst would note that this pro-administration agenda is advanced through the very structure of the article. Figure 4.1 shows the order of the quotations in the article.

As suggested by the structure of Figure 4.1, Planning Minister Salih's quotation is being presented as the final term in a thesis–antithesis–synthesis structure, where the synthesis is one favourable to the Bush administration's position. This line of analysis is strengthened by the fact that the trajectory of the argument is inscribed in a moral space, tracing a rhetorical path from sources most opposed to the American position to those most favourable to it. First quoted are the views of Sunnis, who are supposed to be most hostile to American efforts. Quotations from Shiites follow; they support the draft constitution but are thought to be theocrats who oppose the secular democracy that the United States hopes will be the outcome of the constitutional

THESIS
Objections to the Constitution
1) Sunni objection, Sunni objection

ANTITHESIS
Support of the Constitution
2) Shiite support, Shiite support, Shiite support

3) Sunni objection, Sunni objection

SYNTHESIS
4) Kurdish support and support from 'many Sunnis'(the quotation in (1) from Planning Minister Salih)

Figure 4.1: Order of quotations from Iraqi spokesmen in Finer and Fekeiki (2005)

negotiations. Sunni voices briefly return, but the final quotation is given to Planning Minister Salih, a Kurd, representing the Iraqi ethnic group seen as most closely allied with American interests. Furthermore, this Kurdish source voices Sunni support, implying that all ethnic groups support the draft constitution, thereby constituting a 'majority'. Note also how Salih is shown as reasoning in the way that an American politician might reason, in advocating a reasonable compromise in an atmosphere of political give-and-take: 'some' Sunnis don't like the draft, but 'many' are happy. This quotation 'resonates' for Americans, and was widely repeated in the American press on 27 August 2005 and after. Indeed, Juan Cole, a University of Michigan historian of the Middle East who runs a blog, *Informed Comment*, that is probably the most authoritative source on the Iraq situation in the US media, blogged as follows on 28 August 2005:

> (2) 'The pro-War talking point on the collapse of the negotiations over the constitution is that "some Sunnis" oppose the new constitution.'[2]

Cole himself assessed Sunni opposition as nearly unanimous. However, it is clear that readers of the *Washington Post* reportage were intended to take Salih's statement to represent his sincere belief, and, therefore, in accordance with Grice's Maxim of Quality, to be true until proven otherwise. After reading the *Post* article, I could report 'Some Sunnis are opposed, but many are happy with the draft constitution' as truth, without even mentioning Planning Minister Salih or any other links in the chain of transfer between his utterance in Baghdad and the language in the newspaper, and be taken to be perfectly coherent – and, indeed, much secondary reportage did exactly that. That is, fundamental to the coherence of the *Post* reportage, and crucial in the kinds of 'uptake' that its reportage stimulated, are personalist language-ideological assumptions that personal beliefs and intentions are fundamental to meaning, that words are direct representations of the beliefs of speakers, and that beliefs are true, so that words are representations of reality. But nowhere in the original reportage in the *Washington Post* is this ideological content made explicit.

4.2.2 An example of explicit reproduction

Linguistic anthropologists debate whether or not a set of ideas must be made explicit in discourse in order to be counted as an 'ideology' (Woolard 1998a; see also Johnson and Ensslin's discussion in Chapter 1). My own intuition is that the most effective and enduring ideological frameworks are precisely those that are implicit, reproduced only in unspoken presuppositions and entailments. However, in the case of personalist language ideology, along with the kind of implicit reinscription illustrated in section 4.2.1, we also find explicit attention to its terms, even where the context is not one of a moral panic. An example appeared in an essay in *The New Yorker* magazine in which the journalist Nicholas Lemann (2005) reports on an exchange between Hugh Hewitt, a right-wing radio host, and Dana Millbank, a reporter for the *Washington Post*, who for several years covered George W. Bush's presidential administration. These are the pertinent exchanges:

(3) Hewitt: Do you think he's [GWB] sincere about his religious belief
... Do you think he's sincere in his religious expression?' [and thus in his controversial decision to rule out research on stem cells from human fetuses]
Millbank: 'Oh, yeah. Who would I be to suggest that anybody is not sincere in what they say about their religion?' (Lemann 2005: 37)

(4) Hewitt: 'Do you think they intentionally misled the American people into [the Iraq] war?'
Millbank: 'That's like asking me, "Is the President genuine about his faith?" I don't want to get into what's the motive in some guy's head. I can't know that. I have to deal in the realm of what's knowable.' (Lemann 2005: 37)

In this exchange Millbank makes explicit a corollary to the first principle of personalist ideology: that meaning emanates from the inner states of persons. The corollary is that the diagnosis of such inner states is very difficult, so that an outsider cannot, as Millbank asserts, know 'what's the motive in some guy's head'.

4.3 Personalism in the discourse of moral panics: introduction and background on two moral panics

Personalist language ideology is especially likely to be made explicit in the 'media firestorms' that are an important dimension of moral panics about utterances by public figures. During such moral panics, explicit statements of the terms of personalist ideology are repeated again and again over days or even weeks, reiterating these terms, reinscribing them and driving them home. I take the examples here from two recent moral panics. The first was precipitated by a racist segregationist remark made by US Senator Trent Lott in December 2000. The second began in June 2003, when several journalists published the name of a covert CIA agent, Valerie Plame. It was widely believed that Karl Rove, chief political adviser to President Bush, had leaked the name in order to discredit Plame's husband, a political enemy. Space constraints on this chapter unfortunately require illustration with only a few texts from each of these panics. However, these are drawn from literally hundreds of similar examples.

In December 2000 a media firestorm that lasted several weeks was precipitated by a remark by US Senator Trent Lott, Republican of Mississippi. Senator Lott, who was to assume the position of Majority Leader of the Senate when that body reconvened in late January of 2001, made his remarks at a 100th birthday party for Senator Strom Thurmond, Republican of South Carolina, the longest-serving and oldest member of the Senate. Thurmond had run for president in 1948 as a 'Dixiecrat', a group that had splintered from the Democratic Party. The Dixiecrat platform had as its main plank the enforcement of racial segregation in the United States. Thurmond's birthday party, on 5 December 2002, was attended by the President of the United States and many other dignitaries and was nationally televised on the cable television network C-SPAN. During his turn at the podium, Lott made the following statement.

(5) 'I want to say this about my state: When Strom Thurmond ran for president, we voted for him. We're proud of it. And if the rest of the country had followed our lead, we wouldn't have had all these problems over all these years, either.'

Many people who heard or read the statement believed that it could be interpreted in only one horrifying way: Lott, one of the most powerful elected officials in the US government, was a racist, who supported a policy of racial segregation that most Americans thought had been discredited and forever abandoned in the 1960s. However, Lott had many defenders who argued that he did not 'intend' to express such support and was not a racist. This question was endlessly debated over nearly a month, ending only when the Senate Republican caucus voted to replace Lott as majority leader (Lott continues to hold an important committee chairmanship in the Senate and remains a major figure in US public life).

The second case is the panic over an accusation made against Karl Rove, President Bush's chief political adviser. It was alleged that, in order to intimidate and discredit former ambassador Joseph Wilson, an outspoken critic of the Bush administration's rationale for the invasion of Iraq, Rove had leaked to journalists the fact that Wilson's wife, Valerie Plame, was a covert CIA operative.[3] Since Plame had been an operative specializing in nuclear proliferation working in the most secret and dangerous 'No Official,

Cover' status, many critics believed that the leak had not only destroyed her career and endangered her contacts, but had genuinely compromised national security, and for the most petty reasons. After several journalists published Plame's identity in July of 2003, the CIA asked the Attorney General of the United States to investigate the possibility that someone in the White House had committed a federal crime by revealing the information. On 6 July 2005, Matthew Cooper, a reporter for *Time* magazine, who had written about Plame's identity, testified to a federal grand jury that Rove had been his source. My data come from July and August of 2005. As of this writing in July 2006, to the great disappointment of Rove's enemies, only Lewis Libby, adviser to Vice President Dick Cheney, has been indicted in the case, although Rove remained under investigation for months after the Libby indictment.

4.4 Dimensions of explicit personalism in two moral panics

I followed the Lott case in 2002 and the Rove case in 2005 in the three leading US newspapers, the *New York Times*, the *Washington Post* and the *Los Angeles Times*. I also followed on the internet a wider range of media, especially the so-called 'blogosphere'. Bloggers often proclaim their distance and difference from, and contempt for, the 'mainstream media' – print and broadcast journalists. Indeed, bloggers are distinctive in some ways. They often use lively and even obscene language and write in a strongly polemical style, scorning what they see as a phoney concern with 'fairness'. However, in the matter of both implicit appeal and explicit attention to the terms of personalist language ideology, I found no difference between bloggers and the print media. The explicit reinscription of personalist ideologies in moral panics not only crosses the lines between old and new media, it also crosses political lines. Journalists and bloggers from right, centre and left all work within its terms.

As discussed above, I take the central terms of personalist language ideology to be, roughly, these: Language is meaningful because speakers say what they believe, and they believe what is true. Thus, what is said is true and reflects reality. As we saw in the case of the *Washington Post*'s report on the Iraqi constitution, these principles are taken for granted in everyday reportage. But in moral panics over language, many people come to doubt that these principles are in fact in play. Thus the chain of principles as a whole, and each link in it, become a matter for explicit attention. Examples are shown in the following sections.

4.4.1 Explicit attention to speaker beliefs and motives

When speech is not true, personalist ideology suggests that the mediating mental state of the speaker cannot be one of 'belief' as this is usually understood. If the speaker does in fact 'believe' what he or she said, this is deeply discreditable. When public figures who exemplify the highest level of the autonomy and agency of the intentional self utter statements that are felt not to match reality, a crisis is created that can precipitate an extraordinary elaboration of attention to what the mediating mental state might be. The examples here illustrate the kind of media discourse that results. In Examples 6–7, both from columnists who contribute regularly to the opinion page of the *Washington Post*, Richard Cohen, a 'liberal' writer and Charles Krautham-mer, a 'conservative', make explicit reference to Senator Lott's mental states while denying that they have access to them.

> (6) I am extremely reluctant to call anyone a racist. I frankly have no idea what's in Lott's head. (Cohen 2002)

> (7) One should be very hesitant about ascribing bigotry. It is hard to discern what someone feels in his heart of hearts. (Krauthammer 2002)

A very high level of elaboration about Lott's mental states is seen in the following quotes. These are all from 'liberals'. Paul Krugman and Harold Meyerson are regular columnists for the *New York Times* and the *Los Angeles Times* respectively. Joshua Micah Marshall publishes a widely-cited blog, *Talking Points Memo*.

> (8) What, exactly, did Mr Lott mean by 'all these problems'? ... Is it possible that a major modern political figure has sympathy for such views? ... Was he also ignorant of the aims of the 1948 Thur-mond campaign? Or was he just, in the excitement of the moment, blurting out his real views? (Krugman 2002)

> (9) Much of the wobbly coverage of this story (and much of the deep unease over this among conservatives) stems from the fact that this obviously wasn't some misstatement or hyperbole or slip of the tongue. It's what the guy believes. You can tell that from lis-tening to his words. (Marshall 2002)[4]

> (10) Ol' Trent had gone and shot of his mouth again at Ol' Strom's cen-tenary toot ... no big deal ... Official Washington had always known that the mental landscape of Trent Lott ... wasn't suitable for inspection by small children or swing voters ... Lott and DeLay were old news. Who really cared about their inner lives? (Meyer-son 2002)[5]

Very similar attention was given by journalists to the motives and mental state of Karl Rove, as shown in Examples 11 and 12 below. Robert

Scheer, at that time a regular columnist for the *Los Angeles Times*, was blogging on the website of the leftist magazine, *The Nation*.

(11) 'If you can't shoot the messenger, take aim at his wife.' That clearly was the intent of White House Deputy Chief of Staff Karl Rove in leaking to a reporter that former Ambassador Joseph C. Wilson IV's wife, Valerie Plame, was a CIA agent. To try to conceal the fact that the President had lied to the American public about Iraq's weapons of mass destruction program, Rove attempted to destroy the credibility of two national security veterans and send an intimidating message to any other government officials preparing to publicly tell the truth. (Scheer 2005)[6]

(12) It was to protect those lies [justifying the Iraq invasion], those exaggerations, that incredible train wreck of incompetence, ideologically induced optimism and, of course, contempt for the quaint working of the democratic process, that everything else stems from. (Cohen 2005)[7]

Mr Rove, of course, had his defenders. The example in 13 is from the *Wall Street Journal*. The notoriously conservative editorial writers for the *Journal* claim that Rove's motives were pure; he was not undertaking revenge against a 'whistleblower', but only attempting to help Americans understand the issues clearly. The example is the obverse of those in 11 and 12, but it shows that attention to motives and intentions of speakers is part of the rhetoric of all parties.

(13) For Mr Rove is turning out to be the real 'whistleblower' in this whole sorry pseudo-scandal . . . In short, Mr Rove provided important background so Americans could understand that Mr Wilson wasn't a whistleblower but was a partisan trying to discredit the Iraq War in an election campaign. Thank you, Mr Rove. (Unsigned Editorial, *Wall Street Journal*, 14.07.05)

Rove was exposed to criminal indictment under several laws. The language of these laws is rich in both implicit and explicit personalism. Thus speculation about whether the federal prosecutor and the Grand Jury would find grounds for indictment generated journalistic attention to Rove's state of knowledge and intention. Both his supporters and his enemies were trying to decide whether his leak would fall within the legal definitions of a criminal breach of national security. For instance, in Excerpt 14, the liberal blogger, Billmon, uses the personalist language of the law to enjoy the possibility that Rove might be indicted for treason, a capital crime:

(14) But Rove's conduct certainly meets the far less demanding elements of the Espionage Act . . .

Under the Espionage Act, the person doing the communicating need not actually know that revelation could be damaging; he needs only 'reason to know'. Classification is generally reason to know, and a security-clearance holder is responsible for knowing what information is classified.

Nor is it necessary that the discloser intend public distribution; if Rove told Cooper – which he did – and Cooper didn't have a security clearance – which he didn't – the crime would have been complete.

And to be a crime the disclosure need not be intended to damage the national security; it is only the act of communication itself that must be wilful.

Gulp. What's the matter, Karl? You look a little pale. (Billmon 2005b)[8]

4.4.2 Explicit attention to the enduring autonomous selves of speakers

The folk psychology of personalism takes speakers to have 'enduring autonomous selves' that imply consistency in their motives and intentions. Because of this assumption, motives underlying utterances that do not satisfy the Gricean Maxim of Quality are taken to index enduring deviant properties of speakers. Thus journalistic attention can shift up from the motives behind a specific statement to the general qualities of the person, to so-called 'character'. In the Lott case, this rhetorical move was often used to defend Lott against the charge of racism. Examples of this type are seen in 15 and 16, where they appear in reportage, introduced as quotations.

(15) On Dec. 11 [George] Allen, 50 (R. VA) issued a statement that called Lott 'a decent honorable man who had an unfortunate choice of words'. (Shear 2002)

(16) [Quoting Walter Scott, Black owner of a computer concern in Jackson, Mississippi] 'I've known Trent Lott for 25 years. He's not a racist.' (Applebome 2002)

In Example 17, Richard Cohen, in an opinion column in the *Washington Post*, hesitates to call Lott a racist, but does elaborate an understanding of his general character beyond the immediate motive for his remarks at Thurmond's birthday party.

(17) But if it's impossible to believe that Lott is a racist . . . Lott is intellectually stunted by a pernicious and – if the Senate had any sense – politically lethal case of Margaret Mitchell [author of *Gone With the Wind*] Syndrome . . . He does not have the slightest empathy for what it once meant to be black in the Jim Crow South.' (Cohen 2002)

The same kind of attention was given to Karl Rove's character. This can be seen in Excerpt 18, again from Richard Cohen in the *Washington Post*, and in 19, from the blogger Billmon.

(18) So I am not predisposed to feel Rove's pain, assuming he has any feeling at all. (Cohen 2005)

(19) Rove isn't really a war lord – just a schoolyard bully with a slightly bigger yard to push people around in. Now he's finally come across the kid he can't intimidate. And so, in classic bully fashion, he and his gang of lickspittles have decided to pick on the weaker kids instead. (Billmon 2005a)[9]

4.4.3 Explicit attention to the relationship between word and reality

One of the very important elements of personalist language ideology is the default assumption that 'beliefs are true', so that speech should reflect truth or reality. We have seen above that alleged deviations from this case stimulate reflections on speakers' motives and character. In moral panics, the default case itself is explicitly reasserted as well. Examples 20–23 reassert the default connection between utterance and reality. Excerpt 20 is from an opinion column in the *Washington Post* by conservative commentator, Charles Krauthammer, writing on the Lott case and characterizing violation of the default match as 'getting [it] wrong'. Note that Krauthammer remarks as well on Lott's general character, as in the examples above.

(20) Had Lott stopped with Thurmond-for-president, 1948, this might have been written off as idle and presumably insincere birthday flattery for a very, very old man. But Lott did not stop there. He added, fatally, that America would have been better off had it embraced Dixiecrat segregation. With that, Lott cut off any retreat. This is not just the kind of eruption of moronic bias or racial insensitivity that cost baseball executive Al Campanis and sports commentator Jimmy the Greek Snyder their careers. This is something far more important. This is about getting wrong the most important political phenomenon in the past half-century of American history: the civil rights movement. Getting wrong its importance is not an issue of political correctness. It is evidence of a historical blindness that is utterly disqualifying for national office. (Krauthammer 2002)

Explicit attention to truth and falsehood also was characteristic of much of the journalism during the Rove panic. Examples 21 and 22 are from reportage; they are quite unusual in that the accusation of falsehood is a departure from reportorial neutrality. Extract 23 is from a liberal blogger, Murray Waas, quoted in another blog, Steve Benen's *The Carpetbagger Report*.

(21) The story he would tell prosecutors did not seem to square with the White House's denial that it had played any role in one of the most famous leaks since Watergate. (VandeHei and Allen 2005)

(22) This approach [trying to discredit Wilson by saying the trip was a boondoggle set up by his wife] depended largely on a falsehood: that Wilson had claimed Cheney sent him to Niger. Wilson never made such a claim. (Hamburger and Efron 2005)[10]

(23) Where'd Rove learn about Plame? He said from a reporter. Which reporter? He doesn't know. When did he talk to this reporter? He doesn't know. How did Rove communicate with this reporter? He doesn't know. For a guy who can remember voter information by the precinct in swing states, Karl Rove couldn't remember the slightest details when a reporter gave him classified information? (Benen 2005)[11]

In technical terms, the examples above attend to the Maxim of Quality. However, attention to the other Gricean maxims can also be found. An interesting discourse developing the Maxim of Clarity involves folk ideas about grammar, and attention to exactly how it is that the compositional nature of utterances might accomplish – or perhaps fail to accomplish – the match between utterance and truth. Two examples of this from the Lott panic are seen in Extract 24, from the conservative blogger Andrew Sullivan, and in 25, from a 'color commentary' piece in the *Post*'s section for local Washington news. In these quotations, it is asserted that words have a 'plain meaning' and that Lott's utterance lacked the ambiguity that would disrupt this.

(24) Everyone deserves a break for a 'poor choice of words' but it wasn't the words that really offended. It was the plain meaning of the words. What other words would have sufficed? (Sullivan 2002)[12]

(25) The problem, of course, is that this response works best when there's some actual ambiguity involved. Unfortunately, Lott's sentence was neatly constructed, with a clean use of the conditional, and very few words open to multiple interpretations. The only words that offer some glimmer of hope on the ambiguity front are 'all these problems'. (Kennicott 2002)

In the American media context, journalistic attention to the Maxim of Clarity today is likely to invoke a famous piece of semantic hair-splitting by former President Bill Clinton. During the Monica Lewinsky scandal, Clinton, in the face of extensive evidence to the contrary, had uttered the following sentence: 'There is no sexual relationship between me and that woman,

Ms Lewinsky'. In testimony before a Grand Jury, Clinton defended this lie using the following rationalization, as quoted in the online magazine *Slate*:

> (26) 'It depends on what the meaning of the word "is" is. If the –
> if he – if "is" means is and never has been, that is not – that is one
> thing. If it means there is none, that was a completely true state-
> ment ... Now, if someone had asked me on that day, are you
> having any kind of sexual relations with Ms Lewinsky, that is,
> asked me a question in the present tense, I would have said no.
> And it would have been completely true.' (Noah 1998)[13]

In the Rove case, Rove and his supporters had argued that Rove had not really revealed the identity of Valerie Plame, the CIA operative, because he had not said her name. In Matthew Cooper's Grand Jury testimony, Rove was said to have referred to Plame as 'Joe Wilson's wife'. The argument that Rove had not 'said her name' was considered by many journalists to be 'Clintonian', constituting a violation of the Maxim of Clarity and the idea that 'plain language' best links truth to reality. Clinton's famous hedge is compared to this failure to use plain language in the following examples. The first is introduced into straight reportage in a quotation, while the second appears in an editorial.

> (27) Rove's allies defend the White House's original denial by saying
> that Rove never mentioned Wilson's wife by name, a distinc-
> tion that Holt [Jim Holt, an Arkansas candidate for Lieutenant
> Governor, who was once employed in the National Security
> Administration] said made no difference. 'It's almost like saying
> it depends on what the definition of "is" is,' he said, referring to
> former President Clinton's defense in the Monica Lewinsky case.'
> (Fournier 2005)[14]

> (28) Mr Rove and White House spokesman Scott McClellan can fairly
> be accused, at the very least, of responding to questions about the
> affair with the sort of misleading legalisms and evasions that
> Republicans once rightly condemned President Bill Clinton for
> employing. 'I didn't know her name. I didn't leak her name.'
> Mr Rove told CNN last year. Technically true, perhaps, but hardly
> a model of straightforwardness and probity.' (Unsigned Editorial,
> 'Mr Rove's Leak' *Washington Post*, 15.07.05)[15]

4.5 Conclusion: why personalist ideology matters for analysts of media discourse

While personalist language ideology is interesting to anthropologists as part of a project of characterizing the foundations of western culture, we might ask whether attention to it is important for the critical analysis of media discourse. I believe that it is, because foundational premises in language ideology constitute the frames that make possible the kinds of mystifying hegemonic discourse that are of special interest to Critical Discourse Analysis, perhaps the dominant approach today to the analysis of media discourse. For instance, in research on White racism in the United States, I've been trying to untangle a central conundrum about American culture: gross racialized inequality persists alongside a nearly universally expressed commitment to racial equality. I have suggested that egalitarian Americans tolerate these inequalities because negative stereotypes about people of colour somehow circulate among them. How does this circulation occur? How does the supposedly unsayable, the racist stereotype, somehow get said? And get said often enough, with sufficiently powerful impact that White Americans behave as they do, tolerating inequality and even actively opposing efforts to address it?

I've hypothesized that personalist language ideology can work to permit racist propositions to circulate, even in a discourse environment where to utter these publicly is very risky (as we have seen in the case of Senator Lott). I believe that one way personalist ideology works is to permit White Americans to understand that utterances of negative stereotypes are somehow not 'meant'. No speaker is responsible for them. Thus people who utter racist statements and commit racist acts often get a 'free pass'. Certainly Senator Lott was given a free pass by many commentators. A dramatic illustration of such a free pass appeared as recently as the 31 August 2005 *New York Times*, in a piece of reportage by Carl Hulse on a new memoir by former Senator Jesse Helms. Helms served for 30 years as a Republican senator from North Carolina. In an article headlined, 'In memoir, Jesse Helms says he was no racist', Hulse summarizes claims made in Mr Helms's new book *Where I Stand*. The book was issued by Random House, a distinguished publisher, and includes a foreword by Senator Bill Frist of Tennessee, the then Majority Leader of the US Senate. Frist called the memoir 'a guidebook for understanding what it means to hold clear convictions and champion them without regard for the mood of the moment' (Hulse 2005).

Hulse (2005) reported, 'Criticized throughout his career for opposition to civil rights legislation and accused of using divisive language and imagery in his campaigns, Mr Helms said he was "not the least bit racist" and stood by his decision to oppose strenuously the establishment of a national holiday honoring the Rev Dr Martin Luther King Jr. Hulse's text stated that Mr Helms is said to have defended a flagrantly race-baiting campaign against an African American opponent in 1990 by saying 'The campaign was never about Mr Gantt being black; it was always and only about him being a liberal.' Needless to say, Hulse's reportage in no way challenges Helms' claim. The only demurral from the widely held view that Mr Helms is a dangerous racist is expressed vaguely in the syntactically and agentively reduced and backgrounded protasis in the first quotation: 'Criticized throughout his career for opposition to civil rights legislation and accused of using divisive language and imagery in his campaigns . . .' (Hulse 2005).

Senator Helms's claim to be 'not the least bit racist' joins a long list of protestations of innocence by White politicians who were among the most important segregationists or, like Helms, major leaders in the backlash against civil-rights advances. When Helms was first elected to the Senate in 1972, he was the first Republican elected from North Carolina since 1876. He personified the Republican Party's 'Southern Strategy', by which the party captured the South from Democratic control by appealing to white supremacists after Democratic presidents from Truman to Johnson supported desegregation and civil rights legislation. Yet the *New York Times* reports his claim to be 'not the least bit racist' virtually without comment, and indeed endows his memoir with considerable importance by reporting on it in the main news section of the newspaper rather than in the book review section. Furthermore, the choice of 'reportage', which is supposed to be value-neutral, rather than 'review', where the expression of opinions and values is expected, as the genre for discussion of the book in the *Times*,[16] virtually guarantees that there will be no overt challenge to Helms's claim. But it is not only the journalistic convention of neutrality that constrains such a challenge. The challenge is made difficult by the terms of personalist ideology itself. Personalist language ideology, which makes Helms the first authority on his own intentions, renders coherent Hulse's bland reportage of a patent falsehood as an assertion with the same status as any other assertion.

Personalist language ideology provides a similar underpinning for hegemonic discourse around a multitude of issues. Personalist ideology underpins media discourse, making it seem simultaneously unremarkable and true to the incautious consumer. So I conclude this chapter by suggesting that attention to language ideologies, pioneered by anthropologists such as Silverstein (1979) and Rumsey (1990), should be added to our repertoire of methods for the analysis of media discourse alongside the methods illustrated in the work of critical discourse analysts who have pioneered the study of media language.

Primary sources

Applebome, P. (2002), 'The record'. *New York Times*, 13.12.02, A22.

Benen, S. (2005), 'Rove and Ashcroft and Fitz . . . oh my', 15.08.05 (available online at www.thecarpetbaggerreport.com, accessed 20.10.06).

Billmon (2005a), 'Slime and defend', 13.07.05 (available online at www.billmon. org, accessed 20.10.06).

Billmon (2005b), 'Better warm up Ol' Sparky', 14.07.05 (available online at www.billmon.org, accessed 20.10.06).

Cohen, R. (2002), 'Leadership requires empathy'. *Washington Post*, 12.12.02, A45.

Cohen, R. (2005), 'Rove isn't the real outrage'. *Washington Post*, 14.07.05, A 25 (also available online at www.washingtonpost.com, accessed 20.10.06).

Finer, J. and Fekeiki, O. (2005), 'Sunnis offer new proposals on constitution'. *Washington Post*, 27.08.05 (available online at www.washingtonpost.com, accessed 20.10.06).

Fournier, R. (2005), 'GOP nervously eyeing Rove and CIA probe'. *Guardian Unlimited*, 14.07.05 (available online at www.guardian.co.uk/worldlatest/story/0,1280,-5139995,00.html, accessed 20.10.06).

Hamburger, T. and Efron, S. (2005), 'A CIA cover blown, a White House exposed'. *Los Angeles Times*, 25.08.05 (available online at www.latimes.com/news/nation-world/nation/la-na-leak25aug, accessed 20.10.06).

Hulse, C. (2005), 'In memoir, Jesse Helms says he was no racist'. *New York Times*, 31.08.05, A8.

Kennicott, P. (2002), 'A "sorry" spectacle', *Washington Post*, 13.12.02, C01.

Krauthammer, C. (2002), 'A clear choice of words'. *Washington Post*, 12.12.02, A45.

Krugman, P. (2002), 'All these problems'. *New York Times*, 10.12.02, A31.

Lemann, N. (2005), 'Right hook'. *New Yorker*, 29.08.05, 34–9.

Meyerson, H. (2002), 'GOP revisits a sordid past'. *Los Angeles Times*, 15.12.02, (available online at www.latimes.com, accessed 02.12.06).

Noah, T. (1998), 'Bill Clinton and the meaning of "is"'. *Slate*, 13.09.98 (available online at www.slate.msn.com/id/1000162/, accessed 20.10.06).

Scheer, R. (2005), 'Column left'. *The Nation.com*, 12.07.05 (available online at www.thenation.com, accessed 20.10.06).

Sullivan, A. (2002), 'Those discarded policies'. *andrewsullivan.com*, 9.12.02 (available online at http://time.blogs.com/daily_dish/, accessed 20.10.06).

Unsigned Editorial, *Wall Street Journal*, 14.07.05.

Unsigned Editorial, *Wall Street Journal*, 15.07.05.

VandeHei, J. and Allen, M. (2005), 'In Plame leaks, long shadows; Rove knew of CIA agent, husband's role in criticizing Bush'. *Washington Post*, 17.07.05, A1.

Notes

1 www.washingtonpost.com/wp-dyn/content/article/2005/08/26/AR2005082601323_3.html. Accessed 27.08.05.

2 www.juancole.com; accessed 28.08.05.

3 Wilson's sin had been to point out, in an opinion piece in the *New York Times*, that the supposed 'intelligence' that Saddam Hussein had tried to buy uranium ore from mines in Niger was emphatically wrong. For more on the discourses around the 'intelligence' that was used to justify the invasion of Iraq in 2003, see Jeffries (Chapter 3, this volume).

4 Joshua Micah Marshall, 10.12.02, www.talkingpointsmemo/dec0202. html; accessed 15.12.02).

5 www.latimes.com; accessed 15.12.02.

6 www.thenation.com; accessed 14.07.05.

7 www.washingtonpost.com; accessed 14.07.05.

8 www.billmon.org, July 14, 2005; accessed 15.07.05.

9 www.billmon.org, July 13, 2005; accessed 15.07.05.

10 www.latimes.com / news / nationworld / nation / la-na-leak25aug . . . ; accessed 25.08.05.
11 www.thecarpetbaggerreport.com, Aug. 15 2005; accessed 25.08.05.
12 www.andrewsullivan.com, December 9, 2002; accessed 12.12.02.
13 www.slate.msn.com/id/1000162/; accessed 03.09.05.
14 www.guardian.co.uk/worldlatest/story/0,1280,-5139995,00.html; accessed 14.07.05.
15 www.washingtonpost.com; accessed 15.07.05.
16 The *New York Times* never published a formal review of Helms's book.

PART II
NATIONAL IDENTITIES, CITIZENSHIP AND GLOBALIZATION

5 The iconography of orthography: representing German spelling reform in the news magazine *Der Spiegel*[1]

Sally Johnson

5.1 Introduction

In 1995 the German 'Standing Conference of Ministers for Education and Cultural Affairs' – the *Kultusministerkonferenz* or KMK – announced that a reform of German orthography had been approved. The proposed changes were an attempt to harmonize what was perceived to be a complex and inconsistent set of orthographic rules, causing unnecessary problems for language users of all ages but particularly for young schoolchildren. The reform was to be introduced from 1 August 1998 to coincide with the start of the new school year, and this would be followed by a seven-year transitional period until 2005, during which time the old orthography would be considered 'outdated' (*überholt*) but not 'wrong' (*falsch*).

The decision to reform German orthography had not been taken lightly. Given that the first and hitherto only set of official guidelines for all the German-speaking countries had been agreed in 1901, the final proposal for their revision in 1996 was the result of almost a century of often heated debate among educationalists, linguists, politicians, writers, journalists and other interested parties (see Jansen-Tang 1988; Küppers 1984). Nor was the 1996 reform an exclusively German affair. From the late 1970s in particular there had been close liaison between what were then the four main German-speaking states – the Federal Republic of Germany, the German Democratic Republic, Austria and Switzerland – with the reform process to some extent facilitated by German unification in 1990. At various points there had also been input from Liechtenstein, the only other country with German as sole official language, and from German-speaking groups in Belgium, Luxembourg, Denmark, Italy, Romania and Hungary. On 1 July 1996, representatives from many of these countries, together with German, Austrian and Swiss officials, met in Vienna to sign the so-called 'Viennese Declaration of Intent' or *Wiener Absichtserklärung*, thereby agreeing to implement the new guidelines.

Although the disputes surrounding the state-sanctioned standardization of German orthography had never entirely abated since they first began in the mid-nineteenth century, by the time the Viennese Declaration was signed in 1996, a new round of public protest had already gathered momentum. In May of that year, Rolf Gröschner, professor of law at the University of Jena, and his 14-year-old daughter, took their case against the reform to the 'Federal Constitutional Court' or *Bundesverfassungsgericht* (BVerfG) in Karlsruhe and, while the Court rejected their claim that the reform was at odds with the 'German Basic Law' or *Grundgesetz*, their highly publicized campaign helped to re-kindle much of what can probably be characterized as a traditional public antipathy (both in the German-speaking countries and elsewhere) towards the idea of orthographic reform (see Federal Constitutional Court, 21.06.96; Sebba 2007). Many protest groups then proceeded to challenge the reform in the regional courts in Germany[2] and in October of the same year, a group of eminent writers and intellectuals, including the subsequent Nobel laureate, Günter Grass, put their signatures to a petition known as the 'Frankfurt Declaration on the Spelling Reform' (*Frankfurter Erklärung zur Rechtschreibreform*) circulated at the annual Frankfurt Book Fair by the Bavarian schoolteacher Friedrich Denk. In November 1996, Denk then went on to form a national 'citizens' action group' or *Bürgerinitiative*, entitled 'WE [the people] against the spelling reform' (*WIR gegen die Rechtschreibreform*), the aim of which was to topple the reform via a series of regional referenda. These protests eventually culminated in a return to the Constitutional Court in May 1998 where, following a comprehensive final hearing, the protests were once again dismissed and it was ruled that the reform should proceed as originally planned (see Federal Constitutional Court, 12.05.98).

In this chapter, it is not my aim to explore the various legal challenges inspired by the reform, nor do I wish to describe the precise details of the orthographic changes that were made in this context (for discussion and analysis of these, see Johnson 1999, 2000, 2002, 2005a, 2005b).[3] What I want to focus on here is the way in which the Frankfurt Declaration, together with the more general disputes surrounding the reform, were represented *visually* on the front cover of an edition of the influential German news magazine, *Der Spiegel* published on 14 October 1996 (see Figure 5.1).[4] The decision to concentrate on this particular image is motivated by two main considerations.

First of all, it is relatively unusual to find an aspect of language metadiscursively represented in a *visual* format (see e.g. Blommaert 1999a; Hyland 2005; Jaworski *et al* 2004b). In this sense, the analysis of the *Spiegel* image constitutes an exciting opportunity to explore the representation and/or construction of a linguistic theme in and by the media against the backdrop of recent debates over multimodality (see e.g. Constantinou 2005; Kress and van Leeuwen 2001, 2006; O'Halloran 2004; van Leeuwen 2004a). This, in turn, presupposes the need to re-think the analytical boundaries between the semiotic modes of (at the very least) language and image. As Kress and van Leeuwen (2001, 2006) are able to show, visual images – or the juxtaposition of textual and visual formats – afford a much greater range of expressive possibilities than is the case for language alone. As such, it will be interesting to analyse the resources that might be activated within a multimodal environment in relation to metalanguage and metadiscourse more generally (Coupland 2004; Meinhof 2004; Richardson 2004; see also Ensslin, Chapter 13, this volume).

Secondly, within the academic literature dealing with the public disputes surrounding the 1996 reform of German orthography, the trend has been towards a predominantly negative appraisal of the *Spiegel*'s treatment of this issue on the grounds of its subjectivity, emotionalism and concomitant inability to deal with the debate in a rational, even-handed manner (see e.g. Johnson 2000; Ledig 1999; Stenschke 2005; Zabel 1997). If, however, we are genuinely concerned to further our understanding of media representations and/or constructions of language-related themes – one of the purposes of this book, as outlined in Chapter 1 – I would argue that an alternative approach might be more productive. While it will be neither possible nor desirable to counter the claim that the *Spiegel* editors engage in an 'emotional' and 'subjective' representation of the reform debate, the aim here will be to explore how and why this might be so. This, in turn, is the kind of scenario that pre-supposes the need to bring into play what I have referred to elsewhere (Johnson 2001: 593–4; 2005a:10) as the methodological principle of *symmetry*, a concept that stems from the field of Science Studies (see Irwin and Wynne 1996; Latour 1993; Hargreaves 2000). Central to this approach is the need to move away from a focus on the public and/or the media as the exclusive source of *mis*-understanding or *mis*-representation, together with a demand for greater reflexivity on the part of scientists/academics themselves (see also Cameron, Chapter 12, this volume). As Simon Pardoe (2000: 149) explains in the context of his own research on student literacies, the 'pursuit of symmetry' demands that researchers attend not only to those beliefs and practices that have traditionally been considered *rational* (e.g. 'expert', scientific discourses), but that they 'expand their repertoires of explanation' by showing 'respect' for those discourses which have simultaneously been dismissed as *irrational* (e.g. 'lay' understandings of science). Thus, following an initial suspension of judgement with regard to pre-conceived notions of rationality, researchers can work towards a greater appreciation of not only those beliefs and practices which have been marginalized by dominant discourses but of the ways in which such dominant discourses have been able to achieve their naturalized status as common sense.

93

It is by unpacking the relationship between the two that researchers can then achieve a degree of symmetry in their work.

In sum, it is against this dual theoretical backdrop that the present chapter aims to explore what might be characterized as the 'alternative' (read: non-expert/non-linguists') rationalities underpinning the representation of the German spelling reform in the *Spiegel* image in question. The next section will now sketch the social and discursive contexts in which this image was produced before proceeding to a discussion based on the analytical framework laid out in Kress and van Leeuwen's (2006) *Reading Images: The Grammar of Visual Design*.

5.2 The 'Frankfurt Declaration' and *Der Spiegel* image in context

The 'Frankfurt Declaration' of 1996 contained a critique of the reform of German orthography on the following grounds. These, it should be noted, are by no means untypical of protests against orthographic reform more generally (see e.g. Fishman 1977; Sebba 2007). However, they are worth stating in detail in order to convey a sense of the context in which the subsequent *Spiegel* feature appeared:

1. The impact of the reform on written German would be too minimal as to merit the inevitable upheaval brought about by its implementation.
2. Many of the new rules were superfluous and did not render German orthography easier to learn.
3. The changes would lead to a reduction in the overall meaning potential of German, notably via the new rules on separate and compound spellings whereby the distinction between formerly separable verbs such as *sitzen bleiben* (to remain seated) and previously inseparable verbs such as *sitzenbleiben* (to repeat a school year) would collapse.
4. The new rules would damage the reputation of German abroad given the high level of confusion caused by the reform, leading to a reduction in the number of foreigners wishing to learn German.
5. The reform would disadvantage less well-educated language users, particularly in view of the uncertainty brought about by the existence of variant spellings.
6. A generation of children/pupils would suffer years of confusion and aggravation as a result of the reform.
7. The new orthography was ugly, particularly those forms containing three identical consecutive graphemes such as *Schifffahrt* (boat trip) or *Kaffeeersatz* (coffee substitute).

8. The consequences for German literature would be catastrophic. The necessary revision of literary works would lead not only to an increase in cost to the reader, but would in many cases actually interfere with the referential potential of such texts, threatening the enjoyment of German literature overall.

9. The new guidelines – frequently glossed as *Neuschreib* ('New-write') – had been imposed by the state upon an unwilling population in an Orwellian fashion.

10. The cost of the reform would run into millions of German Marks/Euros. Only printers, publishers of dictionaries and schoolbooks, and software manufacturers would benefit, while the tax-payer stood to lose via the many working hours consumed by the introduction and acquisition of the new spellings. (Adapted from Johnson 2005a: 100 and Denk 1997: 41–4)

A summary of the Frankfurt Declaration, together with some 400 signatures, was later published in the *Frankfurter Allgemeine Zeitung* newspaper (19 October 1996), calling for a halt to the reform and highlighting the way in which the new guidelines had been drawn up by a 'primarily anonymous group of experts' (Denk 1997: 46). One week later the Education Ministers replied with their own so-called 'Dresden Declaration', containing a detailed refutation of the Frankfurt accusations (KMK, 25.10.96). Particularly disputed by the ministers was the claim regarding insufficient consultation. They noted how not only had drafts of the reform proposals been made available to the public in 1988 and 1992, but that these had been widely commented upon in the press. Moreover, in May 1993, a public hearing had been organized and many interested parties invited to submit their views in writing. While some had indeed responded, there had been no reply from the German branches of the international writers' association, PEN.[5]

However, it was undoubtedly the pre-eminence of a number of its signatories that allowed the Frankfurt Declaration to gain widespread media coverage. Among those who had signed were leading writers such as the Nobel laureate Günter Grass together with Siegfried Lenz, Martin Walser, Hans-Magnus Enzensberger and Walter Kempowski, along with many other well-known German-speaking intellectuals, publishers, academics, journalists and historians. And it was in this context that the title page of the influential news magazine, *Der Spiegel*, famously implored its readers to 'Save the German Language!' (*Rettet die deutsche Sprache!*), while the header dismissed the reform as 'nonsense' (*Schwachsinn*), proclaiming 'The Writers' Revolt' (*Der Aufstand der Dichter*). The accompanying illustration, with echoes of the March revolutions of 1848 (more on this later), depicted a group of writers armed for battle, amidst a pile of books alongside the Duden spelling dictionary impaled on a bayonet. Towering above the scene as a whole stood a resolute Günter Grass proudly bearing the German national

Figure 5.1: *Der Spiegel*

flag, thus constituting an overall image that perhaps more than any other intervention in the reform debate captured the extent to which this was by no means a dispute about orthography alone, or even the written language more generally. What was clearly at stake here – for some at least – was the German language in all its force as a symbol of cultural and national unity.

96

In the 14-page feature accompanying the image and dedicated to the protest more generally, the reformers were referred to as 'stubborn orthographic terrorists' (*Die sturen Orthographie-Terroristen*) (p. 262) as well as being accused of a multitude of sins against the German language by various writers. Siegried Lenz complained of 'linguistic decline' (*Sprachverfall*) (p. 268). Martin Walser, on the other hand, declared all spelling norms to be the product of 'centralistic fetishes' (*Zentralismusblüten*), designed only to create errors, and went on to urge everyone to spell as they pleased (p. 270). Hans-Magnus Enzensberger dismissed the nineteenth-century lexicographer and spelling reformer Konrad Duden as an 'armchair fart' (*Sesselfurzer*) and, citing Shelley, proclaimed that poets were probably better 'linguistic legislators' (*Gesetzgeber der Sprache*) than ministers or publishers of schoolbooks (p. 266). Meanwhile, Walter Kempowski (who even admitted to not having familiarized himself with the details of the reform prior to signing the Frankfurt Declaration) insisted that people learned to spell 'visually' rather than according to rules (*sic*). Besides, he maintained, we should be grateful that anyone wanted to write at all nowadays before proceeding to agree with campaigner Friedrich Denk that the dispute was ultimately about 'the loss of national identity in a united Europe' (*den Verlust der nationalen Identität im vereinten Europa*) (pp. 276–80).

These, among others, are the kinds of themes that are taken up in the illustration presented on the *Spiegel* cover in question. The feature is unashamedly anti-reform and in the accompanying editorial the *Spiegel* editors stoically declared that the new orthography would never be employed in their own publication, which would continue to adhere to traditional patterns of spelling and punctuation. The key question at this juncture is: how are such anti-reform sentiments represented in the multimodal environment constituted by the image in question?

5.3 'Save the German Language' – visually representing the reform

In *Reading Images*, Kress and van Leeuwen (2006) propose that the structure and effects of visual/multimodal texts can be usefully analysed in terms of three main dimensions: (1) the representation of social actors and positioning of the viewer; (2) modality markers; and (3) composition of image. The following sections will explore the *Spiegel* image in terms of each of these categories.

5.3.1 Representation of social actors and positioning of viewer

According to Kress and van Leeuwen (2006: 116–24), the depiction of one or more *characters* is central to the way in which social relations between text producers and viewers are enacted in visual imagery. Here the 'real' authors of the image are removed from the context of interaction and their views transmitted via substitutes or 'represented participants' in much the same way as the voice of an author might speak in the guise of a narrator or character(s) in prose fiction. Of key importance in this regard is the *gaze* of such participants. In some cases, for example, imaginary eye contact between participant and viewer can function as a form of address or 'visual you'. Here the image act in question constitutes a 'demand' to the viewer as subject. This contrasts with those cases where there is no eye contact and the viewer is in receipt of an 'offer' to peruse the image from the perspective of an invisible onlooker (ibid.: 118–19).

The nature and intensity of any such demand or offer on the part of represented participants has also to be seen in conjunction with the facial expression depicted, e.g. smile, laugh, grimace, etc. Moreover, as in other visual media such as film and theatre, the structuring of a participant's gaze is closely linked to the attempted positioning of the viewer in terms of subjectivity and/or objectivity of anticipated response. As Kress and van Leeuwen note (ibid.: 120–1), it is in this sense that image acts are also closely tied up with social power relations – the demand, for example, generally presupposes an entitlement to address the viewer which not everyone has. While viewers are under no obligation to accept the constructions of social relations on offer, it is generally assumed that they will at least recognize those constructions provided they belong to the cultural community addressed by the image and/or publication in question.

The participants represented on the *Spiegel* cover image are Günter Grass (at the centre) and four further authors to his fore, namely (from left to right) Martin Walser, Siegfried Lenz, Walter Kempowski and Hans-Magnus Enzensberger, all of whom are well-known figures on the German literary and cultural scene. The image presents an interesting juxtaposition of gaze types. For example, Grass, Lenz and Enzensberger all look away from the viewer, and their earnest facial gestures are redolent of characters 'lost in thought' whose deliberations are on offer for interpretation to the viewer as onlooker. These compare markedly to Walser on the far left and Kempowski (second from right) whose direct eye contact with the viewer, coupled with their earnest facial expressions, appear to demand a more immediate and subjective response to the scenario depicted.

This juxtapositioning of the viewer as subject/object and participant/ onlooker, respectively, is replicated in the *Spiegel* image in a number of further ways. For example, the size of frame used to portray the five authors varies such that differing levels of (imaginary) social distance are simultaneously constructed between participants and viewers. On the one hand, the long shot used to depict the full figure of Grass indexes a sense of 'far social distance', which, as Kress and van Leeuwen (ibid.: 124–5) note, is generally deemed appropriate (at least in western cultures) for the conduct of more *impersonal* social and business interaction. On the other hand, the close head and shoulder shots of Walser, Lenz, Kempowski and Enzensberger construct a sense of 'far personal distance' that is conducive to business of a more *personal* nature. Such contrasting representations are then underpinned by the disparate positioning of the viewer in terms of perspective or 'camera angle' (ibid.: 129–43). Whereas Grass (at the centre) is depicted from a slightly lower angle, creating an imposing figure who looks down on the viewer thereby demanding respect, the remaining four participants are represented more or less at eye level, thereby diminishing potential power differentials. This is a juxtaposition that is further replicated in the use of the horizontal camera angle. Here, the combination of frontal and oblique shots melds with the use of direct and indirect gaze so as to construct a relationship that seems to suggest an alignment of participants and viewer as part of a shared world, on the one hand, while simultaneously representing the five authors as part of a discrete and more distant social space, on the other.

5.3.2 Modality

A second feature of the grammar of visual design described by Kress and van Leeuwen is that of modality (ibid.: 154–74). As in language, modality in visual imagery is concerned with perceptions of what counts as 'real' and, by implication, 'true'. In such contexts, potential modality markers can include i) the use of colour; ii) the level of contextualization, representation of detail, and use of depth; and iii) illumination and brightness (ibid.: 160–3).

Leaving aside the not unproblematic relationship between modality and truth value here, Kress and van Leeuwen (ibid.: 158) propose how present-day western judgements of modality tend to be primarily grounded in a 'naturalistic coding orientation' as the dominant mode for the expression of authenticity. In other words, high modality is more often accorded to seemingly naturalistic images whose features most closely correspond to a typical 35 mm photograph in terms of colour, depth and perspective. However, there are many exceptions to this. For example, 'sensory coding orientations', though typically characterized by a pleasure principle where certain colours such as reds and blues are used to affect emotional states, may also be accorded high modality as in advertising or interior design (ibid.: 165). Meanwhile, 'technological coding orientations' characteristic of, say, a drawing or diagram are frequently perceived to be more objective than a photograph of the same event – here the effectiveness and/or truth value of an image may well be judged in terms of its ability to function as a 'blueprint' (ibid.). In a similar vein, more 'abstract coding orientations' tend to dominate those modes favoured by socio-cultural élites such as scientific/academic discourses or 'high' art (ibid.). As Kress and van Leeuwen point out: 'In such contexts modality is higher the more an image reduces the individual to the general, and the concrete to its essential qualities. The ability to produce and/

or read texts grounded in this coding orientation is a mark of social distinction, of being an "educated person" or a "serious artist" ' (ibid.).

With a circulation that reaches around 8 per cent of the German population, *Der Spiegel* is certainly pitched at the élite end of the print media market and sees itself as addressing a predominantly well-educated readership with a keen interest in current affairs.[6] It is therefore no surprise to find the image in question drawing on many of the features typical of a more abstract coding orientation. For example, we encounter an interesting use of colour differentiation that draws on a limited range of shades (ibid.: 160), characterized, on the one hand, by a small number of bold, highly saturated colours (red, orange, yellow) that might be interpreted as exaggerated or unreal. These combine, on the other hand, with a series of less highly saturated blues, greys, pinks and yellows whose overall effect verges on the monochrome, thereby conveying a sense of the ghostly or surreal. In sum, we might see this use of colour as effecting a high level of modality by attempting to capture the reform debate, in a predictably intellectual manner, in terms of its more abstract essence. However, such high modality is not, I believe, achieved by an abstract coding orientation alone – the image simultaneously draws on elements of a more sensory coding orientation typical of, say, modern consumer advertising or historical forms of political placarding. Accordingly, the use of the bolder colours such as red, yellow, and orange – the latter echoed by the *Spiegel*'s prototypical orange frame – help to inject a strong sense of urgency and emotionality into the magazine's depiction of the reform debate, an urgency not untypical for cover images, which stand (quite literally) alongside their competitors in retail outlets and need therefore to catch the eye of potential consumers/readers. Meanwhile, elements of a more naturalistic coding orientation – notably, the faces of five authors – simultaneously add a touch of realism to the image that is essential for its content to be recognized by the magazine's intended audience.

The overall effect of high modality in the *Spiegel* image is further underpinned by the use of contextualization, the representation of detail, and the depth of image (ibid.: 161–3). Whereas in more naturalistic coding orientations, the absence of contextualization typically affects low modality, here the absence of background appears to reference the generic rather than the particular. This effect is then bolstered by the sense of 'hyper'-reality conveyed by the almost excessive detail of the image's foreground that contrasts with the lack of backgrounding. Similar effects are created by the overall lack of depth to the image together with the almost complete absence of illumination – note how the represented participants cast no individual shadows. These then work together with the use of brightness and focus to create what is a rather misty, hazy effect that seemingly contributes to an overall attempt to capture the essence, as opposed to the specifics, of the reform debate.

5.3.3 Composition of image

In this final part of the analysis, I now turn to the composition of the image in question. As Kress and van Leeuwen (2006: 204–8) note, in western textual modes, so-called linear reading paths are generally compulsory, whereby written texts must be read along a horizontal axis of left to right and a vertical axis from top to bottom. By contrast, reading paths for visual images are much more flexible and may, for example, be diagonal, spiralling or even circular (though some will be more marked than others). It is through the sequence of the chosen reading path that cultural information and perceptions of salience within an image are then decoded. However, the inherent potential for variability on the part of individual readers, coupled with the possibility for disparate readings from one act of viewing to another, necessarily presuppose a high degree of subjectivity where interpretations of the composition and meaning of any given image are concerned.

It is not within the scope of this analysis to conduct an empirical investigation of reader reception in terms of variability of reading paths and perceptions of salience vis-à-vis the *Spiegel* image. However, informal discussions with colleagues and students do seem to point towards either a predominantly diagonal reading path that moves from the top left-hand side of the image down to the bottom right (and sometimes back to the centre) or, alternatively, a spiralling path that again commences at the top left of the image, proceeds clockwise, and ends in the centre. This would appear to support Kress and van Leeuwen's claim (ibid.: 179–93) that, in western modes, and in line with Hallidayan assumptions on the ordering of grammatical constituents in language, old information is typically placed to the left and/or top of an image, with new information located on the right and/or at the bottom. Accordingly, we might see the written text contained at the top left of the *Spiegel* cover as constituting the Given or theme, with the image of the authors itself and the text at the bottom right as New information or rheme. This would imply a metaphorical encoding of the presupposition that the reform is indeed 'nonsense' and that the German language is in need of 'saving', all of which underpins the self-evidence of the 'writers' revolt'. The dispute as a whole is then glossed by the reference on the bottom right-hand side to what might initially appear to be an unrelated feature on the crisis surrounding German *Telekom* shares. However, the intertextual relevance to the spelling reform is evident when one considers that the slogan *Top or Flop?* applies equally to the reform, itself in crisis in view of the various challenges to its authority on the part of writers, lawyers and other social groups that were ongoing at the time of publication.

The overall composition of the image in terms of possible reading paths has also to be seen in conjunction with those features that are accorded particular salience within the image as a whole. Here, the positioning of elements in conjunction with the use of colour, size etc. all contribute to the emphasizing of some features over others. In the *Spiegel* image, we can probably single out the figure cut by Grass as accorded primary salience both in terms of its size and centrality. However, the representation of Grass (the most renowned of the five authors but ironically the only one with whom there is no interview in the accompanying article) works together with a number of other features. These include the German flag whose black/red/gold tones are replicated on the cover of the Duden spelling dictionary and are subtly interspersed throughout the foregrounded image of the writers and books as well as in the reference to the *Telekom* share crisis on the lower right-hand side. Moreover, the deep red of the flag is also picked up in the orangey/red of the traditional *Spiegel* frame as well as the slogan 'Save the German Language' whose font type and size are further redolent of the political sloganizing of the 1960s student movement to which all five writers were in some way linked. Also pertinent in this regard is the use of the familiar second person plural form of the verb 'to save', i.e. *rettet*, that is similarly evocative of student movement discourse and whose function here is an attempted positioning of the viewer as a member of a shared political community and/or reading 'public' whose own rejection of the reform as a nonsense is taken as given (see Gal and Woolard 2001; Lee 2001).

Finally, the salience of certain features within the image cannot be seen in isolation from the overall use of 'framing'. While the trade-mark orangey/red of the *Spiegel* border itself helps to create the sense of a self-contained, unified image within it, we might again see the figure of Grass, the national flag, and the headline '*Rettet die deutsche Sprache*' as framing the image overall, both in a literal and metaphorical sense. In this way, the image encodes a strong sense of the debate over German orthography as much more than a mere dispute over spelling and punctuation. This was a dispute over authority, democracy and German national identity as a whole . . .

5.4 1848 and all that – 'provenance' and the iconography of orthography

This last point leads neatly into a discussion of media representations and/or constructions of the 1996 reform more generally. This is because one of the key criticisms on the part of many pro-reform linguists was related to the purported inability of 'non-linguists' or 'lay' language users, notably many politicians, writers and journalists, to disentangle issues of orthography, on the one hand, from written language, language per se, culture and even national identity, on the other (Hoberg 1997: 98–9, for discussion, see Johnson, 2005a: 156–62).

Yet if the public disputes surrounding the 1996 reform illustrate just one thing, it is that, in the real world, orthography tends not to be compartmentalized in the socially decontextualized manner demanded by the autonomous, structuralist approach of many expert linguists – an approach, moreover, that typically relegates orthography to the level of speech representation, thereby denying its status as part of the 'real' language system at all. On the contrary, as highlighted in the *Spiegel* image in question, nonspecialists' views are much more likely to be characterized by a holistic approach, i.e. one where orthography, written language, culture and even national identity are conflated within the discursive complex that, in its totality, comprises language (see also Cameron 1995; Lippi-Green 1997). This is a phenomenon closely related to what Alexandra Jaffe and Shana Walton (2000: 582) refer to as 'orthographic metonymy', whereby patterns of spelling and punctuation as only a *part* of language appear especially conducive to the indexing of language and culture as a *whole*. As Jaffe notes elsewhere (2000a: 503): 'Orthography is a tool in the symbolic fusion of language and identity: in Decrosse's terms, it is orthography that creates the idea of the "Mother Tongue": a potent metaphor of self and community united in a shared primordial attachment to a language (1987: 32).'

This notion of orthographic metonymy goes some way towards explaining the image of the 1996 reform debate depicted by *Der Spiegel*, not least in terms of what Jaffe and Walton (2000: 582) refer to as the 'striking leap from part to whole' so typical of language ideological debates around orthography generally. Moreover, in accordance with the 'principle of symmetry' discussed earlier, the concept of metonymy facilitates a greater appreciation of this particular instance of anti-reform coverage in the German media that was so readily dismissed as an irrational and exaggerated response to the revised orthography. But while the predominantly structural analysis of the image conducted thus far has certainly been useful, such an approach can tell us little about the broader historical and political discourses that are evoked in and by this particular piece of visual meaning-making. In other words, we still need to know more about where this image and its constituent discourses are, quite literally, 'coming from'. This is something that can be explored in terms of Kress and van Leeuwen's (2001) concept of *provenance*.

Drawing on Barthesian notions of connotation and myth (Barthes 1972, 1977), Kress and van Leeuwen (2001: 10) describe 'provenance' as a significant component of any meaning-making process according to which '[. . .] we constantly 'import' signs from other contexts (another era, social group, culture) into the context in which we are now making a new sign, in order to signify ideas and values which are associated with that other context by those who import the sign.' As an example, they note the use of the sitar by the Beatles in the late 1960s to signify the values of the psychedelic youth culture typical of that era. Provenance is therefore a useful concept with which to explore the themes or values characteristic of one discourse that are invoked in a new text or image. However, as emphasized by Kress and van Leeuwen (2001: 73–4), such inter-textual or inter-discursive (and, one should add, inter-*medial*) invocations are rarely realized in any complete

103

sense such that the phenomenon of provenance tends to be both 'unsyste-matic' and 'ad hoc'. Accordingly, there can be no general rules for the inter-pretation of signs imported in this way except to say that the associated themes and values do tend to be linked to strong emotional states (ibid.).

So what are the broader themes and values invoked by the *Spiegel* image under discussion? Inter-textually, i.e. with specific reference to the structural composition of the image itself, the question of provenance is straight-forward. The picture is in fact a re-working of a nineteenth-century wood engraving by Johann Jakob Kirchhoff entitled *Barrikadenszene am Alexander-platz* ('Scenes from barricades on *Alexanderplatz*') (see Figure 5.2). Of course, the image, which depicts a barricade in one of Berlin's famous centrally located squares, *Alexanderplatz*, that formed part of the popular uprisings of 1848–9, has been subject to significant digital manipulation. Gone is the corpse at the centre of the original and, in a textual intervention not without its own metaphorical significance, the paving stones stockpiled as missiles have been supplanted by books. Also new to the image is the use of colour. But, overall, the provenance of the text and its point of reference are clear: imported into the controversy over spelling and punctuation surrounding the *Frankfurt Declaration* of 1996 are, by analogy, the multi-faceted dis-courses surrounding the political upheavals known as the *Frankfurt Revolu-tion* of 1848–9. Such effects are further reinforced by the textual reference of Kirchoff's own image to Eugène Delacroix's canvas, 'Liberty leading the people', itself a response to the French revolutionary upheavals of 1830.

The *Spiegel*'s own interpretation of this crucial period of German politi-cal history is usefully summarized in a long feature published in 1998 and dedicated to the 150th anniversary of Germany's so-called 'failed' revolution (*Der Spiegel*, 09.02.98; see also Blackbourn 2003; Breuilly 2001; Siemann 1998, 2001). The feature describes how the mid-nineteenth century saw

Figure 5.2: Scenes from barricades on Alexanderplatz

the European order established by the Vienna Congress of 1815 severely disrupted as popular uprisings in a number of major European cities challenged conservative political systems, accompanied by demands for greater democratic rights for individual citizens in the context of independent nation-states. However, comparisons between the German uprisings of 1848–9 and the French revolution of 1789, while commonplace, were largely untenable. By the late eighteenth century, France had 'only' to rid itself of its monarchy – the existence of the French nation-state had been firmly established since the Middle Ages. Conversely, by the mid-nineteenth century, Germany (still divided into 39 separate principalities) struggled not only to achieve greater democratic and constitutional rights for its citizens, but was simultaneously dogged by the question of the very shape of a potentially unified state, involving *inter alia* fraught debates over the status of the area surrounding Posen (now Poznań in Poland) together with Danish-occupied Schleswig-Holstein. Moreover, the general preference for a so-called 'Pan-German solution' (*großdeutsche Lösung*) that would incorporate both Austria and the territories of Bohemia into a unified Germany would have simultaneously presupposed the end of the Habsburg Empire.

Against this complex political backdrop, and following the Paris upheavals of February 1848, the first demands for a democratic, unified German state were drawn up by the liberal revolutionaries, Friedrich Hecker and Gustav von Struve. By early March, significant public demonstrations were taking place in the south-west German town of Karlsruhe and these were quickly followed by uprisings in Vienna leading to the flight of the Austrian Chancellor, Metternich. It was in this context that, in March 1848, the Prussian King Friedrich Wilhelm IV had his troops quell similar uprisings in Berlin with a death toll of 277. Recognizing, however, that his actions had served only to provoke his subjects further – as illustrated by the barricade depicted in the Kirchhoff image – the Prussian King quickly succumbed and withdrew his troops. By April, a unified German state had been proclaimed by Hecker with its parliament based in Frankfurt, and in mid-May the first ever German national parliament assembled in Frankfurt's St Paul's Church (*Paulskirche*). But while Friedrich Wilhelm IV was declared as the first monarch of the newly founded state, the offer of the German crown was rejected. And despite repeated attempts by the architects of the Frankfurt parliament to persuade the other German states to adopt the new national constitution over the coming year or so, the requisite support was ultimately not forthcoming. Thus, in the wake of counter-revolutionary actions on the part of the various German monarchs, culminating in a return to the status ante by mid-1849, the first real 'home grown' attempt to establish a modern, unified and democratic German nation-state had seemingly failed.

The reasons behind, and consequences of, this historical failure on the part of liberal revolutionaries to establish a democratic state at this precise point in German history are also explored in *Der Spiegel* (09.02.98). By the time that a unified Germany was achieved by Bismarck in 1871 (albeit without the inclusion of Austria and the Bohemian territories, i.e. a so-called *kleindeutsche Lösung*), it seems that the new state could pay only lip-service to the democratic impulse underlying the liberal uprisings of 1848–9, even allowing for the fact that a number of demands from that time had been incorporated into the new constitution. The consensus thus appears to be that the uprisings were simply not underpinned by the level of grass-root support and/or revolutionary leadership that is presupposed by truly radical social and political change (both Marx and Engels were scathing in their dismissal of the bourgeois preoccupations of Hecker and Struve). From a latter-day perspective, we might therefore see the significance of the Frankfurt Revolution for *Der Spiegel* as embedded (rightly or wrongly) in two main discourses. First of all, there is the fundamental sense of a failure to achieve a truly democratic nation-state based on the popular will of the people, a failure that is attributed to an inherent unwillingness and/or inability on the part of the German people to exert their own democratic will. This is then accompanied by a second and related discourse consisting of a teleological view of 1848–9 as a historical crossroads, whereby an alternative outcome might well have placed German politics on a radically different course – possibly, for example, one that might not have seen its twentieth-century apotheosis in two world wars and the rise of National Socialism. It is against this backdrop that this turbulent period of German history is popularly and somewhat ironically known as 'the turning point at which Germany simply failed to turn'.

In this context, there are many elements of inter-discursivity afforded by the reference to the Frankfurt Revolution that are visually indexed by the *Spiegel's* representation of the disputes surrounding German orthography. Within the much broader discursive complex that, from the mid-nineteenth century onwards, saw ongoing and sometimes violent debates over the shape of the nation-state and the right to control it, disputes over orthography revolved, and continue to revolve, around the specification of the correct form of the (written) German language of that nation-state together with the most appropriate site of linguistic authority. Who has the right to define the norms of a standard German orthography: linguists as agents of the state, or writers, as self-proclaimed representatives of the people? Whether the *Spiegel* image similarly encodes a metaphorical understanding of the Frankfurt Declaration on the spelling reform as doomed to failure in the manner of the Frankfurt Revolution is open to interpretation (but highly likely). Moreover, did the Frankfurt Declaration similarly represent an historical crossroads from which there would be no turning back should the writers' revolt fail to bring about a democratic, bottom-up process for the establishment of orthographic norms that presupposed the transfer of orthographic authority from state to *demos*? Or did the disputes surrounding the reform amount to little more than a case of 'hot air' on the part of a vocal minority of bourgeois intellectuals equally doomed to failure in the face of widespread popular apathy?

5.5 Discussion and conclusions

I began this chapter with two main aims. The first of these was to take advantage of the relatively unusual opportunity afforded by the *Spiegel* image in question to explore the visual representation of a linguistic theme in and by the media against the backdrop of debates over multimodality. The second was to re-think the binary division of emotionality and rationality that has typically underpinned the dismissal of this image, by spelling reformers and academic linguists alike, as a subjective distortion of debates over German orthographic reform. By means of a detailed structural inspection of the image in question, it has in fact been possible to bring these two aims together. This is in so far as the analysis has revealed how the *Spiegel* image draws on a wide range of meaning-making strategies in relation to the representation of social actors, modality and image composition that simultaneously – and, I would argue, quite *cleverly* – position the intended viewer as both detached onlooker and actively participating subject in this debate. Moreover, the analysis of the textual-discursive structure and provenance of the image reveals the underlying analogies that are being drawn between the Frankfurt Declaration of 1996, on the one hand, and the Frankfurt Revolution of 1848–9, on the other. This is a view of orthography as much more than simply a discrete feature of the language system that operates in isolation from broader social, cultural and political contexts.

As Gunther Kress (2000a: x) reminds us: '[Spelling] has always served as a potent metaphor for social values, structures and practices. Spelling is that bit of linguistic practice where issues of authority, of control, of conformity can be most sharply focused.' If, however, we are to appreciate as linguists how and why such issues become part of a debate over orthographic reform, it is essential to go beyond traditional, autonomous understandings of what constitutes a valid intervention into such debates per se, i.e. one that focuses on the structural dimensions of spelling and punctuation (notably phoneme–grapheme correspondences and/or morpho-phonemic principles) and no more. It is in this sense that notions of subjectivity versus objectivity as applied by many linguists and spelling reformers in their *dismissal* of non-linguists' interventions into this debate emerge as especially problematic. As Susan Gal and Kathryn Woolard (2001: 1–10) remind us, the very notion of 'aperspectival objectivity' or a 'view from nowhere' is itself one that is in constant need of critical scrutiny. And, as has been widely argued elsewhere (e.g. Cameron 1995; Niedzielski and Preston 2000; Johnson 2001, 2005a: 9–11), a more focused and theorized attempt to explore so-called 'folk' conceptualizations of language is especially pertinent in cases such as these. This is in so far as there is much that can be learned by linguists about the nature of language (and language reform) by exploring the views of precisely those social actors in the 'real world' whose views have been traditionally sidelined within the discipline, as well as by acknowledging that our own

work *as linguists* is itself always historically and socially situated (see Blommaert 1999a; Kroskrity 2000). As Gal and Woolard emphasize (2001: 3),
the aim of this critical project is neither to privilege folk understandings of
language, on the one hand, nor to discredit traditional forms of scholarly linguistic endeavour, on the other. Moreover, such reflexivity need not entail a
denial that there are indeed *facts* of language that can themselves be subject to
processes of distortion and/or *mis*-representation by, for example, the media,
in line with classical Marxist definitions of ideology and false consciousness
(Lippi-Green 1997: 66). Rather, the aim is to explore the nature of the *claims*
about language that are proffered by disparate groups of ideological brokers
in the context of the discursive struggles that invariably ensue as these compete for hegemony (Blommaert 1999a).

In practice, this more critical approach invites a re-appraisal of not only
mainstream academic perceptions of the *Spiegel*'s intervention into the
debate over orthography, but an equally critical engagement with the interpretation of German political history and/or orthography seemingly on offer
to viewers of the image in question. In fact, there are many competing and
arguably more nuanced interpretations of the legacy of the Frankfurt Revolution of 1848–9 for German political consciousness than that put forward by
Der Spiegel. For example, as the historian Wolfram Siemann is at pains to point
out, the dismissal of the Frankfurt Revolution as an outright failure is one that
is itself severely in need of re-calibration:

> The more we contemplate all those dimensions which are revealed
> when we view the different levels of action, the less able we are
> simply to state that the revolution failed utterly. The revolution gave
> the impetus to a long-term wave of modernization. National unity
> remained a real prospect, both experienced and recalled. The peasants
> remained victorious in any case: they were finally and irrevocably freed
> from their dependence on their landlords. The legal system had chan-
> ged fundamentally at all levels. Political participation was established
> despite the subsequent reactionary Restoration. Prussia had become a
> constitutional state. The Frankfurt constitution remained exemplary
> for a hundred years, up to the time of the Parliamentary Council in
> 1948–9. The national revolution also had the effect of altering rela-
> tions between the various German states in ways which are important
> for a study of Germany as a federal political system, although much
> more research is needed on this. To see the revolution simply as a failure
> would mean underestimating its meaning and importance in German
> history. (Siemann 2001: 136)

Moreover, as Siemann reminds us elsewhere (ibid.: 134), the apparent failure
of the revolution of 1848–9 was *not* a uniquely German phenomenon given
that revolutionary uprisings at this time were thwarted, with the sole exception of Switzerland, right across Europe. It is in this context that a critical

reading of the *Spiegel* image presupposes a consideration of the extent to which the analogies drawn between the Frankfurt Declaration, on the one hand, and the Frankfurt Revolution, on the other, are in fact invoking what Siemann himself refers to as the much broader and popular '*national myth of the barricade*' (ibid.) – albeit a myth whose invocation lends itself rather well to the metaphorical exposition of orthographic reform as a site of ideological struggle between 'people' and 'state'.

Finally, I would argue that, in order to appreciate an image such as the *Spiegel* cover, we need as linguists to acknowledge at the very least the legit-imate self-perception of the media producers behind such images as language experts in their own right (see also Thurlow, Chapter 11, this volume). In this sense, many German-speaking journalists and editors, just like any other group of language users who have honed their writing craft over a long period of time, were always likely to feel aggravated by a reform that not only re-aligned notions of orthographic (read: *linguistic*) correctness, but simultaneously threatened to destabilize the social, cultural and economic capital metaphorically inscribed into extant orthographic structure – a shift that formed part of what Gal and Woolard (2001: 8) refer to as a broader pro-cess of 'strategic re-contextualisation' necessarily implied by any language reform. It has not been the concern of this chapter to explore the extent to which the predominant conservatism of such groups of ideological brokers was morally justified in the context of the reformers' very real attempts to har-monize the rules of correct German orthography, primarily with younger and/or less experienced users of the written language in mind. (For the record, I do not believe that it was.) However, it is clearly counter-productive in terms of language planning processes more generally to overlook the man-ifestations of such conservatism – as embodied in the *Spiegel* image in ques-tion – if we are to understand more fully the symbiotic relationship between the ideational and interpersonal functions of language for not only producers of media texts but for language users everywhere.

5.6 Postscript

Despite the claim by its editors in October 1996 that *Der Spiegel* would adhere to the pre-1996 orthography, the magazine's publishers, *Gruner + Jahr*, did in fact insist that the editors adopt the new orthography along with the majority of the German print media in the summer of 1999. However, this decision was dramatically reversed in the summer of 2004 when the editors of *Der Spiegel* and the *Süddeutsche Zeitung* together with those newspapers published by the *Axel-Springer Verlag* opted to revert to the old orthography (or, strictly speak-ing, their own in-house versions thereof), although this was a decision subse-quently retracted by the *Süddeutsche Zeitung* and one which, at the time of writing (November 2005), has yet to be implemented by *Der Spiegel*.

Primary sources

Der Spiegel
   '1848 – Die halbe Revolution: Beginn des deutschen Desasters?' (No. 7, 09.02.98).
   'Der Aufstand der Dichter: Rettet die deutsche Sprache!' (No. 42, 14.10.96).
Federal Constitutional Court (*Bundesverfassungsgericht*) (21.06.96) BVerfG, 1 BvR
   1057/96 – *Rechtschreibreform. Beschluß der 3. Kammer des Ersten Senats.*
Federal Constitutional Court (Bundesverfassungsgericht) (12.05.98) BVerfG, 1 BvR
   1640/97 – Rechtschreibreform. Urteil des Ersten Senats vom 14. Juli 1998. Rep-
   rinted in *Entscheidungen des Bundesverfassungsgerichts.* 98. Band (1999) (pp. 218–
   64). Tübingen: J. C. B. Mohr.
'Frankfurt Declaration on the Spelling Reform' (*Frankfurter Erklärung zur
   Rechtschreibreform*). *Frankfurter Allgemeine Zeitung*, 19.10.96. Reprinted in
   F. Denk (1997), 'Eine der größten Desinformationskampagnen', in H.-W. Eroms
   and H. H. Munske (eds), *Die Rechtschreibreform: Pro und Kontra.* Berlin: Erich
   Schmidt Verlag, pp. 41–6.

Notes

1 Many thanks to Tommaso Milani for his detailed comments on an earlier draft of
   this paper. I would also like to thank Oliver Stenschke for locating the Kirchoff
   image and Mark Sebba for drawing my attention to the Delacroix reference.
2 For details of similar debates and forms of protest in Austria and Switzerland, see
   www.rayec.de. The discussion here will restrict itself to an analysis of the protests in the Federal Republic of Germany.
3 The changes can be categorized into six main groups as follows: (1) sound-letter
   classifications (e.g. *Känguruh → Känguru* – 'kangaroo'); (2) separate and compound spelling (e.g. *radfahren → Rad fahren* – 'to cycle'); (3) hyphenation (e.g.
   Hair-Stylist → Hairstylist/Hair-Stylist); (4) capitalization (e.g. *in bezug auf → in
   Bezug auf* – 'with respect to'); (5) punctuation (i.e. a reduction in the number of
   formal punctuation rules); and (6) the separation of words at the ends of lines
   (e.g. *Zuk-ker → Zu-cker* – 'sugar') (for further details and discussion, see Johnson
   2005a: 45–86).
4 I would like to express my gratitude to *Der Spiegel* for granting permission to
   reproduce the image in question.
5 At that time, there were still two branches of PEN, one in eastern and one in western Germany.
6 *Der Spiegel* describes itself (www.media.spiegel.de) as characterized by in-depth
   information with a focus on events in the political and social sphere. According
   to a poll conducted by *Der Spiegel*, readers dedicate on average 2 hours, 30 minutes to each issue. Of the magazine's readership, 39 per cent have the equivalent
   of 'A' levels, 39 per cent are in 'leading' professional positions, and 42 per cent
   had in 2004 a net monthly household income of more than 2,500 Euros.

6 A language ideology in print: the case of Sweden

Tommaso M. Milani

6.1 Introduction

As a substantial body of recent sociolinguistic research has illustrated, Europe at the beginning of the twenty-first century was marked by the progressive emergence of public debates on the introduction or amendment of language policies relating to the naturalization of migrants (see e.g. Piller 2001; Black-ledge 2005; Shohamy 2006a; and Stevenson 2006).[1] Marilyn Martin-Jones (personal communication) suggestively describes this diffusion of discourses on language and citizenship as a powerful wind which swept across Europe, ultimately having a 'real' impact in several national contexts insofar as they resulted in more restrictive language requirements for citizenship applicants (as in Denmark, Germany, Great Britain and the Netherlands).[2]

Sweden, which is often referred to as a prime example of pluralist recognition of the ethnic, religious and linguistic diversity resulting from migration (Koopmans and Statham 2000: 196), also witnessed a heated public debate surrounding the potential introduction of a compulsory Swedish language test as part of the naturalization process. This debate emerged in the context of the campaign preceding the parliamentary election in 2002, when Lars Leijonborg, leader of the Swedish Liberal Party (*Folkpartiet Liberalerna*), made public a report entitled 'A New Integration Politics' (*En ny integrations-politik*) (*Folkpartiet* 2002). In this context, the Liberal Party suggested that Swedish naturalization policies should be revised, and advocated the introduction of a Swedish language test as a prerequisite for the granting of Swedish citizenship. Although language testing was only *one* of the measures advanced by the Liberal Party in its proposals for a more 'integrated' Swedish society, it ultimately became *the* major topic of the electoral campaign, triggering a range of reactions from politicians, cultural figures and the general public. Most interestingly, despite the fact that the introduction of a language test for naturalization was originally advanced by the Liberal Party, the many attempts to buttress this language policy proposal crossed the boundaries of political affiliation. A few representatives of other political parties (e.g. the

Moderate Party, the Center Party, but also the Social Democratic Party) expressed their support for the idea of such a test, while, on the other hand, some members of the Liberal Party itself dissociated themselves from the proposal. Also notable was the change of opinion put forward by the Social Democratic Prime Minister, Göran Persson. After being asked during a chat with the listeners of the radio programme *EKO* (13.08.02) whether he shared the Liberal Party's position on language testing for naturalization, Göran Persson replied that he did not (*Dagens Nyheter*, 29.08.02). Nevertheless, in an interview published only two days later in the influential Swedish daily *Dagens Nyheter*, he declared: 'I am not exactly for a language test: that would be to approach matters the wrong way round' (my translation) but added that nor was he strongly opposed to the idea (*Dagens Nyheter*, 15.08.02a). However, this was followed by a further change of mind, when the prime minister proceeded to condemn the Liberal Party's proposal.

Immediately following the election, the language testing issue was pursued further. On 16 October 2002, 13 members of parliament belonging to the Liberal Party submitted a motion in which they argued that an 'acceptable knowledge of the Swedish language should be a requirement for citizenship', and suggested that the parliament should 'initiate an official inquiry about the possible design of language tests' (*Motion*, 2002/03: Sf 226). A few months later, on 18 February 2003, just before the parliamentary Committee on Social Insurance (*socialförsäkringsutskott*) was to take the aforementioned motion into consideration, the Liberal Party published a further report entitled 'A Reform of Language Requirements is Urgently Needed: New Facts and Arguments'(*Språkkravsreform brådskar – nya fakta och argument*) (*Folkpartiet* 2003), which underlined the idea that a language test would be a helpful measure with which to enhance integration in Sweden. This debate ended with the parliamentary rejection of the Liberal Party's proposal. As a consequence, Swedish naturalization policies were not amended and no language test for naturalization was introduced.

Although the debate described above did not have any actual impact on Swedish policies, I argue in the present chapter that an analysis of the claims advanced in support of the introduction of a language test for naturalization can help us to understand the relationship between three contentious concepts that are under scrutiny in the present volume, namely *language, ideology* and *media representation(s)*. Furthermore, given the role of the *print* media as a contextual space in which the Swedish debate took place, an investigation of a sample of extracts taken from Swedish newspapers articles will also give a sense of the ways in which a particular language ideology is (re)produced and disseminated in the press. Before delving into the analysis of relevant texts, however, I set out in the next two sections to define the notion of language ideology to be discussed here and then go on to provide an overview of the data on which the study is based.

6.2 Disentangling common sense: A Bourdieuan approach

Over the past 20 years or so, the notion of language ideology has been increasingly drawn upon by scholars in sociolinguistics and linguistic anthropology in an attempt to capture the complex nexus between how people think about, label and evaluate linguistic practices in various socio-political contexts. At the same time, the aim of such an approach is to explore how such conceptualizations are enmeshed in other broader cultural processes of, say, delimiting social and ethnic groups, imagining the nation or defining aesthetics, morality and common sense (see, for example, Gal and Woolard, 2001: 3). As Judith Irvine puts it, language ideology is a 'cultural (or subcultural) system of ideas about social and linguistic relationships, together with their loading of moral and political interests' (1989: 255). Drawing on the notion of language ideology, the primary aim of this chapter is to show how and why the proposal to introduce a Swedish language test for naturalization constitutes a tangible manifestation of one particular language ideology – an *ideology of language testing*[3] – according to which the need for migrants to undergo a language test in order to become Swedish citizens is not only represented as good and necessary but also *self-evident*. The relevance of the surfacing of this language ideology, which ties a language test for naturalization to both *morality* and *common sense*, can be understood if read against the backdrop of the Swedish context where since the 1980s ideologies of multilingualism and multi-culturalism have dominated political discourse (Koopmans and Statham 2000; Piller 2001). In particular, these ideologies have led to the underscoring in policy documents (cf. SOU 1999; Prop. 1997/98) of the importance of Swedish language skills for all residents in Sweden coupled however with a rejection of Swedish language requirements for citizenship applicants given that these were considered *unjust* and *discriminatory* (Milani, in press). In this sense, we can see how, in the claims supporting a language test advanced in 2002, we were witnessing the emergence of a competing ideology that attempted to defy and criticize some of the main ideological grounds on which Swedish political management had traditionally been based during the previous two decades.

I have already explored elsewhere (Milani, in press) the language ideological paradox between the explicit arguments that a language test would create a more cohesive Swedish society, and the exclusionary effects that such a test would in fact have given its role in actually (*re*)*producing* boundaries between Swedes and migrants. Here, by contrast, I want to adopt a different approach. First, instead of concentrating on one particular set of arguments, a broader range of intertwining discourses of language testing will be investigated. Second, I take as a point of departure Pierre Bourdieu's (2000: 181) observation that 'tangible self-evidences' are the manifestation of the processes whereby commonsense agreement on the meaning of the social world is produced and reproduced. Bourdieu also reminds us that such processes 'tend to give to an illusory representation the appearance of being grounded in reality' (2000: 181). By bringing together Bourdieu (2000) and the linguistic tools provided by Critical Discourse Analysis (Fairclough 2003; Blackledge 2005), my aim is to turn 'tangible self-evidences' into an empirical research target, and thereby reveal the processes whereby an ideology brings into life a *regime of representation* (Gal and Woolard 2001: 4), that is, a structured pattern of semiotic resources, which misrecognizes what is merely *arbitrary*, and re-signifies it as intrinsically *natural*, *logical* and *morally good* (see also Blackledge 2005, and Stevenson 2006, for a similar approach to the British and German/Austrian contexts, respectively). Specifically, the aim is to make transparent the ways in which coalescing discourses *(mis)represent* and *signify* the link between language skills and language requirements, thereby constructing a social world in which it is seen as *common sense* that applicants for Swedish citizenship should have to take a language test.

6.3 Data

The texts analysed for the purpose of this study encompass extracts of newspaper articles taken from a large corpus of data related to the Swedish debate on language testing for naturalization.[4] There are three main reasons behind the choice of these specific texts. First, the extracts have been selected because they are representative of the most common arguments advanced (and the values indexed) by the supporters of a language test. Second, the choice of newspaper articles is motivated by the role of the print media as a crucial arena in which the Swedish debate was enacted and disseminated. Third, as Norman Fairclough (1995) and Susan DiGiacomo (1999) point out, newspaper articles are important sites of ideology production in so far as they do not only cite and repeat, but also strategically recontextualize (Gal and Woolard 2001: 8) texts and discourses originally produced elsewhere in and by other media such as TV, radio and the internet. This means that, through citation, newspaper articles situate existing texts and discourses 'into a chosen meta-discursive context and hence indicat[e] the preferred way(s) of 'reading' these texts [and discourses]' (Blommaert 1999b: 9). The producers of print media texts are therefore important *ideological brokers* (Blommaert 1999b), not only because they frame reality – the event 'out there' – by foregrounding, backgrounding or even erasing some aspects of it (cf. Fairclough 2003: 53–5). This is also because, in representing reality, text producers may incorporate, and thereby indicate, a particular interpretation of existing ideologically laden discourses on this very reality. This, together with the authoritative status typically accorded to newspaper discourses means that print media 'can have a powerful influence on [. . .] [people's] understanding of, and attitudes to, the social world' (Blackledge 2005: 67). Finally, newspapers are arenas to which only a relatively limited number of people have access in terms of actual production processes. In other words, social groups which wield social power are likely to have privileged or exclusive admission to the production of media texts (van Dijk 1993; Blommaert 2005). At the same time newspaper editors, in particular, may elect to invest with authority the statements of those who would not generally be given the floor, that is, private individuals or the so-called 'man in the street'. Accordingly, not only news reports and editorials have been included in my corpus but also letters to the editor since these represent a fruitful, though not necessarily exhaustive, site for the exploration of grass-root opinion within the public sphere.

At this juncture, it is essential to point out that the texts analysed below belong to different genres, were written by different authors, under different constraints and in different contexts.[5] However, as the main focus of this particular study is to account for the range of discourses in which the ideology of language testing takes shape, the present chapter will concentrate on the arguments of the texts and their linguistic realizations, rather than seek to trace authorial intentionality and/or audience responses. As Adrian Blackledge (2005: 21) puts it: '[w]hat we have is the text itself, and what we know we can identify is its intertextual relationship to other texts, genres and *discourses*' (emphasis added). In the following sections, I will explore three such discourses in the context of the debate over language testing and citizenship in Sweden: the educational discourse, economic discourse and discourse of governance.

6.4 Discourses of language testing and citizenship

6.4.1 Educational discourse

As I have already highlighted elsewhere (Milani, in press), the common denominator – be it explicitly stated or implicitly presupposed – of the claims proffered by the proponents of a language test is that migrants in Sweden *lack*, either totally or partially, knowledge of the Swedish language. This presumed lack is not envisaged as a linguistic deficiency of some individuals, but rather as a widespread phenomenon and a major societal problem to be resolved through language testing. What already emerges here is one of the most recurrent ambiguities in the claims made by the supporters of a test. Given that, from a strictly legal perspective, the language testing proposal refers only to *applicants* for citizenship, it is reasonable to ask ourselves the following questions: (1) What about other migrants who will not, or do not want to, apply for citizenship?[6] (2) Is their alleged lack of Swedish less important than that of those who do apply? (3) How is a language test assumed to affect migrants' language skills? Unfortunately, no clear answers to such questions can be provided from a review of the articles in the corpus. Rather, a few extracts can be taken in order to illustrate some of these ambiguities (note that all translations are my own).

> **Extract 1**
> The Liberal Party suggests that people with a non-Swedish background who do not easily manage to speak Swedish **need to be helped** in order to learn the language. [...] No one will ever be deprived of his or her Swedish citizenship. This means that no language test in the world will ever fail someone who is already Swedish citizen. By contrast, those who apply for Swedish citizenship will **receive help** to cope with Swedish, unless they already master it, so that they will not find themselves outside of civil society, will understand letters from public authorities and news reports, or be able to apply for jobs. In brief, **acceptable Swedish is required in order to be an integrated part of Swedish society**. The proposal does not enhance segregation, but it counteracts it. (*Borås Tidning*, 30.08.02 – my emphases)

This extract is taken from a letter to the editor written by a representative of the Liberal Party in response to a previous article criticizing the language testing proposal. The starting point (first sentence) is a general comment on the significance attributed to migrants' Swedish language skills. It is important to observe that (1) no direct reference is made to a language test, and (2) modality, together with the lexical choice, invests the statement with seemingly tolerant credentials (cf. Blackledge, 2005: 98). In fact, unlike in many other texts in the corpus (see for example Extracts 2, 6 and 7 below), migrants are not *required*, but *need to be helped*, to learn Swedish. This means that Swedish language skills are assumed to be of principal importance. Nonetheless, the responsibility of the language acquisition process in this context does not lie exclusively with the individual migrant, but implicitly with institutions of the state that ought to provide the necessary assistance.

Having established that Swedish language skills are for the 'good' of all migrants in Sweden, the author then moves on to consider the particular case of those who might want to apply for Swedish citizenship. Beside the fact that a language test is now explicitly referred to, it is interesting to note the subtle ways in which the author frames the links between language proficiency and language testing. After clarifying that a test would not pertain to those migrants who have already been naturalized, the author goes on to argue that citizenship applicants will receive *help* to 'cope with' Swedish. Once again the topic of help/assistance is reiterated, but what is not made explicit is whether it is assumed that a language test would itself assist in the learning of Swedish or whether new educational programmes would be introduced in order to accompany the proposed test. However, what is relevant here is that some kind of connection between language test and language proficiency is assumed. Or, to put it another way, the argument runs as follows: if a language test is introduced, migrants will (be helped to) learn

Swedish. Moreover, this argument is shored up via the reference to the social benefits which proficiency in Swedish might provide, i.e. ability to read letters from public authorities, to apply for jobs, and ultimately to be an integrated part of Swedish society. In sum, the author presupposes that there is a positive correlation between language testing, language skills and participation in Swedish society. Nonetheless, apart from the vagueness surrounding the way in which a language test might actually impact on language learning, it is not unequivocal what level of language proficiency migrants are expected to achieve in order to qualify as citizens. Nor is it clear whether those migrants who are already proficient in the Swedish language would need to undergo a test or not.

Another example of a presumed positive correlation between a language test and language skills is provided by Extract 2, which reports on an exchange of opinions between representatives of the Liberal Party and the Social Democratic Party at an electoral meeting in Angered (near the city of Gothenburg).

Extract 2

One of the first questions directed at the Liberal Party was: what about the language test (for naturalization)?

Cecilia Nilsson (Liberal Party) answered that the party did not want to introduce a language test but **make demands on language skills** in order to **stress** the importance of the Swedish language.

Ewelina Tokarczyk (Social Democratic Party) wondered why the Liberal Party thought that people did not want to learn Swedish.

'We do not think that, but **there must be pressure**. Of course, there would be many exceptions: for example, if someone were 80 years old and came here to live with his or her children', answered Nilsson. (*Göteborgs Posten*, 05.09.02a)

This extract is particularly significant because it provides us with a fairly typical example of a news report which alternates between authorial account, indirect report and direct report, through which different contrasting voices are pitted against each other. In addition, the extract also contains other relevant arguments in support of the language testing proposal. Remarkable here are the lexical items 'demand' and 'stress'. As we will also see in relation to the discourse of governance below, 'demand' is one of the keywords of the whole debate, and a language test is presented as a concrete example of such a demand. It is therefore interesting in this context to look at the presuppositions underlying the linguistic expressions containing the lexical item 'demand'.

As the indirect report of the response of the representative of the Social Democratic Party convincingly illustrates (third sentence), the recurrent emphasis put by the Liberal Party on 'making demands' presupposes the idea that migrants are *unwilling* to learn Swedish unless they are obliged to do so.

This view, according to which migrants need a push of some kind in order to learn Swedish, is also forcefully reiterated in the last sentence of the extract where, by way of the strong marker of deontic modality 'must', a degree of 'pressure' on migrants is represented as an absolute necessity. Furthermore, by arguing that such demands underpin the importance of the Swedish language, the representative of the Liberal Party makes it clear that the language testing proposal is not just about enhancing migrants' communicative skills in Swedish: it also has a *symbolic* dimension. In this regard, Bourdieu's (1991) conceptualization of language as a form of capital can be a useful tool with which to investigate the meaning of language testing in this context, and to understand the way in which the instrumental function of language is inextricably linked to its symbolic/identity function (cf. May 2003a).

In a well-known account of the symbolic power of language, Bourdieu (1991) argues that social relations can be understood in terms of economic exchanges between social actors in possession of differing amounts of capital. Bourdieu distinguishes between four forms of capital: economic capital (i.e. material resources), social capital (i.e. class), cultural capital (i.e. all forms of cultural knowledge, including language skills) and symbolic capital (i.e. prestige). Drawing on the notions of cultural and symbolic capital, one can see how the proposal to introduce a language test for naturalization attempts to reinforce the value of Swedish as cultural capital. This is in so far as a certain level of proficiency in Swedish would eventually be sanctioned as an indispensable prerequisite for the gaining of citizenship. Bourdieu also reminds us that all forms of capital transform into symbolic capital 'when they are perceived and recognized as legitimate' (1991: 230). This means that an eventual recognition of a language test as an official and legitimate practice would not only enhance the value of Swedish language skills but, given the legitimacy of such a test, would also increase the value of Swedish as symbolic capital, in other words, its *prestige* (cf. Shohamy 2006a: 95). Against this backdrop, one can conclude that, in the claim that language testing is a marker of the importance of Swedish, language testing becomes a *sign* that itself points to and reasserts the value of Swedish as cultural and symbolic capital in Sweden.

In conclusion, the above examples illustrate how some of the claims proffered by the supporters of a language test are based on the assumption that migrants lack knowledge of the Swedish language because they are generally *unwilling to* learn it. Consequently, they need a stimulation/obligation in the form of a statutory language test. As it is also assumed that there is a positive correlation between a language test and language proficiency, a language test is presented as if it were a reasonable educational tool through which to enhance migrants' language proficiency. Furthermore, it was also possible to show that the obligation to pass a language test is not tied exclusively to the function of Swedish as a resource which enables communication between individuals from whatever linguistic background. Rather, drawing

118

on Bourdieu's notion of language as symbolic capital, we see how the very proposition of a language test for citizenship helps to (re)emphasize the role of Swedish as a symbolic national resource (see also Milani, in press, for a detailed analysis of the relationship between language testing and processes of imagining the nation).

6.4.2 Economic discourse

We saw in the previous section how proposals for the introduction of a language test were motivated at least partly by the positive social effects this would ultimately have on Swedish society. In particular, it was argued that migrants' entry into the Swedish labour market would be enhanced (see Extract 1). The key assumption underpinning this argument is that there is a relation of causality between language skills and access to employment opportunities. Put simply, if an individual knows Swedish, he or she will more readily find a job. As we shall see, however, the relationship between language skills and language requirements is not always unambiguous in this discourse. This becomes clear in Extract 3, which is taken from a report on a series of interviews conducted with representatives of different political parties on the language testing issue.

Extract 3
'[...] They must leave behind **their dependence on subsidies** and enter the labour market', argues Jacobsson, who claims that the **cause** of the higher unemployment rate amongst immigrants **is not the result of discrimination so much as the fact that they cannot speak Swedish**. (*Hufvudstadsbladet*, 29.08.02)

Here, as in Extract 2, we see how news reports can constitute interesting examples of textual interactions between different voices – in this particular case, between the authorial voice of the journalist and the voice of a representative of the Moderate Party (*Moderaterna*). While the first two clauses are part of a longer direct report which is supposed to reiterate the actual words uttered by the politician, the remainder of the extract is an indirect report of the interview worded by the journalist. Nevertheless, the repetition of the reporting verb, and the relative pronoun, which cohesively links the direct to the indirect report, contribute to a blurring of the boundary between the voice of the politician and the authorial voice, thereby giving the impression that the whole extract is a faithful reproduction of the interview. Content-wise, it is noticeable that migrants' lack of Swedish language skills, rather than discrimination, is singled out as the *cause* of high unemployment rates among migrants – from which one can infer that migrants would find employment more readily if they learned Swedish.

That knowledge of Swedish is *conditio sine qua non* for access to the job market is also reiterated later in the same article (Extract 4) by a

119

representative of the Liberal Party, who maintains that migrants must 'learn the language' in order to be able to work.

Extract 4

'There are too few of us here and we need more immigrants. But **in order to work they must learn the language.** This is not an **unreasonable** requirement.' (*Hufvudstadsbladet*, 29.08.02)

Through the dense use of modality, one can infer that language knowledge is assumed to be an indispensable prerequisite of employability. Moreover, the definite article 'the' together with 'language' triggers the presupposition (Fairclough 2003: 56) that there is only one language, i.e. Swedish, through which a migrant can qualify for employment. It should also be highlighted here that, in asserting that 'there are too few of us', this politician overtly expresses his positive attitude towards immigration and, by implication, migrants themselves. Accordingly, he frames the argument with anti-discriminatory connotations, thereby protecting himself from potential accusations of xenophobia. In this apparently liberal context, however, the demonstrative pronoun 'this' not only semantically links the second to the third sentence in the extract, it also operates as a logical connector, which transforms proficiency in Swedish as a prerequisite for employability into a 'not [. . .] unreasonable requirement'. Similarly, in Extract 5 below, a Bulgarian woman, Haklime Hassan, who has been awarded a prestigious prize for business people with a background of migration, asserts that it is 'obvious' that migrants should learn Swedish. In this context, she goes on to argue that she does not employ people who do not speak Swedish, and that a language test would be a positive measure, albeit not for people over the age of 50.

Extract 5

'It is **obvious** that immigrants **must** learn Swedish. I do not employ people who cannot speak Swedish. To introduce a language test as a requirememt for Swedish citizenship is OK as long as it does not apply to people over 50,' claims New Businessperson of the Year, Haklime Hassan. (*Göteborgs Posten*, 05.09.02b)

Whereas language skills are evidently taken to be a *prerequisite* of employability, from which it logically follows that migrants have a *duty* to learn Swedish if they want to enter the economic sphere (Extracts 3 and 4), it is less clear in what sense language *skills* and language *requirements* are specifically inter-related (Extracts 4 and 5). Undoubtedly, there is a widespread argument in Swedish popular discourse which runs as follows: migrants need, should, or must – depending on the degree of obligation/ necessity the speaker or writer commits to (Fairclough 2003: 170) – learn Swedish in order to be able to find work. However contentious that might be, this apparently commonsense argument, according to which it is desirable or even necessary for migrants' entry into the job market to learn the language historically used in the political entity they have moved to, is evidently different from the argument that, in order to be employed, migrants need to have their language skills assessed through a test administered by the state. Nevertheless, what the extracts above show is a recurrent pattern of argumentation in the claims to support a test, according to which these two distinct arguments are conflated or juxtaposed, and the link between them is obscured. This, in turn, leads to the erasure of the boundary between the desirability or duty to learn Swedish, on the one hand, and the necessity to undergo a Swedish language test, on the other.

In order to further substantiate this claim, I want to draw attention to an opinion poll conducted by the customer market research consultancy, SIFO, at the beginning of the electoral campaign (7–13 August 2002) (www.sifo.se). A random sample of 1,000 people were asked: 'Is it right or wrong to require some degree of competence in the Swedish language in order to be able to become a Swedish citizen?' Of the respondents, 71 per cent thought it was right, 22 per cent considered it wrong, and 6 per cent were undecided. Evidently, the question does not ask if it is right or wrong to introduce a *test*. Rather, by means of the verb 'require' and the vague expression 'some degree of competence', the question alludes to a vaguer duty, rather than a legal requirement, to achieve an unspecified level of competence in Swedish. Interestingly, the results of the opinion poll were interpreted in one of the largest Swedish dailies, *Dagens Nyheter*, as evidence of the fact that 'The majority [of citizens] support the language test' (15.08.02b). Likewise, the evening paper *Expressen* claimed that 'Swedes agree with Leijonborg on the language test' (15.08.02). Here, as in Extracts 4 and 5, the more general duty to learn Swedish alluded to in the opinion poll seems to be conflated with a requirement for language testing.

In sum, the analysis above illustrates that the economic discourse, traces of which are contained in the extracts analysed, is based upon the argument that there is a causal relation between Swedish language skills and employment. From this, it logically follows that migrants should learn Swedish if they want to access the labour market, and if the state wants to reduce unemployment rates. Furthermore, the presupposed common representation (cf. Chilton 2004: 181) that it is 'desirable' or even 'necessary' to know the state language in order to be able to enter the labour market is conflated with the argument that a language test is not 'unreasonable'. In this way, not only is emphasis put on language skills, and accordingly a range of social variables which might affect employment devalued (perceived ethnic origin being one of them). Through *erasure* of the distinction between knowing Swedish and providing institutional proof of such knowledge, a language test is also represented as a *self-evident* measure, which would have a positive effect on migrants' entry into the Swedish labour market.

6.4.3 Discourse of governance

While the focus of the two discourses investigated so far is on social and economic integration as an *object* or *goal* of political action, the discourse of governance, which will be explored in this section, deals with the *way* in which integration should be achieved. I employ the term governance, and not government, because the language testing proposal more or less implicitly and simultaneously permeates a multiplicity of social domains (e.g. labour market, inter-ethnic cohesion, etc.). Therefore, it does not only regard government, in the sense of *vertical* relations between the state and its citizens but pertains more widely to governance, understood as the regulation and management of a range of *horizontal* relations between social actors involved in intertwined networks of social practices (Fairclough 2003; Stroud and Heugh 2004).

That the discourse of governance is inextricably linked to the economic discourse appears manifest in Extract 6, which is taken from a letter to the editor written by a candidate of the Liberal Party.

> **Extract 6**
> In those countries which have a language test [for naturalization], unemployment is lower among immigrant groups, and it takes less time to enter the job market. [. . .] It is a known fact that immigrants who came to Sweden in the 50s and 60s **integrated** into society more quickly than today's immigrants. There are of course many reasons for this, but a partial explanation is that the **demand** to **adapt** [to Swedish society] was stronger during that time. Obviously, the **requirement** for acceptable proficiency in Swedish in order to gain citizenship is only a part of a larger package of changes which are necessary for Swedish policy on immigrants and asylum seekers. But the introduction of a language test sends a **signal** that the **time of laxity** is now over. (*Kvällsposten* 11.08.02)

In the opening sentence, the author (as in many of the previous extracts) seems to ascribe a relation of causality between language testing and employment rates. This argument is afforded additional substantiation (though in a weaker sense only) by reference to allegedly encouraging examples of those countries in which a language test is already an obligatory requirement for naturalization. From the economic argument, the author then moves on to the issue of integration and social cohesion. Notable here is the meaning of the term *integration*. The overtly positive evaluation of Swedish policies in the 1950s and 1960s, which were undeniably assimilatory (Hyltenstam 1999), and the lexical choice of 'adapt', which forcefully conveys the image of migrants bending to a pre-given set of rules governing Swedish society, clearly reveals that integration here is taken to be synonymous with assimilation. However, what is most noteworthy is the repetition of the word 'demand/requirement', which is placed in opposition to a purported 'laxity'.

In order to fully grasp the meaning of 'demand' in this context, it is important to understand its connotations. An insight is provided in the following extract, which is suggestively entitled 'Demands for more demands', taken from an article reporting on the Liberal Party leader's campaign tour of southern Sweden.

Extract 7
Demand for more demands
And why should it be contradictory for a liberal [candidate] to become famous by [calling for] **demands for more demands**, he [Lars Leijon-borg] wonders. One of his co-workers is hanging Liberal Party billboards on the meeting rooms' walls saying: Yes – **to make demands is to care**. (*Borås Tidning*, 07.09.02)

The first sentence is a peculiar example of 'quasi-direct discourse' (Voloshinov 1973:151) or 'free indirect reporting' (Fairclough 2003:45), which can be described as a hybrid form of direct and indirect speech. This particular type of speech usually lacks a reporting verb or clause, and displays the features of tense and deixis shift which are typical of indirect speech (Voloshinov 1973; Fairclough 2003). Interestingly, in this example, the reporting verb is retained, but the question attributed by the authorial voice to the leader of the Liberal Party is not put in quotation marks, thereby narrowing the distance between authorial account and attributed speech (cf. Fairclough 2003: 50). Moreover, from the content and the reporting verb, we understand that the question is rhetorical, and no answer is expected. As Blackledge points out (2005: 87–8), a rhetorical question has two main functions: (1) it engages polemically with a non-present critical voice, and (2) it attempts to create *commonsense agreement* with an assumed audience. In the case of this extract, the rhetorical question presupposes the existence of a non-present competing voice questioning the link between being 'liberal' and making 'demands', as if the latter did not accord with the former. However, the voice of the politician also presupposes the supportive response of an ideal listener/reader, which, in this specific example, would go as follows: 'Surely, it is not contradictory to be liberal and, at the same time, make demands'. But the clue which finally reveals the uncontroversial aspect of a demand for a liberal politics is provided by the content of the electoral billboard at the end of the extract, in which 'demand' is compellingly equated to 'care', and is thereby infused with morally positive connotations.

Given that to 'demand' is taken to be morally good for a society, by implication, its converse is presupposed to have negative connotations. Against this backdrop, and bearing in mind that the Social Democratic Party has been almost uninterruptedly in power since the Second World War, it is now possible to understand that the time of laxity criticized in Extract 6, as well as in many other texts within the corpus, refers to the official management of immigration and integration carried out by Social Democratic governments during the previous 30 years.

To sum up, the examples illustrate that a new type of political management is advocated by the supporters of a language test. This form of governance differs from that of the Social Democrats because it focuses on demands and obligations, and thereby bears the trait of toughness. Yet, it is advanced as morally good for Swedish society because firmness is conflated with care. This means that language testing is employed in this discourse as a *symbol*, which stands for a transition from a non-demanding, and by implication sloppy Social Democratic, to a demanding, and by implication caring, Liberal governance. This finding in the Swedish context adds credence to Shohamy's (2001: 41) remark that: 'Tests [may] provide those in authority with visibility and evidence of action.' Or to put it another way, regardless of their actual effects, tests may be employed as the tangible manifestation of a political will to take measures against certain educational, social or economic problems in a given society.

6.5 Conclusions: language, citizenship and common sense

We know that naturalization requirements vary considerably throughout the world, and that proficiency in a state's official language(s) as a prerequisite for naturalization is far from being a *natural* or *commonsensical* requirement typical of all societies (cf. Piller 2001, for an overview). We also know that naturalization practices may undergo historical shifts in one and the same polity. Therefore, the link between proficiency in a state's official language(s), on the one hand, and citizenship, on the other, is based on a relationship of contingency. Following Bourdieu, such a link can be seen as a historically and socio-culturally situated outcome of political struggles between different discourses and ideologies which compete for hegemony in the 'production and imposition of principles of construction and evaluation of social reality' (Bourdieu 2000: 187). And one potential site for political struggle is the media, in this case, newspaper discourse.

As for Sweden, I have already mentioned in 6.1 how ideologies of multilingualism and multiculturalism have had a dominant position in political discourse since the 1980s (see also Milani, in press) leading to the official dismissal of any form of language requirement for citizenship applicants 'for reasons of justice' (SOU 1999: 313). Having said that, the extracts above reveal the existence of a more recent and competing language ideology, according to which a language test is viewed as a good and self-evident requirement for becoming a Swedish citizen. Drawing on Bourdieu's (2000: 181) claim discussed earlier that 'self-evidences' are the result of processes of *misrecognition* according to which 'illusory representations' are made to look as though they were 'grounded in reality', and by examining the connections between the arguments advanced by the proponents of a language test, the aim of this chapter has been to deconstruct, and thereby make transparent, the way in which such a language ideology, by way of three intertwined discourses, *misrecognises* arbitrary links between language skills and language requirements, *(mis)represents* them as intrinsically natural and logical, and finally invests them with a moral status.

Through close textual analysis of various newspaper extracts, it has been possible to show that the educational discourse is built on a rather controversial assumption that migrants' knowledge of Swedish is deficient because they do not want to learn the language of the country to which they have moved. Apart from being discriminatory in so far as it evokes the image of migrants as lazy or generally unwilling to 'enter' Swedish society, this assumption does not take into consideration that successful second-language acquisition is not just the result of personal will, intention or motivation, but is also affected by a wide range of social and economic factors. No less contentious is the presupposition that there is a positive correlation between language requirements, language skills and societal integration between different ethnic groups. Though at first glance seemingly commonsensical, the argument that if a language test were to be introduced, migrants would learn Swedish, overestimates the power of tests to encourage or motivate language learning, while at the same time failing to recognize the negative impact language tests may have on test takers. The recently developed scholarly tradition of Critical Language Testing (CLT) (see Shohamy 2001, for a comprehensive overview) has not only demonstrated that language tests are far from being objective and accurate instruments for measuring certain skills or competences, but are deeply ideological in so far as they help determine what counts as legitimate knowledge, and may ultimately function as disciplinary tools of hidden political agendas that reproduce social inequalities in the name of scientific objectivity (Shohamy 2001, 2006a, 2006b; see also Spolsky 1997). More specifically, CLT theorists have also emphasized how the high stakes associated with certain institutional language tests, such as in the case of tests for naturalization, rather than being an incitement to language learning, may well have negative psychological effects on test-takers, thereby affecting their language performances in such tests (and elsewhere). In addition, CLT has provided us with ethnographic insights into test-takers' life experiences (Shohamy 2001; McNamara 2005; Piller 2006). After recounting a sample of personal narratives of individual test-takers, Elana Shohamy forcefully proposes that:

> The personal experiences and reactions of test takers towards tests [...] provide convincing evidence of the centrality of tests in their lives of test takers. [...] Test takers are threatened by tests as they view them as powerful, authoritative and leading to detrimental consequences. (2001: 13)

Although Shohamy's standpoint might appear somewhat radical (after all, not every test leaves an indelible mark on an individual's life), a critical approach to language testing not only helps to highlight the high symbolic, social and economic stakes underlying specific types of tests. Such an approach also underscores the non-negotiable control over knowledge which is inherent in institutional language tests, thereby (re)producing power inequalities between testing institutions and test takers. In this way, CLT helps undermine and problematize the rather simplistic view according to which language tests are a self-evident educational panacea for societal problems in multiethnic and multilingual societies.

Analogous to what has been observed in relation to the educational discourse, the representation of a language test as having a positive impact on Swedish society is also at the core of the economic discourse which is built on the presupposition that there is a *necessary* and *causal* link between Swedish language skills and employment. This, coupled with the conflation of Swedish language skills with a language testing requirement, leads to the misrepresentation of Swedish language requirements in the tangible form of a language test, as a *necessity* if employment is to be achieved. In other words, not only is language proficiency singled out and treated as if it were *the* social variable which can explain certain socio-economic circumstances, while all other relevant variables are either obscured or devalued. Proficiency in the majority language (Swedish) is also presented as an *inevitable* prerequisite of social mobility and economic integration. This can be taken as a typical example of what Stephen May (2003a, 2005, 2006) calls the trope of (im)mobility, an apparently commonsensical set of arguments which rests on the idea that '[l]earning a majority language will [. . .] provide individuals with greater economic and social mobility' (May 2003a: 102), while '[l]earning [or preserving] a minority language [. . .] delimits an individual's mobility; in its strongest terms, this might amount to actual "ghettoization"' (ibid.). As May convincingly demonstrates, this trope of (im)mobility is flawed with two main inconsistencies. First, the ascription of ineluctably higher instrumental value to majority languages is not an ideologically neutral account of a reality existing 'out there'. Instead, it derives from, and at the same time reproduces, the misrecognition of the socio-political processes which constantly lead to the privilege accorded to some language varieties over others in the public sphere (ibid.: 112). Second, May does not deny that proficiency in the dominant and most powerful language in a given polity may facilitate access to the job market and enable political participation. Nevertheless, an *exclusive* emphasis on such proficiency as the *necessary* prerequisite of social and economic integration 'confuses cause and effect' and disregards 'the central question of the wider structural disadvantages facing minority-language speakers, not least racism and discrimination' (ibid.: 114) (Extract 4 above is a most manifest example). Last but not least, in the case of the economic discourse of language testing, the conflation of language skills with language requirements arbitrarily equates the commonsensical, albeit contentious, argument that proficiency in the dominant language is necessarily conducive to socio-economic privileges, on the one hand, with the no less controversial argument that migrants should pass a language test, on the other, thereby masquerading a language test as an emancipatory practice in the interest of migrants themselves and ultimately of Swedish society as a whole (cf. Blackledge, 2005: 209).

Finally, another central aspect which needs to be addressed is the moral dimension which permeates the whole issue of a Swedish language test for naturalization. The analysis of the discourse of governance shows that language testing is invoked as a marker of transition from an allegedly lax Social Democratic to a more demanding but caring Liberal regime. Here we are witnessing another process of misrecognition whereby an ideology misrepresents a demand as intrinsically synonymous with 'care', and thereby envisions 'toughness' as *the* moral attribute of managing a polity. As Susan Gal and Kathryn Woolard (2001: 3) remark: 'images of linguistic phenomena gain credibility when they create ties with other arguments about aspects of aesthetic or moral life'. In fact, in tying a language test to the moral values of governance, a linguistic, social and economic issue is signified as an ultimately moral concern, and thereby infused with a sense of *gravitas*. To put it simply, a language test is not just a matter of language skills per se. Nor is it a mere question of alleged 'enhancement' of communicative and economic relations between ethnic groups who share a given territory. A Swedish language test for naturalization functions ultimately as a proxy for *how* one envisages Swedish society and its management in a broader sense.

To conclude, in accordance with the observation that 'language ideology is not about language alone', but is 'a mediating link between social forms and forms of talk' (Woolard 1998a: 3), this chapter has illustrated that, in the claims advanced by the supporters of a language test for naturalization, language testing is employed as a semiotic resource through which some social actors envision and structure links between value-laden images of what count as language skills in a polity, and other representations of social, economic and moral aspects of this polity. In this way, analogous to the debate described by Blackledge (2005), these social actors, with the help of and via the print media, become *public* voices, who attempt to bring into life a *regime of representation* in which an arbitrary logic is disguised as natural *common sense*, thus buttressing the legitimacy of particular set of political proposals.

Primary sources

Borås Tidning
Anna Svalander, 'Om de bara lyssnat på Leijonborg' (30.08.02).
TT, 'Leijonborg svävar i det blå' (07.09.02).

Dagens Nyheter
Peter Sandberg, 'Invandrarpolitik: "Svenska lär man sig på jobbet"' (15.08.02a).
Thomas Hall, 'Invandrarpolitik: Majoritet stöder språktest' (15.08.02b).
Expressen
Erik Pettersson, 'Svenskarna ger Leijonborg rätt om språktest' (15.08.02).
Folkpartiet
En ny integrationspolitik (2002).
Språkkravsreform brådskar – nya fakta och argument (2003).
Göteborgs Posten
Per Sydvik, *'Förstågångsväljare grillade politiker'* (05.09.02a).
Anna-Lena Laurén, 'Jag anställer ingen som inte kan svenska' (05.09.02b).
Hufvudstadsbladet
Jeanette Björkqvist, 'Liknande valfrågor – olika lösningar. Integration första gången på bordet' (29.08.02).
Kvällsposten
Mats Lithner, 'Insändare' (11.08.02).
Motion 2002/03: Sf 226, En ny integrationspolitik.
Prop. 1997/1998. *Proposition 1997/1998:16. Sverige, framtiden och mångfalden – från invandrarpolitik till integrationspolitik.*
SOU (1999), *Statens offentliga utredningar 1999:34. Svenskt medborgarskap.* Stockholm: Fakta info direct.
Statistiska centralbyrån (2005), *Statistisk årsbok för Sverige 2005.* Örebro: Statistiska centralbyrån.

Notes

1   I employ the term 'migrant' throughout the chapter, but use 'immigrant' in the translations of the extracts in order to remain textually faithful to the Swedish term *'invandrare'* (immigrant).
2   I would like to thank Kenneth Hyltenstam (Stockholm University) and Will Turner (University of Leeds) for their invaluable comments on previous drafts of the chapter.
3   The use of 'ideology' here in the singular as opposed to 'ideologies' in the plural, is not intended to convey that we are dealing with a perfectly coherent set of ideas, values and representations programmatically and intentionally developed by the Swedish Liberal Party, and shared by all supporters of a language test. Rather, the singular form ideology attempts to capture the dissonant coherence of intertwined discourses resting on interrelated arguments, values and assumptions.
4   The corpus consists of the following texts: (1) policy documents related to a parliamentary committee on citizenship appointed in 1997; (2) opinion polls conducted during the electoral campaign in 2002; (3) policy documents produced by the Liberal Party on the language test issue; and (4) 148 newspaper articles retrieved from two electronic databases (*PressText* and *Mediearkivet*) through a search for the keywords *språktest* (language test) and *medborgarskap* (citizenship) covering the period 1 April 2002–31 March 2003, conducted on 1 June 2005. The two databases cover a wide range of newspapers which can be taken as

representative of the Swedish media landscape (including the most important Swedish-written national daily published in Finland *Hufvustadsbladet*).

5 Despite their heterogeneity, none of the data sources is committed to extreme right-wing political opinions. Moreover, all sources are conditioned by the same societal constraint, namely the unlawfulness of explicitly racist or discriminatory public discourse in accordance with the so-called 'Act on Agitation against Groups of People'.

6 According to the most recently available statistical data on the number of non-nationals and naturalized nationals (31.12.03), the percentage of naturalized nationals tends to be higher with regard to people from Hungary, Poland, the former Yugoslavia, and the southern hemisphere as opposed to other 'western' countries such as Spain, Italy, the UK or the USA (*Statistiska centralbyrån*, 2005).

7 Global challenges to nationalist ideologies: language and education in the Luxembourg press[1]

Kristine Horner

7.1 Introduction: language in the Luxembourgish print media

The representation of Luxembourg as an inherently multilingual and multi-cultural nation-state – an image widely circulated in media discourses directed towards an international audience and/or in relation to the international arena – is rooted in the belief that students in Luxembourgish schools have the opportunity to acquire greater amounts of linguistic capital, i.e. more 'languages', as well as a more profound appreciation of 'cultures' together with the associated values of openness and tolerance in comparison to their counterparts in other EU member-states. The Luxembourgish educational system is sometimes held up as a model, as for example in newspaper articles covering the 2001 *European Year of Languages*, in which Luxembourg is portrayed as being the forerunner in meeting the EU target of *Muttersprache plus zwei* ('mother tongue plus two') (Horner 2004: 216–19).

The Luxembourgish print media itself is also characterized by multilingualism; on the whole, German is the main language of the press, though texts also appear in French and occasionally Luxembourgish or even English. With a circulation rate of over 81,000 (and the closest competitor at 25,500) the *Luxemburger Wort* (renamed *d'Wort* in 2005) is the dominant newspaper on the national market. It is a conservative paper with close links to the Catholic Church and the *Chrëschtlech-Sozial VolleksPartei* (CSV), the dominant political party in Luxembourg.[2] Given its centrality on the national market, it constitutes a key site where national debates are both represented and carried out, including that over Luxembourg's poor results on the first *Programme for International Student Assessment* (PISA) tests, which posed a

130

serious challenge to the idealized model character of the Luxembourgish state-run school system often equated with Luxembourgish nationhood.

In his discussion of the nation as an imagined community, Benedict Anderson ([1983] 1991) emphasizes the pivotal role that the print media plays in the discursive propagation of nationalisms. With particular attention to language ideologies, Susan DiGiacomo takes this line of argumentation a step further by underlining the fact that the print media plays a dual role in the flow of ideological processes; first, it is a forum where selected positions about language are perpetuated or debated, such as links between language and nationhood. Second, the production of written texts involves ideologies of 'orthography, syntax and usage' (1999: 105). The latter point resonates well with constructive critiques of the naturalized way in which Anderson represents linguistic standardization (Irvine and Gal 2000; Kroskrity 2000); language needs to be viewed both as discourse and as a 'material thing' (Blommaert 1999c: 425). In the following two sections, I discuss these theoretical issues in greater depth before turning, in the later part of the chapter, to an exploration of how nationalist language ideologies underpin media discourses about the Luxembourgish educational system.

7.2 Metalanguage, language ideologies and the 'end of innocence'

Sociolinguistic research is currently marked by a heightened interest in the 'meta' dimensions of language (Jaworski *et al* 2004b; Hyland 2005) or the indexical meanings produced in language use, which are ubiquitous in discursive exchanges (Blommaert 2005: 11ff.). Given the interrelationship between epistemology and world events (cf. Ricento 2000; Rampton 2001), Adam Jaworski, Nikolas Coupland and Dariusz Galasiński (2004c) sketch the ways in which academic and non-academic currents are serving as an impetus for the augmented study of metalanguage. Of central importance has been the move towards viewing context as dynamic and multifaceted, which implies that it is not *limited* to the confines of the text itself nor to other objects in the material world, i.e. things that can be pointed to (see e.g. Goodwin and Duranti 1992). This approach to context situates discourse at the heart of scholarly inquiry due to its capacity to reflect, reproduce and sometimes challenge perceptions of reality as well as the organization of social life (see also Johnson and Ensslin, this volume). Moreover, challenges to long-standing theoretical concepts and research paradigms are best understood in relation to the accelerated processes of globalization and the transformations of social life associated with the late-modern period (see Wallerstein [1991] 2001). Drawing on the work of Anthony Giddens (1991) and Lilie Chouliaraki and Norman Fairclough (1999), Jaworski *et al* (2004c: 6) point out that increased instability and uncertainty allow for the 'questioning [of] dominant ideologies'.

Notwithstanding recent productivity in the area of metalinguistic research, Coupland and Jaworski (2004: 16, original emphasis) describe present-day sociolinguistics as characterized by 'a state of tension between more *and less* metalinguistically-oriented perspectives'. Their closing remarks under the rubric 'the end of innocence' point to ongoing epistemological struggles in the social sciences. Among contemporary sociolinguists, there exist varying degrees of discontent with the dominance of positivist approaches to research and/or structuralist views of language, despite calls from diverse camps to maintain these approaches. Although linguists are aware of the fact that all discourses are inescapably bound up with the 'meta' dimensions of language, the acknowledgement that there is no 'view from nowhere' (Irvine and Gal 2000: 79), e.g. with regard to the representation of language, remains a major point of contention, especially when 'expert' discourse is questioned or subjected to analysis. Sally Johnson's (2001) dialogue paper dealing with the 'public understanding of linguistics' raises a series of important questions in relation to the seemingly clear boundary that is sometimes constructed between 'rational' linguists and 'emotional' laypersons. In James Milroy's (2001: 620) response, he asserts that we 'need to put our own house in order' and that we should acknowledge laypersons' understandings of language in the real world. As linguists, can we continue to assume that laypersons are simply misinformed about language because certain views appear to stand in contradiction with linguistic perspectives? Is it not possible that there is something to be learned from lay perspectives on language? Is it not time for the study of metalanguage – and more specifically language ideology – to be acknowledged as a fundamental dimension of linguistic research?

Parallel to the developments described above, there has also been increasing activity in the area of language ideology over the past decade, mainly on the part of linguistic anthropologists (Woolard 1998a; Kroskrity 2000) but also by scholars crossing disciplinary boundaries (Coupland and Jaworski 2004; Blommaert 2005). Studies emphasizing how language ideologies operate as mediating links between social structures and forms of talk are of particular value as they have opened up inroads towards understanding the negotiation of language policy (e.g. Wee 2002) and language planning (e.g. Johnson 2005a), as well as group relations and responses to social change (e.g. Stevenson 2005). The ideological potential of metalanguage is rooted in its predominantly evaluative nature, which in turn is anchored in the semiotic processes of categorization (Cameron 2004). Categorization is based on the dynamics between sameness and difference and, more often than not, feeds into social inequality (Blommaert 2005: 69ff.).

As with all forms of 'meta' meaning, categories are constructed via the indexical properties of discourse. Some of these categories become so naturalized that they are taken for granted, the constructed boundaries appear fixed, and certain groups are homogenized and, in many cases, 'othered'. Judith Irvine and Susan Gal (2000) discuss three specific semiotic processes involved in the construction of 'ideological representations of linguistic difference', the first of which is iconization or the process in which 'linguistic features that index social groups or activities appear to be iconic representations of them, as if a linguistic feature somehow depicted or displayed a social group's inherent nature or essence' (ibid.: 37). The second is fractal recursivity, which 'involves the projection of an opposition, salient at some level of relationship, onto some other level' (ibid.: 38). The third process they discuss is erasure, which serves to 'render some persons or activities invisible' (ibid.: 38). This framework provides a concrete means of fine-tuning a discourse-based, micro-oriented analysis of language ideologies but not at the expense of understanding the macro-processes at work, both of which are crucial to understanding the mediation of language debates.

7.3 Nationalisms, globalization and language ideological debates

In his response to the case studies discussed in *Language Ideological Debates* (1999a), Blommaert (1999c: 427–31) highlights the role of the mass media as key sites for the debates, together with the centrality of nation-building in relation to those various debates. Given the prominence of the nation-state model during the modern era as well as its (albeit shaky) persistence in the late-modern period, this observation does not come as a surprise; however, it does underline the need to further interdisciplinary scholarship. Nationalist ideologies, whether they are mobilized to perpetuate or to challenge particular images of nation-state congruence, are bound up with two highly entrenched language ideologies: the *one nation, one language ideology* and the *standard language ideology*. In their comparative study on nationalist ideologies in the European print media, Jan Blommaert and Jef Verschueren (1992: 362) underline the presence of a related concept, 'the dogma of *homogeneism*', i.e. the view that the optimal societal structure is one that is culturally and linguistically uniform. Underpinning this constellation, of course, is a belief in clearly definable cultures and languages that are frequently 'labeled and ranked' (Blommaert 1999c: 431). The naturalization of categories such as 'language' and 'nation', with which idealized, bounded cultures are commonly equated, is the ongoing work of multiple discourse strategies. Jürgen Spitzmüller (2005), for example, discusses the strategic use of the language as container and the language as organism metaphors (see also Heywood and Semino, Chapter 2, this volume). Hector Grad Fuchsel and Luisa Martín Rojo (2003) illustrate how similar processes operate with regard to countries – be they imagined as nations, nation-states, or multinational states – by means of personification through the use of metonymy, to name just one of the strategies that they discuss.

The normalization of ideologies is potentially enabled by their discursive reproduction in the sense that they are circulated, as Blommaert (1999b: 10) explains, 'by means of a variety of institutional, semi-institutional and everyday practices'. To illustrate this point, he cites Pierre Bourdieu's (1991: 46–9) well-known discussion of the standard language as a '"normalized" product'. The legitimation and institutionalization processes connected with the construction of standard languages, i.e. named national and/or official languages of the state, intersect with the propagation of nationalist ideologies (May 2001: 150–64). As Monica Heller (1999c: 11) puts it, 'the imagining of the nation includes ideological struggles over its most central values, and these struggles take place not only with respect to what monolingualism and multilingualism represent, but also with respect to the very shape of the language to be privileged'. Lesley Milroy describes the *standard language ideology* as beliefs about language that are:

> typically held by populations of economically developed nation states where processes of standardisation have operated over a considerable time to produce an abstract set of norms – lexical, grammatical and (in spoken language) phonological – popularly described as constituting a standard language. The same beliefs also emerge, somewhat transformed by local histories and conditions, in these states' colonies and ex-colonies. (Milroy 1999: 173)

With their origins in European nationalisms, the *standard language* and *one nation, one language* ideologies have been exported to all corners of the globe (cf. Woolard 1998a: 16ff.), and it follows that social actors draw on them to mediate between forms of language use and the organization of social life in multifarious ways and in a wide range of sites, including the mass media and educational system. This observation also applies to the European continent, although – in line with contemporary commentators such as Bernhard Giesen (2001) and Stephen May (2001) – I reject structuralist attempts to maintain a clear-cut, bipolar split between the constructs of ethnic and civic nations based respectively on the so-called German and French models. While there exist different ways of imagining the nation, they are not – and never have been – confined by state borders in spite of the fact that they took shape in relation to specific historical and cultural conditions (Heller 1999c; Giesen 2001). Hence, different manifestations of nationalism can be seen to draw on the two language ideologies discussed above. In fact, by bringing both language ideologies simultaneously into the picture, it becomes obvious that nations cannot be neatly divided up into ethnic and civic categories. This is due to the ways in which nationalist language ideologies are intertwined with one another: neither of the two can exist on its own, although sometimes they complement one another whereas at other times they contradict one another.

The two nationalist language ideologies are linked to the construction of boundaries between 'us' and 'them', yet this happens in different ways, as can be observed by considering relationships posited between spoken and written forms of language by both linguists and laypersons. On the one hand, 'the language' may be viewed as consisting of all 'its varieties' or 'its dialects'; this is related to Heinz Kloss's (1978) model of *Überdachung* – 'over-arching' or 'roofedness' – which, if translated in the latter way shows affinities with the language as a container metaphor; everyone in this container speaks the same 'language' and therefore is considered a member of the same family. Conversely, certain varieties are sometimes viewed as deficient or corrupt versions of 'the language', and indeed mainstream linguistic research continues to lean toward treating standardized written forms of language as the default. Thus, both members of linguistic minorities as well as speakers of so-called 'dialects' may be targets of 'othering' processes by means of language ideologies bound up with the nation-state. The former strategy may be called upon to unite the imagined ethnic nation, whereas the latter fractures it by perpetuating social stratification among members of the ethnic core in the interest of maintaining the status quo (Heller 1999c: 14). Educational systems have frequently played a key role in these linguistic 'othering' processes in light of their historical orientation towards the nation-state (May 2001: 167ff.). In the late-modern period, the nation-state has come under increasing pressure, yet the state continues to function as 'a major centering institution' and thus continues to play a key role in the organization of social life (Blommaert 2005: 76ff.). In connection with accelerated globalization – bound up with the processes of time–space compression affecting people across the world in diverse ways (Bauman 1998) – there exist challenges to nationalist (language) ideologies together with calls to restructure state institutions, especially educational systems.

Globalization notwithstanding, such tensions are not unfolding everywhere identically due to the multiplicity of historical traditions and present-day patterns of social life. It may be argued that fluctuations linked to the processes of globalization impact upon the lives of people residing in small states in a particularly intense manner. As a small state that has been historically dependent on foreign capital and labour, Luxembourg provides an interesting case in point. In 2001, multiple, yet interrelated debates erupted mapping patterns of language use onto social change, including the debate over language requirements for Luxembourgish citizenship (cf. Milani, this volume), and the so-called 700,000 residents 'spectre' in response to a projected population increase (Horner 2004). It was in the wake of these debates that the first *Programme for International Student Assessment* (PISA) results were published. Heated reactions to these results – and the tests

135

themselves – are best understood in relation to greater societal transformations linked to the expanding EU infrastructure and accelerated processes of
globalization, as well as long-standing discourses about language and education in Luxembourg. Before turning to the media discourses debating the
PISA results, I will first provide some information about the Luxembourgish
educational system.

7.4 Language and the Luxembourgish educational system

The structure of the Luxembourgish school-system demands that students
meet high language requirements in the standardized, written varieties of
German and French from primary school upward. Following two obligatory
years of preschool, where mainly Luxembourgish is spoken, standard German
gradually becomes the predominant medium of instruction in primary school
and is used for teaching basic literacy to all pupils, regardless of what is
spoken in the home environment.[3] Luxembourgish is taught as a subject for
one hour a week throughout primary school and in the first year of secondary
school (*septième*), after which it is discontinued altogether. Students are not
required to use Luxembourgish for functions associated with standardized,
written forms of language, although Luxembourgish is used frequently to
write text (SMS) and email messages, cards and informal letters and, by a
small segment of the population, literary texts. Formal texts are usually written in German, French and – increasingly – English, especially in the private
job sector. In the schools, speaking Luxembourgish does not index social
stigma, and Luxembourgish sometimes continues to be used by teachers as
an additional medium of instruction throughout primary school and even at
later stages. On the other hand, the inability to perform certain combinations
of standard French, English and German is frequently stigmatized and,
furthermore, severely limits one's options on the employment market (see
Hartmann-Hirsch 1991; Davis 1994; Fehlen 2002; Klein 2003).[4]

The teaching of French is introduced at the end of the second school
year and constitutes a major component of the curriculum by the third year.
As students approach secondary school, or the *lycée*, there is a gradual shift
from German to French as the medium of instruction, especially in the case of
students who continue their studies in a classical *lycée*. English is usually
introduced in the second year of the *lycée* and the amount of English language
instruction depends on various factors; for example, students in the classical
lycée receive more English lessons than those in the technical *lycée*. The Luxembourgish educational system is marked by a clear division into classical
and technical *lycées*, thus creating two separate educational tracks that
usually provide students with rather different career opportunities upon completion of their studies.

136

Over the past three decades, a number of reforms have been implemented, although these mainly concern the technical *lycée*, while the basic structure of the classical *lycée*, as well as the primary school, has undergone minimal changes. Two reforms specifically concerning the classical *lycée* are of relevance to the following data discussion: the first involves the decision to provide all students with a choice between the so-called modern and classical tracks within the overarching framework of the classical *lycée*. This option signalled a move away from Latin towards more English language instruction and took place in the 1970s, i.e. during the earlier stages of the transformation from an industrialized towards a more service-oriented job market. Secondly, at the close of the 1993–4 school year, obligatory oral language testing was introduced for school leaving (*première*) exams in all classical *lycées*. In a similar fashion, a shift towards a slightly more communicatively-oriented approach to the teaching of French has been taking place at the primary school level.

In addition to other factors, *the relatively inflexible way in which language is used and taught* in the schools creates and/or compounds problems for many students, both autochthonous 'Luxembourgish' students as well as the increasing number of so-called 'foreign' students, the largest group of whom is of Portuguese origin.[5] Children whose parents were not born and raised in Luxembourg are disproportionately represented in the technical *lycée*, as are students from working-class families who use Luxembourgish as a home language (Davis 1994: 112–16). Furthermore, a large percentage of students drop out of school without obtaining the final secondary school leaving diploma (the equivalent of the French baccalaureate). In this light, it is questionable as to whether the Luxembourgish educational system may be held up as a model worth emulating. Given the success of numerous bilingual educational programs (Baker 2001: 229–43), any shortcomings with respect to the Luxembourgish educational system cannot be directly attributed to the bilingual German–French structure per se but rather can be traced to ideologies informing curriculum design and methodological approaches. Despite various forms of resistance on the part of certain individuals involved in the teaching profession, Luxembourgish educational policy tends to strive towards homogenizing students rather than recognizing and working with them as individuals; the implications of such an approach are more noticeable in relation to the classical *lycée* than the technical *lycée*. Historically speaking, the Luxembourgish school-system has been dominated by a mixture of classical humanism and utilitarianism, with other ideologies such as progressivism and social reconstructionism sidelined (Ho 2002; Horner and Weber 2005). In an analysis of print media discourses, the following section deals with the interface between these educational ideologies and the *standard language* and *one language, one nation* ideologies in relation to economic, political and social change.

7.5 Drawing on nationalist language ideologies to discredit the PISA results

Problematic aspects – as well as national controversies – concerning the Luxembourgish educational system are not widely circulated on the international level and, generally speaking, they are not usually subject to extensive public debate in the national press. After the results of the first *Programme for International Student Assessment* (PISA) tests were publicized in December 2001, however, various discussions took place to try to come to terms with the fact that the scores for students in Luxembourg were third from the bottom in all three subject areas: reading, mathematics and natural science.[6] As these results are potentially damaging to positive self-presentation strategies linked to the 'model' school system, attempts are often made to invalidate the results. The overarching strategy is to rely on the widely shared presupposition that countries are unique – and ideally homogeneous – cultural and linguistic entities and consequently there is nothing to be learned from tests administered on an international level. In this case, a further step is taken by positioning Luxembourg as *even more unique* than other countries due to the use of more than one language in the schools and due to the high number of resident foreigners in the Grand Duchy.[7] The following data discussion, based on the three semiotic processes outlined by Irvine and Gal (2000), is divided into two parts.[8] The first deals with discourses attempting to construct a cohesive ethnic Luxembourgish nation, united by both the use of Luxembourgish as the mother tongue and the trilingual ideal. The second section shows how the trilingual strategy can cut both ways: members of the imagined ethnic nation can also be subjected to the 'othering' process by being represented as undermining the trilingual ideal.

7.5.1 Uniting the nation: the naturalization of languages and group boundaries

According to Lionel Wee (2002: 210), 'the relationship between language and identity is made iconic by virtue of the kinds of values supposedly contained within the respective languages'. In his analysis of Singaporean official discourse, Wee describes how certain values are discursively linked to Chinese language varieties and others to English. The situation in Luxembourg is not entirely dissimilar to that in Singapore in the sense that certain values are discursively linked to Luxembourgish, the mother tongue of the idealized, homogeneous ethnic nation, whereas others are linked to the trilingual ideal, i.e. the presupposed mastery of the standardized, written varieties of German and French by Luxembourgish-speaking pupils in state schools. The indexing of either pattern of language use provides a means of self-identification. The following editorial, circulated during the *European Year of Languages*, illustrates these parallel strategies (all translations are my own):

Text 1 (German original)

It [the mother tongue] is one of our roots in society, which is worth nurturing. A mother tongue is identity forming, tells a person out of which historical and sociological context he/she comes and where he/she belongs. Precisely our own historical experience clearly bears witness to what value and strength the mother tongue can have. [. . .] In addition to his/her mother tongue, a person should acquire other languages, so that he/she does not only find his/her way within a limited [bordered] geographical and social milieu but also can look out beyond the edge of the plate into the world. However, foreign languages are only really of use, are only an enriching means of meeting 'foreign' people, if they are learned properly and not in quick doses like 'fast food' reduced to a few empty words or phrases. (*Luxemburger Wort*, 12.03.01)

The values bound up with the mother tongue and those with the mastery of 'foreign' or 'other' languages allow for the formation of two iconic links to be made here between language and members of the imagined ethnic Luxembourgish nation, thereby facilitating the construction of two layers of seemingly immutable boundaries between 'us' and 'them'. The collective memory of the Second World War serves as the catalyst for the creation of an iconic link between the Luxembourgish language and the values of courage and strength, which are embodied by the *Stacklëtzebuerger* or 'rooted, authentic Luxembourger'. The reference to 'our own historical experience' in Text 1 flags the historical event of the Second World War and, more specifically, that of the 1941 census known as *dräimol Lëtzebuergesch* (three times Luxembourgish), which directly connects the mother tongue to the imagined ethnic nation and the present-day independent state.[9] A second iconic link is made between the mastery of 'foreign' or 'other' languages and members of the imagined ethnic Luxembourgish nation; as carriers of several languages it is possible to self-identify as 'good Europeans', which in turn entails the embodiment of the related values of openness and tolerance. In some cases, the process of 'becoming trilingual' is portrayed as coming naturally to members of the imagined Luxembourgish ethnic nation (Horner 2004: 210–16). However, most texts circulating on the *national* level include the added twist that the mastery of German, French and other standardized, written forms of language is the result of discipline and hard work, as for example in Text 1. In this second scenario, therefore, the boundary between 'us' and 'them' is connected to the mastery of artificial, standardized varieties rather than natural, organic mother tongue language use, as is the case in the first scenario.

The arguments that 'we' could not use 'our' mother tongue and that 'we' learn more languages than people in 'other' countries served as two of the principal means of discursively discrediting the results of the 2000 PISA tests. This dual strategy, based on the two iconic boundaries, serves as a means of uniting the imagined ethnic nation in a moment of crisis, and it relies upon the construction of boundaries between 'Luxembourgers' and the 'foreigners':

Text 2 (German original)

Luxembourg is the only country in which students were not allowed to answer in their mother tongue, and one must not forget that Luxembourg in particular also has to deal with [fight] the problem that many foreign children have to learn not only the language of the country but also the foreign languages studied here, and thus they have a much bigger task than their peers in other countries. [...] One cannot simply standardize the cultural knowledge of 32 different countries and try to reduce it to a common denominator. One also cannot compare pears and apples. (*Luxemburger Wort*, 06.07.02)

Text 3 (French original)

We speak Luxembourgish and not German [...] In Munich the German language, the 'high/standard language', is ubiquitous. Children may speak Bavarian at home but they are likely to hear the high/standard language all around them: in the shops, on the streets, in nursery school. In Luxembourg children hear Luxembourgish or French and many other languages. But unless they watch German TV, they will hear German for the first time in their lives in primary school. [...] **We have more children who do not speak the language of the country than our competitors.** We are the only country that has 35% of children who do not speak Luxembourgish at home. [...] **The situation concerning children of foreign origin is very complicated in Luxembourg, more complicated than in other countries** [...] 'Romanophone' children learn French by interacting with people who all speak – to put it mildly – a deficient [full of gaps] kind of French. [...] In addition, it is important to bear in mind that students in Luxembourgish schools have the great opportunity to learn two languages in a quasi-parallel manner to which English is added. (*Luxemburger Wort*, 15.06.02: original emphasis)

Despite the use of more than one language in the schools, the authors of the above texts – an excerpt from a contribution to the educational supplement and a letter to the editor respectively – present arguments informed by the *one nation, one language ideology*. Echoing the perspective brought forth by the journalist who wrote Text 1, they take spatially oriented perspectives, as illustrated by the contrasts between 'here' and 'in other countries' in Text 2 and between 'in Luxembourg' and 'in other countries' in Text 3. Geographical space is carved up into culturally meaningful places because named states are perceived as synonymous with organically grown nations and 'their' languages; the naturalness of this state of affairs is underlined by the analogy between countries and types of fruit in Text 2. If the mother tongue provides people with inner stability and orientation as if it were some kind of internal and unalienable compass (see Text 1), it follows that the world is in order when people are 'where they belong', e.g. the 'Luxembourgers' in Luxembourg, the 'Germans' in Germany and the 'Portuguese' in Portugal. When people are not 'where they belong', they automatically constitute a problem because they are perceived as being out of place (cf. Blommaert and Verschueren 1998). This conceptualization of the world naturalizes the boundary between 'Luxembourgers' and the 'foreigners' who, it is claimed, are largely responsible for Luxembourg's poor PISA results. Thus, the iconic link between mother tongue and national group membership provides a widely tapped basis for self-identification and categorization of the 'other'.

While multiple options are available for self-identification, i.e. as a mother tongue speaker of Luxembourgish or as a carrier of the trilingual ideal, both strategies may be mobilized to essentialize the 'other'. Although there is the disclaimer that mastery of the trilingual ideal requires time and effort – yet another strategy to discredit the PISA results – there is also the presupposition that 'Luxembourgers' are better equipped for this than 'foreign children' (Text 2) or 'children of foreign origin' (Text 3). In Text 3, there is a clear assumption of superiority of 'Luxembourgers' over the 'foreigners' as the latter are portrayed as speaking 'bad' French due to their contact with people who allegedly speak 'a deficient [full of gaps] kind of French'; this statement could well reflect the perception of non-standard language varieties as deficient or corrupt. While Texts 2 and 3 follow a similar line of argumentation in the attempt to unite and defend the imagined ethnic nation, they differ in the respect that Text 2 – written by a group of students – also calls for pedagogical reform. Text 3 – written by a teacher – constructs sophisticated arguments against potential structural reforms, including that of introducing the option of French-based literacy programmes. Issues of literacy, however, are normally erased, which in turn simultaneously erases links between Luxembourgish and German, as well as difficulties encountered by both Luxembourgish and non-Luxembourgish-speaking students. The goal is to maintain a clear boundary between 'Luxembourgers' and the 'foreigners'. Similarly, more complex dimensions of linguistic diversity are also usually erased, thus maintaining the image that it is clear as to who is a *Stacklëtzebuerger* (despite the high incidence of mixed marriages). Discourses in this section portray the PISA tests as illegitimate because, it is argued, they are insensitive to the (alleged) uniqueness of patterns of language use in Luxembourg. At a closer glance, however, Luxembourgish trilingualism does not appear to be linked to openness and tolerance, but rather to the propagation of a certain social order.

7.5.2 Fragmenting the nation: the loss of 'good' language and moral 'decline'

While the iconic link between the trilingual ideal and the values of openness, tolerance and hard work provides one potential strategy to unite the nation – as presented in the texts under discussion – the same strategy may fragment the nation in certain discourses, thus illustrating the semiotic process of fractal recursivity. In this case, the blame for the bad PISA results is put upon students and their parents as well as advocates and practitioners of methods viewed as deviating from the predominant classical humanism paradigm and/or potentially disrupting the status quo. In such discourses, a frequent trope is that of declining standards and the desire to return to what Milroy (1998: 60) describes as 'the Good Old Days of strong moral discipline' or the 'Golden Age'. Although debates about educational issues in Luxembourg differ from those in the UK in multiple respects, they rely on widely shared ideological underpinnings, including the *standard language* ideology:

Text 4 (German original)
School is stressful. School is boring. Memorizing vocabulary. Correcting mistakes. Preparing for tests. Where's the 'fun'? Where's the 'action'? [...] Away with the stressful lectures! What is that? – Well, that is the [teaching] methodology through which we all learned something! Become active yourself! Finding something out for oneself is of course not so frustrating! But it takes a terribly long time! Some never understand the mystery. Long live soft pedagogy! Neat [clean] handwriting, manners, discipline, respect ... old-fashioned concepts! [...] At that time one still deducted 3 points for one grammatical error. And nowadays? Errors should not be considered to be all-important. The main thing is that one understands what is meant. Not too many red marks on the test paper! That is frustrating! (*Luxemburger Wort*, 26.01.02)

Text 5 (French original)
How did we get to this point, whereas from the nineteenth century our students admitted to the universities of our neighbouring countries without an admission exam were able to take courses there and indeed were often extremely successful? [...] Unbelievable but true: a recent report has shown that for a specific regular French verb ending in -er, only 40% of the students in the last year of primary school knew the correct forms. O tempora, o mores! In the past, we used to recite all the irregular verbs in all the tenses by heart. [...] Whereas in the past we even required a teacher of history to speak an error-free French, nowadays one even has to forgive teachers of French for making such errors, at least as long as they are not too numerous. (*Luxemburger Wort*, 19.12.01)

In contrast to the texts discussed in 7.5.1, it is the trajectory of time rather than space that is foregrounded in Texts 4 and 5, as is illustrated by the deictics 'at that time' and 'nowadays' in Text 4 and by the contrast between the past and the present in Text 5. Whereas the iconic link between 'Luxembourgers' and the trilingual ideal was salient in Texts 1, 2 and 3, the claim made in Texts 4 and 5 is that only certain 'Luxembourgers' are true carriers of the trilingual ideal and therewith embody the related ethics and morals, as for example is illustrated in Text 4, where an iconic link is made between students who use and value certain forms of language, i.e. 'neat [clean] handwriting', and their behaviour, i.e. 'manners, discipline, respect'. In Text 5, the allegation of moral decline is signalled with the use of the Latin phrase *O tempora, o mores!* Whereas Latin indexes the 'Golden Age', English sometimes indexes the changes bound up with late-modernity, as with the analogy made between certain types of language learning and 'fast food' in Text 1. The spread of *international* English – frequently linked to global capital – may be viewed as disrupting nationalist language ideologies, as it cannot be regarded as the mother tongue of an imagined ethnic nation, i.e. 'the English', and it is somewhat unclear as to what the idealized, standard reference point is, especially in terms of spoken language use, where such a standard seems to have lost relevance altogether in certain situations.

In Text 4, the insertion into the original German text of the English loans 'fun' and 'action' into stereotypical utterances implicitly attributed to students, parents, or 'othered' individuals involved in the teaching profession indexes multiple sources of change. Furthermore, the insertion of the mixed French and English phrase 'Long live soft pedagogy!' (French original: *Vive la pédagogie soft!*) may be understood as indexing the widening gap among adherents of traditional, classical humanist educational paradigms and advocates of changes perceived as utilitarian in nature, which in turn are linked to globalization. This is depicted as a generational split, thus disrupting the continuity and coherence of the imagined (ethnic) Luxembourgish nation. Texts such as 4 and 5 – a letter to the editor written by a retired primary school teacher and an op-ed written by a retired secondary school teacher respectively – may be understood as warning calls from the elders to the younger generations: if the trilingual ideal is not maintained, there will no longer be a difference between the 'Luxembourgers' and the 'foreigners'. The perceived problem is that 'they' are not doing now what 'we' did then. But is it possible or even desirable to return to the past? Indeed, socio-economic stratification among ethnic Luxembourgers in the past and present is often erased from this kind of discourse, although Text 5 does deal with this issue, justifying it with the claim that not everybody can obtain high-level jobs. In such discourses, the changing demands on the workforce and the decline of jobs in the industrial sector are almost always erased.

While the 'foreigners' constituted the 'other' in 7.5.1, reference to an explicit 'other' is absent from the data in this section. The data in both

143

sections show that responses to the PISA tests point to an awareness of, and uneasiness with, change although the writers find it difficult to point the finger at who is responsible. Most significantly, the PISA tests are viewed as having disrupted the ways in which individuals position themselves in relation to others and their environment.[10]

7.6   Conclusion: sociolinguistic stances in the new millennium

Based on the indexical properties of discourse, the semiotic processes of iconicity, fractal recursivity and erasure provide us with useful strategies to explore the construction of boundaries (Irvine and Gal 2000). The metalinguistic discourses in the media dealing with Luxembourg's PISA results show how people are represented as responding to change at a critical moment in time, as well as the ways in which these responses are anchored in a specific historical tradition. Language ideologies and nationalist ideologies are intertwined, thus making it impossible to clearly distinguish between ethnic and civic nations. Both constructs are available and are drawn upon at different times. While the media discourses discussed in the chapter reflect and reproduce nationalist language ideologies, they also suggest that the accelerated processes of globalization create challenges affecting the lives of real people – with modernist space and time trajectories being disrupted (Giddens 1991).

This chapter has also shown that lay perspectives on language – be it in relation to specific forms or ideals of language use – are much too valuable to ignore because they provide a window to real-world social dynamics, including the valorization and stigmatization of specific linguistic repertoires. As linguists, are we studying *real* language varieties instead of named 'languages'? Are we exploring the ways in which power and identity are bound up with *real* language use? Given the fact that linguistic perspectives on language are constructed and challenged in relation to the same constellation of media discourses and world events as those of laypersons, it follows that traditional linguistic paradigms will be subjected to further questioning in relation to the greater processes of reflexivity bound up with the late-modern period.

Primary sources

Luxemburger Wort
    G.W. 'Die Sprache, ein Wert an sich'. (12.03.01: 3).
    R.S. 'Zéro pointé pour nos élèves'. (19.12.01: 4).
    R.D. 'Ein lehrreiches Desaster! . . .'. (26.01.02: 26).
    M.-P.M. 'En route pour PISA II!'. (15.06.02: 10).
    D.S., A.H., S.T. and L.C. 'Die PISA-Studie – ein Debakel?'. (06.07.02: 37).

Ministère de l'Education Nationale, de la Formation Professionnelle et des Sports (MENFPS) (2001), *PISA 2000: Kompetenzen von Schülern im internationalen Vergleich, Nationaler Bericht Luxemburg*. Luxembourg: Ministère de l'Education Nationale, de la Formation Professionnelle et des Sports.

Statec (2006), *Chiffres-clés du Luxembourg* (available online at www.statistiques.public.lu/fr, accessed 20.10.06).

Notes

1 I wish to thank Jean Jacques Weber for engaging in thought-provoking discussions about the Luxembourgish educational system and for assistance with questions regarding translation. I am also grateful to Tommaso Milani, Spiros Moschonas and Jürgen Spitzmüller for their insightful and constructive comments on this chapter. I remain fully responsible for any remaining shortcomings or errors.

2 The dominance of the *Luxemburger Wort/d'Wort* on the national market is reflected and reproduced by the frequent reference to it as *d'Zeitung* 'the (news)-paper' in everyday talk. The Luxembourgish print media is characterized by the fact that most dailies are linked to political parties. Unlike other European countries, it may be argued that the print media constitutes a more important source of *national* news than television in Luxembourg. For further details on the Luxembourgish print media, see Berg (1993), Hirsch (1997) and Horner (2004).

3 Luxembourgish language varieties are Germanic and bear similarities to Moselle Franconian language varieties spoken in parts of Germany, Belgium and France. Luxembourgish speakers in the Grand Duchy thus acquire basic literacy in a similar fashion to speakers of other Germanic language varieties that are *perceived* as distinct from standard German, e.g. Swiss German speakers who tend to refer to standard German as *Schriftdeutsch* (German for writing) and regard it as separate from spoken *Schwyzertüütsch* (Swiss German) varieties (cf. Watts 1999: 89–94). In spite of the significant number of students who use Romance language varieties in the home, there exist no (full) French language literacy programmes in state-run schools.

4 This state of affairs is further reflected and reproduced by patterns of language use in the print media (see 7.1).

5 I have put the frequently used label of 'foreign' between scare quotes as it may well include large numbers of people born in Luxembourg and/or with Luxembourgish citizenship, but whose parents immigrated to Luxembourg. Similarly, the category 'Luxembourgish' may well include people whose mother or father immigrated to Luxembourg and/or uses a language other than Luxembourgish in the home. As with all binary oppositions, the categories of 'Luxembourgish' and 'foreign' are socially constructed. This dichotomy is particularly salient in media discourses circulating on the national level (see 7.5.1).

6 The PISA tests are organized at the level of the OECD based on input from experts in participating countries. The first set of tests was administered in 2000. The tests are given to 15-year-old students with the goal of determining how well they are prepared for their future careers (MENFPS, 2001: 11). Although discourses about students' test results were widely circulated in the

national press following the release of the first set of test results, discussion of the students' responses to questions about the school-system and teaching methods rarely made it into print. Luxembourg also scored well below the OECD average in this respect (ibid.: 84).

7   Both factors are linked to the small size of Luxembourg (2,586 square kilometres and a total population of 459,500). 40 per cent of the population consists of resident foreigners, i.e. non-Luxembourgish passport holders, who are predominantly Portuguese citizens. In addition, *frontaliers* (border-crossing commuters) from Belgium, France and, to a lesser degree, Germany make up 41 per cent of the workforce (Statec 2006). The small size of Luxembourg also has an impact on print media production and uptake: national newspapers in Luxembourg bear similarities with local papers in larger countries.

8   Articles, editorials and letters to the editor from the *Luxemburger Wort* – published within a year of the release of the first PISA results – in which language issues were raised in relation to the first set of PISA results totalled 51 in number. For a discussion of the discourses scapegoating the 'foreigners', see Horner and Weber (2005).

9   During Nazi-German occupation (1940–44), a census was carried out which included questions on *Jetztige Staatsangehörigkeit* (current citizenship), *Muttersprache* (mother tongue) and *Volkszugehörigkeit* (ethnicity). Many people answered these questions with '*Lëtzebuergesch*', thus symbolically resisting incorporation into the Third Reich, though the exact numbers of people who responded to the census and percentage of people who answered in the above way are matters of historical debate. Articles and editorials referring – explicitly or implicitly – to the Second World War are widely circulated in the present-day Luxembourgish print media; it is also a prominent historical 'event' that appears in other sections, including letters to the editor and the monthly column of *Actioun Lëtzebuergesch*, the non-profit organization established to promote the language (Horner 2004, 2005). Media producers thus play a central role in bringing the collective memory of the Second World War together with present-day nation-building processes. A most interesting example occurred on 31 August 2002, when the *Luxemburger Wort* appeared with a reprint of the original front page of 31 August 1942, where it was first officially announced that (former) Luxembourgish citizens were to be drafted into the Nazi-German army.

10 The discursive discrediting of the PISA tests in the media was fairly effective in blocking constructive debates about the educational system; however, calls for methodological reforms may well lead to further, albeit rather minor modifications. Structural changes, including the option of introducing French language literacy, continue to be firmly ruled out at the time of writing (June 2006).

PART III

CONTACT AND CODESWITCHING IN MULTILINGUAL MEDIASCAPES

8 Corsican on the airwaves: media discourse in a context of minority language shift

Alexandra Jaffe

8.1 Introduction

In contexts of minority language shift and revitalization, the media are of interest for a number of reasons. First, the media constitutes a public, popular forum for the discussion of linguistic issues; these metalinguistic discourses reveal circulating attitudes and ideologies about language. Secondly, the media are a site for status, corpus, and even 'acquisition' planning (Cooper 1989) in the minority language. As many analysts of the Breton and Irish media point out, there are inherent tensions built into these multiple roles since these different objectives imply different programming and linguistic choices (Kelly-Holmes 2001; Ní Neachtain 2001; Ó Laoire 2001; see also Kelly-Holmes and Atkinson, Chatper 9, this volume). With reference to status and corpus planning, minority language practices on radio and television raise central issues and debates within the society about language standards, authority and authenticity. These issues are of course related to fundamental questions about how the minority language speech community is collectively imagined, and what kinds of speech and speakers are considered authoritative and/or authentic. The introduction of acquisition planning as a mandate for minority broadcast media adds complexity to this situation by introducing the learner or 'semi-speaker' into the picture either as a 'voice on the air' or as a consumer of minority media products. The presence of audiences and *potential* audiences with different linguistic competencies pushes minority language media to confront issues of linguistic diversity. This diversity includes not only 'competence' in the minority language but also dialectal diversity and mixed language practices (codeswitching and other contact phenomena) that arise out of language contact and shift (see Cotter 1999).

In this chapter, I explore the way that the media are involved in 'the public construction of languages, the linguistic construction of publics, and the relationship between these two processes' (Gal and Woolard 2001: 1). The focus is on the creative, constitutive role of media practices and representations vis-à-vis the languages/codes of the community, the audiences/identities/publics indexed by those languages, and the way that language and identity are assumed to be connected. With reference to the public construction of languages, I examine language practice on the regional Corsican radio, RCFM (*Radio Corse Frequenza Mora*), looking at the way that differing language policies and practices in news versus informal programming represent Corsican as more or less 'pure' and bounded. The analysis of news programming in Corsican and audience evaluations of the appropriateness and authenticity of news language illustrates tensions between different models of authority and authenticity in corpus and status planning efforts, and provides a dynamic perspective on the interaction between media practices/representations and audience reception. Data from informal radio programming provides insight into the way that linguistic practice can construct a public through the projection of identities/competencies. Finally, I turn to a complex filmed event that I observed and recorded during ethnographic research in a Corsican bilingual school. The analysis focuses on the way that the political and social context of Corsican language revitalization oriented the media professionals, on and the teachers and children of the school towards a monolingual representation of a bilingual space.

The Corsican data illustrates that the introduction of minority languages into the discursive and social space of the media does not have a single, predictable outcome for those languages – either in linguistic terms (the effect of media usage on the code) or in sociolinguistic terms (the effect of media on minority language attitudes and practices, including 'revitalization'). As a public, representational arena, media practices have the power to amplify dominant ideologies and representations of languages and linguistic communities of practice, in which singular identities are mapped onto homogenous codes and monolingual practices. At the same time, less scripted practice in the media also puts on stage and potentially validates much more heterogeneous linguistic forms, practices and identities.

8.2 The Corsican sociolinguistic context: why and how media matters

Over the last few generations, language shift from Corsican to French has been quite dramatic. In the early part of the twentieth century, the first language of most Corsicans was Corsican. Today, the first language of over 90 per cent of Corsican children is French. The language, however, still has a significant presence in the society among middle-aged and elderly speakers. It is also taught as a subject at all levels of the school system, and approximately 10 per cent of Corsican schoolchildren attend bilingual schools where they receive instruction in Corsican and French.

Since the 1970s, language revitalization efforts have been most intense in three domains: literacy activities, in particular the creation of a literary corpus; the broadcast media; and education. The teaching of Corsican is intended to work on both the practical and the symbolic levels. In practical terms, it is an attempt to compensate for the lack of intergenerational transmission. At the same time, the insertion of Corsican in the public education system as a subject or as a medium of instruction in the bilingual schools is a form of status planning. The hope is that the legitimation of Corsican in the public eye may help to reverse language shift by undermining diglossic attitudes. That is, if Corsicans shed the notion that the language is subordinate to French, Corsican speakers will be more likely to make an effort to pass on the language to their children and grandchildren, and non-speakers or semi-speakers will be motivated to learn it themselves. Thus the school plays an important role with respect to the public representation of the Corsican language as legitimate and authoritative.

The media are also significant as a strategy of Corsican status planning that challenges the historical French–Corsican diglossia that excluded Corsican from the public domain. Whereas Corsican language education replaces language acquisition in the family with formal instruction of Corsican as an authoritative code, radio and television are often seen by Corsican language planners as an extension of the 'street' – the informal public domain – which is where many middle-aged Corsican speakers say they learnt to speak the language.

The media have also been given particular importance by Corsican language activists in terms of their potential to be persuasive and influential for a wide audience. Here, there has been an implicit comparison to the other area of intensive corpus planning activity in the 1970s and 1980s – the creation of a Corsican-language literature. Corsican language activists were aware that Corsican literary production had outstripped the pace at which a Corsican reading public was being trained in the schools. Middle-aged Corsican speakers were far less likely to read a Corsican novel than to watch or listen to Corsican language broadcasts. Media productions were also much less likely to be perceived as 'too highbrow' or inaccessible; this was not always the case for Corsican literature. The electronic media are also, of course, associated with modernity, and for this reason, Corsican language planners saw their potential to transform negative views of the minority language as backward and inferior (see Cotter 2001b; Eisenlohr 2004a; Ó Riagáin 1991).

8.2.1 Challenges of media practice

Using Corsican on radio and TV poses a number of challenges. For media professionals, whose training is in French, using Corsican to report on the news or to do DJ chatter requires an adaptation of the Corsican they have learnt in the family or 'on the street' to a new register and to new speech genres. For some, using Corsican professionally stretches their Corsican competencies to their limits; they must learn a language at the same time as they learn/develop a media register for that language.

Secondly, the novelty and visibility of Corsican used in the media, coupled with the importance attached to it, has led to intense scrutiny of both the use of Corsican, and the kind of Corsican used by language activists and the general public. This is far from uncommon (see, for example, Gardner *et al* 2000; Hornberger and King 1999; Peterson 1997) and underscores the way that media broadcasts in minority language contexts are never 'just' about communication or entertainment; they are always interpreted as representations of language within politically and ideologically charged frameworks. For both activists and ordinary listeners, media Corsican has been subject to extremely high expectations. While the precise linguistic content of these expectations differ, they have all related to notions of 'correct', 'pure' and 'authentic' language. People look to the Corsican language media not just to inform and entertain, but to represent, legitimate and instruct. This role has been the source of considerable tension, sometimes embraced, sometimes rejected, by media professionals. In an interview, the director of the regional radio station told me, 'We are *Radio Corse Frequenza Mora*' – the name of the radio station – 'not *Radio Corse Sorbonne*'. He went on to say that they were radio professionals first, not linguists or educators.

But there was no doubt that the radio station director – and all those working in the Corsican broadcast media – could not take a neutral position with respect to using Corsican themselves or incorporating Corsican segments or speakers into their broadcasts. The very incorporation of Corsican into a broadcast has been a cultural and political statement, given the history of French dominance of the media. The same is true for all dimensions of Corsican language use, which include, as we will see below, choices of linguistic form as well as of how often Corsican is used, who uses it, and what functions it. As we will explore below, the language ideological implications of these choices are even more intense for broadcasts whose topic is language or language teaching.

The cultural and political context of broadcasting in Corsican has an impact on both practice and attitudes, acting as a selective frame with ideological implications that, in turn, have consequences for:

1. *Production*: the linguistic choices/practices of professional practitioners as well as non-professional participants in broadcast events (these include people being filmed or recorded; listeners or viewers who call in on the telephone and so on). Production choices include programming decisions about what to broadcast in Corsican, as well as individual decisions about language choice on the air.

2. *Editorial selection*: this process is most visible in broadcasts that are not live. Producers make selections at the moment of filming or recording, choosing where the eye of the camera or the arm of the microphone will point. In documentaries, this creates a corpus of 'rushes' that are then subject to a second selection process in which the producer chooses and assembles a subset of those recordings into the final product.

3. *Audience evaluation*: how the Corsican used in the media is evaluated by viewers/listeners.

In the remainder of this chapter, I address issues 1 and 3 with reference to radio broadcast data, followed by a discussion of all three of these issues in an analysis of a television broadcast.

8.3   Radio broadcast data

The first set of data that I will consider is a corpus of radio broadcasts that includes both scripted, serious, formal genres such as documentaries and news broadcasts, and unscripted interactions in less formal programming that includes interviews, listener call-ins, contests and music. This data was collected in the late 1980s and early 1990s from RCFM (*Radio Corse Frequenza Mora*), the regional branch of France's Radio Bleu network. Starting in 1986, this station began to use a significant amount of Corsican in its programming. The imprint of the ideological and political context of Corsican language revitalization can be seen from the very beginning of RCFM's bilingual programming in the relative purism of the different broadcast genres. Corsican newscasts fell on the 'high' end of the continuum of broadcast types: they were the most formal and the most scripted. These newscasts also represented a kind of authoritative public speech that had been thoroughly dominated by French up to that point; as such, they played an obvious focal role in establishing Corsican as an equal and legitimate language. This role was reflected in their placement in the schedule: throughout the peak listening hours of the morning, the Corsican news alternated on the half hour with French-language versions of the same stories. The central role of the news in the work of legitimation was also reflected in a self-conscious effort not to use *any* French in these broadcasts and in doing so, to create an equivalent Corsican monolingual broadcast space. As a consequence, brief interviews in which the interviewee used French appeared in the French-language versions of the news but were excluded from the equivalent Corsican reports on the same topic.

8.3.1   News language: lexical choices

Presenting the news in a 'pure' Corsican required two kinds of linguistic intervention with respect to names, expressions, acronyms and phrases that

153

Table 8.1: Translation from French in news broadcasts

French	English	Corsican
mesures de compensation	*measures of [financial] compensation*	misure di cumpensazione
Coordination Rurale	*Rural Coordination [Agency]*	Cuurdinazione Rurale
politique agricole commune	*common [EU] agricultural policy*	pulitica agricula cumune
reprennent haleine	*[they] are getting a second wind; catching their breath*	ripiglianu fiatu

were most frequently expressed in French in everyday conversational Corsican. In some cases, these expressions were translated relatively directly (usually very rapidly, since the writers were working from the French language Agence France Press (AFP) dispatches that came in early in the morning); in other cases, neologisms were created. Table 8.1 illustrates some of the phrases found in Corsican newscasts (right-hand column) that were more or less a direct equivalent to the language of the original French dispatch. This does not mean, of course, that the same writers would not have produced the same phrases if they had been composing directly in Corsican; it simply means that the French phrases and structures are transparently represented in the Corsican.

Table 8.2 shows some examples of neologisms. In the first case, the radio term 'spegnifocu' was coined by compounding the verb 'spignà' (*to extinguish*) and 'focu' (*fire*). This word is intended to avoid the influence of French on everyday usage, where people either use the French word 'pompiers' preceded by the Corsican plural definite article 'i' (this renders 'i pompiers') or use

Table 8.2: Neologisms in news language

Corsican news	English	Popular Corsican usage	French
spegnifochi	*firemen*	pompieri I pompiers	pompiers
scrivacciulate	*graffiti*	graffiti	graffiti
Ministru di u Circondu	*Environment Minister*	?	Ministre de l'Environnement

a Corsican adaptation of the French word: 'pompieri'. In the second case, 'scrivacciulate' was coined to replace 'graffiti', an Italian word used in both French and English. The neologism was formed from the verb 'scrive' (*to write*) and the pejorative suffix 'accia', rendering *'bad writing'* or *'scribblings'*. With respect to language purism, it is interesting to note here that the word being avoided is not even a French one: 'graffiti' is just as plausibly Corsican as it is Italian. In short, what we see is a form of hypercorrection motivated by Corsican language purism. The last example in the table shows a Corsican word, 'circondu' (*surroundings* or *area*) being pressed into service as a more technical and more general term, 'environment'.

Finally, Table 8.3 shows some of the non-Corsican words that were included in Corsican newspeak despite purist efforts to the contrary. The first example has to do with pronunciation of the official French designation for the national mountain trail that bisects the island: the GR 20 in French, the 'GR20', where 'G-R' stands for 'grande randonné' (*major trail*). In the news broadcast, the newscaster used the French pronunciation [je ɛr] for the letters G-R instead of the Corsican pronunciation of the two letters: [ji ɛre]. This was followed by 'vinti', the Corsican word for *'twenty'* instead of saying 'vingt' in French. The second two examples, 'supporters' and 'overdose', show English loan words into French being retained in Corsican. The last example documents the use of 'ordinanze', the contemporary Corsican word for *'prescriptions'*. In this case, a 'traditional' word, 'repice', has been more or less supplanted by a product of language contact with French, as 'ordinanze' is derived from 'ordonnances' (*prescriptions*).

What these brief examples in Table 8.3 show is that creating a 'pure' Corsican linguistic space in the news broadcasts in the practical conditions of rapid translations from AFP dispatches causes radio professionals to draw on multiple linguistic resources as they select, reject and recombine elements from 'traditional' Corsican, contemporary Corsican usage, French, Italian and English. The result is a set of texts that are by their very nature

Table 8.3: Non-Corsican words and calques in news broadcasts

French	English	Corsican news
GR Vingt [je ɛr]	*major mountain trail – French Park service designation*	GR Vinti [je ɛr]; not [ji ɛre]
supporters	*fans*	supporters
overdose	*overdose*	overdose
ordonnances	*prescriptions*	ordinanze (ordinanze = pop. usage; repice = 'old' term)

heterogeneous. First, they are never completely consistent (as in the examples of French words that 'slipped in' despite a purist philosophy). Secondly, and perhaps more importantly, the social and sociolinguistic contexts of production make the processes of entextualization visible (or audible). That is, because news language is a new register for Corsican, and because a purist approach contrasts with most everyday conversational practice, almost every linguistic choice on the air is accompanied by the shadow voices of other possible languages, codes or forms. In the absence of a recognized linguistic academy with the power to define the boundaries of good usage in this new media, newscasts thus constantly evoke the idea of a Standard, but cannot, by definition, embody it authoritatively.

8.3.2   The language of less formal programming

The language of the Corsican radio news contrasted with the language of the less formal programming on RCFM. People who spoke on the air included disc jockeys, comedians, writers of informational short radio spots for the station and listeners who called the station to request a song, take part in a contest or contribute to listener fora on current events. Compared to the news, these speakers created a much more heterogeneous linguistic space where codeswitching and dual-language conversations were common and where there was much less attention to using a 'pure' Corsican. This aspect of the radio reflected the desire the RCFM station director expressed to me in an interview: to make RCFM a 'radio of proximity' that reflected the interests and practices of the people who listened to it. This included, for him, replicating the 'language of the café' and of the 'street' although he acknowledged that that language was mixed (cf. Kelly-Holmes and Atkinson's discussion of the Irish context, Chapter 9, this volume). The following transcript represents just one example of this kind of mixed practice. In it, a woman called Marilou calls in to request the song 'The Show Must Go On' by the rock band Queen.

> **Transcript: Marilou**
> normal typeface = Corsican; **bold** = French; _underlined italics_ = English
> in the original recording
>
> DJ: Avemu subitu Marilou. **Marilou bonjour. Vous allez bien**?
> _Now we have Marilou coming up._ Marilou, hello. How are you?
> **Très bien, et vous même?**
> **Well, and yourself?**
> DJ: **Oui oui, avec le soleil ça va toujours bien.**
> **Yes yes with the sun it's always good.**
> **Marilou, d'où vous appelez?**
> **Marilou, where are you calling from?**
> M: **De Migliacciaru.**
> **From Migliacciaru.**

DJ: **Migliacciaru. A Migliacciaru il y a du soleil?**
Migliacciaru. In Migliacciaru is it sunny?

M: Iè, iè
Yes, yes

DJ: Sicuru. Hè in u Fiumorbu, Migliacciaru?
Of course. Migliacciaru is in the Fiumorbu [region], right?

M: **Voilà**, in Fiumorbu, **oui.**
Exactly, *in the Fiumorbu,* ***yes.***

DJ: Bè, ci hè u sole in u Fiumorbu.
So, it's sunny in the Fiumorbu.

M: Oui.
Yes.

DJ: Allora, tuttu va bè. Migliacciaru, **c'est en plaine. Voilà, voilà, c'est tres [čre] bien.**
So, everything's fine. Migliacciaru, ***its on the plain. So, so, it's very good.***
Chì vulete sente voi?
What do you want to hear?

M: **Queen. Le groupe Queen.**
Queen. The group Queen.

DJ: **Po po po po, Queen. Vous êtes dans le vent, eh?**
Oh, oh oh oh, Queen. You're trendy, eh?

M: Ah, oui.
Ah, yes.

DJ Vi piace à Queen.
You like Queen.

M: **Dommage qu'il soit mort jeune, oui?**
It's a shame that he died young, isn't it?

DJ: Ah, ma quessa, **c'est la vie**, chì vulete?
Ah, but that, ***that's life***, *what can you do?*

M: **C'est la vie.**
That's life.

DJ: **C'est la vie, on ne peut pas faire autrement [cough]. Pardon, excusez-moi.**
That's life, you can't avoid it [cough]. Pardon, excuse me.
Le titre de la chanson, c'était?
What was the title of the song?

M: **Ah, bah, le titre anglais, je ne m'en rappelle plus.**
Ah, bah, the title in English, I can't remember it anymore.

DJ: **Alors, je vais vous le faire dire. Je le dis, et vous le répétez:**
OK, I'm going to have you say it. I say it, and you repeat:
The show must go on.

M: *The show must go on.*

DJ: Micca *'de show'*: **la langue entre les dents**: *'the show'*.
Not 'de show': ***the tongue in between the teeth:*** *'the show'.*

a) *The show*

DJ: *Must go hon.*
M: *Must go hon.*
DJ: **Voilà, c'est très bien**. Allora, vi sbrugliate ancu in inglese ind'è u Fiumorbu!
   There, that's very good. *So you can get along in English as well in the Fiumorbu!*
M: Iè, iè. **Merci alors**.
   *Yes, yes. **Thanks then.***
DJ: **Non, merci** à voi d'avè chjamatu. Vi sentimu subitu?
   No, thanks *to you for having called. Will we hear from you soon?*
   Iè. **Allez ... Bonne journée**.
   *Yes. **Well ... have a nice day.***
DJ: **Bonne journée**. Avvedeci O Marilou.
   Have a nice day. *Goodbye O Marilou.*

Even a casual glance at the fonts in this transcript, which represent the different languages used, shows that both Corsican and French are present in high doses, and that there is even a humorous introduction of English. Moreover, the interaction is imbalanced: the two participants do not share the same level of use of Corsican, and most probably do not share the same level of competence in that language. Nevertheless, the exchange goes on quite successfully with the caller Marilou speaking almost exclusively in French and the DJ alternating between Corsican and French. I have argued elsewhere (Jaffe 1999a: 256) that the DJ's use of Corsican is not random, but creatively accommodates to Marilou's uncertain competence in Corsican. He does this by using Corsican almost exclusively in contexts that maximize the potential for comprehension. Corsican is thus used for place names (in particular, 'Migliacciaru' where Marilou lives); in formulaic and habitual utterances/ questions about the weather; to repeat content already established in French; and in highly predictable conversational slots (such as when he asks her what song she wants to hear). As an interaction, then, the exchange acknowledges and validates the varying levels of Corsican language competence that can be found in Corsican society as a result of language shift, and provides a framework in which partial and passive competence is interactionally validated. It creates a dual-language space in which the use of Corsican is an element, but not a prerequisite of cultural membership, community and inclusion (see Woolard 1998b, for comparable strategies in the management of Catalan and Castilian on the radio).

To summarize, then, the contrast between language policy and practice in formal versus informal radio broadcast genres maps onto – and shows the inherent conflict in – the dual goals of Corsican language planning, which are oriented both towards making Corsican an authoritative and legitimate public language and towards its intimate, affective value as a language of culture and heritage. The relatively more purist approach to news broadcasting does the work of legitimation by creating a monolingual linguistic space which indexes a bounded and homogenous speech community. In contrast, the scope for mixed language practices in the informal sphere implicitly defines the speech community in broader terms that accommodate the linguistic and cultural outcomes of language domination and shift.

8.3.3   Audience evaluation of broadcast language

In the brief analysis above, the focus is on the production side of minority language broadcasting and the way that those practices index ideologies of language and corresponding ideologies of identity and thus constitute both language and public. But as Spitulnik's (1996) account of the social circulation of media discourse in Zambia shows, the public is not just a passive recipient of broadcast projections of linguistic identity. As a consequence, the impact of minority language use in the media on popular usage and attitudes – and vice versa – has to be studied empirically. In my research on Corsican radio data, I focused on the evaluative, attitudinal dimension of audience reception, conducting lengthy interviews with approximately 30 people in which they listened to and evaluated nine news segments, three comedy sketches and two interactions between DJs and listeners who called on the phone. This research is described in more detail elsewhere (Jaffe 1999a, 2005), but there are several general findings that concern the argument being made here.

First, with respect to the language of the newscasts, all interviewees offered critiques of Corsican usage they considered 'gallicized'. But while everyone could identify gallicisms, there was little consensus on which specific words or phrases were *too* French and little coherence within each individual's set of judgements. With reference to some of the terms listed in Table 8.1, for example, one interviewee might find 'misure di cumpensazione' completely unacceptable, but pass over 'Cuurdinazione Rurale' without comment; the next person might judge both of those to be acceptable but take great issue with 'ripiglianu fiatu'. And while listeners identified a total of 36 words or phrases as gallicisms, they were able to offer more 'authentic' alternatives for less than half. They were also relatively accepting of French words (some, as Table 8.2 shows, of English origin) that were introduced into the news unaltered, like 'supporters' and 'overdose'. Three older respondents offered 'repice' as a possible substitute for 'ordinanze' but none of them had strong negative feelings about 'ordinanze'. And finally, while listening to the news prompted several people to voice their disapproval of what they considered gratuitous neologisms, they also almost unanimously accepted the neologisms for *fireman* ('spegnifocu') and *graffiti* ('scrivacciulate'), though no listeners claimed to use them. If we look at these evaluations in the light of patterns of production in the news broadcasts, we see the same phenomenon: the presence of a purist language ideology accompanied by an absence of unambiguous and consensual criteria for defining the pure and the impure.

Second, listeners perceived the mixed language of informal programming as an accurate reflection of everyday practice; it was the language of 'proximity' the radio director was aiming for. The on-air interactional frame, moreover, appeared to validate a wide spectrum of Corsican language competencies, both passive and active. For example, one of the reasons I had included the sequence between Marilou and the DJ in the interview corpus was that I had evaluated Marilou as a non-speaker and thus was curious about how Corsicans would evaluate the DJ's use of Corsican with her. I wanted to know whether they would think it was a violation of the sociolinguistic etiquette that calls on speakers to accommodate to the dominant or preferred language of their conversational partner. However, almost none of the people I interviewed characterized Marilou as a non- or semi-speaker, and no one criticized the DJ's use of Corsican and French with her. It was on the basis of these judgements that I reanalysed the interaction, and came to the conclusion that the DJ's careful management of his use of Corsican not only accommodated to Marilou but actually projected onto her a Corsican-speaking identity. Put another way, the DJ's practice disconnected language preference from strict measurements of language competence, which made it possible for accommodation to take place without one speaker converging towards the other speaker's dominant language.

The third general finding is that the broadcast genre influenced listener judgements. Listeners were more critical of language form in their response to the news than they were in their response to informal programming. This is in part because people have different expectations about more and less formal genres. It is thus likely that listeners would have been critical of more informal and mixed usage on the news. At the same time, these listener judgements were also very likely shaped by the overtly purist ideology of the newscasts themselves, which set up a framework for evaluation in which most of the choices open to Corsican language broadcasters could be negatively evaluated with respect to some criterion of purity or authenticity.

Finally, there was a difference between the critical stance of radio audiences during what I would call ordinary listening versus during the evaluative frame of the sociolinguistic interview. Not surprisingly, asking people questions about language and its quality, appropriateness, etc. activated dominant language ideological frameworks; most notably their purist dimension (Jaffe 2000b). It is difficult to provide direct empirical evidence for the experience of what I am calling 'ordinary listening' that took place at the very beginning of interview sessions, before I asked participants any questions at all. However, we might consider the inconsistencies in people's evaluations of what they considered gallicisms as indirect evidence, in that these inconsistencies may reflect fluctuations in listeners' attention to language form. This attention is very hard to sustain even in an interview, and even less likely to occur during 'ordinary listening'. Another kind of indirect evidence involves my assessment of nonverbal responses. Particularly for the

160

informal programming – which included comedy sketches – there was a contrast between positive nonverbal responses during respondents' first listening and the more serious and critical way that they reacted in an evaluative mode.

8.4 The mediatization of bilingual education

I turn now to the way that Corsican and its speakers are represented in programming devoted explicitly to the language. The focus here is on the way that the media as a frame structures the language practices and representational choices of both producers and subjects of media broadcasts. The specific data I will consider is drawn from a year of ethnographic fieldwork conducted in a bilingual Corsican school in 2000. This village school had 27 students between the ages of three and 11, divided into two multi-age classrooms that were taught by two teachers. The language backgrounds of the children reflected the wider sociolinguistic context: four of the 27 students had Corsican as their first language, another four or five came from homes in which Corsican was used frequently, and the rest were French monolingual when they entered school. These numbers reflect general patterns of Corsican competence among children. The teachers in this school were highly committed Corsican language activists who had been among the first to volunteer to teach bilingually in 1996, the first year of implementation of a new French educational policy permitting such instruction. They were both seasoned teachers, who were held up in the Corsican Academy as master practitioners of bilingual education. One of the by-products of their reputation was that they had a great deal of experience with the media, since Academy administrators tended to send to their school those journalists from continental France and elsewhere who expressed interest in Corsican language education. This school also got a disproportionate share of important guests (politicians, for example) and student teachers. As a consequence, the teachers were particularly conscious of the role that their school played in the public representation of bilingual education. They were concerned to legitimate the use of Corsican in all academic subjects, to show that significant Corsican learning could take place in a bilingual format, and to promote the value of the bilingual and bicultural person as a better learner and as a better citizen of the world. They were also acutely aware that they did not have the full support of the society at large, and that diglossic attitudes were still the source of resistance to Corsican as a public language of power in the schools. The public sphere of the media, therefore, was an opportunity to try to change those popular attitudes.

Both of the teachers were also committed to 'cooperative pedagogy' and believed in the value of 'bottom-up' rather than top-down, teacher-directed learning. Every week they held a cooperative meeting in which children were prompted to recount past events, discuss social norms and rules, articulate ongoing academic projects and set priorities for work and extracurricular activities. The teachers made it clear to the children that the ideal cooperative was one in which children took an active role, and the ideal student in the cooperative classroom was one who displayed personal initiative and responsibility for carrying out the projects identified by the group. Since this was a routine activity, I observed and videotaped many weekly cooperative meetings. These meetings varied in the extent to which they were student-run, but they were typically organized by the teacher. Teachers' language practices in the cooperative meetings reflected a pattern of language choice I observed frequently: they spoke primarily in Corsican, but switched freely in and out of French. Children were more likely to speak French than Corsican, and for the most part, teachers did not make an issue of language choice. They were far more focused on the level of the students' engagement in discussion and planning. Thus teacher–student interactions during these meetings often resembled the dual-language exchange between the DJ and Marilou described above.

8.4.1 Media as a frame for student and teacher linguistic production

In the autumn of 2000, the regional television station in Corsica decided to make a documentary on bilingual education, and chose the school described above as their primary site for one week of filming. The teachers made it clear that the cooperative structure was an integral part of their pedagogy, and on this basis, the producer said she wanted to film one of their cooperative meetings.

During the professional filming, I was also videotaping the classroom. The following transcript is an excerpt from the 'made-for-TV' cooperative. The discussion revolved around an ongoing project called 'The Forest School', which had a number of smaller components, all concerned with the flora and fauna in forests. The class had been planning a back-to-school night for parents in which they were going to have several different interactive displays about their work, including an electrical game that lit up when players correctly matched leaf and bark patterns to specific trees. They had also invited a Corsican-speaking carpenter to the school to talk to them about his profession.

Transcript: Made-for-TV Cooperative
Note: French is represented in bold face.

1	Teacher:	Altr'affare à ammintuvà per a	Other things to remember for the
2		Scola di a Furesta? Iè? non. va	Forest School? Yes? No? Ok, So
3		bè. Allora passemu à u secondu	let's go on to the second point, the
4		puntu, u bancalaru?	carpenter?
5	Children:	Iè	Yes
6	Teacher:	Allora, u bancalaru, ùn hè micca	So, the carpenter, isn't this still the
7		dinò listessu prughjettu	same project?

8	Pasqua	[?]	[?]
9	Teacher	[Allora vi dumandu, eiu, avà.	[So, I'll ask you now.
10	Child:	[ùn hè micca listessu	[No, it's not the same
11	Teacher:	Un hè micca listessu prughjettu	Isn't it the same project as the
12		chì a Scola di a Furesta?	Forest School?
13	Children:	Iè, iè	Yes, yes
14	Teacher:	**Oua, c'est pas grave, c'est pas**	**Yes, it's not serious, not serious**
15		**grave** Un face nunda, vale à dì,	It's no problem, that is to say, that it
16		ci hè dinù, allora vidite chì si	is also, so you see we can move
17		pudera avanzà appena di piu, eh,	ahead a bit further, eh, from what
18		al di là di ciò chè n'avemu	we've already planned. Pasqua, yes,
19		previstu. Pasqua, iè, voli dì	do you want to say something?
20		qualcosa?	
21	Pasqua:	Iè. Ci vole . . . priparà i	Yes. We have to . . . prepare the
22		quistione . . .	questions . . .
23	Teacher:	Iè	Yes.
24	Pasqua:	(unintelligible, very soft)	(unintelligible, very soft)
25	Teacher:	Va bè, va bè, emu capitu	Ok, that's good, we've got the idea
26	Pasqua:	perchè ghjè::ra, venderi u . . .	Because it wa::s, Friday the . . .
27		u vinti.	The 20th.
28	Teacher:	u vinti	The 20th
29		addessu hè u vinti d'ottobre.	Now it's October 20th.
30	Pasqua:	allora passa prestu	Well it's passing quickly
31	Teacher:	Ah passa prestu, u tempu?	Ah, time's passing quickly? So!
32		Allora! Pasqua parla pocu, eh?	Pasqua doesn't speak much, eh? So,
33		Allora, ci vole à pensà	we have to think
34		Mettimu, um 'priparà dumande	Let's put, um, 'prepare questions
35		per u bancalaru, ch'hà da vene	for the carpenter, who will come on
36	Julie:	venderi	Friday
37	Teacher:	Allora ma, ci vulerebbe fissà u	Well now, we ought to set a time
38		mumentu avà. Pudemu sceglie.	right away. We can decide. When
39		Quandu emu à priparè ste fiscie,	will we prepare these worksheets,
40		ste dumande pè . . . u bancalaru.	questions for . . . the carpenter.
41	Julie:	Dumane, dumane mattinu.	Tomorrow, tomorrow morning
42	Teacher:	Allora, pudemu dì cusì: pigliemu	Ok, let's say: we'll take
43		un mumentu dumattina per	a moment tomorrow morning to
44		priparà e dumande per u	prepare the questions for the
45		bancalaru.	carpenter.
46	Children:	Iè	Yes.
47	Teacher:	Va bè, chì hà da vene, hà dettu	Good. who is coming, Julia said –
48		Ghjulia – cuandu hà da vene o	when is the carpenter going to come
49		Lesia u bancalaru?	Lesia?
50	Lesia:	euh . . .	euh . . .
51	Teacher	Non, ùn sai piu.	No, you don't remember any more.
52	Pasqua:	Venderi	Friday.
53	Teacher:	Venderi. Venneri u vinti, eh. Va	Friday. Friday the 20th. OK.
54		bè.	
55	Pasqua:	Perchè tutte e mattine, u,	Because every morning, um it, um,
56		si . . . euh . . .	

57	Teacher:	Allora, hà messu, uh, iè? Passa	So, she put it (on the board), right?
58		prestu u tempu,	Time is going by quickly,
59	Pasqua	**non mais on se met, on se met**	**no but we all, we all get together**
60		**tous ensemble, et c'est, c'est un**	**and**
61		**groupe,**	**it's, its a group**
62	Teacher:	Iè	Yes
63	Pasqua	**et alors comme ça on peut**	**and so that's the way we can do**
64		**faire les questions.**	**the questions.**
65	Teacher:	Eccu, pè un mumentu cummunu	Right, a moment that's shared by all
66		tra tutti i gruppi cusì, à tutti i	of groups like that, in all the age
67		nivelli di a scola pudemu priparà	groups in the school we can prepare
68		e dumande. Eccu.	the questions. Right.

The issue that I want to address here is how the media frame influenced the teacher's, and most dramatically, the children's practice. If we consider what it meant to children to be filmed by a television crew, these children – like students in any other classroom – undoubtedly assumed that they should be on their best behaviour when in the public eye. But more specifically, in this particular school, being selected to be filmed for TV clearly framed the school as a site of 'best practice': as an exemplar of what a *bilingual* school should be. This was clear to the children not just because of this particular media event; it was also part of the apprenticeship they had as media subjects due to the frequent visits of the press, visitors, student teachers and researchers that I have mentioned. All of this put the children on notice to present their best linguistic behaviour, and we will see that they tried to live up to this expectation. It was also the case that the process of being filmed by the crew was, even for children who had spoken to radio reporters and been videotaped by me, an intense experience of 'staging' which framed linguistic behaviour as 'performance'. In the cramped quarters of the school, the presence of cables, lights and equipment was quite dramatic. The cameraman often brought the lens of his camera only inches away from the faces of children who were speaking. Some children were also fitted with radio microphones, and when those who did not have these microphones spoke, the sound technician swung a huge boom microphone on a pole above their heads. In several cases, because of technical problems, the director had the teacher re-enter the room and re-start a particular classroom sequence – which thus became a 'take' rather than 'real school'.

If we look at how the children responded to this call to perform as ideal bilingual students in a cooperative school, we can see contrasts between everyday cooperatives and the filmed event in both student leadership and language choice. First of all, in the TV cooperative meaning, Julie, the elected student president of the cooperative, led the meeting from the front of the room, where she wrote down key points on the blackboard. While this was not completely irregular behaviour, it was usually the teacher who played this role. Julie was thus enacting the *ideal* of the student-led cooperative. Her classmates contributed to this image by demonstrating ideal hand-raising behaviour, and by refraining from the calling out, which was otherwise quite common during these meetings. This enactment of ideal cooperative behaviour supports an interpretation of their use of Corsican in the filmed meeting as an enactment of a linguistic ideal. The amount of Corsican spoken by the children during the filming was in fact a dramatic contrast with everyday practice. In the transcript above, both the teacher and Julie use Corsican only. Another student, Pasqua, is notable for his extraordinary effort to contribute in Corsican. We see this on lines 21 and 55 where his struggle to express himself in Corsican can be seen in his hesitations and pauses while he searches for words. This struggle frames his use of French starting on line 59 as a last resort. This effort is implicitly recognized by the teacher in two places. On line 32 she says 'Pasqua doesn't speak much, eh?', which implies that he *usually* doesn't, but is trying to on this occasion. A few minutes later in the meeting (not seen on this transcript) the teacher encourages him to continue speaking in Corsican by using a diminutive and affectionate form of address. Particularly given the fact that Pasqua is one of the older children in the class, this use of the diminutive can be seen as exceptional encouragement acknowledging an exceptional effort.

As a frame for the children's linguistic production, then, the television broadcast translated into an imperative to speak as much Corsican as possible and to only use French as a last resort. For some of the children, like Pasqua, this meant making an extra effort to mobilize his ability to speak Corsican – something he often did not do under ordinary circumstances. For other children who were more shy or who were less confident in Corsican, the challenge of speaking in front of a TV camera (and a potential future audience) in Corsican was too daunting, and they remained silent during the filming. It is significant that the children, without being told to do so, performed being bilingual through monolingual practice.

If we turn to the teachers, being filmed for television also framed their everyday teaching practice as performance. With respect to their teaching roles, being recorded did *not* change the way the teachers distributed their use of French and Corsican across the weekly curriculum; they in no way avoided doing lessons in French. However, the teacher who was filmed in the television cooperative meeting did reduce her habitual use of codeswitching, adapting the TV frame by creating a more homogenous and 'pure' discursive space for Corsican. The teacher of the younger children did not change her practice in front of the classroom at all. However, both she and her colleague used Corsican exclusively when they were interviewed in front of the camera about aspects of their practice. The following is an extract from one clip that appeared in the final documentary in which the teacher of the younger children engaged in an explicit discourse about bilingual education for public consumption:

Secondu mè, l'insignamentu bislingu copre una nuzione chì hè assai
più larga ch'insignamentu. Si parlerebbe piutostu d'educazione bislingua. Dunque, quandu si parla d'educazione bislingua, vogliu dì, vogliu
dì chì i dui codici ghjuveranu à custruì una persona.

In my view, bilingual teaching covers a concept that is much wider
than just teaching. It would be better to call it a bilingual education.
Thus, when we're talking about bilingual education, what I want to
say is that the two codes will function to construct a single person.

In one sense, the exclusive use of Corsican in this and all the other filmed
interviews was not a break with these teachers' professional practice: both of
them had extensive experience in writing and speaking about theoretical
aspects of bilingual pedagogy in Corsican. However, in their everyday professional practice – talking with other teachers, talking with pedagogical coun-
sellors, participating in continuing education courses – they engaged in a
bilingual discourse about bilingualism. In other words, the choice to use Corsican to discuss pedagogy was not induced by the media frame, but the choice
to exclude the possibility of using French was.

8.4.3 The professional selection process: media as a filter for representations of Corsican

The media frame, then, shaped both teachers' and students' orientation
towards a monolingual Corsican norm. This orientation was even more pro-
nounced in the choices made by the television producer, both in the selection
of activities and practices to film, and the further selection and manipulation
of recorded data that appeared in the final programme.

First, if we look at the collection of video data, the TV crew took a great
deal of footage throughout the week, capturing children and parents arriving
at school, a variety of classes, the playground and the lunch room. It was
clear, however, that inside the classroom, their priority was to film Corsican-
language activities. So, for example, a Corsican maths lesson was recorded,
but there were no recordings of maths lessons in French, and in this school,
maths was done almost equally in both languages. During the week, the crew
did film one recording of a 'pre-reading' lesson in French with five- and six-
year-olds, and segments of this lesson appeared in the final programme.
However, the selection of this sequence and the emphasis in the final narration was on the teacher's switching into Corsican, and on her comments
about the values of biliteracy. In contrast, there was no filming at all of the
older children's French literacy work, which was done in French with little
or no codeswitching into Corsican.

We can also see a clear ideological orientation at work in the final documentary, which is the result of the producer's selection and composition
of sound and images from all of the film 'rushes' together with the addition of

voice-over narration, texts and other visuals. First, there is the introductory voice-over, in which the narrator says:

> A lingua corsa, si sa chì ùn hè quasi più imparata indè e famiglie. Ferma a scola. Quì si vede chì mittendu i mesi è a vulinta, l'imparera pò esse efficace è sfaticata. A scola bislingua di a Riventosa hè un bellu esempiu di ciò chì si pò fà.

> The Corsican language: everyone knows that almost no children learn it any more in the home. Only the school is left. Here, you'll see that with the right resources and will, its instruction can be efficient and easy. The bilingual school of Riventosa is a good example of what can be done.

Here, the school is clearly identified as being a success story. That success is defined solely in terms of Corsican language outcomes: the extent to which the school has been able to take over lapsed intergenerational transmission of Corsican. The focus is thus on the bilingual *individual* as a product of schooling, rather than on bilingual practice as a central element of pedagogical practice or social interaction. It is this emphasis that helps to explain the monolingual bias of the programme: given the fact that all schoolchildren in Corsica speak French, demonstrating their bilingualness demands maximal use of Corsican; something the children's own performance acknowledged.

8.4.3.1 Emphasis on literacy

The second thing of note in the final programme is the emphasis on and representation of literacy. Some of the very first images that appear in the documentary, even before the introductory narration include a five-year-old girl writing in her notebook. Her teacher takes up a stance behind the student's back, reaches around her and positions the child's supporting hand on the desk and her writing hand on the page. This is followed by a close-up of a girl writing in her notebook: the viewer can see the individual letters of Corsican words. Viewers then see a head shot of small boy (age four or five) smiling and holding a pen and paper. A child's voice-over narrates in Corsican:

> Datemi un fogliu ancu, è datemi una penna.
> Vogliu scrive u mo nome, d'induve ne sò è di quale ne sò.
> Datemi un fogliu; vogliu risponde anch'eiu.

> *Give me a piece of paper too, and give me a pen.*
> *I want to write my name, where I am from and who is my family.*
> *Give me a piece of paper; I too want to respond.*

A teacher's voice then fades in, giving instructions in Corsican about forming letters: 'it goes up, then drops below the bottom line. A straight line, a curve, and the accent ...'. The title of the show then appears, written in cursive on a graphic depiction of a child's notebook. As the cursive letters form on screen, the teacher's voice is heard behind, again narrating how to form letters.

The emphasis on literacy is related to the shared role of the media and the school as agents of minority language legitimation, since literacy is both a high-status school practice, and because literacy is a powerful embodiment of linguistic authority. The media representations of literacy project two contrasting images of Corsican literacy in the bilingual school. Consider the visual focus on the act of inscription – the images of cursive writing by the children in the school, and in the titling of the programme. We can interpret this focus of the camera's eye in two ways; both are relevant to the functions of the broadcast with respect to the representation of Corsican language literacy. The starting point is of course that a close-up shot insists that the viewer pay attention to a particular thing being filmed; it defines the subject of the shot as interesting. In some cases, things that are camera-worthy/interesting are framed as novelties: the camera's eye simulates a moment of visual discovery for the viewer by 'stopping to look' at a curiosity. At the same time, in so far as the documentary makes a claim to represent habitual practice, there is also an implicit claim that the material depicted is a representative sample of what the filmmakers observed as 'routine'. But in the documentary of the school, where depicted practices are understood to be routinized and habitual, I think that the focus on writing – and even the choice of the French literacy sequence where Corsican was used – carried both kinds of representational weight. The exoticness of Corsican literacy helped to drive home the message of the school's success whilst the routineness of it encouraged viewers to understand Corsican school practice as 'normal'. These two representational axes thus met language planning goals of normalizing Corsican as a legitimate language in the public eye.

At the same time, the documentary introduced an element of affective identification in its carefully managed representation of the diminutive writer mentioned above. The pairing of the child's voice-over saying 'Give me a paper ...' with a picture of smiling boy invites the viewer to hear the lines as words said by an eager learner. What the viewers could not know, however, is that the child's voice-over was not spoken spontaneously by the actual child depicted, but rather, was rehearsed and recited by one of the older children in the classroom, who was a good Corsican speaker. As a representational strategy, the voice-over conflates the conversational roles of animator, author and principle, indirectly attributing both a homogenous set of literacy orientations and a homogenous set of Corsican language competencies to all of the children in the class. The choice of the older child narrator and the use of a rehearsed discourse thus subtly masks the varying levels of Corsican competence among the children in the classroom that were quite obvious to the documentary producer.

8.4.3.2 Language as a filter for selection of final segments: French filtered out

We can see similar representational strategies in other parts of the programme that filtered out both the children's use of French, and variation in
different children's choice and ability to use Corsican. This is not to say that
the producer edited out *all* instances of children speaking French in the classroom, but a great deal more French language use was recorded than was ultimately used. One example of this can be seen in the depiction of children's
recreational activity during a physical education lesson and on the playground. The PE lesson in the documentary shows the teacher conducting an
adult-directed activity: the teacher gave directions, asked the children to
repeat them back, and then gave them verbal commands to race to pick up
objects and to place them inside or outside plastic hula hoops. For the most
part, then, the activity was heavily scaffolded and structured by the teacher,
involved receptive language skills, and used structures that were very familiar to the children and maximized their ability to respond in Corsican. The
children who were selected to answer open questions on camera ('how
many hula hoops do we need?') were also among the most competent, and
the linguistic demands placed on them relatively limited. The overall picture
of competence displayed by this footage was an accurate depiction of the children's collective, receptive competence in Corsican. Like the voice-over, however, it was a subtle over-representation of the children's productive
competence in that language.

The second segment in the documentary involving children on the playground was one of the programme's closing sequences. It showed the very
smallest children exiting the school to go out on the playground. The camera
panned and then zoomed in on a group of girls giggling in a corner; as the
camera closed in on them, they broke into a rendition of a Corsican language
song that they had sung countless times. As in the PE sequence and the child's
voice-over discussed above, highly scripted oral performances stand in, in this
segment, for spontaneous use of Corsican. This spontaneity is indirectly
indexed, in the playground scene, by the casual setting, 'outside' formal
school activities, where children's language choice is presumably unfettered.
This was in fact true of playground talk in this bilingual school, but in the
absence of any constraints, children almost always chose to speak in French
during outside play. The girls' choice to sing when approached by the camera
may have been a spontaneous choice, but its inclusion as the sole representation of playground language was a highly selective misrepresentation of overall patterns of spontaneous language choice.

The girls' song is followed by a screen with the following quotation from
the linguist Claude Hagège, which ends the programme:

> Les unilingues de l'Europe de demain risquent d'apparaître comme des
> sinistrés de la parole. Les multilingues seront, au contraire, le ciment du

monde. Comment refuser de donner aux écoliers, dès les premières années, en y introduisant le bilinguisme, ce surcroît d'humanité qui fait tout l'enchantement de l'enfant à deux langues?

Monolinguals in the Europe of tomorrow risk being viewed as linguistically damaged. Multilinguals, on the contrary, will be the cement of the world. How can we refuse to introduce bilingualism from the very earliest years of school and in doing so, to give our schoolchildren that extra measure of humanity that makes the bilingual child so enchanting? (1996)

This retroactively frames the girls' use of Corsican song – and in fact all of the depictions of children in the documentary, as examples of bilingualism, implicitly understood to be balanced.

8.5 Conclusions

Here, I would like to return to the issue of how the broadcast media act as a frame for minority language practice and representation on Corsica. On the one hand, it is clear that in this particular context of language shift and revitalization, the broadcast media can be a vector for conservative, dominant language ideologies because of the role of legitimation these media inevitably play. That is, because using Corsican is conceived of as a way of upsetting the diglossic model and displacing the hold of French on public space, criteria of legitimacy tend to be framed in dominant terms. Specifically, we see media practices and representations in more 'formal' genres advancing a monolingual, purist Corsican norm. This appears in (albeit inconsistent) efforts to purge Corsican news language of French and French influences as well as in listeners' convictions that there are illegitimate gallicisms to be found in news language. In the documentary on the bilingual school, we have seen how the combined effects of children's and teachers' language choices and the television producer's editorial process conspired to edge French out of the final product and to over-represent children's Corsican language use and competence. Ultimately, this represented the bilingual school as a site of two coexisting monolingualisms. This contrasted both with practices in the school, and with the teachers' explicit commentary on the documentary, in which they talked about the integration of identities in the bilingual individual, and about the bilingual practice in the school as a social and ideological choice rather than just a means by which Corsican speakers could be produced. In this rather pluralistic model, one did not have to have perfect competence to participate as a bilingual, nor did one have to strictly separate the two languages in practice.

Given the French dominance of most Corsican schoolchildren, and the historical dominance of French within the school system, we can understand the Corsican monolingual bias of the documentary in political terms: as a discursive counterweight to the French monolingual norm that dominated public institutions until very recently. The intense focus in the documentary on the use of Corsican in high-status school activities like maths and literacy was a way of maximizing broadcast time to make public, and potentially normalize something that the public did not take for granted: the use of Corsican as an academic register.

Despite the monolingual bias of the representations of practice in the final documentary, the programme did not exclude the plural perspective on bilingual identity and practice that the two teachers promoted in their on-air discourse about practice. Nor did it exclude the French literacy sequence in which the teacher used Corsican to teach French reading. This broadcasted a practice that constitutes a significant break with the overall 'Corsican-only', monolingual representation of the school and illustrated the explicit message that the teachers pushed in every interview opportunity: that bilingual education was very much about validating two or more languages in the life of the individual, and multiple forms of identification and citizenship.

In this respect, the documentary was the vehicle for both a monolingual and a plurilingual ideology. We can see the same dual focus in Corsican radio broadcasting practices. Here, it is clear that the broadcast media represent a vibrant and dynamic marketplace for diverse linguistic forms and practices that include both the 'pure' and 'mixed'. Moreover, the media's vocation to inform and entertain can be contrasted with the school as a site of minority language revitalization. Even though language choice and linguistic form in the media are subject to scrutiny in minority language contexts like Corsica, we have seen that there are modes of audience reception in which issues of form do not take centre stage. In contrast, the issue of norms and standards is never far away in educational contexts. We get a glimpse of this range of evaluative modes and sensibilities in the audience response data mentioned above. Even listening to the 'pure' and formal end of the spectrum of Corsican broadcast genres gives rise to a wide variety of reactions; ranging from acceptance to rejection of neologisms, 'gallicisms' and the inclusion of French or other-language terminology.

Informal programming and broadcast performances also project into the shared, public sphere the full and complex range of linguistic productions, performances and interactions that take place in contexts of language shift and revitalization. This range incorporates multiple forms of variation in both dominant and minority languages, as well as patterns of mixing and switching and interactional language choice. It includes moments in which speakers orient towards more or less monolingual or plurilingual norms, as well as instances of 'stylization' in which speakers self-consciously deploy socially significant elements of the shared sociolinguistic repertoire for a variety of expressive and interactional purposes. As Nik Coupland points out, 'cultural reproduction is nowadays linked to mass-mediated representations and performances' (2001a: 31). Media practices – including stylization – both reflect and feed back into 'everyday talk' (see also Spitulnik 1996).

In this respect, the accumulation of broadcast practice in Corsican, both for producers and consumers, may also influence popular understandings of, and expectations related to, genre and register. At the time that I did my audience research, it was clear that the people I interviewed evaluated the news using the same criteria of authority, acceptability and authenticity that they would apply to any other speech domain. For example, there was quite a lot of discussion of prosody, and respondents claimed that the stress patterns of Corsican news language did not 'sound right'. There were also some direct and indirect references in interviews to the 'over'-nominalization of newscasts, which some more linguistically oriented interviewees contrasted with a 'verbal bias' in Corsican. This compares with the way that people hear and evaluate the language of the news in dominant languages, where they take for granted differences between their prosody and sentence structure and the way that people speak in casual conversation. Over time, then, Corsican broadcast media may help to differentiate registers of Corsican – and hence to develop differentiated criteria of linguistic evaluation – in the public ear.

These perspectives show that the media's involvement in the public construction of languages both comforts and resists dominant language ideologies that link bounded speech communities with equally homogenous linguistic codes. Broadcast media also target, construct and invoke multiple linguistic 'publics', imagined in more or less homogenous ways. Finally, those publics are not simply passive subjects of media representations of language, but play a more or less active role in processes of self-representation and critical evaluation of media language.

9 'When Hector met Tom Cruise': attitudes to Irish in a radio satire

Helen Kelly-Holmes and David Atkinson

9.1 Introduction

The popular Irish television presenter Hector Ó hEochagáin is often credited with increased television viewing figures for Irish language programmes among second-language speakers and for challenging the traditional media boundaries within which the language operates in Ireland. Testimony to his popularity is the fact that he is among a number of public figures parodied in the satirical 'Gift Grub' sketches that feature on Today FM, a national commercial radio station. The focus of this study is an episode of 'Gift Grub' involving a fictional meeting between Hector and Hollywood actor Tom Cruise, which relies for its success on common attitudes to the Irish language in Ireland and on the interplay of both inferiority and superiority complexes in relation to the language.

The chapter begins with an overview of the presence of Irish in the broadcast media in Ireland, with reference to two distinct but related aspects: first of all, the use of the language in the media, and secondly the presence of Irish as a topic in the media, particularly in relation to the attitudinal aspect. The 'Gift Grub' radio satire sketches will then be discussed before the episode of Hector's fictional encounter with Tom Cruise is presented and analysed.

9.2 Irish as a medium[1]

Mass media are a particularly volatile domain for [...] battles over representation, because of their high visibility and because of the inherent publicity function. As mass media build the communicative space of the nation-state, all of the nation's languages, dialects, and language varieties, and the speech communities associated with them are automatically drawn into relations with one another. (Spitulnik 1998: 106)

The 'communicative space' created by the Irish broadcast media both reflects and reinforces a complex sociolinguistic situation.[2] It is a context in which one and the same language can at times be privileged and dominant while at other times marginalized. Despite the constitutional status of Irish as the first official language, English is the dominant media language in Ireland. There are two dedicated Irish-language channels, one is a radio channel, *Raidió na Gaeltachta*, which is primarily aimed at first-language speakers living in the Irish-speaking *Gaeltacht* areas and which was set up in 1972 as a result of a linguistic human rights campaign. *Raidió na Gaeltachta* has something of a reputation for 'linguistic purism'. For example, it is only in recent years that the station has relaxed its recruitment policies in relation to language. Previously only L1 Irish speakers were employed. However in recent years fluent second-language speakers have also been recruited, although they still seem to constitute a minority. In terms of general content, the station is predominantly focused on serving the needs of people living in the Irish-speaking areas (the *Gaeltacht*), providing news as well as current affairs and community programming. Outside of the *Gaeltacht*, an Irish-language community radio station, *Raidió na Life*, also operates in Dublin (cf. Cotter 1999 and 2001b, for a discussion of these issues).

Raidió na Gaeltachta's content, language policies and audience are quite different to those of the other Irish-language channel, TG4, which is a television station. *Teilifís na Gaeilge* was established in 1996, but was relaunched as *Teilifís na Gaeilge 4* or TG4 in 1998, in an attempt to reposition itself as the fourth national television channel. Although described as an Irish-language channel, it is really only during children's television time and during evening prime time viewing that Irish is the sole language. At other times English programmes are shown. In addition, most Irish-language programmes on the channel, including the very popular soap opera, *Ros na Rún*,[3] provide English-language subtitles. One of the stars of TG4 is undoubtedly Hector Ó hEochagàin, whose programmes primarily target L2 speakers (see below).

Apart from these two channels, all of the other media broadcast in English, but have some content in Irish to varying degrees. For example, the first national state radio and television channels (RTÉ 1 and RTÉ Radio 1) broadcast news and current affairs plus some continuity announcements in Irish. The Irish-language content then decreases along a continuum from public to private sector stations. For example, the private national radio station, Today FM, broadcasts 30-second vignettes in Irish entitled *Creid é nó ná creid* ('believe it or not'), but not much else. It is worth noting that the provision of some Irish-language content is a condition for the awarding of a broadcasting licence for all of these private stations. However, the Minister for Communications is not seen publicly to penalize or even criticize these channels for failing to live up to their commitment to the Irish language.

A recent study of attitudes to Irish-language radio programming (MORI, 2005) identified the following five groups, who illustrate well the complexity of attitudes to the Irish language in the media in general:

- 'core Irish audience' (14%);
- 'conforming conservatives' (25%), who are 'keen on the concept of listening to Irish language programmes' but 'less eager to actually avail of these services';
- 'open-minded bilingualists' (27%), who are L2 speakers with a higher than average level of Irish and of education in general. They will listen to Irish language programmes if the content is of interest;
- 'disengaged rejecters' (12%), who represent the 'Irish is a waste of money' type argument (see below), and do not feel that Irish-language programming should be promoted or supported.

One final group is of particular interest to this current study: a cohort identified as 'generation Hector' (22%). They are younger than the conforming conservatives, their Irish is not as good as the open-minded bilinguals, and they are also less likely than this latter group to watch/listen to Irish-language programmes, but they are probably more likely than the conforming conservatives to watch Irish-language programmes and do see a need for them. The group is named in honour of Hector Ó hEochagáin, who is credited, in some circles, with popularizing Irish and improving attitudes to the language through his media presence. Significantly, Hector is an L2 speaker from Navan (not from the *Gaeltacht*), who has been criticized for using Irish in a non-L1 and even far from perfect way. He uses a high degree of code-mixing and English loan words in his Irish, and in a media context in which viewers are used to the 'native speaker' model, his approach is certainly a challenge to established norms of Irish-language broadcasting. In fact, one of the recommendations of the MORI poll mentioned above was that Irish-language programming should 'reflect the heterogeneity of Irish language radio listeners, who are not necessarily proficient Irish speakers nor are they necessarily involved in Irish language activities' (MORI, 2005; (cf. Jaffe's discussion of the Corsican context, Chapter 8, this volume).

A significant point worth making in the context of the presence of Irish in the broadcast media, is that although Hector presents programmes on both the Irish-language television channel, TG4, and on the main national station, RTÉ 1, it is inconceivable to think of him presenting programmes on the all-Irish radio channel, *Raidió na Gaeltachta*, which, as mentioned above, still has a reputation for linguistic 'purity', and which does not appeal to non-fluent L2 listeners of the kind described in the MORI study. Nevertheless, or maybe even because of this, Hector's irreverent brand of codeswitching, his highly accented Irish-English slang and his own particular idiom are very successful.

He has become not only a popular media celebrity, but also a powerful media brand himself, endorsing advertisements for whiskey and horse racing, and attracting sponsorship from international brands such as Vodafone.

9.3 Irish as a topic

Despite the relatively fragile presence of Irish on the broadcast media outlined here, the Irish language is frequently the subject of media debates in Ireland. A recent media event serves to illustrate this and to highlight the prevailing ideologies about Irish that are both reflected by and reflective of the role of Irish in the broadcast media.[4] Despite extensive status planning for Irish, something that is generally considered to have a positive effect on language attitudes (see, for example, Woolard and Gahng 1990), Enda Kenny, leader of the main opposition party in Ireland, recently called for a reversal of compulsory Irish in school, articulating the fairly common perception that this is having a detrimental effect on the language, and urged that Irish should become optional in post-16 education:

> As one who speaks Irish, I believe we must acknowledge that our language is in trouble. [. . .] Compulsion is a blunt tool. Forcing students to learn Irish is not working, and is actually driving many young people away from any real engagement with this beautiful language. After the Junior Certificate, young people should have a choice whether they continue to learn Irish. Those who decide to continue will share classes with those who want to be there, learning Irish, rather than those who wish they were somewhere else, learning something else. (Fine Gael 2005).

His speech was widely reported, and, as is generally the case with any statement to do with the Irish language, caused a minor media storm, with the president of *Conradh na Gaeilge*, the Irish language learning association for adults, claiming that the proposal would 'diminish the status of the language in the eyes of pupils' (O'Neill 2005). In a similar vein, Ciarán Mac Fhearghusa, Chairperson of *Na Gaeil Óga*, 'the Irish language pressure group, set up to promote Irish among young people' responded as follows:

> The Irish government is looking at improving the maths curriculum, fixing problems rather than doing away with the subject altogether – why can't Fine Gael adopt the same positive and innovative approach to Irish – the ancient and native language of Ireland and its most precious and unique cultural asset? (Ó hAdhmaill 2005)

Pat Carey, a TD or member of parliament for the governing Fianna Fáil Party, called upon the Labour Party and the Greens to 'stand by their native language and support the protest against Fine Gael's plans to downgrade the Irish language' (Fianna Fáil 2005). His words were as follows:

> As one of the many people throughout the country who wish they were fluent in our native tongue and as a former teacher myself I believe there is an arguable case for changing the way Irish is taught, with perhaps a greater emphasis on the spoken form. However, removing our own language as a compulsory subject is not an option. (Fianna Fáil 2005)

Contained within the lines of these few brief press statements is the complexity of attitudes to and ideologies of Irish. A pattern emerges in the comments and this is reflected elsewhere in media discussions of Irish. This 'pattern' of attitudes and ideologies is best described in terms of two continua: the first relates to competence in the language; the second to status, concerning the role and importance of Irish in the world. These two continua, which are constructed and reinforced by media discourse about Irish, run between two extremes of superiority and inferiority. For example, Enda Kenny places himself firmly at the superiority end of the *competence* continuum with his statement, 'As one who speaks Irish'. The fact is that anyone who has gone through the Irish education system from start to finish speaks Irish to some degree. However, to make this statement in the context of the Irish sociolinguistic situation is actually to make a claim that one speaks it well, fluently in fact. The learned behaviour is that to 'speak Irish' means to speak it properly or not at all (something that will be discussed below). Here, Enda Kenny is in fact aligning himself with the Irish language élite, while, Pat Carey, on the other hand, is aligning himself with the majority of the population, situated towards the inferiority end of the continuum, who claim not to be able to speak Irish 'properly', 'one of the many people throughout the country who wish they were fluent'.

As regards *status*, all of the statements, both for and against compulsory Irish, situate their authors at the superiority end of this attitudinal continuum about the place of Irish in the world together with its role and status within Ireland: it is 'our language', 'our own language', 'the ancient and native language of Ireland and its most precious and unique cultural asset', 'our native tongue' and 'this beautiful language'. Here we see the symbolic role of Irish (Edwards 1985), which makes 'us' what 'we' are, different to 'them' (primarily the British). This identification aspect is a common feature in bilingual and/or diglossic situations, whereby the minoritized language performs an integrative function, while the dominant language fulfils the instrumental role (cf. Ros-I-Garcia 1984; Dorian 1999; May 2003b).

Only Enda Kenny moves towards the inferiority end of the status continuum by alluding to the fact that not all pupils want to learn Irish, that they might prefer to 'be somewhere else, learning something else'. He is, we would argue, able to do this because he has not only claimed superiority for the language, but also for himself as a fluent speaker. The discourse of 'Irish as a waste of time' and as 'a language of no relevance in the world' is not a new one, having its origins in post-famine nineteenth-century Ireland, and persisting to this day. For instance, in his recent autobiography, acclaimed Irish writer John MacGahern, writing about his schooling in the 1940s, articulated the following view:

> a great many school hours were wasted on the teaching of Irish, to the neglect of other subjects, at a time when most of the children would have to emigrate to Britain or America to find work in factories or on building sites or as domestics. (MacGahern 2005: 9).

Many media controversies highlight this attitude. For example, in an article entitled 'Irish speakers forced "as gaeilge" number plates', readers are told that 'Irish speakers' (in other words Irish-language enthusiasts) have pushed through Irish-language registration plates. The article comments that:

> The minister responsible for road traffic has said that motorists are forced to display Irish lettering on registration number-plates because of a Government-brokered deal with Irish-language devotees. [. . .] The junior transport minister added that he could see why many people thought the situation was 'farcical'. (Williams 2003).

The 'number plates' controversy highlights this perception that Irish is unnecessary – and even incompatible with – modern life. Another indicator of this is the fact that the Health and Safety Authority has recently introduced radio advertisements highlighting the need for workers to be aware of health and safety regulations and their own rights on construction sites. The advertisements are in English, Polish and Turkish, the latter two language options reflecting recent migration by workers from Poland and Turkey to Ireland, but there is no advertisement in Irish. The choice of languages seems a reflection of the utility argument in relation to Irish, the commonsense notion that it is not necessary, since Irish speakers can speak English anyway. Ads in English, Polish and Turkish are necessary to save lives (cf. HSA, 2005); ads in Irish would only waste money, like school hours. The superiority/inferiority continuum in relation to the status and functions of Irish is also often expressed in terms of a living/dying dichotomy, as for example, in the following report in *The Kingdom* newspaper about a survey of intergenerational transmission of Irish in *Gaeltacht* areas: 'The study highlighted the importance of the role of the parents in promoting the native language and passing it on to their children as a living modern language' (*The Kingdom*, 2003).

What is most interesting about the media coverage of Irish as a topic is the conformity of attitudes and the pattern in which they are presented. There is more often than not a declaration in relation to competence, if an individual is making a statement, followed by some claim in relation to the status of Irish and its role in the world. In the next section we will explore the extent to which this pattern is reflected in another media product, although of a very different nature, a satirical sketch.

9.4 'When Hector met Tom Cruise'

Hector Ó hEochagáin is not only a successful media personality himself, he is also, as mentioned earlier, among a number of public figures satirized in 'Gift Grub',[5] an early morning sketch on national commercial radio station Today FM. 'Gift Grub', the Today FM website boasts, 'is an essential mood booster for dark winter mornings' (Today FM, 2005), and listeners are urged to 'tune in every morning at 8:10 am to hear the latest adventures of Bertie and his friends Roy, Michael D, Johnson . . .' (Today FM, 2005). The Bertie mentioned here is Irish *Taoiseach* (or prime minister) Bertie Ahern, Roy is the internationally known Irish football player Roy Keane, Johnson is his brother, and Michael D. is the colourful Labour Party TD (member of parliament), poet, Irish speaker and intellectual Michael D. Higgins. As would be expected with radio satire, language and accent are key factors in the construction of characters, relying on the fact that 'people perceive, and react to, sensory input on the basis of various types of social, often stereotypical, filters' (Edwards 1999: 107). For example, Roy Keane's mixed Cork-Manchester accent and Bertie Ahern's Northside Dublin accent are hyperbolized in the sketches.

An additional aspect to 'Gift Grub' is the use of Irish, which is employed to construct characters in a number of different ways. For example, former Minister for Education Mary O'Rourke, herself a former schoolteacher, is featured in one sketch calling out the register in the *Dáil* (Irish parliament) in Irish, and the language choices of the characters responding help to construct their characters, and Mícheál Martin, considered in general to be a politician free of corruption and less cynical than the average politician, answers in Irish, unlike his colleagues. Furthermore, Irish is used to construct Michael D. Higgins, referred to above, as a cultural artefact. In addition, the Irish language is sometimes featured as a theme in itself. For example, Roy Keane's character, who regularly hosts a quiz, held it in Irish during *Seachtain na Gaeilge* (Irish language week), while the Michael D. Higgins character hosted an Irish-language version of the British television quiz show 'Never mind the Buzzcocks' (*Ná bac leis na Buzzcocks*).

The character of Hector, a parody of Hector Ó hEochagáin, features regularly in the Gift Grub sketches, and the primary way in which his character is constructed is through a hyperbolizing of his characteristic codeswitching. The sketch of interest in this study features a fictional meeting between Hector and Hollywood actor Tom Cruise. The sketch relies on the audience's knowledge of the English-medium prime-time television show 'Hanging with Hector', in which the real-life Hector 'hangs' with celebrities, and in this fictional episode of the series Hector gets to 'hang' with Hollywood actor Tom Cruise. The sketch is rich in various linguistic features, for example, Hector's use of English is also key in constructing his character and equally reflects attitudes to accents and slang. As Rachel Hoare (2001) has pointed out in relation to the Breton context, Breton-accented French plays an equally important role to Breton itself in constructing group identity, and the same can be said of English with an Irish accent. However, for the purposes of the study, the focus of attention here is the character's use of Irish and its relationship to attitudes to Irish. The sketch is too long to reproduce in full here, so we have selected four excerpts for the purpose of analysis. The first is the introductory section, with the Hector character setting the scene for his audience by driving a New York yellow taxi on his way to meet the Tom Cruise character. The Irish-language lexical items and constructions are transcribed in block capitals and an English-language translation is given on the line beneath. Hector is the only speaker in this opening sequence.

Excerpt 1: Opening sequence

1. **Howya folks**	**Hector here**	**TÁ ME**	**Completely**	**AS MO BHOSCA**
		I'm		out of my box
2. **MAR**	**TÁ MÉ**	**ANOIS I**	**New York City**	**LÁR Apple MÓR**
2. Because	I'm	now in		centre Apple big
3. **TÁ SÉ**	**great craic**	**altogether**	**AGUS FÉACH**	**scobers**
3. It's	great fun		And, look	
4. **TÁ MÉ**	**AG TOMÁINT**	**me own**	**yellow taxi.**	
4. I'm	driving			
5. **Hector's**	**taxi BUÍ.**			
5.	yellow taxi			
6. **AGUS today**	**and this is**	**massive**	**Folks**	
6. And				
7. **BEIDH**	**Hector gonna**	**be**	**hangin'**	**LE Tom Cruise**
7. Will be				with Tom Cruise
8. **Star**	**MÓR INS AN**	**Hollywood**		
8	big in			
9. **TOMÁS**	**CÁ BHFUIL SÉ**	**chiefy?**		
9.	Where is it?			

The hyperbolized code-mixing (for example in lines 1, 3 and 4) and the 'nonsense' calques (for example, 'Centre Apple Big' in line 2) created by the Hector character serve a number of functions. First of all, they contribute to the construction of his character in a medium that is entirely based on aural perception. As John Joseph (2004: 25) has pointed out 'all of us instinctively make

[...] decisions about the people with whom we come into contact largely on the basis of their language – indeed, wholly on that basis if the communication is by telephone or email or some other form of writing', or in this case some other form of hearing, namely radio. Furthermore, in bilingual and/or diglossic situations, speaker language has been found to 'strongly affect perception of speakers' character, status and education level' (Bentahila 1983). However, the codeswitching here serves a wider function than simply constructing and identifying Hector, and that function of course has to do with the real Hector's role and place in the 'communicative space' afforded to Irish in the linguistic hierarchy of national broadcasting in Ireland, something we will discuss in more detail below.

In the second excerpt transcribed below, Tom Cruise is talking about his work with fellow Hollywood actor Dustin Hoffman, whom he refers to simply as Dustin. However Hector is confused about this and thinks that Tom Cruise is talking about Dustin, the well-known turkey from Irish children's television in Ireland and media personality in his own right. Tom clarifies by naming the film he and Dustin Hoffman worked on (*Rain Man*), and Hector proceeds to 'translate' the title literally into Irish (in line 6) as 'man raining', providing another source of amusement for the audience:

Excerpt 2: Rain Man/Man Raining

1. **Hector:**	**FAN NOIMÉAD**	**TOMÁS**	**TÁ MÉ**		**confused.**
1.	Wait a minute	Tom	I'm		
2. **Hector:**	**CÉN SORT**	**film LE**	**Dustin?**		
2.	What sort of	film with			
3. **Tom:**	**Rain Man**				
4. **Hector:**	**Ah, Rain Man**				
5. **Tom:**	**Great movie.**				
6. **Hector:**	**SEA, SEA, SEA**	**FEAR AG**	**CUR BÁISTÍ.**		
6.	Yes, yes, yes	Man	raining		

In the third excerpt, the integrating function of Irish is employed as a means of ridiculing Tom Cruise. Here we see the superiority attitude being called into play, whereby Cruise is constructed as an outsider because he does not understand Irish. The excerpt begins with Hector flattering Tom about his teeth, using the Irish word *fiacla*, which Tom does not understand. By way of explanation, Hector offers a number of Irish-English slang synonyms, further reinforcing Tom's outgroup status. Finally, language itself becomes a theme in the discussion. Hector is criticizing Tom Cruise's Irish accent in the film *Far and Away*, a saga about Irish emigrants in America set in the nineteenth century. (It is worth noting that Cruise's accent was widely mocked in

Irish media circles and in critical reviews of the film at the time.) However, because Hector uses both Irish-English slang ('cack') and Irish-language words (*liathróidí*) contained within Irish-language constructions (lines 10, 11, and 13), Cruise does not understand and assumes that Hector is in fact praising him:

Excerpt 3: Far and Away

1. Hector:	You've a fine	set of FIACLA	on you,	TOMÁS
1.		set of teeth		Tom
2. Tom:	What d'you say,	'FIACLA'?		
		teeth		
3. Hector:	FIACLA			
4. Tom	What does that	mean?		
5. Hector	Gnashers,	chops, laughin'	gear,	bosco.
6. Tom:	That's like eh	Gaelic again?	Huh?	
7. Hector:	Magic carpets.	Far and away,	TOMÁS.	
8. Tom:	Great movie.			
9. Hector:	That's a	fantastic	SCANNÁIN,	TOMÁS.
9.			film	
10. Hector:	AGUS DO	accent ...		
10.	And, your			
11. Tom:	My accent?	In Far and Away?		
12. Hector:	DO accent,	BHÍ SÉ	complete cack	TOMÁS
12.	Your accent	it was		
13. Tom:	Really?	Thank you.		
14. Hector:	A load of	LIATHRÓIDÍ	now.	
14.		balls		
15. Tom:	That's real nice	of you to say.		

The use of Irish in the worldly domain of Hollywood is the source of humour in the final extract, whereby Hector translates 'Show me the money', the well-known line from Cruise's film *Jerry Maguire* into Irish. However, this aspect is counterbalanced by the use of Irish to exclude – and even ridicule – Tom Cruise because of his inability to understand Hector's simple Irish (line 2) and his frustrated attempts at pronunciation (line 4). Again, Hector stops short of a complete translation, which would have been *Taispeáin dom an airgead*:

Excerpt 4: Show me the money

1. Hector:	Show me the	money, Hector	AS GAEILGE
1.			in Irish
2. Tom:	What's	AS GAEILGE?	
2.		in Irish?	
3. Hector:	TAISPEÁIN	DOM the	AIRGEAD
3.	Show	me	money
4. Tom:	TAISPEÁIN	DOM the	AIRGEAD
4.	Show	me	money

9.5 Discussion

As Kathryn Woolard points out,

> simply using language in particular ways is not what forms social groups, identities, or relations (nor does the group relation automatically give rise to linguistic distinction); rather, ideological interpretations of such uses of language always mediate these effects. (Woolard 1998a: 18)

In relation to the Hector/Tom Cruise sketch, the ideological interpretations that mediate the comedic effects of the particular use of Irish in this satire[6] are, we would argue, intimately tied up with the competence and status continua that feed an inferiority-superiority complex in relation to Irish in Ireland, which is reflected in and reflective of the role and presence of the language in the media and elsewhere. Significantly, the Hector/Tom Cruise sketch follows the pattern of the media articles and press releases cited earlier, by making statements about competence and status.

9.5.1 Competence and prescriptive attitudes

In terms of competence, Hector's frenzied mixing/switching is used to parody the real Hector Ó hEochagáin's code-mixing style and attempts at communication in less than perfect Irish, something not previously attempted by Irish-language presenters. The extensive codeswitching is humorous because it plays on the feeling of failure many L2 speakers have about the language and their learning experience. The school association is reinforced by Hector's translation of Tom's name into Irish, *Tomás*, since school is one of the few domains – if not the only one – in which this happens. Hector's colourful calques remind the average speaker of their own efforts to search for Irish-language vocabulary in oral exams and classroom situations and their having to resort to English words, something that was frowned upon by language purists. This purism fetish is not uncommon in minority language and revival/revitalization situations (cf. Jaffe, Chapter 8, this volume) since, in the words of Kathryn Woolard (1998a: 18): 'another tenet often clustered with the Herderian ideology in both folk and scientific views demands linguistic purism as essential to the survival of minority languages, and a kind of policing of the boundaries that have been drawn to create distinct linguistic forms'. The illegitimacy of the Irish-English mix was up to recently left unchallenged even though the reality of life in the *Gaeltacht* is in fact bilingual because it was felt that this kind of mixing was a threat to the revival of Irish. Kathryn Woolard (ibid.: 17) makes the point that: 'An equation of change [...] with decay also pervades judgements about the status of languages. Language mixing, codeswitching, and creolization thus make speech varieties particularly vulnerable to folk and prescriptivist evaluation.'

However, as John Edwards (1999: 108) has indicated, the 'culturally relevant stimuli' that inform perceptions of and attitudes to languages can and do change, and while the attitude outlined above, which equates purism with preservation, did persist and does still to a certain extent exist. On the other hand, the metaphors of decay and death are now more often associated with the purists, while mixing has come to be seen as the expression of a 'living' language: 'Some purists are still trying to keep Irish pure but if you're going to speak it as a living language it needs to be more modern' (Fergus Seoighe, principal of a *Gaelscoil*, in Harrison 2005). This revision of prevailing attitudes, as indicated, for example, in the MORI poll discussed above, is quite revolutionary and, in many ways, the real Hector is both a product and producer of this more 'relaxed' attitude. For example, the slogan of *Seachtain na Gaeilge* (Irish language week) in 2005 was a mixed Irish-English one: '*Croí na Teanga*: it's you'. The Irish phrase means 'heart of the language', and the bilingual phrase goes some way to showing people that keeping the language alive can also take place through mixing. The negation of this mixed code is, however, still widespread, as illustrated by the following quotation from a web portal that is intended to give access to links in Irish:

> Anghaeltacht.net concentrates on the sites in which the language is treated as an adult medium. If Irish is the first language or if it receives its rightful position or an honest effort is made to include Irish as a working language, we are happy to include it here. (Foras na Gaeilge, 2005).

The assumption seems to be here that to use Irish in anything other than first place or 'in an honest effort' is not 'adult', something that reinforces the attitude that if you cannot speak fluently you should not try, an attitude that has fed the inferiority-superiority complex. Even though, as the Gift Grub sketches, the MORI study and other examples discussed here highlight, the competence ideology is currently being questioned and revised, the fact that the hyperbolized mixing is such a source of humour in this sketch shows how deep-rooted this particular perception is. Hector is open to parody because he subverts and challenges the competence ideology and because his standard of Irish, as he presents it in the media, is closer to that of an average L2 speaker. Such a person would typically claim not to be able to speak Irish, yet Hector uses this Irish in a media context.

9.5.2 Status in the modern world

Turning to the question of status, the other aspect of the inferiority complex that makes the codeswitching and calques humorous is the commonsense attitude that Irish is an unworldly language, a dying language not a living language, and that it is incompatible with modern life. The translation, then, or attempted translation of words from global media and places that have global media meaning (such as New York, 'The big apple', and its yellow taxis) rather than just local or national meaning is inherently humorous. In fact, this inferiority complex underlines the entire sketch since the idea of a global media personality such as Tom Cruise being 'interviewed' in Irish would seem to most Irish people not just unlikely, but rather ludicrous.

However, the sketch also invokes the other extreme of the status continuum: Irish is still 'our own language', it makes 'us' special, different to 'them', and 'we' are superior because 'we' understand it and 'they' can be laughed at because 'they' do not. While Hector is ridiculed because he does not speak perfect Irish, Tom Cruise is ridiculed because he speaks none at all. In this particular construct, Hector becomes again part of the in-group of not just Irish speakers but Irish people who can understand the language (cf. Horner's discussion of trilingualism in Luxembourg, Chapter 7, this volume).

What is interesting about this invoking of apparently contradictory attitudes towards Irish is the fact that the two ends of the status continuum frequently collocate together in media coverage of Irish. For example: 'While children who attend *Gaelscoils* may have a firm grasp of the native language in reality they have little use for it outside the classroom' (Harrison 2005). In this one sentence from an article about Irish-medium primary schools, or *Gaelscoileanna*, we see the reference to the inherent superiority of Irish as 'the native language', followed immediately by the reference to its lack of utility in the modern world. However, as in the case of the competence issue, attitudes towards the status of Irish are also changing, as evidenced for example in the press coverage of the success of the *Gaelscoileanna* movement and the excellent academic record of Irish medium schools (Flynn and Faller 2005). *Foras na Gaeilge*, a cross-border Irish-language agency, presents the following picture of the changed and changing perception of Irish:

> The image of the Irish language has changed a great deal in recent years [...] Irish was awarded official status within the European Union as a result of sustained public pressure in 2005 [...] TG4 has awoken, or re-awoken, many people's interest in Irish [...] it has one of the youngest staffs of any television station in Europe and this adds to its cool and vibrant image. [...] The Irish language was also associated in the past with rural life and traditional work [...] Who would have imagined twenty years ago, for example, that one could order a cappuccino through the medium of Irish in a modern fashionable café in Dublin. (Foras na Gaeilge, 2005)

Although the text is, not surprisingly, resolutely upbeat, the claims made do in fact reflect a changing reality in relation to Irish. However, again, as in the case of changing perceptions of mixing, this image alteration is far from universal and negative attitudes still exist side by side with positive ones.

9.6 Conclusion

Hector's fictional meeting with Tom Cruise may constitute a very different media genre to the speeches, press releases and reports about Irish in the media. However, the attitudes operationalized and the pattern by which these are presented are remarkably similar. The Irish speaker, in this case Hector, is situated on the competence continuum, and through content and language use his character exploits both extremes of the status continuum, from the notion that Irish is a dead, unworldly language with limited utility to the perception that it is at the heart of Irish identity and essential in defining otherness. Far from being incompatible, both of these ends of the continuum have come to be established as almost necessary in any discussion of Irish in the media, the one counter-balancing the other and providing a check so that a point of view can be mainstreamed, that is, made to seem more reasonable and less extreme. The success of 'When Hector met Tom Cruise' lies in the exploitation of complex and often ambivalent attitudes, not only in the Irish context but in all bilingual and diglossic situations.

Primary sources

Fianna Fáil (2005), 'Lab & Greens must support protest against FG plan to downgrade Irish', *Fianna Fáil Press Releases*, 15.11.05 (available online at www.fiannafail.ie/policy_page.php4?topic=255&id=5130, accessed 20.10.06).

Fine Gael (2005), 'FG Leader outlines reform agenda to energise Irish language', *Fine Gael Press Statements*, 11.11.05 (available online at www.finegael.ie/downloads/Conf.Speeches/enda%20kenny%20-%20irish%20compulsion%20%20111105.doc, accessed 20.10.06)

Flynn, S. and Faller, G. (2005), 'Free schools score highly in third level feeder list', *Irish Times*, 21.11.05 (available online at www.ireland.com/newspaper/front/2005/1121/pf1630273000HM1FEEDER.html, accessed 20.10.06).

Foras na Gaeilge (2005), 'The Irish Language Today' (available online at www.bnag.ie/language/default.asp?catid=16, accessed 20.10.06).

Harrison, M. (2005), 'Making Irish a Living Language', *Western People*, 18.05.05 (available online at www.westernpeople.ie/news/story.asp?j=25432, accessed 20.10.06).

HSA (2005), 'Mind Yer Language for New Safety Push', *Health and Safety Authority of Ireland Press Releases July–December 2005* (available online at www.hsa.ie/publisher/index.jsp?&1nID=427&2nID=427&3nID=427&4nID=427&nID=429&aID=1452, accessed 20.10.06).

The Kingdom (2003), 'Parents vital in promotion of native tongue', *The Kingdom Newspaper*, 16.10.03 (available online at www.the-kingdom.ie/community/story.asp?j=10996, accessed 20.10.06).

Today FM (2005) (available online at www.todayfm.com, accessed 20.10.06).

Williams, E. (2003) 'Irish speakers forced "as gaeilge" number plates', *Sunday Independent*, 23.10.03 (available online at www.unison.ie/irish.independent/stories.php3?ca=9&si=1067620&issue.id=9957, accessed 20.10.06).

Notes

1. For a comprehensive overview of Irish-language broadcasting, see Watson (2003). See also Kelly-Holmes (2001) for a comparison of television in Breton and Irish and a discussion of minority language broadcasting.
2. For a detailed insight into the sociolinguistic situation of Irish, see Hindley (1990); Ó Laoire (1995); Ó Riagáin (1997); Crowley (2005); and Mac Giolla Chríost (2005).
3. The title of the soap opera is the name of the fictional town in the Galway *Gaeltacht*, where it is set.
4. Research on language attitudes in relation to Irish has tended to focus on attitudes of L2 speakers to learning/speaking the language in order to examine the success or otherwise of the revitalization programme that has been in various modes of operation since the Republic gained independence from the UK in 1921 (see, for example, Murtagh 2003). In addition, there have been studies of accent in Irish-English (see, for example, Edwards 1977).
5. We had hoped to interview the writer of the sketches Mario Rosenstock. However, this proved not to be possible.
6. Cf. Jaffe (2000b) and Woolard (1987).

10 Dealing with linguistic difference in encounters with Others on British television

Simon Gieve and Julie Norton

10.1 Introduction

In a recent programme broadcast on BBC4, a UK-based TV channel for 'upmarket' programming, Jonathan Ross, a popular BBC presenter who recently hit the news headlines for his huge salary, was sent to Japan to present an hour-long analysis of contemporary Japanese cinema. Obviously a good deal of time, effort and money went into this production: Ross prowled the streets of Tokyo enthusing about the renaissance of Japanese cinema; he showed us clips from modern Japanese films; and interviewed writers and directors. But since Ross apparently knew no more than a few words of Japanese, how did viewers suppose he communicated with them? In a typical interview he sat across a table with a renowned director, in a room otherwise empty of people; this was an exclusive interview, we were led to understand, not a press conference. As we watched, Ross asked a question in English. The Japanese director responded in Japanese, and a voice-over speaking in Japanese-accented English interpreted for us, not through dubbing over the original – we can just about hear Japanese being spoken – but it was as if we had our own simultaneous interpreter whispering in our ear. Without hesitation Ross asked a follow-up question, and he got an instant response. They appeared to being having a long, thoughtful dialogue, the one in English the other in Japanese. As far as we could see, there was nobody else present at the interview, there were no headphones, wires, ear-pieces, awkward pauses for any unseen interpreter to translate between them, and yet there were no apparent communication difficulties or breakdowns of any kind.

How can we explain the fact that, in a programme dedicated to demonstrating the Otherness of Japanese culture, language has become transparent? Of course, we know that there must have been an interpreter present, that they couldn't have made the programme without one or many linguistic intermediaries setting up interviews, negotiating, translating and interpreting. Why

188

did the producers go to the trouble of erasing all evidence of linguistic difference when they must have gone to enormous trouble to deal with it themselves? The evidence of linguistic difference has not been hidden from us, so why has it been made to appear as if communication across linguistic difference is not difficult, problematic, or even of interest, in a programme in which Tokyo street scenes are lingered over in fascination? There are some simple, obvious, answers: it may be assumed that we don't want to see participants in the programme embarrassed by their struggles to speak in a language they are not fluent in; as an audience we don't want to endure the same delays and awkwardness of communication across linguistic difference that the programme makers themselves had to deal with, when air time is short and precious, and we know they had interpreters, we don't need to be constantly reminded, the programme is not about that. These may be sensible reasons within the terms of television, but if this minimization of the effects of linguistic difference in English-language broadcasting is the norm, and we believe it is, we are concerned about its possible effect.

The analysis we present in this chapter will relate to programmes broadcast on British television, where an English-speaking audience is assumed. It is based on a small corpus of televised programmes in travel, documentary and lifestyle genres filmed outside the UK, and broadcast between 2003 and 2005 (see Appendix for a list of items in the corpus). These were selected opportunistically, including individual programmes from series such as *Dream Home Abroad* (a series on Channel 5 about British buyers of foreign property), *A Place in the Sun* (a similar series on Channel 4), *No Going Back* (a Channel 4 series about a British family attempting a new start after buying a house in Tuscany) and some one-off documentaries such as *Headmasters and Headscarves*, a programme on BBC2 about the debate within one French school over the ban on Muslim girls wearing the hijab. The corpus excludes programmes made originally for non-native English-speaking audiences. We are not including here the way in which native speaker–non-native speaker interactions are represented in comedy or fiction genres, although the frequent exploitation of their comic potential is clearly of interest. We have concentrated on programmes and particular scenes in programmes in which we would expect protagonists (which include interviewers, presenters and the principal subjects of programmes, such as British people who have moved or are intending to live in another country), to interact with non-native speakers of English. We are using the terms native speaker and non-native speaker here only because they offer a convenient marker of linguistic difference; we acknowledge that the terms are problematic (see, for example, Christophersen and MacArthur 1992; Davies 1991; Rampton 1999). There are examples in the corpus of linguistic mediation (usually subtitling) when speakers would probably not regard themselves as non-native speakers. Our strategy has been to make subjective judgements based on the broadcast evidence of linguistic ability, and adopt the role of 'ideal viewers' in the sense of uncritically accepting constructions of Otherness (marked by lack of English language skills) offered by the programme. Thus, for example, we would suspend our faculties for critical deconstruction and go along with the implication in a programme that a person of Chinese appearance shown in a food market in Beijing is probably a Chinese speaker with limited English language ability, in the absence of any positive evidence to the contrary. We consciously bracket this initial construction, and focus on what happens next.

It is apparent that there is a general tendency on British broadcast television to minimize the effects of linguistic difference, that is, not to show interactions with Others who are not competent English speakers. For example, in *vox pop* news interviews on the streets of foreign cities commonly found in news broadcasts covering international stories, interpreters rarely appear and the presenters themselves do not make use of foreign language (FL) skills. Usually the interviews that are broadcast are with fairly competent English speakers, who are simultaneously represented as identifiably different (not British). Thus we are led to assume that an interviewee on the streets of Paris, for example, is French, and are perhaps encouraged in that view by the appearance of a French accent, while also understanding that her Frenchness is no impediment to her ability to communicate in English. While there may be pragmatic, financial and time-constraint reasons for this, we see this minimization as ideological. It can serve to promote the belief that on the one hand language is not a dimension of difference between people, and that therefore we – the audience, ordinary people – don't need to deal with it. Yet, the very avoidance in broadcast television of interactions across linguistic difference indicates that language is an important dimension of difference, and the production work needed to pull off such encounters suggests that we do need to work on it. On the other hand, when linguistic difference cannot be avoided we find in the corpus a reluctance to engage with it positively and for protagonists to settle for minimalist attempts at communication.

Previous discussion in this area has centred on decisions to either dub (voice-over interpretation) or subtitle non-English native speaker voices. The concern in Translation Studies has been with the accuracy of translation and interpretation, the role of the interpreter, technical constraints in the choice between subtitling and dubbing, and how local and individual voices can be represented in translations (Katan and Straniero-Sergio 2003; Kilborn 1993; Koolstra *et al* 2002; Piette 2002; Taylor 2002). Scholars in Modern Foreign Language Studies, by contrast, have been concerned with the accessibility of authentic second-language speech, which allows FL speakers to make their own interpretations uninhibited by media interventions, and the effects of media representations on people's attitudes to FL learning (see Conclusion). Richard Kilborn (1993: 649), for example, states that: 'In Britain [. . .] acquiring foreign languages has never been accorded high cultural significance and there is the somewhat arrogant assumption that the majority of life's activities – including broadcasting – can be satisfactorily conducted in English.'

However, the issue is wider than a choice between dubbing, narrating or subtitling foreign language encounters; it also raises questions about how cultural groups are constituted, insider/outsider status, the nature of cultural difference, and how our relationships with cultural Others are ideologically constructed. There are also issues about how people relate to, and communicate with, each other across cultural and linguistic difference. These perspectives can benefit from insights developed within Critical Discourse Analysis on the construction of the social subject and the role of power in constructing relationships (see also Burger 2002). In televised situations of linguistic difference, the power which determines the choice of code to be used in interaction is augmented by the non-native speakers' lack of knowledge about the nature of the programme and its intended audience, and their relative inability to communicate with the production team. Television, like more traditional forms of ethnography, wants to find its subjects naive, authentic, natural, not playing up to the cameras, while the presence of the camera (and that of the researcher) is an immediate threat to authenticity (see Thornborrow and van Leeuwen 2001, for studies on the importance of authenticity in media discourse, and also Leishman 2001). Another relevant issue is the interest within Critical Discourse Analysis in the colonization of media discourse by the imperative for entertainment over information, analysis and argumentation (Fairclough 1995). This topic has been largely ignored within applied linguistics and sociolinguistics, however; to our knowledge, only Adam Jaworski *et al* (2003) have dealt with any of these issues.

In this chapter we will first present a framework for analysing broadcast TV programming which includes communication or potential communication across linguistic difference, focusing on the triangular relationship between protagonists, audience and FL speakers, and the presence or absence of linguistic mediation. We then outline eight strategies for dealing with such difference that we have found in our corpus of broadcast material: (1) minimization by omission of encounters across linguistic difference; (2) overheard FL talk; (3) protagonist – Other talk in English; (4) non-verbal engagement; (5) 'getting by'; (6) mediated interaction; (7) protagonist – Other talk in an FL; and (8) pseudo-interaction. We will for the most part illustrate these strategies with short descriptions of relevant scenes from a small number of productions, with some limited use of transcript.

10.2 Modelling the relationship between protagonists, FL speakers and the television audience

We can represent this relationship in the form of a triangle (Figure 10.1). At the bottom left are the protagonists: hosts, narrators, travellers abroad who are relaying their experiences back to the audience; they are usually

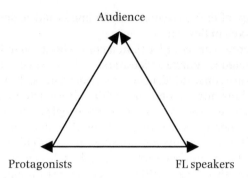

Figure 10.1

but not always monolingual English native or near-native speakers – and in that respect representative of the target audience. At the bottom right are the Others: the FL speakers, those with whom the protagonists may not be able to communicate. At the top we have the target audience.

It is rare for the subjects of television programmes (those observed or encountered) whatever their cultural or linguistic attributes to assume or be granted right of direct address to the audience; they speak only to and through the protagonists. This triangular relationship is revealed in the common practice of filming interviewees speaking not directly to the camera but to one side of it, so that the audience finds itself addressed in the proxy form of a seen or unseen interviewer. But interviewers and presenters not only stand in for the audience as addressees; they usually have a voice of their own and speak directly to the audience.

In contexts of (potential) linguistic difference an additional level of mediation is required. The production team has to decide on the means and extent of mediation in four directions: FL speaker to audience (if ever); FL speaker to protagonist; protagonist to FL speaker; and protagonist to audience.

This mediation may serve to either:

1. erase linguistic difference by ignoring its existence;
2. background linguistic difference;
3. 'thematize' linguistic difference (foreground the procedure of talk between speakers of different languages, making it the topic or content rather than the vehicle); or
4. present linguistic difference as an ordinary, everyday interactive accomplishment, unthematized, as in common subtitling and dubbing practices.

Mediation of the fourth type can be problematic if, instead of showing communication across linguistic difference as an ordinary accomplishment, it only 'pretends' to do so. How we judge whether or not an encounter includes genuine interaction or only pseudo-interaction (where the protagonist's

192

primary concern is not the communication between them and their interactants but between them and the audience, while a show of genuine interaction is made) is a difficult problem in the context of television, where everything is to a certain extent contrived. We will be looking at examples of this from our data set, and considering how much space is allowed for subjects to construct identities and voices for themselves; how to distinguish between 'authentic' interactions between protagonists and FL speakers and pseudo-interactions; and whether and how the relationship between protagonists and FL speakers is constructed differently from that with speakers who share the same language as protagonists and audience.

Linguistic mediation may occur either prior to filming, during filming, or post-filming as follows.

1. Pre-filming interventions may anticipate problems likely to arise from linguistic difference and preclude them, by avoidance or mediation strategies.
2. Mediation during filming may also be, and usually is, required to allow the protagonist to interact with FL speakers, but interpreters are not always made available.
3. Post-filming mediation may allow the audience different degrees of direct access to the voices of FL speakers without them having been mediated by a protagonist.

Our original diagram in Figure 10.1 can now be used to represent what we see of the interaction as it happened: whether protagonists demonstrate a primary orientation to the audience (see Figure 10.2) or to those with whom they are in the presence of and interacting with (Figure 10.3).

Similarly, for the subjects of the programme (Figures 10.4 and 10.5). The diagram can also be modified so as to represent how the production as a whole articulates and mediates the relationship between the protagonist, audience and the FL speaker *as broadcast*, through pre-, during- and post-filming strategies; we will make use of heavy dashed arrows (➖ ➖ ➖ ➤) to

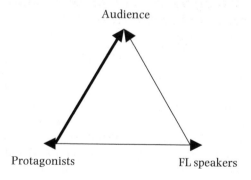

Audience

Protagonists   FL speakers

Figure 10.2

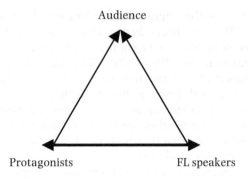

Figure 10.3

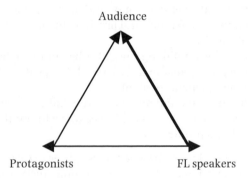

Figure 10.4

signify the effect produced by the production as broadcast (after editing, subtitling and dubbing) rather than by the interaction as it happened. A thinner line is used to indicate that less prominence is given to that dimension of the interaction.

10.3 Eight strategies for dealing with linguistic difference on broadcast television

We have identified eight strategies for the representation of linguistic difference. The whole taxonomy will be presented, but we are concerned in particular with how two of these strategies, 7 and 8, are accomplished. While the taxonomy has been established on the basis of the whole corpus, the examples we use will be taken mainly from single episodes of (1) the travel entertainment series *Around the World in 80 Days* (BBC1), presented by the popular broadcaster and comedian Michael Palin, in which he travels around the world from country to country; (2) *Around the World in 80 Treasures* (BBC2), presented by historian Don Cruikshank, a tour of some of the world's cultural treasures; and (3) a documentary *The Dark Heart of Italy* (BBC4) in

194

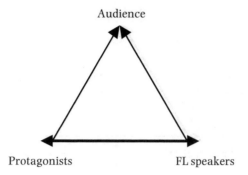

Figure 10.5

which Tobias Jones presents a personal view of the Italian national character, based on his experience of many years of residence in Italy. The first was selected because of the high frequency of Palin's interactions with FL speakers in his travel programme: not only does Palin visit a lot of different places, he makes a point of talking to a lot of people, and the entertainment value of these programmes is in large part derived from the way he interacts with people he comes across. The Cruikshank programme has been selected because, although the main focus is not on the people he meets but on valuable and beautiful artefacts found in various countries, some attempt is made to locate the artefacts in a cultural context. He, or the programme makers, do of course need to talk to people just to get to see these objects, but he asks local experts to talk about them too. The Jones programme has been selected because, unusually, the presenter speaks the language of the place that the programme is about – Italy – and he is constantly interacting with Italians. Indeed, the BBC has given him air-time because he is to a certain extent an insider to Italian culture; this is unusual because television tends to rely on in-house presenters who are, or become, known faces to the audience rather than local experts. (The use of the well-known cultural issues presenter Kirsty Wark in the *Tales from Italy* series on BBC2 is a case in point. As a non-Italian speaker she is reduced to interviewing only English-speaking Italians.) On the more 'up-market' BBC4 channel, where ratings are less of an immediate concern, it has been possible to risk an unknown, non-professional presenter for this one-off programme.

10.3.1 Strategy 1: omission of encounters across linguistic difference

In many of the programmes in our corpus, such as those involving British people buying property abroad or moving abroad to start new lives (*A Place in the Sun, Dream Home Abroad, No Going Back*), interactions with non-native English speakers are actually rather rare or even non-existent. It is not uncommon

195

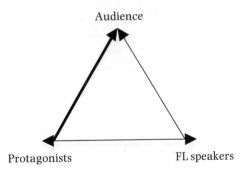

Figure 10.6

in an entire episode of a programme on, say, buying a home in Spain, not to hear a single word of Spanish spoken, even in the background. Local English-speaking estate agents are sought out, and local English expatriates are interviewed to talk about the area, rather than Spanish-speaking neighbours. In one episode of *Around the World in 80 Treasures* featuring Chinese porcelain, Cruikshank often refers explicitly to negotiations to get access to various sites in Beijing, but we never see or hear them taking place. It is hard, of course, to be certain about what has been excluded. We do at one point get a glimpse of his interpreter, however, and hear him explain to Cruikshank why a particular item cannot be seen, at which point it becomes apparent that the negotiations have been extensive. We represent this strategy in Figure 10.6, where the protagonist is shown addressing the audience only.

10.3.2 Strategy 2: overheard FL talk

This strategy is frequently used when it is important to demonstrate that the protagonist is in a 'foreign' place – foreign-sounding, as well as foreign-looking, foreignness. Both Palin and Cruikshank are often shown wandering about in public places; we see and hear the people around them talking, but there is no interaction, and the protagonists often look slightly bemused.

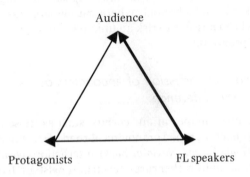

Figure 10.7

While the FL speakers are in a sense directly accessible to the audience, as in Figure 10.7, they are unmediated either through interaction with the protagonist or with subtitles, narration, summary or any form of interpretation, and it is without their involvement. Like the protagonists, the audience become 'over-hearers' or eavesdroppers rather than party to interaction. The alterity of the FL speaker is found in the impossibility of communication.

10.3.3   Strategy 3: protagonist–Other talk in English

This is a frequent strategy when protagonists do interact with people whom we take to be FL speakers, and we have noted it already in the context of *vox pop* news interviews on the streets of foreign cities. Here there is a tension between the apparent foreignness of the location and the interlocutor, which is constructed visually, and lack of difference in linguistic terms. A 'foreign' accent may be apparent but interactants are usually selected for their proximity to English native-speaker language skills. There are numerous examples in the data; one such occurs when Palin has been observing a parade of soldiers in Greece. We are given lots of contextualizing shots of the street scene so we know it has not been staged for the camera. Palin then interviews one of the soldiers, who 'happens' to be a highly proficient Greek speaker of English (see Figure 10.8).

10.3.4 Strategy 4: non-verbal engagement

In this strategy interaction does take place between the protagonist and FL speakers, but it is non-verbal. There is a kind of faux innocence here; despite the resources of the production team on location, which we imagine must include interpreters, the protagonist is allowed to wander freely among 'the locals', as in strategy 2, and is shown interacting wordlessly. It is the kind of situation we can easily imagine ourselves in – smiling and gesturing, often exaggeratedly in acknowledgement of the fact these are not 'normal' smiles and gestures. It can also take the form of negative engagement, often sensationalist, as in scenes of English football supporters fighting in the streets with

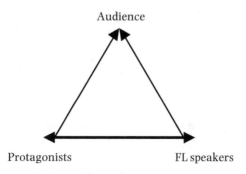

Figure 10.8

Turkish fans shown on British television in the run up to the 2006 football World Cup, but documentary and travel programmes usually avoid such negative images, and protagonists and interactants display exemplary benevolence towards each other. There is an example in an episode of *Around the World in 80 Treasures* where Cruickshank is seen observing some Chinese people dancing silently in the park in the summer palace; at first he only watches from the side but later he is shown joining in with the dance as best he can. It is difficult to diagram this strategy simply; in Figure 10.9 we have shown a weak interaction between protagonist and FL speakers, which the audience simply observes.

10.3.5 Strategy 5: 'getting by' across linguistic difference

In a step beyond strategy 4 we sometimes see the struggle for communication across linguistic difference actually taking place. As we know, it can be difficult, time-consuming and embarrassing, and it is often therefore exploited in the media for its entertainment potential. Palin is a frequent user of this strategy for this very reason. For example, when he takes a horse-drawn taxi from the quay to the railway station in Alexandria we are treated to an extended conversation between himself and the driver, who speaks idiosyncratic English. He is then given the 'Palin treatment', which includes asides for the benefit of the audience, exploiting occasional linguistic oddities. In other genres, such as sitcom, FL speakers are often introduced solely for the comic potential of their accents, amusing lexical errors (which are often rather contrived), communication failures and misunderstandings, which are seen as the inevitable outcome of interaction with FL speakers. On other occasions the interaction, and the difficulty of interaction, is treated as ordinary. Thus, for example, we observe Cruikshank in Beijing, having been disappointed in his attempt to see some porcelain in a museum, shopping for a teacup in various antique shops; he tries to ask passers-by where the shops are, he asks about the dates of various items, he bargains, all in 'foreigner talk' attuned to the presumed

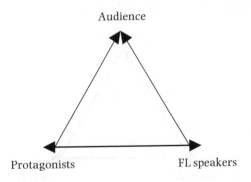

Figure 10.9

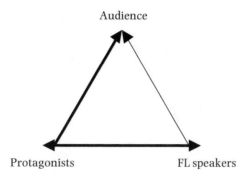

Figure 10.10

English abilities of his interlocutors. Later he tries eating silkworms and fried snake from a local food stall. In the absence of an interpreter he behaves like most British travellers abroad, getting by with no knowledge of the native language. Cruikshank negotiates his relationship with both audience and market vendors simultaneously, both parties combining gesture, 'foreigner talk', shifts of orientation between the camera and his interactants, and utterances which can be considered to be part of the interaction as it happens, apparently directed at interlocutors rather than the camera but evidently not understandable to them. These may be solely for the benefit of the audience (and thus exploitative of interlocutors who do not know what he is saying, as we sometimes find with Palin) or simply to enact phatic communication, understood as such by the foreign language speakers who may reciprocate in like manner.

In contrast to Figure 10.9, Figure 10.10 shows the greater extent of protagonist–FL speaker interaction, with a simultaneous orientation to the audience by the protagonist.

10.3.6   Strategy 6: mediated interaction across linguistic difference

This strategy is used when the content of the talk produced by the FL speaker (rather than the protagonist) is important or central to the programme, and the protagonists – in this case presenters and interviewers – are not FL proficient. We find it in documentaries, current affairs programmes and news reports from foreign locations, and in programmes such as the example with which we opened – Jonathan Ross reporting on new trends in Japanese cinema. Mediation is inevitable in these cases, and the most common form is post-production. That is to say, it is rare to find interpretation taking place on-screen, with the interpreter who was present during filming appearing in the broadcast version, but it does sometimes occur. It is more common for whatever interpretation that took place between protagonist and FL speaker at the time of filming to be edited out and replaced by subtitling, dubbing, voice-over translation or narrator summary. The interpreter is often not

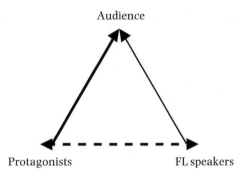

Figure 10.11

visible on-screen, and the peculiar situation of two people apparently speaking to each other in different languages has become normalized on British broadcast TV. There can be some degree of direct access on the part of the FL speaker to the British audience, unmediated by either protagonist or post-production, in so far as the audience has FL proficiency and subtitling has been chosen over dubbing or voice-over. However, the most common device is to start with the first few words of the speaker audible to demonstrate that an FL was being used but almost immediately obscured by voice-over translation or narration. This may particularly frustrate members of the audience who are speakers of the language, and it also deprives the rest of the audience of exposure to the sounds and cadences of foreign tongues.

Figure 10.11 shows the limited but unmediated link between FL speaker and audience, mediated protagonist's interaction with the FL speaker, and unmediated talk for the audience (visually, addressed to the FL speaker), which is usually both preceded and followed by direct to camera talk by the protagonist.

10.3.7   Strategy 7: protagonist – Other talk in an FL

It is rare to see protagonists on British TV speaking any language other than English, but it does occasionally happen. Some English native-speaker protagonists in the British media do have FL skills[1] and very occasionally (though not in our corpus) a non-native bilingual protagonist may have been selected. In the case of the Tobias Jones programme, the protagonist appears to have been selected specifically because he was a bilingual cultural insider. In these cases the linguistic difference is not so much between protagonist and FL speaker as between them and the audience, and some form of mediation may be required for the latter's sake. In fact mediation is not always provided, and this can give the impression of showing off by the protagonist: we are being shown that they are second-language proficient, and this fact is more important than what they are saying. For example, listeners were once treated to a brief clip on radio news of the British Prime Minister, Tony Blair, speaking some words of French at a European meeting, apparently solely to demonstrate that he could do it.

The Channel 4 series *Jamie's Great Escape* featured 'celebrity chef' Jamie Oliver travelling around Italy in his camper van, staying with Italian families, being shown how to cook by local people in small towns, and also cooking for them. There are a good many scenes showing Oliver interacting with Italians on the streets, in restaurants and in family settings. He has a basic knowledge of Italian, and is communicative if not accurate or fluent; above all he is unselfconscious and makes the best of his limited Italian language skills. The Italians he meets respond conversationally rather than as interviewees, making use of foreigner talk, their own knowledge of English, or speaking in Italian (standard or dialect) as if they understood each other perfectly well. His amiable on-screen persona and the mood of congeniality that is achieved in these on-screen interactions is a major part of Oliver's appeal as a celebrity (rather than, say, his authority, expert knowledge, or good taste). Little attempt is made to mediate these interactions for the sake of the audience; there is some subtitling but no voice-over. He does not appear to have an interpreter with him, although he sometimes enlists English-speaking local people to help him out. While there is also a good deal of talk by Oliver that is purely for the sake of the camera rather than involving the people he is with, he does try to preserve a sense of *being with* the Italian speakers rather than *making use of* them. A common device is for Oliver to repeat in English his own or his interlocutors' Italian for the sake of the audience, either at the time of the interaction or in the form of voice-over narration. There is also occasional narration in his own voice which sometimes reports interactions he has had. His comfortable style of engagement with FL speakers making use of basic second-language skills is rarely found on British broadcast TV. We show these encounters in Figure 10.12.

Palin also has some command of Italian, possibly better than Oliver's, and in an early episode of *Around the World in 80 Days*, we observe him speaking

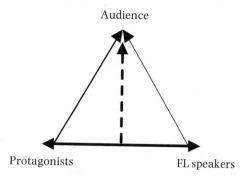

Audience

Protagonists   FL speakers

Figure 10.12

Italian as he registers for a hotel room in Venice and takes a parcel to the post office. This is done in a similarly unselfconscious way; it is seen as a normal and unremarkable thing to do to speak Italian in service encounters in Italy. When he later spends half a day with Venice dustmen on their rounds, his genial interactivity and the gentle leg-pulling that have led to him being called 'the nicest man in Britain', and are perhaps the main appeal of the programme, emerge. The limitations of his Italian quickly become apparent, however, and the refuse collection team speak no English, but his enthusiastic manner and interactive skills make it possible to film encounters which seem to go well, with his good humour being shared by the work crew. However, his talk is laced with an additional layer of commentary to camera. This is partly to report to the audience in English what has just been said in Italian, thus avoiding the need for later mediation (subtitling or voice-over). This preserves audience involvement in the event as it unfolds and maintains the appearance of intimacy in their relationship with Palin. There is also another aspect of his talk, which lends to the encounter the appearance of strategy 8 – a pseudo-encounter in which the FL speaker is being used as a foil to support the protagonist in his own relationship with the audience.

This suspicion that the FL speaker is being 'used' is much less evident in *The Dark Heart of Italy* in which Tobias Jones interviews Italians on the streets and in cafes to provide illustrative evidence for his arguments. It is clear that he already knows what he wants to say, however; he is not forming his judgements as he reports what each interviewee says. The technique is to introduce a topic which contributes to his theme (the nature of Italians and Italian society and culture), interview an Italian without any linguistic mediation, and then turn to camera and report what has been said in English, adding his own commentary, often prefaced with 'you hear this a lot in Italy ...'. Jones's reports are not direct translations of what interviewees have said, however, and Italian speakers in the audience may accuse him of misrepresentation. Non-Italian speakers can only trust him, and we are encouraged in this trust by his obvious fluency and the appearance of unproblematic and authentic interaction; he *appears* to be simply talking with Italians and telling us what they are saying.

There is a certain degree of orientation by the protagonist to the audience as well as to the FL speaker in both the Palin and Jones examples discussed above, much more obviously so than in the Oliver case because of the real-time alternation between talking to/with the FL speakers and direct address to camera. We might represent them as in Figure 10.13.

FL programmes that occasionally appear on British TV, such as the French language documentary *Être et Avoir* ('To be and to have') about a school-teacher in a small village in France, are useful 'end cases' against which the degree of Othering in different cases can be judged. In *Être et Avoir* there is no linguistic mediation during filming, and no voice-over, narration or dubbing; the dialogue is subtitled from start to finish.

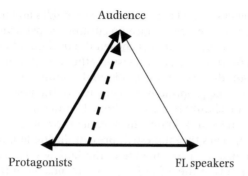

Figure 10.13

10.3.8 Strategy 8: pseudo-interaction

The tendency that we noted under strategy 7 for Palin to make use of interaction with FL speakers for his own purposes can be found more fully elsewhere in the data. In this case the protagonist's orientation is primarily to the audience, and the interaction with FL speakers is largely fake – they are there as a prop. This is not unusual in broadcasting that does not include FL speakers of course, and those who agree to appear on TV are aware of the fact that their own role is only ever a supporting one. When FL speakers are involved, however, the degree and extent of this synthetic 'using' is more apparent because of the asymmetry involved in linguistic mediation. While the protagonist always knows what is being said, and the audience is kept in touch through various strategies either during or after filming, the FL speaker is left comparatively in the dark during the interaction. They may not even be aware of the genre of the programme in which they are taking part, the audience at which it is directed, or the personality, expertise and reputation of protagonists. They may be depending entirely on whatever cues they can pick up from the interaction as it unfolds as to what they can assume as shared knowledge and values, what register is appropriate, how long a turn they can expect to have, what role they are being granted as speakers, and what status they have. Whatever linguistic mediation we see is provided for the benefit of the monolingual English-speaking audience, though we cannot of course know what has been communicated to FL speakers before or even after filming. English-speaking participants are handicapped in these ways to a lesser extent, and they have relatively greater opportunity to regulate their own voice.

In fairly 'normal' encounters such as those we see in Oliver's Italian journey, this has less importance: the cues that the FL speaker picks up from the encounter as it happens are the same as those found in normal conversation, and the interaction is filmed as a 'normal' interaction (not forgetting, of course, whatever effect the presence of a camera will inevitably have). In Cruikshank's *Around the World in 80 Treasures*, however, his encounters are with FL speakers in a wide range of roles – guides and interpreters, shop assistants, people on the street, museum curators, experts and craftsmen.

In one scene Cruikshank has chosen the traditional Japanese samurai sword as one of his treasures, and is visiting the workshop of a contemporary master craftsman, dressed in full traditional costume, to see how they are made. Ritsuo (an inappropriately familiar use of the first name of a master craftsman by Cruikshank) has a very limited knowledge of English, and it is apparent that Cruikshank knows no Japanese. No interpreter is visible or audible, and it appears that none was present during filming. While he has done some homework on the making of the Japanese sword, Cruikshank is not the expert and is in the difficult position of mediating the master crafts-man's expert knowledge without the linguistic resources to do so. The fact that he was put in this position is perhaps symptomatic of the attitude of Brit-ish television producers towards FL subjects. Cruikshank tries to maintain his authority as presenter and his privileged direct access to the audience, and the result is the sidelining of a participant who has every right not to be side-lined and apparently also no desire for this to happen.

Palin follows a middle path between Oliver's encounters with ordinary people, which we could imagine ourselves sharing, and Cruikshank's access to expertise. When he takes a boat to Alexandria he is seen on the bridge talk-ing to the captain; he then appears in the kitchen making brioches with the cook, which we see him later eating in the dining room as an ordinary passen-ger, talking to the waiter as any passenger might. The following transcript is taken from the scene in the ship's kitchens.

	Palin	**Franco**
Establishing shot of ship's kitchens. Palin and Franco are in background bent over a dough mixer		
Voice-over	There are now 300 passengers for Franco and his team to cook for and he needs all the help he can get	
Close-up of dough being mixed in the machine		(unclear) (in Italian)
Palin out of picture, semi-audible	Looks very satisfying	
Shot of Franco's hands making a brioche. Voice-over	Franco's one-man bakery sets a furious pace	

	Palin	**Franco**
Palin direct to camera,	He *has* been doing it for 27 years	
Palin glances at Franco, and Franco looks back at Palin		Che?
Close-up Palin's hands copying Franco making a brioche	Slightly like making dirty Fidos .. do you know?	
		Aah!
	Dirty Fidos we have in England . I'm sure you have them in Italy but. there we go. sort of twiddle it a bit . speciality of yours Franco?	
		Eh?
	Specialista?	
		(?) (Italian)
	Lei specialista?	
		(?) (Italian)
Close-up of Palin's face looking at the table as he speaks	You're vetting them aren't you Franco you're getting rid of all mine you're just being nice to me at the moment	
Close-up of Palin fashioning a P out of dough	Now I'm going to do a big P. It's a bit sort of .. egotistical I know but .. let's see if would work .. how about that .. there we are .. a P . a little blob at the end there for that artistic touch . there we are a nice P . there we are	
		Wrong
Palin direct to camera	How about that Now this bit's very boring so if you'd like to go away and film nice arty shots of sea	
Looks at Franco and nods	I'll have half a bottle of chianti	

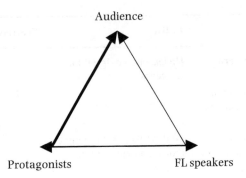

Figure 10.14

The scene is set up to appear as if Palin was joining Franco's team to help him make brioches for three hundred passengers, but in fact he is little help and amuses himself by making his initials in dough. While Palin is apparently talking to him it seems clear that Franco understands little of what Palin says but this does not appear to matter to Palin, who is actually speaking for the benefit of the audience, and Franco seems to accept this. It is clear that Franco has no idea what a dirty Fido is, for example, and Palin has no interest in explaining it to him. When Palin asks Franco if making this style of brioche is one of his specialties, Franco's responses are hardly audible and restricted to one or two words of Italian. Thus while appearing to be maintaining an on-going relationship with Franco by using his name and referring to him directly (as 'you'), glancing at him and using an occasional word of Italian, the main relationship is between Palin and the audience, from which Franco is almost totally excluded. In a final joke Palin appears to be addressing the camera crew, whom he tells to go off and film elsewhere while he has a drink with his new friend Franco.

Figure 10.14 shows the protagonist's predominant orientation to the audience, but it is parasitic on the secondary relationship between protagonist and the FL speaker.

10.4 Ways of dealing with encounters across linguistic difference

Within the eight overall strategies for dealing with encounters across linguistic difference described above, we have identified certain elements, which are summarized in Table 10.1. Those most commonly found in our current corpus (which excludes news reports and political interviews) are in bold in the table.

Further research will allow a quantitative study of the extent to which each strategy is to be found in British broadcast television overall or in particular broadcast genres, but at present our assessment of their relative dominance is necessarily subjective. They apply only to programmes in which

Table 10.1: Summary of strategies used in dealing with encounters across linguistic difference

Pre-filming strategies	During-filming strategies	Post-filming strategies
Selecting English speakers as informants	**Intermittent report / narration / explanation by protagonist**	**Voice-over interpretation and dubbing**
Avoiding interaction with non-English speakers	**Non-verbal communication**	**Subtitling**
Providing interpreters	***Pseudo-interaction***	**Narration**
Selecting a presenter competent in the FL	Use of an interpreter, on- or off-screen	**Editing out real-time interpreter participation**
	Consecutive translation by protagonist	
	Foreigner talk	
	Lingua franca talk	

encounters across linguistic difference might be expected to occur, and we realize that this may be a problematic judgement, as the salience of linguistic difference is likely to be affected by the presence of the camera, or indeed of the protagonist. For example, a speaker who would normally speak one language in her home or work environment might normally switch to another language in a context she considered more formal or in the presence of an outsider. A speaker who might be quite comfortable speaking a second language in some circumstances might not want to try it in front of a camera – or the opposite case might apply. We are only describing situations in which encounters or potential encounters are perceived by producers and protagonists as involving linguistic difference, and are dealt with as such.

10.5 Conclusion

Generally speaking, British television does not do well in its broadcast representations of encounters across linguistic difference, and our personal observations indicate that in other contexts the situation is not much different. Certainly, comparative research is called for here. In normal programming a monolingual world is largely assumed. Even in programmes when a multilingual environment is to be expected, the workings of cross-linguistic communication are largely avoided, eliminated or obscured. We assume that this is in order to preserve a professional appearance of seamlessness (Scannell 1991), in which things do not 'go wrong' and where time is not wasted in the process of communication itself. Naturalistic encounters are given the appearance of scripted ones, in which speakers do not lose their train of thought, hesitate, repeat themselves, or have to struggle very much to make themselves understood, unless for the sake of a particular dramatic point. Thus an everyday fact of life for many people – and increasingly many people – who communicate across linguistic difference is naturalized as something 'going wrong' as far as television is concerned. When we do get to see and hear FL speakers in interaction with 'people like us' (in whatever language, however mediated), it is frequently exploited for its entertainment value as linguistic disorder.

Arguably, minimization of the intrusion of the effects of linguistic difference into programmes is justifiable in television's own terms. In the genres we have selected for our corpus, however, the content of the programmes in travel, relocation abroad, international documentary and current affairs programmes is ostensibly the experience of going beyond what we can find at home. In these programmes it is less easy to justify avoiding representations of linguistic difference or adopting strategies to minimize the implications of linguistic difference. Equally unsatisfactory are representations of Others as unreachable, irredeemably different, marked by linguistic difference before all else, such that it is impossible to have meaningful interaction with them, and all attempts at interaction are evidence of its very impossibility, hence a cause only of humour or frustration. Our ideal approach is rarely found; it would recognize that linguistic difference does exist, in predictable as well as unpredictable contexts; that it is important to recognize it, because language and linguistic difference are central to being human; and that it is not an impossible divide. Ways to mediate difference, and ways to be with other people even in the absence of fully adequate linguistic mediation, would be unselfconsciously represented.

We can only speculate on the effects of these representations on the British viewing public. It may make attempting communication across linguistic difference seem to be something to be avoided, as it is made to appear that attempts to communicate across linguistic difference are hazardous and potentially embarrassing. Just as FL speakers' attempts to speak English are a cause for our own amusement, we would be exposing ourselves to similar ridicule. Alternatively, or in addition, communication across linguistic difference may be seen as unnecessary. The way it is represented may reinforce the perception of English as a global language which can be used anywhere, with anyone, on any occasion, and reduce the perceived need to learn other languages. This is a view that has been expressed elsewhere, for example on the *lingua-net* forum, an e-list devoted to discussion of the teaching and learning of foreign languages. The following posting was made here with regard to the programme *The Headmaster and the Headscarves*, part of the BBC2 *This World* current affairs series, about the debate within one French school over the legal requirement for Muslim girls not to wear the hijab in school. This was a British production but filmed entirely in France in a 'roving eye' style without a presenter, and mediated for the UK audience by a British narrator and voice-over translation of all dialogue:

> what stopped me giving the programme 10/10 was the way in which the recorded voices were dubbed – as per usual. Why can't we allow all speakers to be heard in their native language, and provide an on-screen transcription with a translation available as teletext subtitles? If TV broadcasters treated all programmes in this way, it might go some way to encourage our insular population to take foreign languages seriously. (Chris Tetley, *lingua-net* forum. 30.03.05)

This may be so. However, none of the 41 comments received from viewers and published on the BBC *This World* 'Have your say' webpage itself made any reference to language issues. A viewer who wrote to a BBC interactive web-page about voice-overs on BBC news broadcasts made a similar point. While much of his critique is only relevant to already fluent speakers of French, he also offers the following comment on language learning:

> I think it's rather impolite to voice over an interviewee who is speaking a language which viewers could well understand. Fluent speakers probably find this to be particularly annoying. [...] With subtitles if you actually understand the language being spoken you can be confident in the quality of the translation or you can see errors if the translation is not very good. [...] When you are actually watching Chirac and listening to his voice and seeing the subtitles you get a much better feeling that you are really listening to the French president you get his emphasis, his tone of voice – it's far, far better than having a translator voice over the top. [...] Is there much surprise that we are famously reluctant to learn other languages because our media tend to isolate us from ever encountering them? (Holdsworth 2005)

Another perspective on this concerns not the effect on the way FL learning is perceived, but on how FL speakers are themselves perceived and are able to represent themselves. Although *all* subjects of the televisual gaze are to a greater or lesser extent objectified and struggle to participate in this public sphere on their own terms and in their own voices, FL speakers are in a potentially even weaker position, as we have already mentioned. This is because of their often limited understanding of the nature of the genre together with the objectives and perspective of the programme-makers, their reduced understanding of what can pass for shared knowledge with the audience, their relative lack of direct access to that audience, reduced opportunities for meaning-making, and relative lack of access to what the protagonist is communicating to the audience. These factors all make it more difficult for FL speakers to speak for themselves and for their voices to be heard. It also makes it easier for programme-makers to construct subjectivities and ascribe skills, knowledge and opinions to them that they may be ignorant of and may not willingly accept. The line between authentic and pseudo-interaction becomes harder to negotiate, and television's ability to exploit its subjects as objects of entertainment is facilitated. In all the examples discussed here our access as an audience is to a simplified, reduced, heavily mediated voice of the FL speaker. This adds to the impression that it is not really worth the effort to communicate with such speakers.

Primary sources

CiLT (2006) 'Promoting Languages: Celebrity Linguists' (available online at www.cilt.org.uk/promoting/linguists.htm, accessed 20.10.06).

Holdsworth, D. (2005) quoted in I. Jolly, 'Are news reports dubbing down?', BBC News Newswatch, 17.02.05 (available online at (www.news.bbc.co.uk/newswatch/ukfs/hi/newsid_4270000/newsid_4273500/4273597.stm, accessed 06.09.05).

Appendix: titles of items in the corpus

A Place in the Sun (series), Channel 4, 2003.
Around the World in 80 Days (series), BBC Enterprises Ltd, 1993.
Around the World in 80 Treasures (series), BBC2, 2005.
Breaking the Silence: Truth and Lies in the War on Terror, Carlton, 2003.
Chaos at the Chateau, Channel 4, October 2004.
Dispatches: Congo's Killing Fields, Channel 4, 17.08.03.
DIY SOS France Special, BBC1.
Dream Home Abroad (series), Channel 5.
French Exchange (series) BBC4, 2005.
French Leave (series) Channel 4, 2003.
Headmasters and Headscarves, BBC2, 29.03.05.
I Want That House (series), Channel 4, 2003.
Jamie's Great Escape (series), Channel 4, 2005.
No Going Back (A Year in Tuscany) (series), Channel 4, 2003.
Tale of Two Alis ('Cutting Edge' documentary series), Channel 4, 2003.
Tales from Italy (series) BBC2, 2005.
The Dark Heart of Italy, BBC4, 08.06.05.
The Day I Will Never Forget, Channel 4, 18.08.03.
The Deal (Panorama documentary series), BBC1, 28.09.03.
The Dollar a Day Dress, (Panorama documentary series), BBC1, March 2005.
The Lost Boys of Sudan, Channel 4, 04.10.03.
The Reign in Spain (Posh and Becks), Channel 4, November 2003.

Notes

1. See, for example, the website of the UK's National Centre for Languages (CiLT), which provides *inter alia* a list of 'celebrity linguists': www.cilt.org.uk.

PART IV
YOUTH, GENDER AND CYBER-IDENTITIES

11 Fabricating youth: New-media discourse and the technologization of young people

Crispin Thurlow

Fears are growing that today's teenagers are becoming 'Generation Grunt', a section of society that has effectively lost the ability to talk or express itself. (1)

We may well be raising the thickest, most incoherent and sub-literate generation for centuries. (2)

11.1 The discursivity of adolescence and the politics of culture

While the period of the human lifespan characterized by the label 'adolescence' is undoubtedly established chronologically and biologically, it is first and foremost a cultural and economic construction. And it is seldom young people themselves who control the mechanisms by which their lives are represented and organized as 'adolescent'. For the most part, therefore, this period

Figure 11.1

of the lifespan is pretty much whatever adults say it is. In her book about the cultural construction of adolescence, Nancy Lesko (2003) demonstrates how adults have in fact fashioned – and come to rely on – adolescence as a crucial *technology* for maintaining the entire social-moral order. One of the most powerful means by which this has been achieved over the past 100 years or so is undoubtedly through scientific and scholarly discourses on adolescence (cf. also Griffin 1993; Burman 1994). More recently, however, it is commerce and the mass media which have arguably come to exercise even greater influence over the discursive constitution of adolescence and the daily experience of young people. These contemporary industries – or discursive orders – therefore demand rigorous examination and critique.[1]

Like Lesko, scholarly critics have noted with concern the violence which is often done to young people by adults seeking to discipline and police them (often quite literally) into the institutional frameworks through which adolescence is organized and normalized. Mike Males (1996), for example, has been outspoken in his criticism of the USA's 'war on adolescents' by which young people have, perhaps more aggressively then ever, become scapegoats for a host of social and moral ills. Johanna Wyn (2005) likewise identifies the tension between cultural narratives preoccupied with 'youth as (violent) threat' in the context of generational change, and those fixated on 'youth as hope for the future' in the context of socioeconomic change. In either case, young people appear to be positioned unfavourably, and social commentary about adolescence, in the words of Henry Giroux (1998: 23), typically amounts to little more than the projections of adult desires, fantasies and interests. In his searing critique of the corporatization and exploitation of young people, Giroux has more recently also concluded that the only appropriate way to understand youth and adolescence is therefore to confront the misrepresentation of young people and what he calls the politics of culture.

> The politics of culture provide the conceptual space in which [youth] is constructed, experienced, and struggled over. Culture is the primary terrain in which adults exercise power over [young people] both ideologically and institutionally. Only by questioning the specific cultural formations and contexts in which youth is organized, learned and lived can educators [and scholars] understand and challenge the ways in which cultural practices establish power relations that shape [young people's] experiences. (Giroux 2000: 4)

In this chapter, what I would like to do is to focus on just one contemporary site where this 'politics of culture' appears to be especially fierce: the consistently negative representation of young people's new-media language in the print media. In doing so, the chapter is intended to fulfil both an academic and advocacy objective. As with all inter-group communication, the social identities and power relations of young people and adults are necessarily

214

co-constituted; these processes are, however, far from mutual. Without doubt, young people are greatly disadvantaged and disempowered by adults' almost total control of the print media. This is simply not an equal playing field; nor are media representations without influence and consequence.

As the examples quoted at the start of the chapter show, adult-driven media commentary can be unapologetically exaggerated and, however humorously sugar-coated, remarkably hostile towards young people. It seems hard to imagine nowadays that it would be appropriate to speak in the same way about any other major social group defined, say, by race, age or sex (cf. Thurlow 2005). Following the lead of Nancy Lesko, Mike Males and Henry Giroux, therefore, I am persuaded that mediatized metadiscourse about young people, language and new technology is likely to say as much about adults as it does about young people. With this in mind, I want to propose that media discourse about young people's new-media language functions in multiple ways as a technologizing resource by which adults are seen not only to be constructing adolescence, but also to be constructing themselves as adults.

There is of course no denying that communication technologies like the internet and the mobile phone are (relatively) new and that their emergence has been (relatively) rapid and dramatic. It would also be inaccurate to suggest that language and communication have remained unaffected by these technological developments. Nonetheless, changes in linguistic and communicative practice can seldom be attributed solely to technology, nor are these technologies only ever the province of young people (cf. Baron 2000). Popular discourse, however, typically talks and writes about young people's new-media language as if this were the case; and to do so is to misunderstand both language *and* technology. It is also to misrepresent young people.

11.2 A little background: the triple whammy

Youth is almost always represented as different, strange and exotic such that the otherwise ordinary, uneventful lives of many young people often end up being eclipsed by the heightened negative images of some young people in popular and some professional discourse (Davis 1990; Griffin 1993). Central to this homogenizing mythology of adolescence is also the notion of the non-communicative or communicatively inept young person, coupled with adult complaints about young people's deleterious impact on received standards of language and communication. Set against the usual backdrop of 'storm and stress' stereotypes about young people, and together with increasingly codified, institutionalized standards of 'good' communication (see Cameron 2000a; Thurlow 2001a), young people's communication nowadays seems to be construed as more problematic than ever, with adults frequently characterizing their interactions with young people as a kind of distinctive inter-cultural communication in much the same way that men and women's exchanges have come to be exaggerated (e.g. Tannen 1990). In my own work, I have been interested in the tendency for these popular (mis)character-izations of young people's communication to become implicated with other public discourses about new technology and language (e.g. Thurlow 2003).

In much the same way that a recurrent cultural narrative exists about youth and adolescence, all technologies appear to be accompanied by heightened popular reactions regarding their social and cultural impact (Kling 1996; Standage 1999). Whether in terms of people's experiences of community life, their standards of morality, or the way they organize their personal relationships, public discourse about emerging technology is also typically polarized by judgements of its being either 'all good' or 'all bad' (see Thurlow *et al* 2004 for more on this point). One major narrative thread in this public discourse about technology is often the way social interaction communication and especially language are negatively affected, and espe-cially language (Baron 2000). Typically, these popular anxieties coalesce around much the same kind of 'verbal hygiene' (to use Cameron's 1995 term) or linguistic puritanism, which characterizes all language change. Added to popular discourses about young people and about new technologies, therefore, one finds the usual 'folk-linguistic' (Niedzielski and Preston 1999) concern about threats to standard varieties and conventional communica-tion practices more generally – that young people ('teen-talk') and new tech-nologies ('netlingo') might be to blame merely compounds matters.

This is particularly true of young people's use of mobile phones and text-messaging, where, as in the journalists' comments quoted below, young people are often understood to be – or rather accused of – reinventing or destroying not only the (English) language but also the entire social order.[2]

> As a dialect, text ('textese'?) is thin and unimaginative. It is bleak, bald, sad shorthand. Drab shrinktalk. The dialect has a few hieroglyphs (codes comprehensible only to initiates) and a range of face symbols. [...] Linguistically it's all pig's ear. [...] Texting is penmanship for illiterates. (3)

> Text messaging [...] is posing a threat to social progress. (4)

It seems, therefore, that adult anxieties about youth, about technology and about language merge into a kind of triple-whammy panic about declining standards of morality and the unwinding of the social fabric. And, to be fair, it is not only lay people and journalists who are responsible for producing this kind of over-stated rhetoric.

> The phenomenon of Netspeak [*sic*] is going to change the way we think about language in a fundamental way, because it is a linguistic singularity – a genuine new medium. [...] Netspeak is something completely new. [...] [It] is a development of millennial significance.

> A new medium of linguistic communication does not arrive very often,
> in the history of the race. (Crystal 2001: 238–9)

In his popular book *Language and the Internet*, for example, David Crystal (2001) appears to dismiss text messaging as simply giving young people something to do, a point of view which seems unfortunately patronizing and which also underestimates the intricate, integral role something like text-messaging plays in their social lives. What is more, for all his millennial rhetoric about 'netspeak', new linguistic/discursive practices seldom spring from nowhere, neatly quashing pre-existing forms and conventions. Just as technologies do not replace each other, nor is it really possible to imagine communicative practices breaking completely, or that dramatically, with long-standing patterns of interaction and language use. There is little doubt, of course, that so-called 'new' communication technologies have emerged, and have been embraced, relatively quickly; it is also true that there are many adults who find themselves compromised by the ease and skill with which many (though by no means all) young people have adopted these technologies. That language change – or perceived language change – is met with public discussion and concern is likewise unsurprising and perfectly understandable. Nonetheless, what I am concerned with here is how young people come to be unfairly and problematically positioned by these largely adult discourses – especially in so far as these discourses are afforded the mainstream recognition and demographic influence of the print media.

11.3 Media metadiscourse and new-media language

In an earlier study, I looked to start challenging this popular discourse about young people's new-media discourse by examining their actual practices in the context of SMS/text-messaging (Thurlow 2003). (Others too have conducted more empirically grounded studies of actual new-media language; see, for example, Hård af Segerstad, in press; Androutsopoulos 2000; Androutsopoulos and Schmidt, 2002). In this modest study, based on a convenience sample of real text-messages, I was able to show that popular discourses about the linguistic exclusivity and impenetrability of this particular technologically mediated discourse appeared to be greatly exaggerated. My chapter here looks to extend this earlier work by undertaking a more systematic, focused investigation of these popular metadiscourses (e.g. media representations) and especially media representations which frame actual practice. Few people read the same newspaper more than once; even fewer people regularly read more than one newspaper. It is really only scholars and media analysts who make a point of reading and re-reading dozens – perhaps even hundreds – of different papers. The advantage of doing this is that it affords an otherwise unusual opportunity to see how a single issue is reported in many different papers, from many different locations and over a substantial period of time. This in turn puts one in a far better position to identify the ideological assumptions by which social practices come to be institutionally organized and popularly understood – or, in this case, misunderstood.

Together with two research assistants, I searched the *ProQuest* and *LexisNexis* newspaper databases for any English-language news articles between 2001 and 2005 covering issues related to young people, language and new technology. (Search terms included 'language', 'teenagers', 'adolescents', 'adolescence', 'youth', 'young people', 'technology', 'email', 'text messaging' and 'instant messaging'.) An initial sample of 156 different news stories was eventually condensed to form a dataset of 101 articles specifically addressing young people's language practices with new media such as the internet and mobile phones.[3] While the majority of these articles were from national and regional British (36) and US (33) newspapers, the rest came from Canada (9), New Zealand (7), Ireland (4), Singapore (3), Malaysia, the Philippines, Hong Kong, Australia (2 each) and Indonesia (1). As is typical industry practice, a handful of news stories in the corpus were based on syndicated reports or had picked up on stories reported by other papers.

In analysing this corpus, my intention was to eschew a strictly quantitative content analysis in favour of a more interpretative, critical review, which highlighted striking themes rather than statistical patterns. As such, my interpretations here do not make claims to representativeness but rather appeal to an informed judgement of typicality, supported by the inclusion of multiple examples selected from a wide range of different data sources. In presenting this material, it is also not my intention necessarily to account comprehensively for the content of my newspaper corpus in its entirety; nonetheless, along with a range of indicative lexicalizations, sequentially numbered extracts from different articles are given as typical examples. All data examples will be indicated in a different font, and, for longer extracts, sequentially numbered.[4]

In a sister publication (Thurlow 2006), I have examined the corpus with reference to the metadiscursive construction of new-media language more generally, with specific reference to folk-linguistic characterizations of its nature, descriptions of its spread and impact, and exemplifications of actual practice. In this chapter, however, I want instead to focus on the three most troubling narrative preoccupations in contemporary media (mis-) representations of young people's new-media language practices. I suggest that each of the metadiscursive themes which follows presents itself as both a product of, and a premise for, the *technologization* of youth.

11.3.1   Theme 1 – the homogenization of youth: 'I txt there4 I am'

With surprisingly few exceptions, the underlying tone of the articles in my corpus was generally unfavourable towards young people, as with the following kinds of labels: 'idiot student', 'fickle teenagers', 'rapid-fire lifestyle of

218

youth', 'impressionable youth', 'dull and spotty', 'yoof market', 'trend-setting teens', 'garrulous youngsters', 'typical teenager chatter' and 'seemingly (*sic*) sophisticated'.

> Across the land, every night [. . .] teenagers and their ilk are yakking online in chat rooms. (5)

Even more consistent with the general homogenization of 'youth culture' (Davis 1990; Griffin 1993), however, was the depiction of young people as a generation defined uniformly and almost solely in terms of its use of communication technologies. Throughout the entire corpus reference was continually made to lifespan labels such as the 'keyboard generation', 'Generation IM',' the gen-txt community', 'Generation Text', 'mobile generation', 'the thumb generation', 'gen.txtrs' and 'GNR8N TXT'. By the same token, young people were described as 'handset-wielding children', 'wired teens', 'internet-connected since birth', 'text-savvy teenagers', 'tech-rich youth', 'computer-fluent', 'cyberliterate' and 'tech-savvy'. What all these labels, unwittingly perhaps, assume is a generation of young people for whom new communication technology is necessarily second nature, their raison d'être even, and whose social lives centre around typed communication. As one article put it, 'texting is ingrained in the psyche of teenagers'. In somewhat more explicitly pejorative terms, young people were also frequently caricatured as 'hooked', 'addicted', 'text addicts', 'feverishly punching in text on cell phones', 'fervent practitioners of text messaging', 'dependent and compulsive users'. Their use of communication technologies was likewise depicted as a 'craze', 'mania', 'youth obsession' or of 'having cult status'. This framing of young people's new-media practices has the added rhetorical value of supporting otherwise empirically unsubstantiated, anecdotally exaggerated claims for the ubiquity (in terms of availability and uptake) and uniformity of any emergent language practices (see Thurlow 2006).

In newspaper articles devoted to discussing new communication technologies, it might seem obvious that young people would be framed so frequently in terms of their technologies; nonetheless, where recent generations of young people have been characterized in terms of their political beliefs, musical and dance styles, ways of dressing and so on, it does seem striking that the current generation has come to be one-dimensionally epitomized (in the minds of adults at least) by the technologies it uses. In fact, popular discourse about young people and new technology typically characterizes them as 'wired whizzes' and/or 'techno-slaves' (McKay *et al* 2005); on the one hand, young people are talked about as being somehow *naturally* technology inspired and literate, on the other hand, an image is promoted of young people being arch-consumers or tragic victims of technology (e.g. Postman 1994). The hype inherent in popular notions like 'cyberkids' and the 'net generation' is, however, problematic since these sorts of generalized and exaggerated depictions of the role of technology in young people's lives conceal major demographic and economic inequalities (Holloway and Valentine 2001; Facer and Furlong 2001). What is more, implicit in most of these representations is the belief that young people are, in either case, technological dupes, unable to control their consumption/use of new communication technologies. That an adult-driven commerce makes it almost impossible for young people to exist otherwise is a point noticeably overlooked by the articles in my corpus, which readily give voice to corporate perspectives (Thurlow 2006; cf. also Thurlow 2003).

11.3.2 Theme 2 – The de-generation of language: 'the grunt generation'

Mediatized representations of young people's new-media language are arguably at their most aggressive when framed as an attack against conventional or 'correct' orthography and 'proper' spelling. Indeed, for over half of the articles in my corpus, the impact of young people's new-media language on conventional standards of literacy was not simply a topic of discussion but the primary focus. Take, for example, the following sample of headlines from a range of different newspaper articles:

> The Queen's English meets the cellphone.
> Communication shortcuts are corrupting teenagers' language skills.
> Teens' love for e-mail is 'ruining' their grammar.
> Texting shortcuts worry examiners.
> Linguists worry about text messaging effects.
> Is text messaging threatening literacy?
> Phone txt chat 'harms literacy'.
> Letters R history thnx to e-mail, teachers fear.
> Globespeak could kill off 'hello'.
> A Langwidge going from bad 2 worse.
> 1 dA wil Nglsh B ritN li this?

Without wanting to rehearse the all too familiar complaints of what Deborah Cameron calls the 'great grammar crusade' (Cameron 1995: 78), the issue of young people's literacy (or lack thereof) was a topic covered extensively in the corpus. Instant messaging, emailing, and especially text messaging were, for example, described throughout as 'destroying', 'impacting', 'harming', 'limiting', 'damaging', 'ruining', 'threatening', 'massacring', 'corrupting' or 'eroding' standard English and received standards of literacy. For the most part, any concern about falling standards of literacy also centred specifically on standards of grammar, spelling, punctuation, capitalization and sentence structure which were usually reported as being 'sloppy', 'atrocious', 'inferior', 'errant', 'improper', 'undisciplined' or simply 'ugly'. Noticeable by its absence was any serious, sustained discussion about the unquestionable sociolinguistic creativity and poetry in many young people's new-media language practices (see also Ensslin, Chapter 13, this volume). In true verbal-puritan style, new-media language was most commonly positioned in opposition to standard language. A good example of this general pattern was one particular concern expressed in several articles for the negative impact of new-media language on the 'art' (sic) of formal writing and, specifically, traditional handwritten letter-writing which, it was feared, were being 'consigned to history'. A similar framing occurs also in perceived threats to the 'art' of conversation, and the fear that the 'art' and 'courtesy' of accurate spelling and well-constructed sentences or messages is being lost. As one might expect, young people's supposed attack on English was, in some articles, reduced to formal markers of received practice and canonical standards of literature:

> Text messaging is hardly the Queen's English. (6)

> SMS [. . .] has little resemblance to Oxford English. (7)

> And to think this happened in the land of Shakespeare. If the bard were alive today, he'd probably write, '2B or not 2B' [. . .] (8)

> While Shakespeare wrote sonnets about love, today's suitors send a text message to declare their devotion. (9)

This type of claim is clearly underpinned by the assumption that newer forms and styles of communication are necessarily inferior to older, more received ones. Ironically, the ideological preference for uniformity, transparency and accessibility (Cameron 1995: 64) which usually promotes 'plain English' as the most desired style seems not to apply to practices like text and instant messaging whose economic and succinct styles receive no credit. For the most part, the generic practices of instant messaging, text messaging and email are conflated and almost always characterized in terms of, for example, excessive abbreviation, the use of lower-case lettering (or the 'loss' of capitalization) and the absence of punctuation. That literacy is thereby apparently rendered by the print media as equivalent to formal aspects of (written) language use is itself of interest; however, it also reflects the common tendency to 'de-discourse' new-media language altogether, isolating linguistic forms from communicative functions and from contexualizing social practices.

It is in this way that this type of metadiscourse makes a number of important, usually erroneous, assumptions not only about language but also about the nature of technology; it also has important consequences for the way technologically mediated communication is underestimated and poorly understood (see again Thurlow 2006, for more on this). In particular, the image of new-media language presented across the current corpus was consistent with the way that computer-mediated communication is usually characterized in lay (and some scholarly) discourse as being necessarily asocial, task-oriented and always falling short of the supposed ideal of face-to-face communication (see Thurlow *et al* 2004; Walther and Parks 2002).

In several cases, the perceived loss of standard grammar and/or received style was frequently presented by journalists (and their invited commentators) as equivalent to a loss of communication per se. Historical, cultural and economic variables in language change were also uniformly overlooked, as in the following extracts which, either explicitly or implicitly, make questionable claims of direct causality:

> *Since* text messaging has become one of the quickest and easiest forms of communication between teenagers and pre-teens, grammar and spelling have deteriorated dramatically. (emphasis mine) (10)

> English teachers bemoan the 'creative' spelling that texting has fostered, saying that writing skills have deteriorated *since* the popular communication tool has been in use. (emphasis mine) (11)

> The text messaging craze is [...] systematically destroying grammar, syntax and even spelling. (12)

What appears most troubling about this type of framing of new-media discourse is less the fact that dismissing it as 'meaningless messages', 'staccato statements', 'short bursts of dialogue', or just generally 'short' and 'shallow' fails to acknowledge its sociolinguistic complexity and variety, but that these comments devalue a way of communicating which clearly has a great deal of interpersonal and symbolic value for many young people. Certainly, few articles in my corpus explicitly commented on the metalinguistic awareness which evidently underpins most young people's use of new-media language – the ironic and self-reflexive quality of much of it, as well as young people's poetic/aesthetic appreciation for its particular orthographic and visual qualities (see also Kress 2000b). Indeed, much new-media discourse is often highly creative, inventive and playful (Androutsopoulos 2000; Palfreyman and al Khalil 2003; see also Ensslin, Chapter 13, this volume). What is more, there is seldom any evidence to suggest that young people's new-media language is also not interactionally and pragmatically meaningful to them – which it most likely is. Instead, however, new-media discourse is typically characterized as a deficient or inadequate form of communication, and most especially when set against idealized modes of communication such as face-to-face conversation.

Journalistic talk about the 'degeneration' of language and literacy at the heart of these print media accounts of young people's new-media language is clearly intended as a resource for bemoaning moral and societal decline. However, one might more reasonably view this as a two-fold *de-generation* of language: first, as an undue metadiscursive separation of every-day discourse into age-related or age-appropriate categories; second, as an inherent denial of the generative, creative potential of language-in-use. In either case, young people are left to feel that their ways of speaking/communicating are bad because theirs are not standard or appropriate ways just as researchers suggest is the case with ethnic-minority dialects and other non-standard speakers (see, for example, Collins 1999, on the Ebonics debate). It is very much in this way also that adolescence reveals itself yet again as a site for administering the social order, for preserving tradition, the status quo, and for preventing moral decay/decline (cf. Lesko 2003). I will return to this point shortly.

11.3.3 Theme 3 – The exaggeration of difference: 'Cracking the code of teenspeak'

Closely allied to both the homogenized image of a tech-savvy or technologically enslaved generation of young people and their deleterious impact on standards of literacy and moral order, the third major narrative theme in my corpus was concerned with the apparent unintelligibility or impenetrability of young people's new-media language. Just as the language used by young instant messagers has been described even by some specialists as a 'new hieroglyphics' (e.g. Pew Internet and American Life Project, (www.pewinternet. org)), scholars too have sometimes tended to exaggerate the uniqueness and exclusivity of text messaging language due to its supposedly code-like inaccessibility (e.g. Kasesniemi and Rautiainen 2002: 183).

Throughout the print media accounts in my corpus, new-media language was frequently depicted as being inaccessible to adults; for example, in the following terms: 'baffling', 'causes confusion', leaving them 'stumped' by the 'misspellings', 'abbreviations' and 'bizarre acronyms'. Accordingly, new-media language can only be understood by those in the know – the initiated, those who understand. It is simply incomprehensible to the untrained reader. For the 'uninitiated', the 'text-illiterate', the 'clueless', new-media language is therefore a 'mysterious lexicon', 'hieroglyphics', 'code', 'technobabble', 'cryptic chat', 'a bizarre activity', 'hodgepodge communication', 'secret code', 'language soup', 'jumble', 'impenetrable', 'ramblings', 'cryptic symbols', 'word jumble', 'quirky, cryptograms', 'garbled', 'encoded messages', 'gobbledegook', 'gibberish', 'opaque', 'secrets', 'argle-bargle', 'cipher', 'exclusive', 'effective code against POS' ['parent over shoulder'], 'code language', 'obscure', and 'a secret language'. No wonder, then, that young people's new-media language usually needs to be 'deciphered'.

Serving the same dual metalinguistic function of establishing new-media language as a 'real' or distinctive variety as well as promoting its apparent unintelligibility, one rhetorical strategy used in over a third of the articles in my corpus was the provision of some sort of glossary or listing of in-text examples of messaging terminology. Where, for example, one article included a 'How to Text' section, another gave readers a chance to 'test your knowledge of the lingo'. By the same token, other articles made reference to so-called text messaging dictionaries or online translation services. In Thurlow (2006), I follow Norman Fairclough's (2003) idea of relations of equivalence, in considering how these rhetorical devices serve to authenticate the characterization of new-media language as a kind of linguistic revolution.

This rendering of new-media language as being somehow unintelligible not only serves to promote its validity as a distinctive, revolutionary sociolinguistic variety, but also plays up its impenetrability or inaccessibility for adults. As such, young people's new-media language becomes a prime resource by which adults are able to exaggerate and fetishize the teen-ness of new-media language, young people's communication more generally, and young people themselves. Indeed, there is something almost self-absorbed or narcissistic in this adult-generated media discourse with its persistent implication that young people are somehow deliberately texting or messaging in order to exclude (or 'foil', as in the example below) adults. Once again, this artful hieroglyphic code must be cracked.

> The evolving language of online chat is leaving parents – as well as grammar and punctuation – behind. (13)

> They have created their own words to foil teachers and other adults. (14)

> The page was riddled with hieroglyphics, many of which I simply could not translate. (15)

A key communicative function of all language use – and arguably more so with slang and other colloquial forms – is its use for social identity maintenance, for ingrouping and outgrouping. In other words, the primary symbolic value of young people's new-media language lies precisely in the fact that it is not meant to be for, or necessarily about, adults. As a young person quoted in one article put it: 'It's a teen-to-teen thing.' In this respect, just as Rosina Lippi-Green (1997) sees the 'burden of communication' being forced onto ethnic minorities, it is young people who are apparently obliged to make themselves understood to adults. Yet, the indignation of the teacher in Extract 15 – 'many of which I simply could not translate' – leaves one wondering if what is being indirectly conveyed here is an adult's frustration (or fascination) with their own lack of technical competence in contrast to the technical capacity of many young people. This possible sense of disempowerment is no doubt also disruptive of the usual power relations which usually characterize adolescence more generally.

Elsewhere in the corpus, journalists found other rhetorical means by which to exaggerate the difference of young people's new-media language, for the most part, resorting once again to over-extended claims for its ubiquity and impact (see Thurlow 2006). For example, largely anecdotal, unsupported claims were made for the way new-media language was supposedly affecting the way people talk to each other, leading to a breakdown in communication and the erosion of traditional conversation, and causing people to lose the ability to talk or express themselves as well as losing the ability to read and write properly.

> Teenagers are more likely to understand this new shorthand language than plain English. (16)

> Young people seem to be throwing out the dictionary in favor of the quick and easy way of writing. (17)

The exaggeration of the distinctiveness of young people's new-media language is thereby represented so as to dramatize adult anxieties about declining standards of literacy as well as to feed adult mythologies about the inscrutability of young people's communication in general (Thurlow, 2005). These two principle myths, or cultural narratives, are encapsulated nicely in the two cartoons below – yet further examples of ways in which social order and control are powerfully rehearsed and exercised through what appear to be harmless and ideologically innocent depictions of young people's new-media language.[6] Where the first depicts the dominant adult anxiety about the impact of young people's new-media language on received standards of literacy and social order, it is the second which relies for its

www.cartoonstock.com

Figure 11.2

humour on the exaggeration of unintelligibility and inaccessibility – as does the Zits cartoon at the start of this chapter. I am therefore inclined to follow Jane Hill's (2001) lead in thinking that this type of apparent playful cele-bration of 'youth culture' ultimately works to elevate and promote the superiority of adulthood; in doing so, young people's communication capital (cf. Thurlow 2001a, after Bourdieu 1991) is simply devalued even further.

11.4 Technologization: styling the teenager

As Deborah Cameron (1995) suggests, the responsibility of academics is not necessarily to evaluate the scholarly merits or accuracy of folk-linguistic dis-course, but certainly to critique those metalinguistic claims to authority by which social/power relations come to be organized and normalized (see also Cameron, Chapter 12, this volume). Where the first position is only ever likely to be a matter of taste, the second is instead a matter of politics. Indeed, all metadiscourse – regardless of its linguistic validity – is always a site of con-stant bureaucratic and interpersonal struggle. Invariably also, the promotion or denigration of certain styles and ways of speaking – the devaluing of com-munication capital, just mentioned – serves as a means of rehearsing or reproducing the social order. In Cameron's terms, verbal hygiene and moral hygiene are always interconnected (Cameron 1995: 114), just as commerce and profit are always closely implicated in the reproduction and maintenance of standard varieties (cf. Bourdieu 1991). In this sense, therefore, style itself becomes a commodity – especially for professional language workers, those who make a living from language, such as dictionary editors, academic lin-guists and, of course, newspaper journalists.

Much of what one sees in the newspaper articles I have looked at is, of course, just a continuation of the age-old 'great grammar crusade' whereby the preservation of standard (written) varieties becomes a rhetorical resource for discussing traditional values, educational discipline, moral certainty and cultural homogeneity. Indeed, discussions about language offer a (meta-)symbolic means for adults to reflect on any number of issues which typically have little do with language per se. For the most part, therefore, it would be impossible to decide which of youth, technology or language is the 'real' worry for society – in my corpus at least they appear largely inseparable. Regardless of whether adults have spoken about young people and their language in similar ways before, it is the apparent intensity and negativity with which they are currently being characterized which is striking. While the popular metadiscourse examined here promotes the idea of an attack being launched by young people, it would seem that, on the contrary, it is young people who are, for various economic, commercial and cultural rea-sons, increasingly coming under attack from adults (Males 1996; Giroux 2000). In this regard, young people's new-media language practices are both easy targets *and* readily available ammunition.

226

Before even turning to consider the literal technologies which appear to preoccupy journalists and their chosen commentators, adolescence can itself also be thought of as a technology in at least two different, but related, ways. Particularly since the early twentieth century, adolescence has been established as a complex of mechanisms or a system of knowledges designed by adults for socializing people into citizenship and for disciplining them into societal hierarchies. Given this, it is also quite understandable that the print media, as a powerful mechanism of representation in itself (Hall 1992), would also be brought to bear on adolescence. In returning to my corpus once more, this broader technological function of adolescence arguably exposes itself in comments such as the following:

> Our society needs people who are able to use English correctly. (18)

> If the already ingrained corruption of the English language is perpetuated, we will soon be a nation made up entirely of grammatical duffers. (19)

> The English language is being beaten up, civilization is in danger of crumbling. (20)

As Nancy Lesko points out, however, the technology of adolescence has a dual function:

> [T]he categories and processes involved in adolescents' identities are simultaneously sites of broader cultural debates about knowledge, identity, representation, and power. In other words, adolescent bodies [are] a terrain in which struggles over what count[s] as an adult [. . .] [are] staged. (Lesko 2003: 50)

In this sense, therefore – and in a similarly Foucauldian way – it is also possible to conceive of adolescence as a 'technology of self'(Foucault 1988) by which adults are, in turn, also able to construct their own identities as adults. It is partly through the constant othering – or outgrouping – of young people as young people, that adults identify themselves socially as adults – as grown ups. Indeed, adolescence is inevitably a site of intense oppositional identification through which adults exercise many of their own hopes for the future and anxieties about the status quo (cf. Wyn 2005). As Cameron also notes, public discussions about language bring into being communities and identities, in this case, adult identities whereby their metadiscourse about the language standards and their exaggeration of language difference become means to establish a sense of identity and social control.

There is, in fact, yet another means by which adolescence might be seen as discursively organized and technologized in the particular context under discussion here. Given the more metaphoric meanings of 'technology' just mentioned, the particular mode of *technologization* I really want to invoke relates to the strategic commodification of young people's new-media practices as a means to further 'stylize' (cf. Cameron 2000b; Fairclough 1997) them as necessarily media rich and media savvy (cf. Thurlow and McKay 2003).[7] Like Deborah Cameron (2000b) and Norman Fairclough (1997), I see this stylization as a prescriptivist imposition or scripting of certain ways of speaking together with the commodification of language as being a matter solely of transactional, utilitarian value. In fact, the link between language, literacy and the marketplace was apparent on a number of occasions in my corpus, where the increasing valorization of the instrumental function of language and communication was revealed, as in these extracts:

> Employers complain they are forced to give remedial lessons ... to hundreds of thousands of school-leavers to help them communicate clearly. (21)

> This verbal slang is exasperating businesses. (22)

> If you can't speak good English, how can you expect someone to give you a good job? (23)

While Cameron focuses her own discussion on the scripting – or 'styling' – of (female) workers, my concern here is obviously with the way adult journalists and other media commentators create and promote a specific image (or style) of 'teentalk' and new-media language – one which often bears little resemblance to actual practice (Thurlow 2003; Thurlow 2006). Not only, therefore, does public metadiscourse on young people's new-media language work to sustain the technology that is adolescence itself and to service the identificational needs of adults, this same metadiscourse technologizes young people by rendering them as uniformly and universally 'wired' or 'hooked'. Lesko (2003) discusses how the administration and disciplining of young people's play in particular has also been central to the technology of adolescence. It would appear to be no coincidence, therefore, that the playful and, for the most part, benign practices of young people's new-media discourse come under fire. Where linguistic puritans are typically dour sticklers for the rules, language here is invariably treated as a dull tool rather than, say, a ludic resource or sensual practice.

In more sinister terms, however, language, and new-media language in particular, are thereby exploited as resources by which adults may, as Giroux (2000: 15) would see it, not only demonize but also commodify youth. Indeed, for Steven Miles (2000), the value of young people in contemporary society lies precisely in their role as consumers. As such, the metalinguistic idealizations and misrepresentations of the print media might be understood as being ultimately focused on the preparation of young people for consumption – as both agents and as objects. Young people and youth are themselves consumable (Wyn and White 1997; also Giroux 2000) and youth itself has nowadays 'been transformed into a market strategy and a fashion aesthetic used to expand the consumer-based needs of privileged adults' (Giroux 2000: 19). Accordingly, the media and marketers work together to exaggerate the separateness of youth culture in order to distinguish young people as a valuable resource and a profitable market (White 1993 in Miles 2000: 120). And technology is central to the consumption of youth, with young people being obliged to position themselves in relation to technology which, in turn, becomes a key way in which their identities are explored (by themselves) and also understood by adults. A central feature of this strategy is therefore the promotion of an image of young people as aggressive brand-chasers and new technology users. The success of adolescence as a technology depends on keeping young people caught unavoidably in series of double-binds, trapped in a limbo of endless 'becoming', according to Lesko (2003). They are neither children nor adults; they are always too old *and* too young. In examining mediatized metadiscourse about young people's new-media language, what is apparent, therefore, is not just the triple whammy of adult moralizing about youth, declining standards of language and the impact of new technology, but also an impossible double-bind which the media forces young people into. On the one hand, young people are confronted by the aggressive targeting of an adult-driven commerce, and on the other hand, they face the constant criticism of an adult-generated media. It seems that young people are once again caught in a no-win situation.

11.5 The hidden agenda of language workers

Given the focus of this volume, I would like to end with a brief observation about the broader institutional conditions under which public metadiscourse about young people's new-media language comes to be produced.[8] For example, it is important to recognize that journalists are a community of professional *language workers* who, like academics, teachers and lexicographers, are especially and explicitly dependent on the crafting of language for their livelihoods. It is also widely known that news-making disproportionately and consistently values negativity (McGregor 2002). Not surprisingly, therefore, the print media predictably generates more than its fair share of language mavens and grammar crusaders invested in upholding and preserving received orthographic or other linguistic standards. It is understandable too if news-makers are more than especially prone to worrying and writing about perceived threats to language. In which case, the endless schooling of the style manual and the disciplining of editors are just too easily redirected to the broader community of language users (cf. Johnson's discussion of the German spelling reform, Chapter 5, this volume).

Notwithstanding this, one empirical benefit of reviewing in detail a corpus of over 100 newspaper articles from around the world has been the opportunity to identify other somewhat more problematic processes of story recycling and what might (kindly) be called 'informal syndication'. It is otherwise hidden processes such as these which reveal something of the institutional processes by which not only the news but also youth itself comes to be fabricated. I offer the following two specific examples drawn from my corpus.

11.5.1 The National Examiners' Report

On 7 November 2004, the British *Daily Telegraph* carried an article under the headline 'Pupils Resort to Text Language in GCSE Exams', in which its education correspondent picked up on a report by one of the UK's major secondary school examination authorities (Assessment & Qualifications Alliance, AQA). In what might be regarded either as an over-interpretation or as a gross misrepresentation, the original article contained statements such as the following:

- examiners have given warning that pupils are using text message language in GCSEs;
- this is the first official acknowledgement that mobile phone shorthand is undermining standard English;
- English GCSE scripts were peppered with abbreviated words which have become second nature to many youngsters;
- the examiners' report suggests that such abbreviations are becoming the norm;
- 'It's quite appalling that school children cannot distinguish between ordinary language and text language.' (24)

In point of fact, the 61-page, official examiners' report (published by AQA in 2004, p. 15) contained only a single statement in the middle of an otherwise long section about general spelling and grammatical issues: 'The usual errors with they're/their; are/our; we're/were; your/you're were frequent, and texting spellings such as U for "you" are increasingly prevalent.' Feeding directly into, and indeed helping to constitute, the continual moral panic about falling standards of literacy, this original article was subsequently picked up in a number of other articles in the current corpus where the original incident was likewise overstated. For example:

Exam papers are 'riddled' with abbreviated words and spellings. Young people seem to be throwing out the dictionary in favour of the quick and easy way of writing. (25)

Examiners have noticed in recent years that the language of text messages has crept into GCSEs and a report published by the largest exam board in the country showed papers were riddled with abbreviated words. (26)

Chief examiners' reports on trends in public examinations have begun to note instances of texting language in exam scripts. Some cases – including a 13-year-old Scottish pupil who wrote an entire description of her summer holidays in text-speak – have provoked concern among some teachers. (27)

In Extract 27, the journalist also (mistakenly) conflates the GCSE-examiners' story with a completely separate incident in which a Scottish schoolgirl reportedly submitted a classroom essay using text messaging style.

11.5.2 The Scottish girl's school essay

On 3 March 2003, the British *Daily Telegraph* had run a story about an anonymous Scottish teacher who claimed to have received from a 13-year-old pupil a composition completed entirely in the style of a text-message. From the original newspaper report, the following is reported:

British education experts have warned of the potentially damaging effect on literacy of cellphone text messaging after a student handed in an essay written in text shorthand. The 13-year-old girl, a student in a secondary school in the west of Scotland, explained that she found it 'easier than standard English'. 'I could not believe what I was seeing,' said her teacher, who asked not to be identified. 'The page was riddled with hieroglyphics, many of which I simply could not translate.' (28)

What is noticeable from this extract is how many of the same metadiscursive tropes arise (e.g., 'damaging effects on literacy', 'riddled', 'hieroglyphics', 'translate'). What is even more telling, however, is how this particular story appeared also in nine other articles in the corpus – in places such as *The Scotsman*, *The London Times*, and *Western Mail* (all UK), the *Ottawa Citizen* and *Montreal Gazette* (Canada), *Reason Magazine* (USA), the *Irish Times* (Ireland), *Jakarta Post* (Indonesia) and *BusinessWorld* (Philippines). Reports of the story could also be found in the online versions of both the BBC and CNN. In fact, a cursory web search at the time of writing this chapter also revealed how the same story was featured as the focus of at least 1,630 different websites. A year and a half after the original *Telegraph* article, a British *Guardian* article, headlined 'Texting is No Bar to Literacy', included the longest reported segment of the girl's supposedly original essay (together with a 'translation') under the sub-heading 'SMS: A Textbook Case'.

My smmr hols wr CWOT. B4, we used 2 go 2 NY 2C my bro, his GF & thr 3 :-@ kds FTF. ILNY, its gr8. Bt my Ps wr so {:-/ BC o 9/11 tht thay dcdd 2 stay in SCO & spnd 2 wks up N. Up N, WUCIWUG - - 0. I ws vvv brd in MON. 0 bt baas & ∧ ∧ ∧ ∧ ∧.

231

> My summer holidays were a complete waste of time. Before, we used to go to New York to see my brother, his girlfriend and their three screaming kids face to face. I love New York, it's a great place. But my parents were so worried because of the terrorism attack on September 11 that they decided we would stay in Scotland and spend two weeks up north. Up north, what you see is what you get – nothing. I was extremely bored in the middle of nowhere. Nothing but sheep and mountains. (29)

Although this might well have been an unfortunate misjudgement of register on the part of the young pupil, what news reports uniformly fail to acknowledge is the undeniable creativity, potential wit and innovative literacy of the girl's piece. Instead, as with the original *Daily Telegraph* article, subsequent articles which ran this story condemned the incident as an indictment of young people's new-media language, tending also to exaggerate and/or extrapolate from the original news report – shifting, for example, from an isolated, individual incident to a statement about the 'current generation of teenagers' (Extract 30). In fact, in the case of one article in the Indonesian *Jakarta Post* (Extract 31), an apparently fabricated excerpt is actually quoted.

> This week we learn that the current generation of teenagers is so estranged from real language that a 13-year-old in the west of Scotland has submitted an essay to her teacher in text-message shorthand. (30)

> A student that was asked to write a short descriptive piece about a recent holiday included the sentence, 'U can get 2 the hotel straight from the beach', while it is possible to decipher what is meant it really is not appropriate for this kind of coding to be encroaching in this way. Grammatical and spelling accuracy are things that are going to be lost if this kind of coding goes on unchecked. (31)

To suggest that this young person's essay represents a 'textbook case' of new-media language is clearly to misconstrue the realities of young people's actual, everyday, usual practices (Thurlow 2003). To further suggest that it might also epitomize the literacies of an entire generation is a gross extrapolation from the facts. That adults get away with *mis*representing young people on such a scale and in such a questionable manner says a great deal about the relations of power that structure youth. Print-media metadiscourse about young people and their new-media language is more than a harmless and perhaps understandable mis-recognition of language, technology, and/or young people; this news-making seems more intentionally and effectively irresponsible. Perhaps it is time for young people to offer these professional story tellers and language workers a little friendly advice: 'Act your age!'

Notes

1. I am very grateful to Mary Beth Kaiser and Hazel Lin for their help with collecting and compiling the corpus analysed here. For their comments on earlier

presentations of this work, I am also indebted to various colleagues at the 10th International Conference on Language and Social Psychology (University of Bonn, Germany, 14–17 June 2006) and the first meeting of the AILA Research Network on Language in the Media (Skipton, England, 6–8 April 2006). Completion of this chapter was made possible thanks to financial assistance from the Department of Communication (travel support, April 2006) and the College of Arts & Sciences (faculty development award, June 2006) at the University of Washington.

2. In countries where English is not a recognized/official language, this mediatized metadiscourse typically centres also on the deleterious impact of young people's use of English – new media or otherwise – on the local/official language (see e.g. Spitzmüller 2005, for a discussion of the German context).

3. Articles in the corpus were distributed as follows: 18 from 2001, 10 from 2002, 24 from 2003, 30 from 2004, and 6 from 2005. An additional 13 articles collected previously (from 1999 or 2000) were also included.

4. A complete listing of the original articles (together with date, newspaper and database source) constituting my corpus has been published along with Thurlow (2006); this can be found online at (www.jcmc.indiana.edu/vol11/issue3/thurlow.html#appendix1).

5. Technology and new-media language clearly have indentificational value also for young people; in the case of this mediatized metadiscourse, however, it is adults who are 'imposing' a social identity rather than young people choosing it for themselves.

6. Although beyond the scope of my analysis here, the type of mediatized adult discourse under discussion here is, of course, just as likely to be found in the broadcast media. Another example is a 2005 broadcast in the United States of NBC's TODAY programme which featured an item with well-known journalist Katie Couric expressing her largely anecdotal, folk-linguistic concerns about young people's new media language. Indeed, her commentary mirrors almost perfectly the metadiscursive themes identified in this chapter and those of Thurlow (2006). A recording of this 6-minute item may be downloaded from my website [WMV file 70.6 MB]: http://faculty.washington.edu/thurlow/materials/today-clip.wmv.

7. In borrowing Deborah Cameron's (2000b) notion of 'stylization', I mean also to reference the role of language – and, no doubt, new-media language – as a key identity resource for the self-styling of young people (cf. Eckert 1989; Marshland 1993: 130 in Miles 2000: 123).

8. This final section of the chapter is taken in large part from Thurlow (2006) and reproduced here with permission from the *Journal of Computer-Mediated Communication*.

12 Dreaming of Genie: language, gender difference and identity on the web

Deborah Cameron

12.1 Language and gender in the media

Linguists often complain about the unscientific approach that dominates media coverage of issues relating to language. In *The Language Instinct*, for instance, Steven Pinker underlines the absurdity of what passes for informed comment on linguistic matters by asking us to imagine a world in which the same approach is applied to TV nature programmes:

> Imagine that you are watching a nature documentary. The video shows the usual gorgeous footage of animals in their natural habitats. But the voiceover reports some troubling facts. Dolphins do not execute their swimming strokes properly. White-crowned sparrows carelessly debase their calls. Chickadees' nests are incorrectly constructed, pandas hold bamboo in the wrong paw, the song of the humpback whale contains several well-known errors and monkeys' cries have been in a state of chaos and degeneration for hundreds of years.
> (Pinker 1994: 370)

Pinker's target here is what James Milroy and Lesley Milroy (1998) call the 'complaint tradition', which is preoccupied with standards and correctness. Complaint discourse does feature prominently in the media's treatment of language: it is found in readers' letters to newspapers, in columns and opinion pieces, and whenever some controversy (e.g. on the teaching of grammar, or Ebonics, or a proposal to introduce language tests for immigrants) propels the subject onto the news agenda. And as Pinker says, complaint discourse is generally pre-, un- or openly anti-scientific. The 'authorities' it recognizes are more likely to be poets, princes and politicians than linguists or anyone else with 'scientific' knowledge (see also the contributions to this volume by John-son, Horner, Milani and Thurlow).

But complaint discourse is not the only kind that appears in the media with some regularity. Some media representations of language (e.g. radio and TV series charting the history of English, or documentaries about polyglot 'savants' and whether language can be taught to apes) are more like the nature programmes Pinker contrasts with unscientific prescriptivism: they belong to a strand of factual programming or journalism in which the author-ity of science is both recognized and exploited. The media rely on experts to provide them with material and sometimes to present it to audiences directly. And the experts, for their part, often solicit media interest in their work: as well as reporting on their research to fellow-experts in conference papers or journal articles, they issue press releases in the hope that the media will dis-seminate their findings to a wider public.

One area of linguistic research which is recurrently placed in a 'scienti-fic' frame is male-female differences in verbal ability and behaviour. Like the staple topics of the complaint tradition (grammar, spelling, slang, (il)literacy, obscenity, language change), language and gender attracts media coverage because the issue is seen to be one of perennial interest to a general audience. Unlike the staple topics of the complaint tradition, however, language and gender is rarely the subject of media opinion pieces. Stories are often sourced from journal articles and conference papers (or at least, from press releases put out in connection with them); audiences are assumed to be interested in the latest research findings and in the views of people with some claim to spe-cialist 'scientific' expertise.

This kind of science-led reporting would seem on the face of things less vulnerable to the charge Pinker levels against media 'language mavens', namely that their endless unscientific grumbling does nothing to inform the public, but merely panders to popular ignorance and prejudice. On inspection, however, things are not quite so simple. To see why, let us examine a typical example of the science-led language and gender story. In August 2005, a study conducted by researchers in Sheffield and published in the scholarly journal *NeuroImage* attracted international media coverage. The news item I reproduce below appeared with minor variations in both print and broad-cast outlets from the UK to Australia and from China to the USA.

Men do have trouble hearing women: research
Men who are accused of never listening by women now have an excuse – women's voices are more difficult for men to listen to than other men's. Reports say researchers at Sheffield University in northern England have discovered startling differences in the way the brain responds to male and female sounds. The research shows men decipher female voices using the auditory part of the brain that processes music, while male voices engage a simpler mechanism. (*ABC NewsOn-Line*, 17.08.05)

At first glance, this story belongs to a familiar journalistic genre of brief snippets presenting the fascinating facts unearthed by boffins toiling in laboratories. But it also belongs to another familiar genre which has nothing to do with science: the 'battle of the sexes' story. In fact, it is that cliché which provides the overarching frame. Beginning with the headline 'Men do have trouble hearing women' – notice that periphrastic *do*, a marked grammatical choice suggesting that the writer is contesting some previous claim to the contrary – the scientists' discovery that 'women's voices are more difficult for men to listen to than other men's' is presented as settling an old argument about whether and why men do not listen to women.[1] According to 'science', both parties have a point: women are justified in complaining that men do not listen to what they say, but men are equally justified in rejecting the charge of sexism: the problem is not their attitudes but the way their brains are wired. So, a popular stereotype concerning language and gender ('men do not listen to women') is shown to be (a) 'scientifically' valid and (b) the result of biological sex differences – from which we may conclude that (c) there is nothing to be done about it. Many stories based on the science of sex and gender follow exactly this formula.

What such examples show is that 'scientific' sources, no less than 'unscientific' ones, can be deployed in media discourse to reinforce questionable popular preconceptions. Indeed, where it is possible, this is a highly effective strategy, exploiting the cultural capital of science to invest common-sense folk-beliefs with added authority and credibility. On the issues that are central to the language complaint tradition, it is not possible to play the science card because the divergence between expert and popular ideologies is virtually absolute. In the case of language and gender, however, certain kinds of science are more compatible with folk understandings (sometimes, indeed, they are the source for them), and the science card, especially the trump card of biology, is regularly played in reporting. If we ask why the Sheffield study, unlike dozens of other language and gender studies, made headlines around the world, the answer is clearly because it aligned so neatly with popular wisdom, and lent itself so readily to the 'battle of the sexes' treatment. Had the researchers found that their subjects processed male and female voices in exactly the same way, that would have been no less interesting or significant from a purely scientific point of view; but we can be pretty sure it would not have interested the media.

In sum, then, I am arguing that the key issue for our understanding of media representations of linguistic issues is not whether they draw on 'scientific' or 'unscientific' sources, it is how they select and frame their source material. 'Science' is useful – and is drawn on extensively – where it aligns, or can be made to align, with popular language ideologies and commonplace media tropes (e.g. 'the battle of the sexes'). Where there is no such alignment, science will be ignored or dismissed. Parenthetically, we might observe that the same considerations apply to the reporting of 'unscientific' opinion – not

236

all opinions or prejudices are equal. If a public figure makes a speech deploring falling standards of grammar and spelling among schoolchildren, journalists will scramble to produce an 'X hits out at falling standards' story; but if a public figure makes a speech praising the excellence of young people's grammar and spelling, there will either be no story or else the angle will be 'who does he think he's kidding?' (see also Thurlow, Chapter 11, this volume).

When we consider the media's representation of any issue, we need to look not only at ideological factors which make some kinds of scientific source material more likely than others to be reported (e.g. what a study is about and whether its premises and conclusions fit with or challenge popular preconceptions), but also at the influence of conventions relating to genre, format and formula (e.g. whether a study can be summarized in the space the media allots such stories, and how easily it can be presented using a familiar formula like 'the battle of the sexes'). But we should also be aware that presentation conventions can change: in the case I am concerned with, the presentation of language and gender in the media, it is evident that they are changing, in line with new ideas about how best to make science accessible and appealing to a popular audience. The reporting of the Sheffield study illustrates the 'traditional' approach; but in the remainder of this chapter I want to focus on the 'new' approach, illustrating the discussion with a more detailed examination of the online interactive text-analysis tool which is known as the 'Gender Genie'.

12.2   Popularizing science: the new interactivity

Popular interest in sex or gender differences is not a new phenomenon, and nor is the mediation of knowledge about them. Throughout the modern period, the media have played an important role in codifying and disseminating ideas about the differences between women and men. Evidence of public interest in linguistic gender differences can be found in print genres going back to early modern times: in grammar books, usage guides and texts on elocution, and in less specifically linguistic genres like conduct books, etiquette manuals and other forms of instructional literature. As science has overtaken religious or moral doctrine as the most authoritative source of knowledge about the nature and behaviour of humans, however, interest in male–female difference has tended to migrate to more 'scientific' media genres. Today, the subject features prominently in self-help and popular psychology texts, as well as in books, magazine articles and television science documentaries dealing with evolution, genetics and the workings of the human brain.

The topic of male–female difference, then, is of enduring interest to the media (and their audiences); and as the case of the Sheffield study shows, certain long-established formulas for discoursing upon it have also endured over time. But recently, we have been seeing the emergence of new formats and formulas. For example, television science producers are increasingly mixing the traditional documentary format with elements from the newer entertainment genre of reality television: gender and sexuality are among the subjects considered especially well suited to this approach. In Britain during summer 2005, the BBC broadcast a series titled *Secrets of the Sexes*, in which experts demonstrated various scientific theses relating to sexual difference by administering tests to a group of 'ordinary' men and women. Channel 5 came even closer to *Big Brother* territory with *The Truth About Female Desire*, a series in which eight women spent a week having everything from their fantasies to their clitorises probed by scientists from the Kinsey Institute. The aim of these formats is to solicit the active interest and involvement of audiences by showing how scientific theories or findings apply to an exemplary group of real people – people viewers can 'get to know', and who they can identify as like themselves or their friends. This contrasts with the traditional approach, in which scientific information is transmitted by expert 'talking heads'. Many media producers believe that younger viewers in particular are bored and alienated by being 'lectured' in this way. The 'reality' approach is held to make science more relevant to their experience, more engaging and more entertaining.

The emphasis on involving the viewer, on not treating him or her as a passive recipient of expert wisdom, is even more marked in the 'new' medium of the web. It has become common for the output of both print and broadcast media to be supported by websites, on which users can register their own responses to an item and interact more directly with its content (see Hill, Chapter 4, this volume). Thus viewers of *Secrets of the Sexes* can go to the relevant part of the BBC's website and test themselves in the same way they have seen the people in the programme being tested. 'Satellite' websites attached to the output of other media are only the tip of the iceberg, however. Numerous freestanding websites cater to popular interest in male–female differences, and many, like the *Secrets of the Sexes* site, feature interactive quizzes based on supposedly scientific sources. Just as you can find websites containing standardized tests of IQ or personality type, so you can find tests purporting to reveal the sex of your brain, or where along the spectrum of possibility your sexual preferences fall. At least some of these quiz sites aim to educate as well as entertain users, on the principle that many people respond better to a concrete, personalized, 'hands on' demonstration of whatever scientific point is being made than to an abstract, impersonal exposition by an expert.

The Gender Genie, which made its debut on the web in 2003, is a variation on the interactive quiz which works on input provided by the user to demonstrate a general point about gender difference. One thing that is unusual about it – and which makes it particularly apt for my purposes – is its specific focus on language. Because of the orthodox view that women on average have better verbal skills and men better spatial skills, and that this difference has a biological basis, language features in many 'brain sex'-type quizzes, but it is seldom their central focus. Also unusual is the kind of input on which the Genie works. Most quizzes involve a mixture of puzzle-solving tasks (e.g. mentally rotating objects in space) and self-report questionnaire items (e.g. recording how far the user agrees with a statement like 'I find it easy to figure out what other people are feeling'). By contrast, visitors to the Genie's website are invited to paste a sample of English prose into a window. They then receive, within a few seconds, the Genie's verdict on whether the author of the sample is a man or a woman. Below I will say more about how the Genie performs its magic trick. First, though, I should explain why it is of interest for the purposes of this chapter.

My interest in interactive websites on the theme of sex and gender began around 2001 when I realized how popular they were with the students I taught in language and gender classes. During the previous few years I had become used to teaching students whose ideas about language and gender came from 'Mars and Venus'-style self-help literature, but now more of them seemed to favour the kind of material available on the web. While some of the sites they frequented were clearly 'just for fun', others were presented as more 'serious'; students would raise, as serious class discussion points, allegedly 'scientific' facts they had gleaned from these sources. It seemed these websites were contributing to an ideological phenomenon whose linguistic dimension I was documenting at the time (see Cameron 2005, 2006): the post-feminist rehabilitation of biological essentialism in discourse on sex/gender. I therefore began to take an interest in their content. But I also became interested in the effects of the medium and format. Two much-commented-upon features of the web as a medium are its interactivity and its democratic or egalitarian quality. I wondered what difference those features might make to the way users engage with what is presented as expert or scientific knowledge. Does being (inter)actively engaged encourage a more incisive and critical stance, or does it, on the contrary, encourage credulity and cause confusion?

I am also interested in *exploiting* the interactivity of the web to investigate those questions, by looking at the uptake of certain ideas by website users. As media scholars have been insisting for decades, text or content analysis on its own cannot tell us what audiences will actually make of the text in question. If we want to talk about the influence or effect of media representations, we also need to consider reception evidence. On the web, where users routinely interact both with and about the content they have chosen to consume – and where this interaction leaves a public record – it is possible to find what you might call naturally occurring reception evidence. The study reported below exploits that, using evidence of the Gender Genie's reception by one group who showed a particular interest in it – bloggers.

Typing 'Gender Genie' into Google yields not only a link to the Genie site itself, but also links to many other sites on which it gets a reference. A large proportion of these are weblogs in which the blogger has made a link to the Genie, and many blogs also contain one or more entries in which the blogger recounts and reflects upon his or her own experiences with the Genie. Some of

239

these entries contain links to similar entries in other blogs and/or extended discussions in which visitors to a blog, using its comments facility, compare notes on the Genie with the blogger and one another. At the end of 2003 I constructed a sample of this discourse by running a web search on the phrase 'Gender Genie' and collecting everything that related to the Genie – entries, comments and links – from the first 100 English-language weblogs the search turned up.

Clearly, this sampling method has limitations and disadvantages. I cannot claim that the sample is representative of the English-speaking population, or even of Genie-users as a sub-set of that population. Indeed, I can only make informed guesses about who, in offline social reality, the bloggers in my sample are: though most, in this context unsurprisingly, did make their gender explicit – 55 per cent were men, 38 per cent women and 7 per cent unclassifiable – few chose to identify themselves in terms of other demographic categories such as class, race, ethnicity, nationality, occupation or geographical location.[2] What I referred to above as 'naturally occurring reception evidence' is in this respect inferior to an audience study using a properly controlled sample. In addition, the researcher is essentially an eavesdropper, and so cannot put her own questions to her subjects. On the other hand, by eavesdropping in this way a researcher can discover what questions subjects themselves consider worth asking or discussing, and that can be informative in its own right.

I found there were clear patterns in the bloggers' responses to the Genie – in what they reported doing with it, in what they understood it to be doing, and in what they found interesting or puzzling about that. My claim is that these responses tell us something about what non-linguists bring to bear when they engage with mediated versions of scientific findings on language and gender difference, and that this may shed light on the implications of the new interactivity for popular understandings of science. I return to the bloggers' responses below; first, though, it is necessary to say something about the science on which the Gender Genie is based.

12.3 The science of the Gender Genie

The Gender Genie derives from the work of a group of computer scientists who specialize in automated text categorization (a technique whose most salient real-world application is designing internet search tools). These researchers have developed an algorithm they claim is 80 per cent accurate in categorizing unseen texts as male or female authored (Argamon *et al* 2003). The Genie uses what is described without elaboration on its site as a 'simplified version' of that algorithm.

The dataset the original researchers developed the program on was a 25 million-word sub-set of the British National Corpus (BNC), a collection of English-language texts which are sub-categorized by genre and

subject-matter and tagged word by word using a 76-item grammatical classification scheme. The group took a sample of written texts containing both
fiction and various kinds of non-fiction, with equal numbers of male and
female authored texts in each sub-category. They carried out statistical analyses on a large number of variables (concentrating on common closed-class
items to avoid confounding the variables of gender and topic) to identify those
that most reliably discriminated the male from the female authored texts in
the corpus subset. They found several. For instance, high frequencies of personal pronouns, especially *I, you, she* and their variants, emerged as markers
of female authorship, while high frequencies of determiners, quantifiers and
nouns post-modified by prepositional phrases with 'of' emerged as markers of
male authorship.

In their published scholarly work the researchers argue that the underlying gender difference here has to do with orientation to entities in the world
which are encoded linguistically as nominals. Men and women do not differ in
the overall frequency of their nominal use, but they do differ in the kinds of
nominals they favour. Men's heavier use of noun phrases containing determiners, quantifiers and 'of' post-modification reflects a tendency to want to specify the properties of objects. Women's heavier use of personal pronouns
reflects a tendency to focus on people and relationships – pronouns as deictics specify both the relationship of the writer to the reader and the relationship of new to given information. The researchers point out that this fits with
some familiar generalizations about gender and conversational speech, for
instance Janet Holmes's (1993) proposal that women are more oriented to
the interpersonal and men to the referential functions of discourse, or
Deborah Tannen's (1990) assertion that men do 'report talk' and women
'rapport talk'. They also point out that their gender markers coincide with
some of the markers of the 'involved–informational' contrast that is one
dimension of register variation in Douglas Biber's influential model (e.g.
Biber 1995). Women's writing is more 'involved' and men's more 'informational'. (The same markers also discriminate fiction from non-fiction: both the
original algorithm and the Genie's version adjust for this.)

When a user pastes a text into the window on the Gender Genie site,
what the Genie does is search it for the forms that have been defined as
gender discriminators, calculate their frequencies and apply certain statistical weightings to different features, so that 'maleness' and 'femaleness' can be
quantified. What the user gets back on the screen is a version of their text with
keywords highlighted, two numerical scores, one for maleness and one for
femaleness, and a message of the form: 'The Genie thinks the author of this
passage is: male!/female!' The guess is based simply on which score was
higher, though if the two scores are identical or very close a user may get a
message that the Genie finds their gender undeterminable. The user is then
invited to tell the Genie if the guess is correct. If it is not, the Genie responds
with one of a range of 'humorous' comments. For instance, where a text

actually written by a woman has been mistakenly attributed to a man, the Genie may comment: 'she only thinks she's a man', or 'that is one butch chick!' The user is also invited to click on a 'view stats' link, which leads to statistical information on the Genie's cumulative success rate. I monitored this periodically from August to December 2003: the percentage of accurate guesses varied from 51 per cent to 68 per cent, far lower than the 80 per cent the original researchers claimed and at the lower end no better than chance.[3] As we will see in the discussion of their responses below, however, few bloggers were primarily interested in evaluating the Genie 'scientifically' – indeed, few appear to have understood its principles and procedures well enough to attempt such an assessment.

12.4 Bloggers respond to the Genie

We may begin this discussion of responses to the Genie by considering how bloggers in the sample used it. Their comments make clear that in the overwhelming majority of cases, the first thing – and often the only thing – they did was to paste in texts written by themselves; if they got beyond that, they pasted material written by friends, co-workers and fellow-bloggers, with very occasional forays into literature or scripture. This suggests that the ostensible question – 'is the author of this text a man or a woman?' – cannot be the question users really want answered. Clearly, they know the answer already. What is it, then, that they are hoping the Genie will tell them?

In some cases users' comments make clear that their main objective in interacting with the Genie was to test whether it really could do what it claimed. These users often deliberately chose texts which they believed would be hard for the Genie to categorize. Far more often, though, users appeared to be most interested in discovering whether their own writing conformed to the Genie's stylistic template for their gender. What the scientists present as a descriptive account of gender differences in written English is evidently reinterpreted by users as normative, as is implied in the following quotation (underlining indicates a hyperlink in the original):

> Found a link to the Gender Genie on Bekah's 'Mixtape Marathon' blog. Go play with it: it's amusing, especially if you're a blogger. *Find out if you write like you're supposed to write.* (*Schteino.com*, 07.10.03 – emphasis added)

It is interesting that most users in the sample maintain this normative orientation in spite of having access to statistics which show that the Genie's judgements are very frequently wrong (from which it also of course follows that a large minority of the sample will themselves have been wrongly categorized). The Genie's unimpressive success rates might be expected to prompt scepticism about its diagnostic criteria, or even the basic premise that gender can be identified from a 500-word writing sample. But while the Genie's errors were the single most common topic in my sample, very few users took the fact that they personally were mis-classified as grounds to dismiss the Genie's claims. Rather, most seemed to feel that the mis-classification said something about *them* – and what it said was often construed as problematic. The quotations below illustrate one common kind of response to being mis-classified or inconsistently classified:

> Everyone's run some prose through the Gender Genie by now, no? I've probably put 15 pieces through it of varying lengths and only ONCE has it ever categorized me as a female. Bad Gender Genie. (*Angelweave*, 11.11.03)

> I tried it a couple times, and both times was declared to be female. There it is. I REALLY have an identity crisis. (*Integrate*, 21.09.03)

> According to it, I must be Gender confused. LOL. (Ron, *Integrate*, 27.09.03)

> Sometimes it said I was a man. Just as often it said I was a woman. Sigh. I'm terribly confused. (David Strain, *Ghost of a Flea*, 15.10.03)

> I think I have a complex. [...] (Danah Boyd, *Misbehaving.net*, 26.10.03)

These comments are marked (by devices like emoticons, 'LOL' [laughing out loud], etc.) as ironic or joking: this is a consistent feature, suggesting the authors have designed their responses to make clear that any confusion about their gender identity is in the Genie, not in them; but the fact such comments are made at all is equally instructive. These users seem to be orienting to a commonsense perception of gender atypicality or ambiguity as marked and accountable: something that calls for acknowledgement and comment, however qualified by distancing devices.

Another kind of comment that recurred is illustrated below. Here a woman who has been identified by the Genie as male seeks an explanation in terms of her atypical personal history:

> I wonder if my expository writing was shaped by a traditional education at what had been an all boys' school. [...]? Exeter had only been co-ed for five years when I got there. (*Woolgathering*, 31.10.03).

Other women who made similar comments referred to their status as 'tomboys' with masculine interests and mostly male friendship networks. An interesting point about such responses is that although they suggest that women's 'natural' dispositions can be overridden by experiences such as being educated at a formerly all-boys' school, they also imply that 'nature' is more fundamental than 'nurture'. Gender atypicality is seen to be socially constructed (i.e. social factors are invoked to explain it), but conformity to the supposed gender norm is not treated as the outcome of any social process. There is only one instance in the entire sample where anyone seeks to explain a correct guess by the Genie (the contributor in question remarks that the Genie's judgement does not surprise her, as she has always been a 'really girly girl').

When men were mis-identified as women, a different kind of explanation often came into play:

> I put *ten of my blog entries to the test* and the program thought me to be female about half the time. (Radley Baiko, *The Agitator.com*, 22.08.03)
> It's because you are gay Radley (not that there is anything wrong with that). (Tom, 22.08.03)

> These things always get my gender wrong. They keep calling me female. (Ewon, *The Ranter's Guild*, 31.10.03)
> Well [...] you ARE gay [...] maybe you're a little effeminate? ☺ (Marlie, 31.10.03)

> I submitted some poems I had written some months ago and this is what I got:
>   Female score: 199
>   Male score: 73
> 'mutter' (Simon Shine, Unicast, 20 November 2003)
> That's because poetry is very gay! ☺ (Guan Yang, 20.11.03)

Once again, ironizing or qualifying devices are used, presumably to disclaim any allegiance to anti-gay prejudices or stereotypes. Nevertheless, the stereotype of gay men as 'effeminate' *is* being invoked as a potentially reasonable or at least intelligible explanation for the Genie's judging a gay man's writing (or a poet's) to be female-authored.

This may help to explain the only difference I found between men's and women's comments in the blog sample: a tendency for men to express slightly more irritation about being judged female than women did about being judged male. For men, being judged female potentially connotes homosexuality, whereas for women, at least in this sample, being judged male connotes only the less stigmatized identity of 'tomboy'. (Lesbianism is not mentioned anywhere in this sample.) Somewhat to my own surprise, the sample contained no evidence of any belief among the bloggers that women's writing is inferior to men's, so that men judged female might consider the judgement a downgrading of their social status: any slur such men perceived was far more clearly to their heterosexual credentials.

So far as one can tell, the prevailing common sense about language and gender among these bloggers is a version of the 'difference model': they find the claim that men and women write differently uncontroversial, and in most cases consider it desirable to fall within the normal range for whichever gender they identify as – though gay men in this scheme are anomalous, with numerous comments suggesting that in their case, gender atypicality would be typical. There are also a few creative writers whose ambition is to be able to write convincingly in both male and female personae, but clearly that ambition entails a belief that distinct male and female styles exist. Only two contributors in the sample seriously questioned that premise, both writing in blogs maintained by techno-literate feminist groups. The first comment raises the technical question of whether the algorithm is confusing gender and genre, while the second poses the more philosophical question of why gender differentiation has been such a consistent preoccupation among designers of intelligent machines:

> It's no surprise that academic writings come up male and personal blogs female – the algorithm looks at the incidence of personal pronouns among other things and obviously in academic-speak that incidence is almost nil. The same thing happened to me, comparing blog posts with thesis chunks [i.e. the blog posts were judged 'female' and the thesis chunks 'male']. (Jean, *misbehaving.net*, 31.10.03)

> [. . .] it's interesting that, however many years after those gender tests that the Turing test is based on, people still think trying to find the 'innate gender' behind the author of an anonymous text is 1) possible at all and 2) possible through formulaic mathematical calculation and 3) a worthy pursuit. (*The Literary Machine*, 26.10.03)

But if most bloggers in the sample take it as common sense that clear-cut gender differences in writing style exist, many find the Genie's diagnostic criteria at odds with their own understanding of how language relates to gender. Numerous comments suggested that the writer had difficulty grasping the notion of style as something constituted by the relative frequency of particular formal variants. Most users who commented on this took the designers of the algorithm to be claiming that some words were 'male' and others 'female'. The use of personal pronouns as diagnostics for femaleness made some sense to these users, presumably because they could see a symbolic connection between 'personal' and 'feminine', but the use of determiners and quantifiers as diagnostics of maleness caused universal bafflement:

> Some of the masculine words are kind of surprising. *The* and *a*, for instance! What do women use instead? (Smiley, *Ranter's Guild*, 30.10.03)

As well as failing to appreciate that the issue is statistical frequency, this blogger clearly does not think beyond words to syntactic constituents. According to the Genie, pronouns are 'what women use instead' – but instead of whole noun phrases containing articles rather than instead of the articles as discrete words.

Another commonly expressed view was that what genders a text is the content, not the form. Several bloggers had used some variation on the strategy humorously described here, and thought it surprising, or in some cases plain stupid, that the Genie took no account of the semantic clues they provided to their gender:

> I typed the following text in the gender genie.
> 'hello, my name is bob! I am a really nice, friendly male. I am married to a woman, and enjoy all kinds of manly things, like punching, watching science fiction films, and raw meat. On top of all that, I really hate tea parties! In sum, I am, most definitely, NOT a woman!'
> the answer: female! (Jonathan, *Integrate*, 21.08.03)

Finally, many users connected gender and genre: poetry was thought to be feminine (or gay), academic writing masculine, and so on. While we might, indeed, want to ask questions about how far the algorithm succeeds in disaggregating gender from genre effects,[4] the connections made by bloggers mostly followed a stereotyped cultural logic rather than the linguistic logic employed by the Genie. For instance, contributors to a blog called *The Ranter's Guild* debated whether 'ranting' was intrinsically masculine. Culturally, that proposal makes sense, since the aggressive expression of strong opinions or emotions which the term 'rant' connotes is stereotypically associated with masculinity. Stylistically, however, one might predict that 'ranting' would fall towards the 'involved' end of the 'involved–informational' continuum, which in the Genie's universe would make it more likely to be classified as 'female'.

12.5 Interactivity, democracy and the public understanding of science

It is my own experience, and that of many other language and gender researchers, that the public reception of research on this topic is shaped by two sets of factors which from a linguist's point of view constitute obstacles to understanding. Both of these are in evidence in the bloggers' responses to the Gender Genie. One set of factors could be called ideological: they include the conviction of many or most people that differences between men and women are both natural and desirable, the tendency to notice (and indeed, exaggerate) gross male–female differences while overlooking both similarities between men and women and variation within each group, the inclination to generalize from stereotypes, and the propensity to interpret descriptive statements about gendered behaviour as normative statements about how real men and women should behave. The other major factor, though, is the difficulty even well-educated non-linguists seem to have in grasping principles like the distinction between linguistic form and content, the idea that a

language is not just a lexicon, or the probabilistic nature of socially conditioned variation. Media representations of language and gender often reproduce these misconceptions, but they can hardly be accused of causing them.
The question may be asked, however, whether problems of understanding are
unwittingly being exacerbated by the current trend towards more interactive
and democratic forms of mediation.

This is not just a question about the web. I noted above that the web as a
medium is interactive and democratic; but it seems clear that these characteristics of newer media are leaking, or being deliberately imported, back into the
older media too, for both technological and cultural reasons. Producers are
now wary of the traditional 'experts talking' approach to science (and other
factual) programming, which as they see it is out of tune with the interests
and expectations of twenty-first-century audiences – not least because of
their extensive experience with new media in which interactivity is the
norm. If science, politics and other serious subjects are to retain any hold on
a mass audience in the long term, the thinking is that new approaches must
be adopted which encourage more active involvement. Getting audiences to
vote or otherwise register their opinions is one way to involve them; another
is to solicit their identification with 'real people'; and yet another is to do what
the Gender Genie and other interactive websites do, namely relate knowledge
directly to the individual by working with user-generated (and typically user-
centred) input.

These strategies may well work to increase interest and engagement.
But do they work to enhance understanding? Arguably, they do not. The problem is that certain kinds of content – expository, abstract and general rather
than interactive and personalized – are difficult to accommodate within the
formats many media producers now favour. But without the didactic 'talking
heads' or their textual equivalent, there is no pre-established frame or context
for the user's personal engagement with science, and nothing to guide the
user in drawing conclusions from that engagement. The consequence may
be to compound errors and reinforce misconceptions.

I have suggested, for instance, that many or most Genie-users in the
blog sample did not understand the basic assumptions built into the algorithm. Users could be quite deeply engaged with the Genie in the sense that
they spent significant time putting samples into it and discussing the results,
and yet at the same time fundamentally mistaken or uncertain about the
claims it was making, and thus unable to formulate any sensible assessment
of them. Many users, unsurprisingly, filled the gaps in their understanding
from a pre-existing stock of folk-linguistic common sense, which sometimes
caused them to arrive at false inferences and to store untrue facts: for instance
that *the* and *a* are 'masculine words', which is both false in itself and a distortion of the claim actually made by the original scientists. It is true that the
Genie was not designed as an educational tool (the blogger who urged his
peers to 'go play with it' was doubtless right about its primary purpose); but

247

it is comparable in both its strengths and its weaknesses to other quiz-type sites which do aim to educate as well as entertain.

The kinds of media formats I am talking about also favour certain kinds of *science* over others. In the case of sex and gender, for instance, even leaving aside ideological preferences, it is obviously much easier to design an interactive quiz or reality-TV-style science programme around the kind of science that takes clear-cut male–female differences for granted rather than the kind which wants to complicate or challenge the binary mindset. Arguments about ontology and epistemology are not good candidates for boiling down into quiz questions, nor is it easy to pursue such arguments via the exploits and personalities of some exemplary group of ordinary people. That, as much as any resurgence of ideological essentialism, may be a reason why media treatments of language and gender lean towards socio-biology and away from sociolinguistics.

But some genies are not easy to put back into their bottles. If we take it that interactivity is now an established feature of the media landscape, the question we must ask is whether linguists too can harness it, to enhance public understanding, and to engage audiences with more complex stories, about the nature, structure and social life of language.

Primary sources

BookBlog (2003–2006), *The Gender Genie* (available online at www.bookblog.net/gender/genie.html, accessed 20.10.06).

Notes

1. In fairness to the scientists, it appears they did not endorse the way their research was presented in reports like this one. I discovered this when I was contacted by a researcher from BBC Radio 4's *Woman's Hour*, who was working on a critical item about the Sheffield study. She told me she had spoken to its authors and they were unhappy about the reporting of their work.
2. My informed guess about the bloggers' demographic characteristics other than gender is as follows, and will probably surprise nobody. They are mostly under 40, educated to at least college level (many are clearly students), from which it follows the sample will be skewed towards the higher end of the socio-economic scale, and currently located in economically advanced western countries, with the largest number resident in the USA (though not necessarily US nationals).
3. Of course, data that depend on consistent and accurate input from users must be treated with caution: it is possible that people are more inclined to report inaccurate guesses. However, my own suspicion is that the original algorithm has been significantly simplified, that much of the text people submit to the Genie falls outside the parameters the researchers were dealing with in the more controlled sample they developed the algorithm on, and that the Genie's success rate really is quite unimpressive.

4. Argamon *et al* were certainly aware of this issue, and attempted to filter out genre and topic effects by sampling equal numbers of male- and female-authored texts in each generic and thematic sub-category. But having consulted the full list of sources which the researchers, to their credit, have made available for the purpose, it is my opinion that the classifications used in the BNC are insufficiently delicate for this filter to be effective. Thus if there is any tendency for some subjects to be written about by women and others to be written about by men, what are really genre and topic effects will show up as gender differences. While I cannot say with certainty that this is what has happened in Argamon *et al*'s study, on the basis of the information given by the researchers I think the possibility cannot be ruled out.

13 Of chords, machines and bumble-bees: the metalinguistics of hyperpoetry

Astrid Ensslin

13.1 Introduction

Following the traditions of concrete and experimental machine poetry, first explored by Augusto de Campos in Brazil and Max Bense and his Stuttgart circle in the 1950s, a new generation of web poets and artists have, since the beginning of the 1990s, sought ways of thematizing and problematizing language- and media-related issues in terms of 'the message for its own sake' (Jakobson 1960: 356). This has been achieved via the creation of artistic forms of digital verse in conjunction with the underlying digital code, as well as other digitized semiotic modes such as image and sound. Not only does such a genre, broadly referred to as hyperpoetry, call out for an alternative aesthetics of medial self-reference, procedurality, interactivity, hypermediality and networking (Block *et al* 2004) (terms to which I will refer in more detail later); it also provides a prolific testing ground for issues surrounding the structural, functional, social and medial dimensions of language per se. As such, hyperpoetry has to be seen in the context of Dell Hymes's (1974: viii) multidisciplinary concept of sociolinguistics, which includes 'not only sociology and linguistics, but also social anthropology, education, poetics, folklore and psychology' (Romaine 1982: 5).

The theoretical aims of this chapter are two-fold. First of all, to provide a media-theoretical background, I want to suggest the need for a re-interpretation of Roman Jakobson's (1960) tripartite concept of mediality. Jakobson subsumes message, code and contact under intra-linguistic communicative factors, and while he explicitly distinguishes between 'physical channel' and 'psychological connection', he does not suggest two different terms or concepts but groups them under 'contact'. My approach addresses this *desideratum* by taking into account the materiality of message, code, (psychological) contact *and* (physical) channel. We shall see that the physicality of the medium (the channel) cannot exist without the abstract assumptions of (representational) 'modeness' (Constantinou 2005: 606), on the one hand, and of the various possible inter-human relations, infrastructures and social practices, on the other (Lukács 1971: 83; Sterne 1999: 504; Levinson 1984: 7; Cook 1998: 262; cf. Jewitt 2004: 184).

Secondly, I will investigate the physical and metaphysical implications of Marshall McLuhan's (1964) seminal slogan 'the medium is the message' (quoted in McLuhan and Zingrone 1995: 151). This then provides the context for my second aim, namely to consider the role of so-called '*aesthetic*' metalanguage in relation to current work within sociolinguistics and discourse analysis with its predominant focus on the *factual* and/or explicatory dimensions of metalanguage (e.g. Jaworski *et al* 2004b; Preston 2004; Hyland 2005). I aim to show how aesthetic metalanguage, as employed by hyperpoets, operates, by contrast, on an *implicatory* basis that presupposes the construction of a secondary, fictional reality (cf. Bell, forthcoming, for a 'Possible Worlds' approach to hypertext).

Against this theoretical backdrop, I will go on to investigate some recent examples of digital poetry with respect to representations of metalinguistic issues such as syntagmatic and paradigmatic relationships, grammatical and biological gender, hypermedia textuality, trans-semiotic signification together with deconstructionist tenets such as the decentralization of meaning, authorship and in fact humanity vis-à-vis the empowered (text) machine (Licklider 1960; Aarseth 1997; Ensslin 2007). These examples are taken from all three generations of hypertext literature (Hayles 2002), i.e. **hypertext** per se, represented by Jim Rosenberg's *Diagrams* and Robert Kendall's *Penetration*; **hypermedia**, exemplified by Ursula Menzer's *Er/Sie* (*He/She*) and Zeitgenossen's *Yatoo*; and **cybertext**, illustrated by Urs Schreiber's *Das Epos der Maschine* (*Machine Epic*). I will explore the five pieces in the fourth section of this chapter. The specific medial characteristics of each of the three generations will be taken into account, and I shall include an investigation of hypertext's idiosyncratic macrotextual features and their implications for the receptive process; hypermedia's interplay between intermediality, intersemioticity and synaestheticism; and cybertext's progressive and innovative potential with respect to changing human–machine communication and subverting traditional receptive power relationships. I will further explore the multiple layers of meaning that 'metalanguage' can assume, as hyperpoets engage creatively in the mediality of language, in modes and in the material as well as abstract properties of the medium (see Constantinou 2005: 609–10). By doing so, they implicitly invite readers, or 'users', to develop critical views on language- and media-related issues (cf. Cameron, Chapter 12, this volume). These issues can be situated on continua such as the formalist-applied and the structuralist-poststructuralist/deconstructivist spectra. Most significantly for this book, hyperpoets present, either directly or indirectly, human beings in a complex relationship between individual social backgrounds, public (e.g. language ideological) debates and the powerful role of the media and their producers, which both condition and are conditioned by user interaction.

13.2 Concepts of metalanguage

In recent years, there has been a growing interest within linguistics, sociolinguistics, stylistics and discourse analysis in language in relation to the New Media including both work into the use of language (e.g. Crystal 2001; Manovich 2001; Shortis 2001; Aitchison and Lewis 2003; Boardman 2005) and, of more direct relevance for the concerns of this volume, *representations* of language-related topics (e.g. Ronkin and Karn 1999; Tattersall 2003; Pfalzgraf 2006). In the majority of reported cases, however, New Media texts such as websites deal with metalanguage in a folk linguistic or pseudo-scientific way (Niedzielski and Preston 1999; Preston 2004; see the contributions to this volume by Cameron, Hill and Thurlow). By the same token, the majority of metalinguistic analyses are factual in nature, a trend which I seek to contravene, or rather supplement, by specifically looking at fictional, aesthetic aspects of metalanguage.

I shall dedicate this chapter to an investigation of aesthetic phenomena found on the internet, which represent metalanguage discourse. These 'hyperpoems', as I will call them, are inextricably linked to semiotic concerns pertaining to the mediality and materiality of the computer, which are assimilated by New Media writers and artists to achieve effects that merge two levels of metadiscourse: metamediality in the macroaesthetic sense of the material medium in its own right (e.g. the computer vs. the book) on the one hand, and metalanguage in a macro- and microstructural sense as it is understood by text linguists in the tradition of Kintsch and van Dijk (1978) on the other. In other words, I deliberately include the distinctive qualities of hypermedia in my discussion, first because the internet is generally associated with *marked* mediality, which sets it apart from the unmarked, i.e. macrostructurally linear, print media (see Ensslin 2007); and secondly because this marked mediality is associated with a range of material and abstract qualities which enable certain discursive modes and processes in opposition to other, more conventional media.

Having said that, I will not restrict my discussion to purely structuralist elements of aestheticized, or simply 'aesthetic' metalanguage. I will also include issues of broader sociolinguistic interest, namely the debate surrounding grammatical and biological gender; semiotic processes that reflect implied notions of intermediality and synaesthesia;[1] and, on a specifically communicative level, the role of the linguistic subject, i.e. the human operator set against a virtual, technological environment. Furthermore, hyperpoetry, like its forerunner concrete poetry, attributes its commitment to language to a social function, in that it investigates the contemporary, techno-ontologically determined communicative situation in a playful, creative manner.

One of my major concerns in this chapter will be the use of aesthetic metalanguage in hyperpoetry. Not only is poetic language unconditionally self-referential in the sense of describing language 'as object'. It is also used in this particular medium to creatively refer to a plethora of specifically sociolinguistic concerns, which are characterized by an inherently language- and media-ideological programme (see Jaworski *et al* 2004b, 2004c; Johnson 2006: 437). This programme may be contextualized in terms of recent theories and debates surrounding folk linguistics (Niedzielski and Preston 1999), language-ideological debates (Blommaert 1999a) and folk metalanguage (Preston 2004). In effect, I argue that, broadly speaking, aesthetic metalanguage as used in hyperpoetry represents a certain kind, or rather modification, of folk metalanguage as described by Preston, who distinguishes between three types of folk metalanguage (see also Johnson and Ensslin, Chapter 1, this volume). 'Metalanguage 1' is, according to him, conscious, 'overt comment about language' (2004: 75) made by non-experts. 'Metalanguage 2' largely corresponds to Jakobson's phatic function of language, i.e. the largely unconscious *'mention* of talk itself' (Preston 2004: 85; emphasis in original). 'Metalanguage 3' may be considered the conceptual, ideological, communal background to 'Metalanguage 1' in that it refers to 'beliefs which members of speech communities share' (ibid.: 87). Leaving aside the highly controversial potential of the term 'speech community', it has to be conceded that none of the three types suggested by Preston can be fully adopted for my approach, although 'Metalanguage 1' would probably come closest to the kind of metalanguage featured in this study. In fact, we are not dealing with explicit, conscious comments made by non-linguists in open discourse. Clearly, hyperpoets mostly are not language experts in the sense of academic 'linguists'; nor, however, do they use language in a prototypically folk-linguistic way. We are indeed concerned with yet another level of conscious linguistic engagement with language, which transcends the traditional notion of 'poetic' by adding a multilayered 'meta'-dimension. This dimension may, in a multitude of possible ways, relate to formal, semiotic, communicative, pragmatic and/or ideological aspects of language.

Contrary to both expert and folk metalanguage as understood conventionally, aesthetic metalanguage, or rather 'metalinguistics', as suggested by the title of this chapter, creates a secondary, virtual, and therefore highly malleable reality into which the reader-user is immersed and which he or she temporarily substitutes for his or her primary reality (see Culler 1997).[2] Even more importantly, poetically represented metalanguage achieves its effects through implicature rather than explicature (see Sperber and Wilson 1986; Blakemore 1992). It operates by suggestive means rather than spelling out the issues it is concerned with. In Wolfgang Iser's terminology, it leaves semantic gaps for the reader-user to fill (see Iser 1978), thereby allowing them to form a holistic mental image of the text and the meta-linguistic issues in question.

13.3 The aesthetics of hyperpoetry

In what follows I will focus on an emergent literary and media genre, which I generically refer to as 'hyperpoetry'. More specifically than 'digital poetry' or 'e-poetry', both of which are used rather broadly to designate a wide range of poetic phenomena, the concept of hyperpoetry feeds on a distinctive set of macro- and microstructural, as well as semiotic features, which I will elaborate below. Suffice it to say at this stage that 'e-poetry' and its cognate 'digital poetry' are understood to relate to any representations of written and oral poetry on the internet, ranging from mere digitizations of formerly printed poems (so-called 'paper-under-glass' adaptations) to highly sophisticated, intricately interlinked and largely machine-controlled manifestations of so-called cybertext – another term which I will explain in more detail.

The immediate forerunners and theoretical foundations of hypermedia poetry can be traced back to the 1950s, when experimental, progressive artists and writers across the world began to show an interest in the emerging field of computer technology. One of the spiritual centres of this innovative international movement was the Stuttgart School around philosopher, physicist and semiotician Max Bense. Following Leibniz's conceptions of generalized mathematics, which suggested the reduction of spirit to form and reflected the predominance of serialized art and architecture during the baroque age, Bense (1954; 1956; 1958; 1960) hypothesized that literature, particularly verse and rhyme, were essentially driven by mathematical concepts. Similarly, in Ernst Jünger's *Praise of Vowels*, Bense observed the atomistic structure of language, with vowels being its smallest constituent units. From this point of departure, Bense developed his concept of 'style' in which he saw the essence of any written work and, according to which, style unites art and technology, liberating language from its semantic ties. By the same token, form, in Bense's view, can only be aesthetic if it categorically controls the sensual/material. Given his emphasis on the aesthetics of formal, linguistic representation, Bense is widely understood to be one of the fathers of concrete poetry, in other words, poetry that neglects the signified and, instead, experiments with the visualizing potential of the signifier, featuring for instance pictorial typography, shape poems and collages.

On a broader, anthropological and philosophical scale, we might see Bense as having redefined the relationship between mankind and nature in terms of a teleologically conceived 'technological' theory of existence. Bense subscribed to expressionist thinking in that he saw the destruction of the social and intellectual world from the early twentieth century as paralleled by the destruction of traditional philosophical ontology. However, this destruction was not to end in 'nothingness', but rather in the replacement of the natural world with an artificial one, i.e. a transition from ontology to technology. By the second half of the twentieth century, humans and machines had arrived at a 'new' technological state, which had transformed human intellectual existence into an amalgamation of machine-like and spiritual components. Bense treated this technological revolution neither euphorically nor pessimistically, as he regarded it as unavoidable and indeed indispensable for the continuous improvement of the world's habitability.

By the same token, Bense and many other form-oriented writers and artists of the 1950s and early 1960s (e.g. the Vienna School, the French group Oulipo and the Brazilian Noigandres Group) turned against the prevailing ideologically governed, mostly content-oriented schools of literary criticism. In Bense's view, the dawning technological sphere would precipitate the deconstruction of both conventional, extralinguistic meaning and traditional literary forms. To highlight a new synthesis of the linguistic elements, which would represent this technological sphere, Bense introduced terms such as 'montage', 'linguistic reduction', 'reconstruction' and 'recapitulation', which became constitutive of his aesthetics of concrete poetry.

As Gottfried Benn, one of Germany's major post-war poets and Bense's kindred spirit emphasized, reflexivity with regard to artistic technique, which includes both medium and style, needs to keep up with its time. The spirit of the computer age (and here I am referring to another seminal document in relation to concrete poetry, Eugen Gomringer's 1955 *from verse to constellation. purpose and form of a new poetry*), is represented by changed conditions and forms of communication, which entail a reduction of language, an augmented use of symbolic signs and images so as to incorporate and thus simplify textual messages, and faster information transfer. According to the manifestos of prominent concrete poets such as Gomringer, the poet's social function is to embrace this new condition by creating verbal art that conforms to this increase in visuality, playfulness, innovation, formulaic experimentation and fluidity and the simultaneous decrease in morphosyntactic complexity.

Concrete poetry, in Gomringer's (1966) view, is conscious of its function in society, as it is not understood in terms of the Wordsworthian 'spontaneous overflow of powerful feelings', but much rather as a linguistic and communicative testing ground. It therefore comes as no surprise that the boundaries between concrete poetry and the language of *advertising* were perceived to be fuzzy, first because of the aesthetic commodification of language in the new media (mostly television at that time) and, secondly, because of the conjunction of language with other semiotic modes such as sound and image. Gomringer considered the traditional verse poem as obsolete, as it failed to reflect contemporary society with its changed communicative situation organically. Concrete poetry, on the other hand, was considered relevant by its representatives in view of its capacity to express precisely that schism between twentieth-century reality and the impossibility of ontological expression thereof. Bense's later works were largely informed by Claude Shannon's Information Theory (Shannon 1948), which considers information only valid if measurable in terms of information units or so-called bits. Using electronic computers and Kaeding's *Frequency Dictionary of German* (1898), Bense experimented with word frequencies, generating machine-produced, stochastically serialized texts of pre-semantic quality. This 'artificial' as opposed to 'natural' form of 'writing' was later picked up by so-called ASCII artists and writers, who set out to create digital works of art and writing based on programming codes. Due to its highly specialized technical approach, however, this poetic form has never gained any real ground. Of much greater pervasiveness have been so-called WYSIWYG (what-you-see-is-what-you-get) products, which are perceived on screen rather than by means of a codified programming syntax.

One of the major characteristics of concrete poetry, which has transferred into hyperpoetry, is the intersemiotic tendency to construct syntactic, visual and acoustic arrangements out of language material with a view to drawing the reader's attention to the essence of (literary) communication, the message itself. Etymologically, the term 'hyperpoetry' is derived from 'hypertext' (Nelson 1984; Nielsen 1990), which in its most generic, macro-structural sense refers to intricately interlinked, digital textual networks, consisting of nodes, or 'lexias' (text units displayed in individual windows; see Landow 1997), and links, which form the underlying pattern of most latter-day web pages. Applied to concrete literary phenomena, the term '(literary) hypertext' subdivides into 'hyperfiction', 'hyperdrama' and 'hyperpoetry'. In what follows, I will use 'hypertext' in the confined sense of 'first generation hypertext' (see Hayles 2002), which comprises literary text networks that emerged before the popularization of the World Wide Web and are far more script-centred than, say, '(literary) hypermedia', which may be conceived of as 'second generation hypertext'. To a significantly greater degree than hypertext, hypermedia combines the idea of textual webs with the digitization of formerly analogue multimedia such as script, image, sound, animation and film, and their joint and mutually supplementary creation of intersemiotic meaning. Cybertext, a term coined by Norwegian hypertext and game theorist Espen Aarseth (1997), is the most recent of the three, notably, overlapping generations and refers to digital literary phenomena that place the machine, i.e. the program code, at the centre of attention, thus implying a reduction of user intentionality and control for the sake of machine empowerment. By 'cybertext', which is derived from Norbert Wiener's book *Cybernetics: Or, Control and Communication in the Animal and the Machine* (1948), Aarseth understands 'the mechanical organization of the text', which posits 'the intricacies of the medium as an integral part of the literary exchange' (1997: 1). Cybertext thereby transcends McLuhan's (1964) aphorism 'the medium is the message' in that it reduces the perceiver's intentionality to a seemingly random interplay of action and,

predominantly, *re*-action, which is ultimately controlled by a textually encoded programme performed on screen before the user's eyes. Interactivity
is governed by the text 'machine' rather than by the user, who finds his or
her own intentional actions undermined by a quasi-humanized, unpredictable text object.

With this in mind, Aarseth proposes an alternative, pragmatic model of
textual communication, which attempts to accommodate all text types, yet
is specifically targeted at texts that incorporate machine-like microcosms
such as hypertexts, MUDs (Multi-User Dungeons) and computer games. Most
significantly, Aarseth places the text machine, a mechanical rather than
metaphorical concept, at the centre of his communicative triangle. This
notion of text integrates the afore-mentioned, binary concept of mediality, as
it feeds on the verbal sign (which forms the encoded basis of digital textuality)
and the material medium. Finally, to enable interaction and textual performance – and a *performance* it is as opposed to any conventional reading
experience – a human operator is required. The elements of this triad are
mutually interdependent, and changes in any of the three elements will
result in changing text types. Most interestingly, however, is the fact that
Aarseth omits two crucial elements: first, the element of reference, of Jakobson's extralinguistic 'context', which would conventionally form part of the
interplay between all three components or even constitute the purpose of
this interplay. Secondly, the model disregards the crucial role of the author-
programmer, who is ultimately responsible for the creation and 'behav-
ioural' mechanisms of the text machine. We may envisage the role of the
author-programmer in terms of a quasi-deistic creator, who withdraws
after the completion of his or her creation, leaving it to its own mechanistic
devices. Unlike a biological organism, however, this mechanism is non-
autopoetic in so far as it can only work provided that it is operated by a
user. Aarseth thus shifts the focus of attention from the traditional triad of
sender – message – receiver to the 'cybernetic intercourse between the various part(icipant)s in the textual machine' (1997: 22). In this conceptual
framework, language and the media, in this case hypermedia, have to be
seen as equivalent interactive components of a neo-pragmatic concept of
textual *performance*. Such a performance then marginalizes traditional issues
of semantics. Instead, it emphasizes the multifarious interplay between the
three major interactants of the text machine, which are quintessentially
human, linguistic and medial. Later in this chapter I will illustrate this principle by means of a prototypical cyberpoem entitled *Machine Epic*.

In their attempt to define hyperpoetic aesthetics, Block *et al* (2004) identify four chief attributes: interactivity, networking, procedurality and medial
self-reflexivity. The first two attributes are mutually interdependent. Interactivity in the sense of communication between different users of a computer
network, which also brings in the element of interpersonal and intertextual
networking, is one of the major principles of the World Wide Web. It has

257

been implemented artistically by online collaborative creative writing projects such as Dragan Espenschied and Alvar Freude's *Assoziations-Blaster*,[3] which invites users to contribute texts associated with given keywords, such as 'compilation' in our example. The second component of interactivity is the interchange between human being and machine, between user and computer, which, due to its contingency upon situational and psychological circumstances, results in highly personalized, unrepeatable aesthetic experiences. Processurality refers to the interest expressed by hypermedia poets in the processes of the 'work in movement', the 'open work', as Umberto Eco (1989) calls it. The term has often been used programmatically by writers of concrete and hypermedia poetry alike (Mon *et al* 1960), referring to the reader's or user's contribution to the construction of text as well as the dynamic nature of linguistic or semiotic processes in a more general sense (Block *et al* 2004: 27–9).

Finally, medial self-reflexivity constitutes, in my view, the central defining characteristic of hypermedia literature. Flagged up by Marshall McLuhan in his discipline-founding tenet 'the medium is the message', the significance of the medium as an extension of human corporeality and spirituality has become the founding principle of media studies and underlies any artistic and literary discourse performed in the New Media. Similarly, medial self-reflexivity implies an at least dualistic concept of the 'medium', namely the materiality of code *and* contact (channel), and their related metalingual and phatic functions, to use Jakobson's (1960) terminology. It is the emphasis on the latter, phatic function in particular which distinguishes hypermedia poetry from other forms of digital poetry and print media in general. Simultaneously, it is precisely the self-reflexive engagement with form/language and substance/medium (see Romaine 1982; cf. de Saussure 1966 and Abercrombie 1965), as well as its variable links to social and psychological concerns, that make hyperpoetry relevant to a discourse-analytical and more general sociolinguistic framework.

Having said that, upon closer inspection, Jakobson's communication model needs further refinement when attempting to adapt it to communicative processes involved in the production and reception of literary hypertext. In fact, hypertext per se implies not only a dual, but an essentially tripartite concept of the 'medium', which encompasses the materiality of message, code *and* contact (channel), and their related poetic, metalingual and phatic functions. As opposed to, for instance, the book, hypertext, takes place in a 'marked medium' (see above), which therefore needs to be thematized and explored creatively. In this respect, Jakobson's theory fails to distinguish sufficiently clearly between 'physical channel and psychological connection' (1960: 353), as he subsumes both aspects under 'contact', the function of which is to enable addresser and addressee to enter and stay in direct communicative contact. However, physical channel and psychological connection are two fundamentally different concepts, which need to be divided into two

258

separate factors within any communicative model. Medial reflexivity primarily draws on the physical side of Jakobson's concept of contact. Message and code, on the other hand, are particularly significant for hyperpoetry, which is indebted to the metalinguistic traditions of concrete poetry and focuses on the message in the sense of the poetic use of language, i.e. 'the message for its own sake' (Jakobson 1960: 356).

13.4 Metalinguistic representations in hyperpoetry

In what follows, I will now discuss five hyperpoems, written in English and German by American, English, Austrian and German poets/poet teams. The poems are taken from each of the three hypertext generations and feature, in a diversity of artistic approaches, aspects of the previously mentioned concept of aesthetic metalanguage. The first two poems represent grammatical and textual ideas (morphology and syntax as linguistic 'infrastructure' on the one hand and antilinearity as an alternative to conventional, sequentialized textuality on the other), thereby featuring the systemic, microstylistic nature of language on the one hand and the macrostructural, procedural side on the other. The third poem forms the perhaps closest link to the majority of issues discussed in this book by thematizing the dialectics of grammatical and biological gender in German and, more importantly, the language ideological debates and language policies surrounding this issue. Poem number four exemplifies meta-semiotics or, as it were, meta-multimodality and is therefore, along with the last poem, the most meta-theoretical, meta-'linguistic' (in the sense of referring to the academic discipline rather than language per se) of all the poems featured in this chapter. Finally, with a view to demonstrating how meta-communicative and meta-medial issues are used to create a digital 'performance', I will introduce and analyse an example of cyberpoetry.

Text 1: Metagrammar – Jim Rosenberg's Diagrams

'Chordal texts' is the name given by Jim Rosenberg to his hyperpoetic *Diagrams* series, a 'work in progress' published between 1968 and 2004. Rosenberg, whose major objective is to depict 'morphemic hypertexts' as 'an association structure for thought' (Kac 1996: 112), views words in musical terms, as notes, which combine into short phrases, or 'chords' and, on a larger level, into 'massively intricate symphonies of word poems' (Larsen and Higgason 2004). These phrases are written on transparent, bi-dimensional 'cards', which are partially superimposed onto each other. This creates an effect which reminds the (informed) reader of the interplay between paradigmatic and syntagmatic relations between linguistic units, whereby the syntagmatic level is reinforced by 'connectors', which are intended to signify the conjunctive relationships between node clusters. Individual cards are activated, i.e. they flash up upon mouse-over. The symphonic impression created by this conglomeration of verbal 'chords', however, clearly evokes the image of contemporary, atonal, dissonant, polyphonic and thus individualizing approaches to symphonic art as pursued by composers like Fartein Valen, Christopher Rouse and John Corigliano.

Rosenberg's deconstructionist approach is grounded in the idea of juxtaposing words in a cluster in such a way as to disrupt syntax and the construction of semantic meaning, an enterprise which provides a rich platform for experimentation with structural concepts non-existent in ordinary syntax. In fact, by turning the reader's attention from extra-linguistic to intra-linguistic signification, Rosenberg evokes an engagement with the aforementioned double-layered meta-level, which involves, on the one hand, the reader's immersion into a non-realistic, alternative virtual sphere based on Coleridge's 'willing suspension of disbelief' and, on the other, an engagement with the very essence of linguistic structuralism, the horizontal and vertical interplay between formal oppositions.

Text 2: Metatextuality – Robert Kendall's Penetration

Perhaps the most prototypically hypertextual of all hyperpoems discussed in this chapter is Robert Kendall's *Penetration* (2000), which forms part of a larger cycle of poems entitled *The Seasons*. As indicated previously, hypertext as a literary New Media art form essentially follows the poststructuralist principle of meta-theoretical engagement. Thus, it ventures to deconstruct conventional notions of textuality, which, in a nutshell, comprise linearity (of language organization), closure, totality, coherence, and, from a cognitive point of view, the meaningful and meaning-creating interplay between bottom-up and top-down processes. Instead, it features lexias (see above) which are arranged in a non-linear way, by means of networked nodes which are interlinked by means of associative connections and, hence, read in a multilinear fashion (see Figure 13.1). All active links are highlighted in this hyperpoem, thus helping readers to navigate through the work. By choosing to visualize and thus facilitate navigation in this way, Kendall sets himself apart from other hypertext writers (e.g. Michael Joyce in *afternoon, a story*[4] and Bill Bly in *We Descend*[5]), who employ, for instance, hidden, 'missing' (fake) and/or 'dynamic'(sporadically active) links (see Bernstein's [1998] taxonomy of links) as a foregrounding technique.

By displaying stanzaic fragments of verse which can be transgressed in any random order, without ever safely reaching a finishing line or developing a reliable mental representation of the perceived textual representation, Kendall experiments with textual coherence and coherence-building cognitive processes. His poems thematize the complex interplay between the construction, deconstruction and reconstruction of coherence, which may be described in terms of bottom-up and top-down processes in mutually

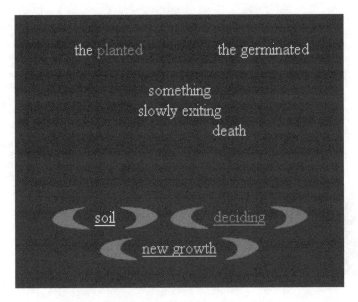

Figure 13.1: Lexia from Robert Kendall's *Penetration*

oppositional as opposed to complementary ways. Implicitly, hence, Kendall hints at the debate surrounding hypertextuality, which is concerned about the fact to what extent one may speak of an altogether new notion of textuality (cf. Kuhlen 1991; Storrer 2002).

Text 3: Gender and language – Ursula Menzer's Er/Sie (He/She)

The so-called 'digital concrete poem' *Er/Sie (He/She)* by Ursula Menzer (2000–2001) represents an early, rather puristic manifestation of the binary materiality of the medium with which hypermedia poets engage. The German poet ludically features the much debated and politicized incompatibility of sex and gender rooted in German morphology (cf. Pusch 1984; Leiss 1994; Eickhoff 1999; Hellinger 2000) in that she submerges the reader-user in a flood of animated, intersemiotically charged lemmata containing morphemic and non-morphemic instances of the pronouns 'er' and 'sie' ('he' and 'she'). (Note that the German first person singular masculine nominative personal pronoun 'er' (he) is homonymous to a personalizing derivational suffix '-er', which has masculine grammatical gender.) The overwhelming majority of 'er' tokens seems therefore to render the German language inherently chauvinistic, which Menzer takes to absurd lengths by demonstrating the randomness of folk linguistic comment, which generally insists on the supplementation of an analogous, capitalized feminine ending in written representations of, for example, professional status, e.g. *'LehrerIn'*

261

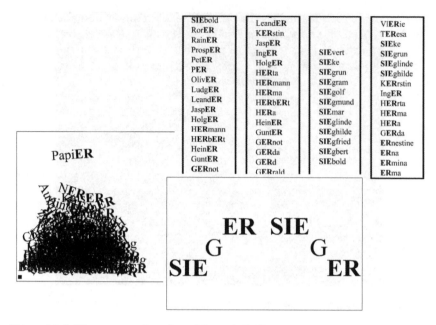

Figure 13.2: Three screenshots from Menzer's *Er/Sie*

(teacher) or '*PolitikerIn*' (politician). Other than in English, this concern is not entirely illegitimate, as the generic (as opposed to biological) '-er' suffix is generally accompanied by a gender-marked determiner such as *der* (the) or *ein* (a). In fact, the debate over appropriate oral and written representations of grammatical and biological gender has been a major site of dispute for feminist linguists and sociolinguists in the German-speaking countries since the 1980s and has been met with much criticism and ridicule in public, not least media, discourse.

Upon closer inspection, Menzer's hyperpoem involves a semiotically more varied, socio-critical message than might at first appear to be the case in so far as it goes beyond the metagrammatical approach to gender. The inherently playful, carnivalesque (Bakhtin 1968) character of the poem is heightened by the use of popular classical music, the effect of which cannot of course be re-invoked in the present print media. Rimsky-Korsakoff's sound-constructed *Flight of the Bumble-bee*, a metaphorical sound-text, for instance, is chosen deliberately to symbolize language on several semiotic layers as an elusive, evanescent phenomenon, which is bound to fall prey to popular hermeneutic appetite. Furthermore, stylized images of popular television are represented, for example, by the linguistic construction of a winner's rostrum. Menzer creates a pun using the German word *Sieger* (winner), which contains a nonmorphemic instance of *sie* and the personalizing suffix *er*. She thereby alludes to media broadcasts of sports events, which are ideologically functionalized to evoke modern-day heroism and feelings of national identity in viewers. Here, sound is used to deliver a satirical message, as an indistinct clicking noise spitefully accompanies the construction of fake linguistic hierarchies together with feminist linguists' equally fake attempts to deconstruct them. The visualized linguistic 'rubbish heap', finally, depicts the 'cognitive overhead' (Conklin 1987: 40) caused by contemporary (hyper-)media consumption and the flood of frequently indistinguishable, commercially ideologized semiotic subsystems (see also van Leeuwen 1999). The metaphor represents language as commodified, commercialized and invalidated to such an extent as to reduce its traditional political and rhetorical superiority over the visual image. The term 'reverse ekphrasis' (literally the recourse to the visual to replace and explain words instead of the opposite, verbalizing procedure; see Bolter 2001) aptly describes this ideologically charged process of increasing visuality in the New Media and its consequence, the debilitation of the verbal sign.

Text 4: Metasemiotics – Zeitgenossen's Yatoo

Hypermedia literature is largely determined by ideas of intermediality and intersemioticity, two interlinked concepts that are concomitant with the digitization process, which ascribes to every (previously analog), art form the same underlying programming code. *Intermediality* designates the concept of unifying, in one medium, a number of different material media as well as their idiosyncratic implications for the reception and production of information. *Intersemioticity*, on the other hand, is understood on a more abstract, hermeneutic level, in terms of an interplay between diverse semiotic modes, their relationships and relative contribution to the meaning-making process (see Heibach 2003). These modes include script, sound (oral language, music, noise), as well as still and moving image (e.g. photography, cartoon, painting, sketch, animation and film; see Conklin 1987). In this context, semiotic theories such as Charles Sanders Peirce's (1931–1958) tripartite distinction between symbol, icon and index have been adapted by hypermedia scholars (e.g. McKillop and Myers 1999; Ensslin 2007) to describe and hermeneutically interpret the multifarious ways in which intersemioticity and intermediality are featured in hypermedia poetry. Some theorists even venture as far as to describe the underlying synaesthetic (multisensory) concept as a *Gesamtdatenwerk* (an integrated intersemiotic data network; see Ascott 1999), in other words a neo-Wagnerian pan-artistic representation of (virtual) life in its own right.

An example that lends itself particularly aptly to the discussion surrounding the overlapping disciplines of literature, poetry, performing and fine art in the digital paradigm is Zeitgenossen's (pseudonym for Ursula Hentschläger and Zelko Wiener, an Austrian team of digital writers and artists) 'roll-over love poem' (Simanowski 2002) *Yatoo*, which was first

263

launched in 2001 and has been further developed to this day. A piece of so-called 'audio contact art', it involves vocalized rather than written language, experimenting with the synergies of roll-over graphic animation and de-sequentialized oral love poetry. The online version of this poetry cycle features a stylized, futuristic visual setting reminiscent of the interior of an overdimensional spacecraft. In the foreground, PANTHA, a hybrid, artificial, male rather than female humanoid creature in a fire-salamander space suit is depicted, who is set against an enormous, sublime landscape featuring digitized, moving geometric constellations. The impression evoked by this visual arrangement may be described as a neo-Romantic cyberspace 'painting', or piece of digital art, where the human individual finds him- or herself confronted with an overpowering, sublime scenery that combines the phenomenology of virtual reality with a new approach to orally transmitted poetry (cf. Clayton 2003, on the congruity between nineteenth-century and postmodern thought, art and literature).

Yatoo is an acronym for 'you are the only one'. Similarly, the hyper-poetry cycle toys with five-word phrases like 'I love you so much', 'I will suffer from you' and 'I want you to escape', read out in turns by a female and a male voice, as the reader activates sound and image simultaneously by rolling the mouse over kaleidoscopic stars consisting of symmetrically organized geometrical shapes. Upon activation, the shapes change colour and form, releasing one of the above words at a time. There is only one way of triggering the original sequence of words by hitting identical shapes in a certain order. Therefore, the first reading experience equals a jigsaw, a game, a play on words, augmented by a transmedial interplay of various semiotic

Figure 13.3: Main user interface in *Yatoo*

modes. The mathematical logic of the geometric shapes diametrically opposes the emotional message delivered by the spoken language in the 'poems'. Visual material is therefore employed symbolically, as it does not share any semantic features with the other semiotic elements conveyed by the text and, rather than complementing verbally revealed information, undermines the emotive nature of the love poems. Figure 13.3 depicts the main user interface with the rotating star at its centre.

Text 5: Metacommunication and metamediality – Urs Schreiber's Das Epos der Maschine (Machine Epic)

As suggested above, recent aesthetic technological developments have shifted the focus within hypertext/hypermedia on the empowerment of language, both in terms of programming code and on-screen representation. This trend has then led to the creation of so-called cyberpoems, a term which derives from Aarseth's concept of 'cybertext' discussed above.

To varying degrees, some of the relatively rare instances of this new genre of cyberpoetry have toyed with the idea of medial self-reflexivity, by focusing on the machine and its relationship with user, medium and language. To exemplify this idea, we can turn to Urs Schreiber's *Das Epos der Maschine* (*Machine Epic*) (1998), in which surface text and programming code operate self-reflexively, by portraying the 'machine' as an anthropomorphic, vivified organism. Schreiber employs audio-visual techniques that

Figure 13.4: Title page and self-creating text sample from *Das Epos der Maschine* (*Machine Epic*)

evoke a rather strident, disconcerting human–machine symbiosis. The representation of a multiply wired human head, which has been deprived of its singular physiognomic features, matches the machine-generated background noise, representing electronic waves of varying degrees of intensity (see Figure 13.4). Text is generated in a quasi-random fashion, at times responding to mouse-click, at times emerging or moving autonomously. The sentence 'his eyes were resting in the head of the machine' (my translation) reflects the amalgamation between human being and machine, which renders the latter complete, self-contained and consistent. The machine in Schreiber's narrative cyberpoem, as well as the text itself, can be operated (but not controlled) by human beings. This then evokes associations with the media as an ideologically governed apparatus used by the general public, but governed from within, through mechanisms established by human 'programmers', or 'ideological brokers', who more often than not remain behind the scenes of the mediated event.

In Bense's terms, Schreiber's poem appears to be generating various styles of language literally of its own accord – styles that merely resemble dialogic, narrative and descriptive discourse. Hence, language is constructed here as a medium that both generates and incarnates technology, or rather the product of human authorial interaction with technology, which renders itself utterly self-centred and thus undermines any meaningful dialogue between the reader and the text.

13.5 Conclusion

In this chapter I have tried to describe some of the main ways in which the metalinguistics of hyperpoetry aestheticizes the representation of language by both drawing on and invoking language as an art form in its own right. I have suggested, moreover, that so-called *aesthetic* metalanguage takes us (far) beyond current theories of (factual) metalanguage. This is in so far as hyperpoetry creates a second layer of reality, i.e. fictionality, into which language users (poets and reader-users) delve and within which metalinguistic discourse (in its characteristic dual sense, i.e. referring to both language *and* linguistics) unfolds in terms of implicature rather than explicature. Given this multi-layered codification, metalanguage producers evoke associations with, rather than comment explicitly on, language-related concerns ranging from metastructuralist, or metagrammatical through metatextual to metacommunicative and metadiscursive issues.

Generally speaking, it can be said that there is a tendency among hyperpoets to revisit McLuhan's slogan 'the medium is the message' by overtly thematizing the tripartite, or rather quadripartite, mediality of language and discourse, namely that of the message, the channel, the contact and the code. In so doing, the more 'conservative' hyperpoets position themselves in the context of concrete poetry, focusing on the systemic nature of language and other semiotic modes (what I have called metagrammar and metasemiotics) and representing them in a ludic, carnivalesque, often satirical manner. Other hyperpoets deal with issues arising from more recent fields of linguistic study, such as questions of textuality (text linguistics) and gender (as part of sociolinguistics). This is achieved by insinuating, rather than explicitly commenting on (in the sense of Preston's 'Metalanguage 1') issues regarding cognitive processes performed by the receiver of (hyper-)text in the case of text linguistics, and the controversy surrounding delicate questions of language policy in the case of language and gender. That said, it cannot be assumed that the poets in question are fully aware of or deliberately draw upon any specific linguistic theories. What they all have in common, however, is a distinctive interest in medial and linguistic reflexivity, which opens up a vast field of interpretation potential exceeding the traditional stylistic scope of 'language' in its narrowest sense.

With respect to *channel* – in other words the material medium which enables human–machine communication – a range of innovative 'cyberpoets', as I have called them, have begun to take advantage of recent technological advances. In doing so, they are venturing beyond the classic communicative dualism of sender and receiver by calling into question the relative authority of the human operator (in the sense of both authorprogrammer and user-receiver) together with the hegemony of the linguistic sign. Instead, they investigate the autonomous, performance-oriented power of the linguistically encoded Frankensteinian text machine, by creating poetic programmes that gradually start to usurp the receptive process per se. This reduction of intentionality on the receiver's side is currently one of the central areas of techno-aesthetic development, with authors experimenting on biologically rather than intentionally driven hermeneutic systems that respond, for instance, to human respiration (e.g. Kate Pullinger's *The Breathing Wall* 2004). However, these concerns while offering a tantalizing glimpse of the potential for future developments take the artistic engagement with the communicative channel, the medium, into hitherto unknown dimensions of cognitive literary theory. As such, they clearly take us far beyond the confines of aesthetic metalanguage as discussed in this chapter. In fact, the very notion of 'reduced intentionality' on the part of the receiver opens up an entirely new dimension within the discourse of ideology and power. Evidently, the conventional idea of media-induced 'brainwashing' is revolutionized by a neo-Orwellian scenario which replaces the hegemony of the ideological broker *behind* the medium with that of the empowered medium itself. In reality, of course, a (text) machine cannot operate without the input of a (human) programmer, whose idiosyncratic fingerprints will be left as an indispensable creative trademark on the code, the channel and the message. In this respect, it is down to consumers themselves to develop a critical awareness of the all-important psychological 'contact' between themselves, media producers and the code-empowered medium itself. After all, of all communicative functions it is precisely this psychological link which can best be controlled by perceivers, for they are in charge of the actual decoding and interpreting process and therefore at liberty to unmask medially concealed ideologies. Assuming that this awareness-raising process is one of the major intentions shared by hyperpoets, we can be assured that their work will indeed remain indispensable for the interests of contemporary sociolinguistics.

Primary sources

Kendall, R. (1999–2000), *The Seasons*. Watertown, MA: Eastgate Systems (available online at www.eastgate.com/Seasons/Welcome.html, accessed 20.10.06).

Menzer, U. (2000–2001), *Er/Sie.digital*, CD-ROM (programmed by S. Orth), in R. Simanowski (ed.) *Literatur digital. Formen und Wege einer neuen Literatur.* Munich: dtv (available online at www.soyosigma.de, accessed 20.10.06).

Pullinger, K. (2004), *The Breathing Wall*, CD-ROM. London: The Sayle Literary Agency.

Rosenberg, J. (1968–1999), *Diagrams* (available online at www.well.com/user/jer/bio.html, accessed 20.10.06).

Schreiber, U. (1998), *Das Epos der Maschine* (available online at http://.kunst.im.internett.de/epos-der-maschine/edmdiemaschine.html, accessed 20.10.6).

Zeitgenossen (2001), *Yatoo* (available online at www.zeitgenossen.com/outerspaceip/, accessed 20.10.06).

Notes

1. In a nutshell, the term 'intermediality' (cf. 'intertextuality') refers to relationships between media and the way in which they are established by the productive, creative interplay of various media and their concomitant semiotic systems either within one (e.g. digital) medium or several separate (analog) media. 'Synaesthesia', which refers to the joint stimulation of various sensory channels (e.g. vision, touch and hearing), is one of the central aesthetic effects of this interplay. Rather than operating on a merely additive level, medial, semiotic and sensory interconnections result in a higher-level conceptual and aesthetic experience, which opens up new cognitive and perceptual dimensions (see Müller 1996: 127).

2. The concept of virtual reality, which might spring to mind in the context of the New Media, does not apply here, as, along with Bukatman (1994), I understand it to be a three-dimensional, visualized simulation of real life, which uses language only as a marginalized communicative and exploratory tool. Hyperliterature, on the other hand, creates secondary realities through language as a mediating code.

3. www.a-blast.org/ (06.07.06)

4. Joyce, M. (1990), *afternoon, a story* (CD-ROM). Environment: Storyspace. Cambridge, MA: Eastgate Systems (first published 1987).

5. Bly, B. (1997), *We Descend* (CD-ROM). Environment: Storyspace. Cambridge, MA: Eastgate Systems.

COMMENTARY

14 Language in the media: authenticity and othering

Adam Jaworski

'Language in the media' *is* an ambiguous title. On the one hand, it may refer to all language use (or discourse) in the domain of the media, while on the other hand, adopting a meta-linguistic perspective, it may refer to more or less overt representations and discussions of language and language-related issues. Both these interpretations must be treated as endpoints on a cline. As has been suggested in earlier work (e.g. van Leeuwen 2004b; Cameron 2004; see also Johnson and Ensslin; Horner [note: all references without the year of publication are to 'this volume']), all language use is in some way metalinguistic in that its production and interpretation depend on the successful deployment and uptake of what has been variously referred to as the framing and keying strategies, contextualization cues, metamessages, code-orientation, and a plethora of other signals and devices exploiting and relying on the reflexive nature of language. The foregoing chapters themselves embody the title's ambiguity by displaying various degrees of orientation to the 'meta' level in their choice of data, but what they all invariably demonstrate is the ideologization of language – a metalinguistic concept *par excellence*, which involves people's ideas, beliefs and attitudes to language with regard to patterns of prestige and standardness, displays of authority and hegemony, acts of subversion and contestation, orientation to the aesthetic dimension of code, and so on. All of these conceptions, which may be articulated explicitly or made manifest in communicative practice, can be always linked to specific contexts of use and the speaker's/writer's sociocultural knowledge (see, e.g. Woolard and Schieffelin 1994; Kroskrity 2004).

Linguistic ideology is not something that only takes place in the media. In fact, as a spectacle of social interaction produced for the observation of readers and viewers, media discourse does not in principle differ greatly from other forms of unmediated interaction (Scollon 1998). However, such is the ubiquity and influence of the media on contemporary societies, including changes in individuals' ways of speaking (cf. Coupland 2007) that it is arguably the single most frequently studied institutional domain of discourse use (including political communication) in sociolinguistics and (critical) analysis of discourse (cf. Cotter 2001a for an overview). The media genres from which the data of all the chapters in this book are derived constitute linguistic and cultural 'rich points' (Agar 1991; Coupland 1995); consider print media news, and comment and analysis sections (Heywood and Semino; Jeffries; Hill; Milani; Horner; Thurlow), political magazine covers (Johnson); TV documentaries (Jaffe) and lifestyle programmes (Gieve and Norton), light entertainment and factual radio reporting (Kelly-Holmes and Atkinson; Jaffe), and last but not least (interactive) internet sites (Cameron; Ensslin). All of these texts are extremely powerful either because of their capability to reach and influence vast numbers of people, or because of their élite, authoritative status, or both (Hill; Johnson; Milani; Horner; Jaffe; Thurlow).

It is also the unquestionable effect of the media to 'pick up' certain issues, however small, and turn them into stories, moral panics and debates, especially, if the *issue* is sufficiently *negative* to increase its news value (Galtung and Ruge 1965). Language-related 'stories' are no exception here. Kristine Horner notes that the national press in Luxembourg does not normally extensively cover problematic aspects of the Luxembourgish educational system, but the publication of the results of the first *Programme for International Student Assessment* (PISA) in 2001, in which the results for students in Luxembourg turned out to be lower than in most other European countries, led to a discussion of these results in the national press together with their potential links to issues of trilingualism. Conforming to the well-established *complaint* tradition (Milroy and Milroy 1998; Cameron), allegations of an emerging crisis in language and communication standards are also at the heart of the media reports discussed by Sally Johnson in relation to a recent German spelling reform, Jane Hill's study of the *personalist ideology* in media reports of public figures' lies and misstatements, and Crispin Thurlow's chapter on young people's new-media communication styles. Generally, and here I am echoing Deborah Cameron's observation, whenever *the standard language ideology* (Lippi-Green 1997) dominates the reporting of any aspect of language, it is always from the position of a threat to the accepted social, political and moral order (see also Milani; Jaffe; Kelly-Holmes and Atkinson). Aberration from the 'standard' is rarely, if ever, praised or even accepted. For example, young people's revelatory and humorous language creativity displayed in new-media discourse is treated with contempt as eroding society's standards of literacy (Thurlow), while the only reason why equally 'shocking' creativity may be at all tolerated in hyperpoetry by 'mainstream' media (evidenced by the absence of ridicule and scorn) seems to be its apparent relegation to the relatively harmless yet marginalized status of 'avant-garde' literature (Ensslin).

Heywood and Semino present us with an amazing, but not at all surprising statistic that in press news reports (based on a sample of the British print media), approximately 50 per cent of the words are used to represent the speech and writing of other people. The preponderance of news items about communicative acts is testament to the key role that language (or discourse, or communication, more broadly), conceived of as a form of social action (Austin 1961), plays in structuring all aspects of social life (e.g. Fairclough 2003). And, as attested by this collection of articles, debating language issues is about debating issues of social structure, political and economic power, and identity positions with concomitant evaluation of social actors (Cameron 2004), and taking sides by all the parties involved, including the chapter authors (Blommaert 1999a).

In stressing 'the increasing culturization of economic life', Scott Lash and John Urry (1994: 109) note that in late modernity, which they also refer to as 'consumer capitalism' (ibid.: 2), traditional consumption patterns of the modern era are exaggerated not only by the quickening turnover of ever disposable objects but also by a significant reflexivity of human subjectivity in the process of consumption, heightened by the consumption of cultural artefacts, or signs, and the crucial role of knowledge and information in the functioning of contemporary economies. This 'reflexive accumulation' (ibid.: 61) privileges 'expert systems' (Giddens 1991) as a basis for establishing and maintaining different regimes of truth (Foucault 1980) with regard to the social and moral order, and is also characterized by the 'aestheticization of everyday life' (Featherstone 1991), which on the one hand is a function of the increased role of research and design in economic production, while on the other allows the 'experts' to bestow cultural capital on consumers. As Lash and Urry suggest:

> The information and communication structures which displace the more traditional social structures are at the same time knowledge/ power structures and underpin what Foucault called normalization and 'individuation'. Isolated from the bedrock of social networks, the 'specialized consumption' of cultural and other commodities is not so much a matter of 'difference' or 'pluralized life worlds' or even 'neo-tribes', but instead a matter of niche marketing and disembedded lifestyle enclaves [...]. (Lash and Urry 1994: 142)

In the past two decades, these roughly sketched ideas from social theory have resonated with critical discourse analysts and ethnographically inclined sociolinguists by focusing on the increasing role of meta-level discourses in regulating the social process (Coupland and Jaworski 2004). As Blommaert (2003, 2005) demonstrates, in the new, global world system premised on the inequalities between 'core regions' and 'peripheries' (Wallerstein 1983, [1991] 2001), specific pronunciations, vocabulary, regional and class varieties (dialects and sociolects), styles, genres, different repertoires of literacy, and other speech and writing forms need to be examined beyond their referential or denotative meanings as indices of social and symbolic values, or in terms of their 'indexical valence' (Ochs 1996; Rampton 2006) as activating the relative positions of power and distance between communicators, evoking

273

their subjectivities (orientation to particular class, ethnicity, gender positions, etc.), access to or inaccessibility of economic, social, cultural and s
ymbolic capital (Bourdieu 1991; cf. Milani), connotations of psycho-social
and cultural ideals, and the types of communicative activities being manifest.
Furthermore, the reflexivity afforded by language allows speakers to engage
in creative enactments of different personae via stylization (e.g. Rampton
2006; Coupland, 2007). However, just as speakers may be free to opt for a
particular voice (cf. Kelly-Holmes and Atkinson; Thurlow), which, following
Hymes, Blommaert (2005: 68) defines as 'the ways in which people manage
to make themselves understood or fail to do so', they are often equally con-
strained by the hegemonic practices of verbal hygiene (Cameron 1995), or
what van Leeuwen (1993) refers to as the *discursive recontextualization* of
social practice (including speech or writing; cf. also Urban's 1996 notion
of *entextualization*, and Iedema's 2003 notion of *resemioticization*). Such
recontextualizations, which involve a sequence of linguistic or non-linguistic
activities, a 'genre', semiotically transform the 'original' social practice by
way of substitutions, (particularization, generalization, objectivation, etc.),
deletions, rearrangements, and additions (repetitions, reactions, goals, legit-
imations, and evaluations). These two approaches bear obvious affinity with
Irvine and Gal's (2000; Gal and Irvine 1995) oft-quoted semiotic processes
for the ideologized construction of linguistic difference (*iconization, fractal
recursivity*, and *erasure*; see Horner), and it is these social practices which,
for me, account best for the pair of complementary key themes that run
through the preceding chapters: *authenticity* and *othering*.

In spring 2004, a well-publicized row erupted between the British artist
Tracey Emin and a London primary school. Emin had been commissioned by
an art charity to produce a work of art with a group of eight-year-old pupils in
the school, and the result was a patchwork quilt, a type of tapestry for which
Emin is well known. Once the project was completed, the finished work of art
attributed to Emin, with the children's assistance, remained in the school.
Subsequently, the school had the piece valued at Sotheby's for £35,000
and decided to sell it as part of its fund-raising activities. On hearing the
news, Emin demanded the return of the quilt (claiming it was hers and the
school had no right to sell it), or to de-authenticate it as not hers, in which
case the piece would be worthless and unsaleable (unless Sotheby's made
its history clear).

In recent years, the question of authenticity in relation to language has
gained considerable interest among sociolinguists and discourse analysts
(e.g. Thornborrow and van Leeuwen 2001; Eckert 2003; Bucholtz 2003;
Coupland 2003b). Not unlike the above example, there appears general
consensus that 'authenticity is an ideological construct that is central to
the practice of both speakers and analysts of language' (Eckert 2003: 392), or
as van Leeuwen (2001: 396) puts it, 'authenticity cannot be seen as an objective feature of talk, or any other form of sociocultural production [. . .]

Authenticity is about validity. [. . .] Indeed, authenticity could be considered to be a special kind of modality, or a special aspect of modality' (cf. Johnson). Although this may explain how Emin was able to manipulate the validity of the quilt as hers, this also allowed the school to contest her decision on the grounds of contradiction, i.e. denying authorship but asking for the quilt back.

The aforementioned articles by Eckert, Bucholtz and Coupland (published as a 'Dialogue' exchange in the *Journal of Sociolinguistics*) demonstrate a recent shift to greater self-reflexivity in sociolinguistics, which acknowledges that language researchers, like other language users and commentators, must acknowledge their own interests and ideological position vis-à-vis the languages and speakers they study (cf. Blommaert's claim quoted above on researchers 'taking sides' in language ideological debates they report on).

Space precludes me from outlining the Dialogue's trio's detailed account of the dominant language ideologies in sociolinguistic research. Suffice it to say that all these authors are in agreement that one of these ideologies, 'and in some ways the most powerful, is that of *the linguist as arbiter of authenticity*' (Bucholtz 2003: 406–7). In this respect, we are not very different from all the media pundits quoted in the chapters of this book and other 'folk linguists' (Preston 2004; see also Johnson and Ensslin; Johnson; Cameron).

In his typology of 'sociolinguistic authenticities', the focal points oriented to in defining languages as authentic, Coupland (2003b: 421, see also 2001b) lists the following six criteria:

Authentic language 1: attested and attestable language.
Authentic language 2: naturally occurring language.
Authentic language 3: language encoding fact and truth.
Authentic language 4: fully owned, unmediated language.
Authentic language 5: language indexing personal authenticity.
Authentic language 6: language indexing authentic cultural
membership.

Far from treating the above dimensions as unproblematic, Coupland provides us with a useful template to consider 'traditional' ways of viewing language (and its users) as authentic.

Authentic language (AL)3 and *AL5* seem to provide a basis for the *personalist language ideology* discussed by Jane Hill in relation to the media coverage of public figures' alleged lies and misstatements. This ideology purports that the 'true' hence authentic meaning of the utterance emanates from the assumed sincerity, integrity and commitment of the speaker (writer), which is significant because, as Hill argues, racist and other hegemonic forms of discourse can be seemingly produced unchallenged if, somehow, they can be claimed not to reflect the moral stance of the speaker.

The chapters by Sally Johnson; Tommaso Milani; Kristine Horner; Alexandra Jaffe; Helen Kelly-Holmes and David Atkinson; Crispin Thurlow; and Deborah Cameron, make evident the media bias in attending to *AL6*. This is only too often steeped in the essentialist view of authenticity resting on two assumptions: '(1) that groups can be clearly delimited; and (2) that group members are more or less alike' (Bucholtz 2003: 400). Thus, both the proponents and the opponents of the German spelling reform may fly the literal or metaphorical German flag of national and cultural unity (Johnson); the advocates of Swedish language tests for Swedish citizenship may claim that a distinguishing feature of migrants in Sweden is their lack of knowledge of the Swedish language (Milani); while the discourses of national identity in Luxembourg may invoke either the *one language one nation ideology* linking Luxembourgish to the 'idealized, homogeneous ethnic nation', or the ideal of a trilingual nation presupposing the 'mastery of the standardized, written varieties of German and French by Luxembourgish-speaking pupils in state schools' (Horner).

AL6 comes into play also in less explicit media representations of language. As Coupland argues (2003b: 424), '*Authentic language 6* gives us a potential differentiation among speech communities on the basis of their "cultural authenticity"', which is probably most acute in the case of ethnic/linguistic minorities undergoing a language shift in the direction of the hegemonic variety. The chapter by Jaffe, for example, demonstrates how the choice of a minority language (Corsican), and the degree to which it is spoken in media broadcasts indexes their audiences as 'Corsican', whether a bounded and homogeneous speech community through hypercorrect, Corsican monolingual, authoritative news radio broadcasts, or a community undergoing a language shift in more relaxed, mixed-language use in light radio entertainment programmes. The same chapter demonstrates how Corsican–French bilingual education in a TV documentary is achieved, somewhat paradoxically, by the editorial process of *erasing* in the final version of the programme most of the French language usage by pupils and teachers to normalize, or authenticate 'the use of Corsican as an academic register'.

Kelly-Holmes and Atkinson demonstrate how the fetish of purism in minority language revitalization situations (see also Jaffe) leads to the othering of a prominent though 'imperfect' minority language user. In a comedy radio sketch, an Irish 'celebrity' is deemed not be an authentic speaker of Irish (cf. Coupland's *AL4*) and is 'othered' through the parodic (hyperbolic, nonsensical and otherwise 'incorrect') representation of his L2-like Irish. Yet, even this ridiculed form of Irish gains some degree of authenticity as an index of Irishness (*AL6*) when another character in the same sketch (a 'Hollywood star') is 'othered' by his demonstrable inability to understand even most rudimentary Irish.

Probably the most evident instance of the media metadiscourse harnessed in the service of *de*authenticating language is illustrated by Thurlow's analysis of the international print media hysteria around young people's new-media language. Here, the questioning of the authenticity of text and online messaging involves *AL1* and *AL2*, which Coupland (ibid.) positions in the context of sociolinguistic theory as the *methodological* criteria. In Thurlow's study, adolescents' new-media language is not an *attestable* language variety as it is contrasted with the *attested* 'standard': 'Text messaging is hardly the Queen's English' (*AL1*), and an artificial code created under abnormal circumstances rather than a 'naturally' occurring language (*AL2*). Furthermore, new-media language is deemed to be not only formally but semantically deficient, and its alleged incomprehensibility makes people who use it morally suspect (*AL3*). Thurlow's chapter is also a particularly good illustration of how the recontextualization of the social practice of text and instant messaging transforms them semiotically to enable the preservation and reproduction of the social, political and economic *status quo*, whereby the powerful adult-run media organizations may keep young people in the double-bind of being targeted as lucrative consumers of the new media and being criticized for doing so.

Representation and evaluation of languages, like all language ideological work, always involves individual and group identity statements. As the well-known quote from Raymond Williams states, 'a definition of language is always, implicitly or explicitly, a definition of human beings in the world' (Williams 1977: 21; quoted in Woolard and Schieffelin 1994: 56). Therefore, in parallel to the (de-)authentication theme running through the foregoing chapters, another dominant theme is that of (de-)legitimating individual language users and/or groups they may want to identified with. Where language ideology is oriented to producing social and political inequality, language users are inevitably 'othered'.

As we have postulated elsewhere (Jaworski and Coupland 2005), in defining different identity positions, we need to distinguish between the 'self', the 'non-self' and the 'other'. The first two categories are premised on *difference*, such as contrasting the speakers of different national languages, say Swedish and Luxembourgish, who by implication are likely to be members of two different, imagined national communities occupying non-overlapping, imagined national territories. This sort of distinction may work well for the adherents of *one nation, one language ideology*, as they are likely to treat these two entities as linguistically and ethnically idealized and homogeneous constituencies. However, national (and other) groups are not homogeneous ethnically, linguistically or otherwise, and this will always present a problem for the 'purists'. This is when a third category is involved in order to make sense of those who may be making claims to the same sorts of identity positions as 'self' but not being accepted as such, e.g. migrants, asylum seekers, and so on. In social anthropological terms, this position is occupied by the ambiguous and anomalous mediator between 'self' and 'non-self':

277

[S]ince any description of the world must discriminate categories in the form 'p is what *not*-p is not' (Leach 1964 and 1969), and since every category system is based on the principle of difference, such primitive logic is seen as intrinsically binary. But, as Leach points out, if the logic of our thought leads us to distinguish *we* from *they*, how can we bridge the gap and establish social, economic, and sexual relations with the *others* without throwing our categories into confusion? The usual answer is that mediation is achieved through the introduction of a third category such as amphibian, which is ambiguous or anomalous in terms of the ordinary categories of land and water animals. Such abnormal middle forms are regarded as dangerous and powerful and are typically the focus of taboo and ritual observance (cf. Leach 1969: 10–11). (Babcock-Abrahams 1975: 169)

Thus, the Other occupies the liminal status of those who are like 'us' and are not like 'us', being stereotyped, dehumanized, diminished, inferior, odd, irrational, exoticized and evil; feared and desired at the same time (cf. Hall 1997; Said 1978; Riggins 1997). Othering of language users is the automatic byproduct of deauthentication and delegitimation of their languages: users of 'lesser' languages are not fully human (like 'us'). As Horner states in her chapter: 'both members of linguistic minorities as well as speakers of so-called "dialects" may be targets of "othering" processes by means of language ideologies bound up with the nation-state'. Being 'inadequate' speakers of the idealized national 'standard' languages is the basis of the media othering 'foreign' migrants in Luxembourg (Horner) and in Sweden (Milani), and L2 Irish speakers in Ireland (Kelly-Holmes and Atkinson).

Thurlow points out how young people are othered by adults as the sub-human 'grunt generation', while the same adults may be displaying a fascination with young people's command of new technologies. In Cameron's chapter, we see how the deeply ingrained belief in linguistic differences between the sexes (a version of the *biological determinism ideology*) leads not so much the media but media consumers (internet bloggers) to acts of *self*-othering. Having their gender identity misidentified by an internet-based quiz 'analysing' samples of texts for the sex of the author, bloggers display an orientation to self- or other-ascribed 'gender atypicality' adhering to, rather than questioning the view that the writing styles of males and females differ (in ways suggested by the authors of the quiz).

The two chapters by Lesley Jeffries, on the one hand, and Simon Gieve and Julie Norton, on the other, are interesting examples of *the linguist as arbiter of authenticity* ideology mentioned above. Jeffries presents newspaper journalists' accounts of a public apology by Tony Blair, which the journalists dismiss as a 'non-apology', a view endorsed by Jeffries' pragmatic analysis (with other approaches available, cf. Lakoff 2001). Gieve and Norton discuss British television presenters' on-screen interactions with non-English-speaking, or English L2-speaking 'hosts' outside of the UK in terms of eight strategies for 'communication across linguistic difference', one of which inevitably involves the presenters and L2 English-speaking hosts interacting in English. However, what is more interesting here, is the fact that the authors find some interactions between presenters and hosts conducted in the local language (i.e. not in English) to be *authentic* or 'normal' ('he does try to preserve a sense of *being with* the Italian speakers rather than *making use of* them'; 'His comfortable style of engagement with foreign language speakers making use of basic second language skills is rarely found on British broadcast TV'; 'The limitations of his Italian quickly become apparent however, and the refuse collection team speak no English, but his enthusiastic manner and interactive skills make it possible to film encounters which seem to go well, with his good humour being shared by the work crew.'). These *unproblematically* construed encounters are contrasted with 'pseudo-encounters', which are 'largely fake', in which hosts appear to be mere props in the presenters' delivery of their scripts for the benefit of the viewing public.

It is not entirely clear what discursive features demarcate 'normal' from 'pseudo-interactions'. In our own work on similar type of data (British TV holiday programmes; see Jaworski *et al* 2003), we have observed presenters' overwhelming disattention to the performance frame and the enactment of a second stream of 'out-of-frame activity' (Goffman 1974: 210) for the benefit of the viewing public. In such instances, presenters disattend verbally and/or non-verbally to their host interactants, depriving them of full *participation status* (Goffman 1974: 224). Instead, they gain the role of what Goffman calls the 'toy status, namely, the existence of some object, human or not, that is treated as if in frame, an object to address, act to or comment on, but which is in fact out of frame (disattendable) in regard to its capacity to hear and talk' (ibid.; see also Dunn 2006).

To conclude, although the explicit focus of the book is on *language* in the media, in specific case studies we are always confronted by meaning which cannot be divorced from its material existence, or 'its mode of actualization', and subsequently from the relation of the material substance of language (or other semiotic modes) and the kinds of meanings which are made (Kress 2000b: 136). Several chapters included here demonstrate cross-modal meta-discursive processes, e.g. speech being represented, recontextualized or entextualized through writing in print media (Heywood and Semino; Jeffries; Hill; Milani; Horner). These print media representations and enactments of speech are authoritative and élitist due to limited access to the actual production process (see Milani). Similarly, Johnson demonstrates how the cover of *Der Spiegel* she's analysed *visually* represents the opposition of five intellectuals to the German spelling reform, encapsulating their protest and conservatism through the image's metaphor of the five men armed and ready for battle (cf. Heywood and Semino's 'communication as physical aggression' metaphor). A skilled reader of the cover would probably deconstruct its meaning (with the probable added element of humour) in a relatively short time, but might miss much of the remaining detail of the debate represented in the 14-page 'cover story'. The trade-off here is a relatively long time needed for the decoding of the written text. Thurlow's cartoon examples may also be seen to add an element of humour to the debate on young people's use of new-media language, though the author opts for a less innocent interpretation, linking the cartoons with a devaluing of young people's communication capital. Finally, Ensslin's orientation to the formal properties of the *mode* of written German and English in hyperpoetry is complemented by her analysis of the contextualizing properties of the digital *medium* though which such poetry is disseminated and consumed.

References

Aarseth, E. (1997), *Cybertext: Perspectives on Ergodic Literature*. Baltimore: The Johns Hopkins University Press.

Abercrombie, D. (1965), 'What is a "letter"?', in D. Abercrombie (ed.), *Studies in Phonetics and Linguistics*. London: Oxford University Press, pp. 76–86.

Agar, M. (1991), 'The biculture in bilingual'. *Language in Society*, 20, 169–81.

Aitchison, J. (1997), *The Language Web: The Power and Problem of Words*. Cambridge: Cambridge University Press.

Aitchison, J. (2001), 'Misunderstandings about language: a historical overview'. *Journal of Sociolinguistics*, 5(4), 611–19.

Aitchison, J. and Lewis, D. M. (2003) (eds), *New Media Language*. London: Routledge.

Anderson, B. ([1983] 1991), *Imagined Communities: Reflections on the Origin and Spread of Nationalism*. London: Verso.

Androutsopoulos, J. K. (2000), 'Non-standard spellings in media texts: the case of German fanzines'. *Journal of Sociolinguistics*, 4(4), 514–33.

Androutsopoulos, J. K. (2006), 'Introduction: sociolinguistics and computer-mediated communication'. *Journal of Sociolinguistics*, 10(4), 419–38.

Androutsopoulos, J. K. and Schmidt, G. (2002), 'SMS-Kommunikation: ethnografische Gattungsanalyse am Beispiel einer Kleingruppe'. *Zeitschrift für Angewandte Linguistik*, 36, 49–80.

Argamon, S., Koppel, M., Fine, J. and Shimoni, A. R. (2003), 'Gender, genre and writing style in formal written texts'. *Text*, 24, 321–46.

Ascott, R. (1999), 'Gesamtdatenwerk: connectivity, transformation, and transcendence', in T. Druckrey (ed.), *Ars Electronica: Facing the Future*. Cambridge: MIT Press, pp. 86–9.

Austin, J. L. (1961), *How to Do Things with Words*. Oxford: Clarendon Press.

Babcock-Abrahams, B. (1975), 'Why frogs are good to think and dirt is good to reflect on'. *Soundings*, 58: 167–81.

Baker, C. (2001), *Foundations of Bilingual Education and Bilingualism*. Clevedon: Multilingual Matters.

Bakhtin, M. M. (1968), *Rabelais and His World* (trans. H. Iswolsky). London: MIT Press.

Bakhtin, M. (1981), 'Discourse of the novel', in M. Holquist (ed.), *The Dialogic Imagination: Four Essays* (trans. C. Emerson and M. Holquist). Austin: University of Texas Press, pp. 259–422.

Baron, N. S. (2000), *Alphabet to Email: How Written English Evolved and Where It's Heading*. New York: Routledge.

Baron, N. (2002), 'Who sets email style? Prescriptivism, coping strategies, and democratizing communication access'. *The Information Society*, 18, 403–13.

Barthes, R. (1972), *Mythologies*. London: Cape.

Barthes, R. (1977), *Image – Music – Text*. London: Fontana.

Bauer, L. and Trudgill, P. (1998) (eds), *Language Myths*. London: Penguin.

Bauman, R. and Briggs, C. L. (2003), *Voices of Modernity: Language Ideologies and the Politics of Inequality*. Cambridge: Cambridge University Press.

Bauman, Z. (1998), *Globalization: The Human Consequences*. Cambridge: Polity Press.

Bell, A. (forthcoming), ' "Do you want to hear about it?" Exploring possible worlds in Michael Joyce's hyperfiction, *afternoon, a story*', in M. Lambrou and P. Stockwell (eds), *Contemporary Stylistics*. London: Continuum.

Bell, A. (1991), *The Language of the News Media*. Oxford: Blackwell.

Bell, A. and Garrett, P. (1998) (eds), *Approaches to Media Discourse*. Oxford: Blackwell.

Bense, M. (1954), *Aesthetica (I). Metaphysische Beobachtungen am Schönen*. Stuttgart: Deutsche Verlags-Anstalt.

Bense, M. (1956), *Aesthetica (II). Aesthetische Information*. Baden-Baden: Agis.

Bense, M. (1958), *Aesthetica (III). Ästhetik und Zivilisation. Theorie der ästhetischen Zivilisation*. Krefeld: Agis.

Bense, M. (1960), *Aesthetica (IV). Programmierung des Schönen. Allgemeine Texttheorie und Textästhetik*. Krefeld: Agis.

Bentahila, A. (1983), *Language Attitudes among Arabic-French Bilinguals in Morocco*. Clevedon UK: Multilingual Matters.

Berg, G. (2003), *'Mir wëlle bleiwe wat mir sin': Soziolinguistische und sprachtypologische Betrachtungen zur luxemburgischen Mehrsprachigkeit*. Tübingen: Niemeyer.

Bernstein, M. (1998), 'Patterns of hypertext'. Watertown, MA: Eastgate Systems Inc.. (available online at www.eastgate.com/patterns/Print.html, accessed 02.11.06).

Biber, D. (1995), *Dimensions of Register Variation: A Cross-Linguistic Comparison*. Cambridge: Cambridge University Press.

Bignell, J. (2002), *Media Semiotics: An Introduction* (2nd edn). Manchester: Manchester University Press.

Blackbourn, D. (2003), *History of Germany 1780–1918. The Long Nineteenth Century* (2nd edn). Oxford: Blackwell.

Blackledge, A. (2005), *Discourse and Power in a Multilingual World*. Amsterdam: John Benjamins.

Blakemore, D. (1992), *Understanding Utterances*. Oxford: Blackwell.

Block, F. W., Heibach, C. and Wenz, K. (2004) (eds), *pOes1s. Ästhetik digitaler Poesie The Aesthetics of Digital Poetry*. Ostfildern-Ruit: Hatje Cantz.

Blommaert, J. (1999a) (ed.), *Language Ideological Debates*. Berlin: Mouton de Gruyter.

Blommaert, J. (1999b), 'The debate is open', in J. Blommaert (ed.) *Language Ideological Debates*. Berlin: Mouton de Gruyter, pp. 1–38.

Blommaert, J. (1999c), 'The debate is closed', in J. Blommaert (ed.) *Language Ideological Debates*. Berlin: Mouton de Gruyter, pp. 425–38.

Blommaert, J. (2003), 'Commentary: a sociolinguistics of globalisation'. *Journal of Sociolinguistics*, 7 (4), 607–23.

Blommaert, J. (2005), *Discourse: A Critical Introduction*. London: Routledge.

Blommaert, J. and Verschueren, J. (1992), 'The role of language in European nationalist ideologies'. *Pragmatics*, 2, 355–75.

Blommaert, J. and Verschueren, J. (1998), *Debating Diversity: Analysing the Discourse of Tolerance.* London: Routledge.

Bloomfield, L. (1944), 'Secondary and tertiary responses to language'. *Language,* 20: 45–55. Reprinted in C. F. Hockett (1970) (ed.) *Leonard Bloomfield Anthology.* Chicago: University of Chicago Press, pp. 284–96.

Blum-Kulka, S., House, J. and Kasper, G. (1989) (eds), *Cross-cultural Pragmatics: Requests and Apologies.* Norwood, NJ: Ablex.

Boardman, M. (2005), *The Language of Websites.* London: Routledge.

Bokhorst-Heng, W. (1999), 'Singapore's speak Mandarin campaign: language ideological debates in the imagining of the nation', in J. Blommaert (ed.), *Language Ideological Debates.* Berlin: Mouton de Gruyter, pp. 235–65.

Bolter, J. D. (2001), *Writing Space: Computers, Hypertext, and the Remediation of Print.* Mahwah, NJ: Lawrence Erlbaum Associates.

Bourdieu, P. (1991), *Language and Symbolic Power.* Cambridge: Polity Press.

Bourdieu, P. (2000), *Pascalian Meditations.* Cambridge, MA: Polity Press.

Breuilly, J. (2001) (ed.), *Nineteenth-Century Germany: Politics, Culture and Society, 1780–1918.* London: Arnold.

Brown, P. and Levinson, S. ([1978]1987), *Politeness: Some Universals in Language Usage.* Cambridge: Cambridge University Press.

Browne, D. (1992), 'Raidío na Gaeltachta: reviver, preserver or swan song of the Irish language?'. *European Journal of Communication,* 7, 415–33.

Bucholtz, M. (2003), 'Sociolinguistic nostalgia and the authentication of identity'. *Journal of Sociolinguistics,* 7, 399–416.

Bucholtz, M. and K. Hall (2004), 'Theorizing identity in language and sexuality research'. *Language in Society,* 33, 469–515.

Bukatman, S. (1994), 'Virtual textuality'. *Artforum,* Jan 1994, 13–14.

Burger, M. (2002), 'Identities at stake in social interaction: the case of media interviews'. *Studies in Communication Sciences,* 2(2), 1–20.

Burman, E. (1994), *Deconstructing Developmental Psychology.* London: Routledge.

Busch, B. (2005), 'Changing media spaces: the transformative power of heteroglossic practices', in C. Mar-Molinero and P. Stevenson (eds), *Language Ideologies, Policies and Practices: Language and the Future of Europe.* London: Palgrave Macmillan, pp. 206–19.

Butler, J. (1990), *Gender Trouble: Feminism and the Subversion of Identity.* London: Routledge.

Butler, J. (1997), *Excitable Speech: A Politics of the Performative.* London: Routledge.

Cameron, D. (1995), *Verbal Hygiene.* London: Routledge.

Cameron, D. (1997), 'Performing gender identity: young men's talk and the construction of heterosexual masculinity', in S. Johnson and U. H. Meinhof (eds), *Language and Masculinity.* Oxford: Blackwell, pp. 47–64.

Cameron, D. (2000a), *Good to Talk? Living in a Communication Culture.* London: Sage.

Cameron, D. (2000b), 'Styling the worker: gender and the commodification of language in the globalized service economy'. *Journal of Sociolinguistics,* 4(3), 323–47.

Cameron, D. (2004), 'Out of the bottle: the social life of metalanguage', in A. Jaworski, N. Coupland and D. Galasiński (eds), *Metalanguage: Social and Ideological Perspectives.* Berlin: de Gruyter, pp. 311–21.

Cameron, D. (2005), 'Language, gender and sexuality: current issues and new directions'. *Applied Linguistics*, 26(4), 482–502.

Cameron, D. (2006), 'Men are from earth, women are from earth', in D. Cameron (ed), *On Language and Sexual Politics*. London: Routledge, pp. 133–45.

Cameron, L. (2003), *Metaphor in Educational Discourse*. London: Continuum.

Cassirer, E. ([1944] 1990), *Versuch über den Menschen. Einführung in eine Philosophie der Kultur*. Frankfurt/M.: Fischer.

Chilton, P. (1996), *Security Metaphors: From Containment to Common House*. New York: Peter Lang.

Chilton, P. (2004), *Analysing Political Discourse: Theory and Practice*. London: Routledge.

Chouliaraki, L. and Fairclough, N. (1999), *Discourse in Late Modernity: Rethinking Critical Discourse Analysis*. Edinburgh: Edinburgh University Press.

Christophersen, P. and MacArthur, T. (1992), *Native Speaker*. Oxford: Oxford University Press.

Clayton, J. (2003), *Charles Dickens in Cyberspace: The Afterlife of the Nineteenth Century in Postmodern Culture*. Oxford: Oxford University Press.

Cohen, A. and Olshtain, E. (1981), 'Developing a measure of sociocultural competence: the case of apology'. *Language Learning*, 31(1), 113–34.

Cohen, S. (1972), *Folk Devils and Moral Panics*. London: MacGibbon and Kee.

Collins, J. (1999), 'The Ebonics controversy in context: literacies, subjectivities, and language ideologies in the United States', in J. Blommaert (ed.), *Language Ideological Debates*. Berlin: Mouton de Gruyter, pp. 201–34.

Conboy, M. (2003), 'Parochializing the global. Language and the British tabloid press', in J. Aitchison and D. M. Lewis (eds), *New Media Language*. London: Routledge, pp. 45–54.

Conklin, J. (1987), 'Hypertext – an introduction and survey'. *IEEE Computer*, 20(9), 17–41.

Constantinou, O. (2005), 'Multimodal discourse analysis: media, modes and technologies'. *Journal of Sociolinguistics*, 9(4), 602–18.

Cook, N. (1998), *Analysing Musical Multimedia*. New York: Oxford University Press.

Cooper, R. (1989), *Language Planning and Social Change*. Cambridge: Cambridge University Press.

Cotter, C. (1999), 'Radio Na Life: innovations in the use of media for language revitalization', *International Journal of the Sociology of Language*, 140, 135–47.

Cotter, C. (2001a), 'Discourse and media', in D. Schiffrin, D. Tannen and H. E. Hamilton (eds), *The Handbook of Discourse Analysis*. Oxford: Blackwell, pp. 416–36.

Cotter, C. (2001b), 'Continuity and vitality: expanding domains through Irish-language radio', in L. Hinton and K. Hale (eds), *The Green Book of Language Revitalization in Practice*. San Diego: Academic Press, pp. 301–12.

Coupland, N. (1995), 'Pronunciation and the rich points of culture.' In J. Windsor Lewis (ed.), *Studies in English and General Phonetics: In Honour of Professor J. D. O'Connor*. London: Routledge, pp. 310–19.

Coupland, N. (2001a), 'Dialect stylisation in radio talk', *Language in Society*, 30(3), 345–75.

Coupland, N. (2001b), 'Stylisation, authenticity and TV news review.' *Discourse Studies*, 3, 413–42.

Coupland, N. (2003a), 'Introduction: sociolinguistics and globalisation'. *Journal of Sociolinguistics*, 7(4), 465–72.

Coupland, N. (2003b), 'Sociolinguistic authenticities.' *Journal of Sociolinguistics*, 7, 417–31.

Coupland, N. (2004), 'Stylised deception', in A. Jaworski, N. Coupland and D. Galasiński (eds), *Metalanguage: Social and Ideological Perspectives*. Berlin: Mouton de Gruyter, pp. 249–74.

Coupland, N. (2007), *Style: Language Variation and Identity*. Cambridge: Cambridge University Press.

Coupland, N. and Jaworski, A. (2004), 'Sociolinguistic perspectives on metalanguage: reflexivity, evaluation and ideology', in A. Jaworski, N. Coupland and D. Galasiński (eds), *Metalanguage: Social and Ideological Perspectives*. Berlin: Mouton de Gruyter, pp. 15–51.

Croft, W. (2002), 'The role of domains in the interpretation of metaphors and metonymies', in R. Dirven and R. Pörings (eds), *Metaphor and Metonymy in Comparison and Contrast*, Berlin: Mouton de Gruyter, pp. 161–377.

Crowley, T. (2005), *War of Words: The Politics of Language in Ireland 1537–2004*. Oxford: Oxford University Press.

Crystal, D. (2001), *Language and the Internet*. Cambridge: Cambridge University Press.

Culler, J. (1997), *Literary Theory: A Very Short Introduction*. Oxford: Oxford University Press.

Cyr, D. (1999), 'Metalanguage awareness: a matter of scientific ethics'. *Journal of Sociolinguistics*, 3(2), 283–6.

Davies, A. (1991), *The Native Speaker in Applied Linguistics*. Edinburgh: Edinburgh University Press.

Davis, J. (1990), *Youth and the Condition of Britain: Images of Adolescent Conflict*. London: Athlone.

Davis, K. A. (1994), *Language Planning in Multilingual Contexts: Policies, Communities, and Schools in Luxembourg*. Amsterdam: John Benjamins.

Day, R. (2001), 'The Irish language and radio: a response', in H. Kelly-Holmes (ed.), *Minority Language Broadcasting: Breton and Irish*. Clevedon: Multilingual Matters, pp. 73–82.

Decrosse, A. (1987), 'Un mythe historique: la langue maternelle', in G. Vermes and J. Boutet (eds), *France, pays multilingue*. Vol 2. Paris: L'Harmattan, pp. 29–37.

Deignan, A. (2005), *Metaphor and Corpus Linguistics*. Amsterdam: John Benjamins.

Denk, F. (1997), 'Eine der größten Desinformationskampagnen', in H.-W. Eroms and H. Haider Munske (eds), *Die Rechtschreibreform: Pro und Kontra*. Berlin: Erich Schmidt, pp. 41–6.

Derrida, J. (1988), *Limited Inc*. Evanston, IL: Northwestern University Press.

de Saussure, F. (1966), *Course in General Linguistics* (trans. W. Baskin). New York: McGraw Hill.

Deutschmann, M. (2003), *Apologising in British English*. Umeå: Umeå University.

DiGiacomo, S. M. (1999), 'Language ideological debates in an Olympic city: Barcelona 1992–1996', in J. Blommaert (ed.), *Language Ideological Debates*. Berlin: Mouton de Gruyter, pp. 105–42.

Dorian, N. C. (1999), 'Linguistic and ethnographic fieldwork', in J. A. Fishman (ed.), *Handbook of Language and Ethnic Identity*. Oxford: Oxford University Press, pp. 25–41.

Duchêne, A. and Heller, M. (2007) (eds), *Discourses of Endangerment: Interest and Ideology in the Defence of Languages*. London: Continuum.

Dunn, D. (2006), 'Singular encounters: mediating the tourist destination in British television holiday programmes'. *Tourist Studies*, 6, 37–58.

Duranti, A. (1992), 'Intention, self, and responsibility: an essay in Samoan ethno-pragmatics', in J. H. Hill and J. T. Irvine (eds), *Responsibility and Evidence in Oral Discourse*. Cambridge: Cambridge University Press, pp. 24–47.

Eagleton, T. (1991), *Ideology: An Introduction*. London and New York: Verso.

Eckert, P. (1989), *Jocks and Burnouts: Social Categories and Identity in the High School*. New York: Teachers College Press.

Eckert, P. (2003), 'Sociolinguistics and authenticity: An elephant in the room'. *Journal of Sociolinguistics*, 7, 392–7.

Eco, U. (1989), *The Open Work* (transl. A. Cancogni). Cambridge, MS: Harvard University Press.

Edwards, J. (1977), 'Students' reactions to Irish regional accents'. *Language and Speech*, 20(3), 280–6.

Edwards, J. (1985), *Language, Society and Identity*. Oxford: Basil Blackwell.

Edwards, J. (1999), 'Refining our understanding of language attitudes'. *Journal of Language and Social Psychology*, 18(1), 101–10.

Eickhoff, B. (1999), 'Gleichstellung von Männern und Frauen in der Sprache'. *Sprachspiegel*, 55, 2–6.

Eisenlohr, P. (2004a), 'Register-levels of ethnonational purity: the ethnicization of language and community in Mauritius'. *Language in Society*, 33(1), 59–80.

Eisenlohr, P. (2004b), 'Language revitalization and new technologies'. *Annual Review of Anthropology*, 33, 21–45.

El Refaie, E. (2001), 'Metaphors we discriminate by: naturalized themes in Austrian newspaper articles about asylum seekers'. *Journal of Sociolinguistics*, 5(3), 352–71.

Ensslin, A. (2007), *Canonizing Hypertext: Explorations and Constructions*. London: Continuum.

Facer, K. and Furlong, R. (2001), 'Beyond the myth of the "cyberkid": young people at the margins of the information revolution'. *Journal of Youth Studies*, 4, (4), 451–69.

Fairclough, N. (1995), *Media Discourse*. London: Edward Arnold.

Fairclough, N. (1997), 'Technologization of discourse', in C. R. Caldas-Coulthard and M. Coulthard (eds), *Texts and Practices: Readings in Critical Discourse Analysis*. London: Routledge, pp. 71–83.

Fairclough, N. (2003), *Analysing Discourse: Textual Analysis for Social Research*. London: Routledge.

Fairclough, N. (2006), *Language and Globalization*. London: Routledge.

Featherstone, M. (1991), 'The aestheticization of everyday life.' In M. Featherstone (ed.) *Consumer Culture and Postmodernism*, London: Sage, pp. 65–82.

Fehlen, F. (2002), 'Luxembourg, a multilingual society at the romance/germanic language border'. *Journal of Multilingual and Multicultural Development*, 23, 80–97.

286

Fishman, J. (1977) (ed.), *Advances in the Creation and Revision of Writing Systems*. The Hague: Mouton.

Fishman, J. (1999) (ed.), *Handbook of Language and Ethnic Identity*. New York and Oxford: Oxford University Press.

Foucault, M. (1980), *Power/Knowledge: Selected Interviews and Other Writings, 1972–1977* (ed. C. Gordon). New York: Pantheon.

Foucault, M. (1988), 'Technologies of the self', in L. H. Martin, H. Gutman and P. H. Hutton (eds), *Technologies of the Self: A Seminar with Michel Foucault*. Amherst: University of Massachusetts Press, pp. 16–49.

Fowler, R. (1991), *Language in the News: Discourse and Ideology in the Press*. London: Routledge.

Gal, S. and J. T. Irvine (1995), 'The boundaries of language and disciplines: How ideologies construct difference.' *Social Research*, 62, 967–1001.

Gal, S. and Woolard, K. (2001) (eds), *Languages and Publics: The Making of Authority*. Manchester: St. Jerome.

Gal, S. and Woolard, K. (2001), 'Constructing languages and publics: authority and representation', in S. Gal and K. Woolard (eds), *Languages and Publics: The Making of Authority*. Manchester: St. Jerome, pp. 1–12.

Galasiński, D. (2004), 'Restoring the order: metalanguage in the press coverage of Princess Diana's *Panorama* interview', in A. Jaworski, N. Coupland and D. Galasiński (eds), *Metalanguage: Social and Ideological Perspectives*. Berlin: Mouton de Gruyter, pp. 131–45.

Galtung, J. and M. H. Ruge (1965), 'The structure of foreign news'. *Journal of International Peace Research*, 1, 64–90.

Gardner, N., Puigdevall i Serralvo, M. and Williams, C. H. (2000), 'Language revitalization in comparative context: Ireland, the Basque country and Catalonia', in C. H. Williams (ed.), *Language Revitalization: Policy and Planning in Wales*. Cardiff: University of Wales Press, pp. 311–61.

Garrett, P. (2001), 'Language attitudes and sociolinguistics'. *Journal of Sociolinguistics*, 5(4), 626–31.

Garrett, P., Coupland, N. and Williams, A. (2003), *Researching Language Attitudes: Social Meanings of Dialect, Ethnicity and Performance*. Cardiff: University of Wales Press.

Giddens, A. (1991), *Modernity and Self-Identity: Self and Society in the Late Modern Age*. Stanford: Stanford University Press.

Giesen, B. (2001), 'National identity and citizenship: the cases of Germany and France', in K. Eder and B. Giesen (eds), *European Citizenship: Between National Legacies and Postnational Projects*. Oxford: Oxford University Press, pp. 36–58.

Giles, H., Coupland, J. and Coupland, N. (1991) (eds), *Contexts of Accommodation: Developments in Applied Sociolinguistics*. Cambridge: Cambridge University Press.

Giles, H. and Powesland, P. (1975) (eds), *Speech Style and Social Evaluation*. London: Academic Press.

Giroux, H. A. (1998), 'Teenage sexuality, body politics and the pedagogy of display', in J. Epstein (ed.), *Youth Culture: Identity in a Postmodern World*. Oxford: Blackwell, pp. 24–55.

Giroux, H. A. (2000), *Stealing Innocence: Youth, Corporate Power, and the Politics of Culture*. New York: St. Martin's Press.

Gitelman, L. and Pingree, G. B. (2001), *New Media: 1740–1915*. Massachusetts: MIT Press.

Goffman, E. (1967), *Interaction Ritual*. New York: Pantheon.

Goffman, E. (1974), *Frame Analysis: An Essay on the Organization of Experience*. New York: Harper and Row.

Gomringer, E. (1966), *manifeste und darstellungen der konkreten poesie 1954–1966*. St. Gallen: galerie press.

Goodman, S. and O'Halloran, K. (2006) (eds), *The Art of English: Literary Creativity*. Basingstoke: Palgrave Macmillan.

Goodwin, C. and Duranti, A. (1992), 'Rethinking context: an introduction', in A. Duranti and C. Goodwin (eds), *Rethinking Context: Language as an Interactive Phenomenon*. Cambridge: Cambridge University Press, pp. 1–42.

Grad Fuchsel, H. and Martín Rojo, L. (2003), ' "Civic" and "ethnic" nationalist discourses in Spanish parliamentary debates'. *Journal of Language and Politics*, 2, 31–70.

Grady, J. (1997), *Foundations of Meaning: Primary Metaphors and Primary Scenes*. Unpublished PhD dissertation. University of California, Berkeley.

Grady, J. (1998), 'The "conduit" metaphor revisited: a reassessment of metaphors for communication', in J.-P. Koenig (ed.), *Discourse and Cognition: Bridging the Gap*. Stanford, CA.: CSLI Publications, pp. 205–18.

Grewenig, A. (1993) (ed.), *Inszenierte Information. Politik und strategische Kommunikation in den Medien*. Opladen: Westdeutscher Verlag.

Grice, H. P. (1975), 'Logic and conversation', in P. Cole and J. L. Morgan (eds), *Syntax and Semantics 3: Speech Acts*. New York: Academic Press, pp. 41–58.

Griffin, C. (1993), *Representations of Youth: The Study of Youth and Adolescence in Britain and America*. Cambridge: Polity.

Hagège, C. (1996), *L'Enfant aux Deux Langues*. Paris: Editions Odile Jacob.

Hall, S. (1992), 'The spectacle of the 'other'.' In S. Hall (ed.), *Representation: Cultural Representations and Signifying Practices*. London: Sage in association with The Open University Press, pp. 223–79.

Hård af Segerstad, Y. (in press), 'Language use in Swedish mobile text messages', in R. Ling and P. Pedersen (eds), *Front Stage-Back Stage: Mobile Communication and the Renegotiation of the Social Sphere*. Dordrecht: Kluwer.

Hargreaves, I. (2000), *Who's Misunderstanding Whom? An Inquiry into the Relationship between Science and the Media*. London: ESRC.

Hartmann-Hirsch, C. (1991), 'Triglossie – Quadriglossie . . . ? Luxembourg: eine mehrsprachige Gesellschaft', in B. Schlieben-Lange and A. Schönberger (eds), *Polyglotte Romania: Homenage a Tilbert Didac Stegmann: Beiträge zu Sprachen, Literaturen und Kulturen der Romania* (Band 2). Frankfurt/M.: Domus Editoria Europaea, pp. 959–74.

Hayles, N. K. (2000), 'Flickering connectivities in Shelley Jackson's Patchwork Girl: the importance of media-specific analysis'. *Postmodern Culture* (available online at www.muse.jhu.edu/journals/pmc/v010/10.2hayles.html, accessed 02.11.06).

Hayles, N. K. (2002), *Writing Machines*. Cambridge, MA: MIT Press.

Hayles, N. K. (2004), 'Print is flat, code is deep: the importance of media-specific analysis'. *Poetics Today*, 25(1), 67–90.

Heibach, C. (2003), *Literatur im elektronischen Raum*. Frankfurt/M.: Suhrkamp.

Heller, M. (1999a), 'Sociolinguistics and public debate'. *Journal of Sociolinguistics*, 3(2), 260–88.

Heller, M. (1999b), 'Heated language in a cold climate', in J. Blommaert (ed.), *Language Ideological Debates*. Berlin: Mouton de Gruyter, pp. 143–70.

Heller, M. (with the collaboration of M. Campbell, P. Dalley and D. Patrick) (1999c), *Linguistic Minorities and Modernity: A Sociolinguistic Ethnography*. London: Longman.

Heller, M. (2003), 'Globalization, the new economy, and the commodification of language and identity'. *Journal of Sociolinguistics*, 7(4), 473–92.

Hellinger, M. (2000), 'Feministische Sprachpolitik und politische Korrektheit – Der Diskurs der Verzerrung', in K. Eichhoff-Cyrus and R. Hoberg (eds), *Die deutsche Sprache zur Jahrtausendwende: Sprachkultur oder Sprachverfall?*. Mannheim: Duden-verlag, pp. 177–91.

Herring, S. C. (2001), 'Computer-mediated discourse', in D. Schiffrin, D. Tannen and H. Hamilton (eds), *The Handbook of Discourse Analysis*. Oxford: Blackwell, pp. 612–34.

Heywood, J. and Semino, E. (2005), 'Source "scenes" and source "domains": insights from a corpus-based study of metaphors for communication', in A. Wallington, J. Barnden, S. Glasbey, M. Lee, and L. Zhang (eds), *Proceedings of the Third Interdisciplinary Workshop on Corpus-Based Approaches to Figurative Language*. Birmingham: School of Computer Science, University of Birmingham, pp. 12–19.

Hill, J. H. (2000), 'Read my article: language ideology and the overdetermination of promising in American presidential politics,' in P. V. Kroskrity (ed.), *Regimes of Language*. Santa Fe, NM: SAR Press, pp. 259–92.

Hill, J. H. (2001), 'Language, race, and white public space', in A. Duranti (ed.), *Linguistic Anthropology: A Reader*. Malden, MA: Blackwell, pp. 450–64.

Hindley, R. (1990), *The Irish Language: A Qualified Obituary*. London: Routledge.

Hirsch, M. (1997), 'Luxembourg', in B. S. Ostergaard (ed.), *The Media in Western Europe: The Euromedia Handbook*. London: Sage, pp. 144–52.

Ho, J. W. Y. (2002), 'Curriculum documents as representation of institutional ideology: a comparative study'. *Language and Education*, 16, 284–302.

Hoare, R. (2001), 'An integrative approach to language attitudes and identity in Brittany'. *Journal of Sociolinguistics*, 5(1), 73–84.

Hoberg, R. (1997), 'Orthographie, Rechtschreibreform und öffentliche Meinung', in H.-W. Eroms and H. H. Munske (eds), *Die Rechtschreibreform: Pro und Kontra*. Berlin: Erich Schmidt, pp. 95–100.

Holloway, S. and Valentine, G. (2001), *Cyberkids: Youth Identities and Communities in an Online World*. London: Routledge.

Holmes, J. (1990), 'Apologies in New Zealand English'. *Language in Society*, 19, 155–99.

Holmes, J. (1993), 'Women's talk: the question of sociolinguistic universals'. *Australian Journal of Communication*, 20(3), 125–49.

Hornberger, N. and King, K. (1999), 'Authenticity and unification in Quechua language', in S. May (ed.), *Indigenous Community-Based Education*. Clevedon: Multilingual Matters, pp. 160–80.

289

Horner, K. (2004), *Negotiating the Language-Identity Link: Media Discourse and Nation-Building in Luxembourg*. PhD dissertation, State University of New York at Buffalo. Ann Arbor: University Microfilms International.

Horner, K. (2005), 'Reimagining the nation: discourses of language purism in Luxembourg', in N. Langer and W. V. Davies (eds), *Linguistic Purism in the Germanic Languages*. Berlin: de Gruyter, pp. 166–85.

Horner, K. and Weber, J. J. (2005), 'The representation of immigrant students within the classical humanist ethos of the Luxembourgish school-system: from *Pour une école d'intégration* to the PISA debates', in A. J. Schuth, K. Horner and J. J. Weber (eds), *Life in Language: Studies in Honour of Wolfgang Kühlwein*. Trier: Wissenschaftlicher Verlag Trier, pp. 241–58.

House, J. (2003), 'English as a lingua franca: a threat to multilingualism?'. *Journal of Sociolinguistics*, 7(4), 556–78.

Humphrys, J. (2004), *Lost for Words: The Mangling and Manipulation of the English Language*. London: Hodder and Stoughton.

Hyland, K. (2005), *Metadiscourse: Exploring Interaction in Writing*. London: Continuum.

Hyltenstam, K. (1999), 'Inledning: ideologi, politik och minoritetsspråk', in K. Hyltenstam (ed.), *Sveriges sju inhemska språk – ett minoritetsspråksperspektiv*. Lund: Studentlitteratur, pp. 11–40.

Hymes, D. (1974), *Foundations of Sociolinguistics*. Philadelphia: University of Pennsylvania Press.

Iedema, R. (2003), 'Multimodality, resemioticization: Extending the analysis of discourse as multi-semiotic practice'. *Visual Communication*, 2, 29–57.

Irvine, J. (1989), 'When talk isn't cheap: language and political economy'. *American Ethnologist*, 16, 248–67.

Irvine, J. and Gal, S. (2000), 'Language ideology and linguistic differentiation', in P. V. Kroskrity (ed.), *Regimes of Language: Ideologies, Polities and Identities*. Oxford: James Currey, pp. 35–83.

Irwin, A. and Wynne, B. (1996) (eds), *Misunderstanding Science: The Public Reconstruction of Science and Technology*. Cambridge: Cambridge University Press.

Iser, W. (1978), *The Act of Reading: A Theory of Aesthetic Response* (trans. W. Iser). Baltimore: The Johns Hopkins University Press.

Jaffe, A. (1999a), *Ideologies in Action: Language Politics on Corsica*. Berlin: Mouton de Gruyter.

Jaffe, A. (1999b), 'Locating power: Corsican translators and their critics', in J. Blommaert (ed.), *Language Ideological Debates*. Berlin: Mouton de Gruyter, pp. 39–66.

Jaffe, A. (2000a), 'Introduction: non-standard orthography and non-standard speech'. *Journal of Sociolinguistics*, 4(4), 497–513.

Jaffe, A. (2000b), 'Comic performance and the articulation of hybrid identity'. *Pragmatics*, 10(1), 39–60.

Jaffe, A. (2005), 'L'évaluation de la radio: perspectives corses sur le purisme linguistique'. *Langage et Société*, 112, 79–97.

Jaffe, A. and Walton, S. (2000), 'The voices people read: orthography and the representation of non-standard speech'. *Journal of Sociolinguistics*, 4(4), 561–88.

Jakobson, R. (1960), 'Closing statement: linguistics and poetics', in T. A. Sebeok (ed.), *Style in Language*. Cambridge, MA: MIT Press, pp. 350–77.

Jakobson, R. ([1955]1985), 'Metalanguage as a linguistic problem', in S. Rudy (ed.), *Roman Jakobson: Selected Writings*. Vol 7. Berlin: Mouton de Gruyter, pp. 113–21.

Jansen-Tang, D. (1988), *Ziele und Möglichkeiten einer Reform der deutschen Orthographie seit 1901*. Frankfurt/M.: Peter Lang.

Jaworski, A. and Coupland, J. (2005), 'Othering in gossip: 'you go out you have a laugh and you can pull yeah okay but like . . .'.' *Language in Society*, 34, 667–94.

Jaworski, A., Fitzgerald, R. and Morris, D. (2004a), 'Radio leaks: presenting and contesting leaks in radio news broadcasts'. *Journalism*, 5(2), 183–202.

Jaworski, A., Coupland, N. and Galasiński, D. (2004b) (eds), *Metalanguage: Social and Ideological Perspectives*. Berlin: Mouton de Gruyter.

Jaworski, A., Coupland, N. and Galasiński, D. (2004c), 'Metalanguage: why now?', in A. Jaworski, N. Coupland and D. Galasiński (eds), *Metalanguage: Social and Ideological Perspectives*. Berlin: Mouton de Gruyter, pp. 3–13.

Jaworski, A. and Galasiński, D. (2002), 'The verbal construction of non-verbal behaviour: British press reports of President Clinton's grand jury testimony video'. *Discourse and Society*, 13(5), 629–49.

Jaworski, A., Thurlow, C., Lawson, S. and Ylänne-McEwen, V. (2003), 'The uses and representations of local languages in tourist destinations: a view from British TV holiday programmes'. *Language Awareness*, 12(1), 5–29.

Jewitt, C. (2004), 'Multimodality and new communication technologies', in P. Levine and R. Scollon (eds), *Discourse and Technology: Multimodal Discourse Analysis*. Washington, DC: Georgetown University Press, pp. 184–95.

Johnson, S. (1999), 'After Schleswig-Holstein. Implications of the "no" vote on the 1998 reform of German orthography'. *Debatte: Review of Contemporary German Affairs*, 7(2), 158–74.

Johnson, S. (2000), 'The cultural politics of the 1998 reform of German orthography'. *German Life and Letters*, 53(1), 106–25.

Johnson, S. (2001), 'Who's misunderstanding whom? (Socio)linguistics, public debate and the media'. *Journal of Sociolinguistics*, 5(4), 591–610.

Johnson, S. (2002), 'On the origin of linguistic norms: orthography, ideology and the constitutional challenge to the 1996 reform of German'. *Language in Society*, 31(4), 549–76.

Johnson, S. (2005a), *Spelling Trouble: Language, Ideology and the Reform of German Orthography*. Clevedon: Multilingual Matters.

Johnson, S. (2005b), 'Sonst kann jeder schreiben, wie er will . . .'? Orthography, legitimation, and the construction of publics', in S. Johnson and O. Stenschke (eds), 'Special issue on the German Spelling Reform', *German Life and Letters*, 58(4), 453–70.

Johnson, S. (2006), 'Review of "*Metalanguage: Social and Ideological Perspectives*. Edited by Adam Jaworski, Nikolas Coupland and Dariusz Galasiński. 2004"'. *Language in Society*, 35(3), 437–40.

Johnson, S., Culpeper, J. and Suhr, S. (2003), 'From "politically correct councillors" to "Blairite nonsense": discourses of "Political Correctness" in three British newspapers', *Discourse and Society*, 14(1), pp. 29–47.

Johnson, S. and Ensslin, A. (2007), ' "But her language skills shifted the family dynamics dramatically." Language, gender and the construction of publics in two British newspapers'. *Gender and Language*, 1(2).

Joseph, J. (2004), *Language and Identity: National, Ethnic, Religious*. Basingstoke and New York: Palgrave Macmillan.

Joseph, J. E. and Taylor, J. T. (1990) (eds), *Ideologies of Language*. London: Routledge.

Kac, E. (1996), *New Media Poetry: Poetic Innovation and New Technologies*, special issue of *Visible Language*, 30(2), Providence, RI: Rhode Island School of Design.

Kaeding, F. W. (1898), *Häufigkeitswörterbuch der deutschen Sprache*. Steglitz bei Berlin.

Kasesniemi, E.-L. and Rautiainen, P. (2002), 'Mobile culture of children and teenagers in Finland', in J. E. Katz and M. A. Aakhus (eds), *Perpetual Contact: Mobile Communication, Private Talk, Public Performance*. Cambridge: Cambridge University Press, pp. 170–92.

Katan, D. and Straniero-Sergio, F. (2003), 'Submerged ideologies in media interpreting', in M. Calzada Perez (ed.), *Apropos of Ideology: Translation Studies on Ideology – Ideologies in Translation Studies*. Manchester: St Jerome, pp. 131–44.

Keane, W. (1997), *Signs of Recognition*. Berkeley: University of California Press.

Keane, W. (2002), 'Sincerity, modernity and the Protestants'. *Cultural Anthropology*, 17, 65–92.

Kelly-Holmes, H. (2001) (ed.), *Minority Language Broadcasting: Breton and Irish*. Clevedon: Multilingual Matters.

Kilborn, R. (1993), ' "Speak my language": current attitudes to television subtitling and dubbing'. *Media, Culture and Society*, 15, 641–60.

Kintsch, W. and van Dijk, T. (1978), 'Toward a model of text comprehension and production'. *Psychological Review*, 85(5), 363–94.

Kittler, J. ([1985] 1990), *Discourse Networks 1800/1900*. Stanford: Stanford University Press.

Klein, C. (2003), *La valorisation des compétences linguistiques sur le marché du travail luxembourgeois*. Differdange: CEPS/INSTEAD.

Kling, R. (1996) 'Hopes and horrors: technological utopianism and anti-utopianism in narratives of computerization'. *CMC Magazine*, February 1996. Available (11.04.03) online.

Kloss, H. (1978), *Die Entwicklung neuer germanischer Kultursprachen seit 1800*. Düsseldorf: Schwann.

Koch, P. and Krämer, S. (1997), 'Einleitung', in P. Koch and S. Krämer (eds), *Schrift, Medien, Kognition. Über die Exteriorität des Geistes*. Tübingen: Stauffenburg, pp. 9–26.

Kövecses, Z. (2002), *Metaphor: A Practical Introduction*. Oxford: Oxford University Press.

Koolstra, C., Peeters, A. and Spinhof, H. (2002), 'The pros and cons of dubbing and subtitling'. *European Journal of Communication*, 17(3), 325–54.

Koopmans, R. and Statham, P. (2000), 'Challenging the liberal nation-state? Postnationalism, multiculturalism, and the collective claims-making of migrants and ethnic minorities in Britain and Germany', in R. Koopmans and P. Statham (eds), *Challenging Immigration and Ethnic Relations Politics: Comparative European Perspectives*. Oxford: Oxford University Press, pp. 189–232.

Koutsogiannis, D. and Misikopoulou, B. (2003), 'Greeklish and Greekness: trends and discourses of "glocalness"'. *Journal of Computer-Mediated Communication*, 9(1), 1–26. (available online at www.ascusc.org/jcmc, accessed 28.12.05).

Kress, G. (2000a), *Early Spelling: Between Convention and Creativity*. London: Routledge.

Kress, G. (2000b), 'Text as the punctuation of semiosis: Pulling at some of the threads', in U. H. Meinhof and J. Smith (eds), *Intertextuality and the Media: From Genre to Everyday Life*. Manchester: Manchester University Press, pp. 132–54.

Kress, G. and van Leeuwen, T. (2001), *Multimodal Discourse: The Modes and Media of Contemporary Communication*. London: Arnold.

Kress, G. and van Leeuwen, T. (2006), *Reading Images: The Grammar of Visual Design* (2nd edn). London: Routledge.

Kroskrity, P. (2000) (ed.), *Regimes of Language: Ideologies, Polities and Identities*. Santa Fe: School of American Research Press.

Kroskrity, P. V. (2004), 'Language ideologies', in A. Duranti (ed.), *A Companion to Linguistic Anthropology*. Oxford: Blackwell Publishing, pp. 496–517.

Küppers, H.-G. (1984), *Orthographiereform und Öffentlichkeit. Zur Entwicklung und Diskussion der Rechtschreibreformbemühungen zwischen 1876 und 1982*. Düsseldorf: Schwann.

Kuhlen, R. (1991), *Hypertext: Ein nicht-lineares Medium zwischen Buch und Wissensbank*. Berlin: Springer Verlag.

Kymlicka, W. and Patten, A. (2003) (eds), *Language Rights and Political Theory*. Oxford: Oxford University Press.

Laforest, M. (1999), 'Can a sociolinguist venture outside the university?'. *Journal of Sociolinguistics*, 3(2), 276–81.

Lakoff, G. (1991), 'Metaphor and war: the metaphor system used to justify war in the Gulf'. *Journal of Urban and Cultural Studies*, 2(1), 59–72.

Lakoff, G. (2002), *Moral Politics: How Liberals and Conservatives Think*. Chicago: Chicago University Press.

Lakoff, G. and Johnson, M. (1980), *Metaphors We Live By*. Chicago: Chicago University Press.

Lakoff, G. and Johnson, M. (1999), *Philosophy in the Flesh: The Embodied Mind and its Challenge to Western Thought*. New York: Basic Books.

Lakoff, G. and Turner, M. (1989), *More than Cool Reason: A Field Guide to Poetic Metaphor*. Chicago: Chicago University Press.

Lakoff, R. T. (2001), 'Nine ways of looking at apologies: The necessity for interdisciplinary theory and method in discourse analysis', in D. Schiffrin, D. Tannen and H. E. Hamilton (eds), *The Handbook of Discourse Analysis*. Oxford: Blackwell Publishing, pp. 199–214.

Landow, G. P. (1997), *Hypertext 2.0: The Convergence of Contemporary Critical Theory and Technology*. Baltimore: The Johns Hopkins University Press.

Larsen, D. and Higgason, R. E. (2004), *An Anatomy of Anchors* (available online at www.sigweb.org/conferences/ht-conferences-archive/ht04/hypertexts/larsen/noflash/rosenberg/, accessed 03.11.06).

Lash, S. and J. Urry (1994), *Economies of Signs and Space*. London: Sage.

Latour, B. (1993), *We Have Never Been Modern*. Hemel Hempstead: Harvester Wheatsheaf.

Leach, E. R. (1964), 'Anthropological aspects of language: Animal categories and verbal abuse', in E. H. Lenneberg (ed.), *New Directions in the Study of Language*. Cambridge: Cambridge University Press, pp. 23–63.

Leach, E. R. (1969) (ed.), *Genesis as Myth and Other Essays*. London: Jonathan Cape.

Ledig, F. (1999), 'Die öffentliche Auseinandersetzung um die Rechtschreibreform von 1996'. *Deutsche Sprache*, 2, 97–117.

Lee, B. (2001), 'Circulating the people', in S. Gal and K. Woolard (eds), *Languages and Publics: The Making of Authority*. Manchester: St. Jerome, pp. 164–81.

Leezenberg, M. (2002), 'Power in communication: implications for the semantics-pragmatics interface'. *Journal of Pragmatics*, 34, 893–908.

Leishman, C. (2001), ' "People know me really well": Jane Macdonald and the construction of authenticity in the Cruise'. *Ecloga*. Department of English Studies, University of Strathclyde (available online at www.strath.ac.uk/ecloga/contents.html, accessed 02.11.06).

Leiss, E. (1994), 'Genus und Sexus. Kritische Anmerkungen zur Sexualisierung von Grammatik'. *Linguistische Berichte*, 152, 281–300.

Lesko, N. (2003), *Act Your Age! A Cultural Construction of Adolescence*. New York: Routledge Falmer.

Levinson, J. (1984), 'Hybrid art forms'. *Journal of Aesthetic Education*, 18, 5–13.

Levinson, S. (1983), *Pragmatics*. Cambridge: Cambridge University Press.

Licklider, J. C. R. (1960), 'Man-computer symbiosis'. *IRE Transactions on Human Factors in Electronics, HFE-1*, 4–11.

Lippi-Green, R. (1997), *English with an Accent. Language, Ideology, and Discrimination in the United States*. New York: Routledge.

Low, G. (2003), 'Validating metaphoric models in Applied Linguistics'. *Metaphor and Symbol*, 18(4), 239–54.

Lukács, G. (1971), *History and Class Consciousness: Studies in Marxist Dialectics*. Cambridge, MA: MIT Press.

MacGahern, J. (2005), *Memoir*. London: Faber and Faber.

Mac Giolla Chríost, D. (2005), *The Irish Language in Ireland: From Goidel to Globalization*. London: Routledge.

McGregor, J. (2002), 'Restating news values: contemporary criteria for selecting the news', in *Proceedings of the Australian & New Zealand Communication Association* (available online at www.bond.edu.au/hss/communication/ANZCA/papers/JMcGregorPaper.pdf, accessed 02.11.06).

Machin, D. and van Leeuwen, T. (2003), 'Global schemas and local discourses in *Cosmopolitan*'. *Journal of Sociolinguistics*, 7(4), 493–512.

McIntyre, D. (2004), 'Point of view in drama: a socio-pragmatic analysis of Dennis Potter's Brimstone and Treacle', *Language and Literature*, 13(2), 139–60.

McKay, S., Thurlow, C. and Toomey Zimmerman, H. (2005), 'Wired whizzes or techno slaves? Teens and their emergent communication technologies', in A. Williams and C. Thurlow (eds), *Talking Adolescence: Perspectives on Communication in the Teenage Years*. New York: Peter Lang, pp. 185–203.

McKillop, A. M. and Myers, J. (1999), 'The pedagogical and electronic contexts of composing in hypermedia', in S. L. DeWitt and K. Strasma (eds), *Contexts, Intertexts, and Hypertexts*. Cresskill: Hampton Press, pp. 65–116.

McNamara, T. (2005), '21st century shibboleth: language tests, identity and inter-group conflict'. *Language Policy*, 4, 351–70.

McLuhan, E. and Zingrone, F. (1995) (eds), *Essential McLuhan*. New York: Basic Books.

McLuhan, M. (1964), *Understanding Media: The Extensions of Man*. New York: McGraw Hill.

McNair, B. (2006), *Cultural Chaos: Journalism, News and Power in a Globalised World*. London: Routledge.

Males, M. A. (1996), *The Scapegoat Generation: America's War on Adolescents*. Monroe, ME: Common Courage Press.

Manovich, L. (2001), *The Language of New Media*. Cambridge, MA: MIT Press.

May, S. (2001), *Language and Minority Rights: Ethnicity, Nationalism and the Politics of Language*. London: Longman.

May, S. (2003a), 'Rearticulating the case for minority language rights'. *Current Issues in Language Planning*, 4, 95–125.

May, S. (2003b), 'Misconceiving minority language rights: implications for liberal political theory', in W. Kymlicka and A. Patten (eds), *Language Rights and Political Theory*. Oxford: Oxford University Press, pp. 123–52.

May, S. (2005), 'Language rights: moving the debate forward'. *Journal of Sociolinguistics*, 9, 319–47.

May, S. (2006), 'Contesting minority language rights: addressing the attitudes of majority language speakers'. Plenary lecture given at *Sociolinguistics Symposium 16*, Limerick, Ireland, 6–8 July 2006.

Meinhof, U. H. (2004), 'Metadiscourses of culture in British TV commercials', in A. Jaworski, N. Coupland and D. Galasiński (eds), *Metalanguage: Social and Ideological Perspectives*. Berlin: Mouton de Gruyter, pp. 275–88.

Meyerhoff, M. and Niedzielski, N. (2003), 'The globalisation of vernacular variation'. *Journal of Sociolinguistics*, 7(4), 534–55.

Milani, T. M. (in press), 'Language testing and citizenship: A language ideological debate in Sweden'. *Language in Society*.

Miles, S. (2000), 'Consuming youth', in S. Miles (ed.), *Youth Lifestyles in a Changing World*. Buckingham: Open University Press, pp. 106–26.

Milroy, J. (1998), 'Children can't speak or write properly any more', in L. Bauer and P. Trudgill (eds), *Language Myths*. London: Penguin, pp. 58–65.

Milroy, J. (2001), 'Response to Sally Johnson: misunderstanding language?'. *Journal of Sociolinguistics*, 5(4), 620–5.

Milroy, L. (1999), 'Standard English and language ideology in Britain and the United States', in T. Bex and R. Watts (eds), *Standard English: The Widening Debate*. London: Routledge, pp. 173–206.

Milroy, J and Milroy, L. (1998), *Authority in Language*. London: Routledge.

Mitchell-Kernan, C. (1972), 'Signifying and marking: two African-American speech acts', in J. Gumperz and D. H. Hymes (eds), *Directions in Sociolinguistics: The Ethnography of Communication*. New York: Holt, Rinehart and Winston, pp. 161–79.

Moal, S. (2001), 'Broadcast media in Breton: Dawn at last?', in H. Kelly-Holmes (ed.), *Minority Language Broadcasting: Breton and Irish*. Clevedon: Multilingual Matters, pp. 6–30.

Mon, F., Höllerer, W. and de la Motte, M. (1960), *movens. Dokumente und Analysen zur Dichtung, bildenden Kunst, Musik, Architektur*. Wiesbaden: Limes-Verlag.

MORI (2005), 'Attitudes to Irish language radio programming', (available online at www.mori.com/polls/2004/irish-jan.shtml, accessed 02.11.06).

Müller, J. E. (1996), *Intermedialität. Formen moderner kultureller Kommunikation*. Münster: Nodus.

Murtagh, L. (2003), *Retention and Attrition of Irish as a Second Language: A Longitudinal Study of General and Communicative Proficiency in Irish among Second Level School Leavers and the Influence of Instructional Background, Language Use and Attitude/Motivation Variables*, Unpublished PhD Thesis, University of Groningen.

Musolff, A. (2004), *Metaphor and Political Discourse: Analogical Reasoning in Debates about Europe*. Basingstoke: Palgrave Macmillan.

Nelson, T. H. (1984), *Literary Machines 93.1*. Sausalito: Mindful Press.

Niedzielski, N. A. and Preston, D. R. (1999), *Folk Linguistics*. Berlin: Mouton de Gruyter.

Nielsen, J. (1990), *Hypertext and Hypermedia*. Boston: Academic Press.

Ní Neachtain, M. (2001), 'Competence and minority language broadcasting: a response', in H. Kelly-Holmes (ed.), *Minority Language Broadcasting: Breton and Irish*. Clevedon: Multilingual Matters, pp. 69–73.

O'Brien, G. V. (2003), 'Indigestible food, conquering hordes, and waste materials: metaphors of immigrants and the early immigration restriction debate in the United States'. *Metaphor & Symbol*, 18(1), 33–47.

Ochs, E. (1996), 'Linguistic resources for socializing humanity', in J. J. Gumperz and S. C. Levinson (eds), *Rethinking Linguistic Relativity*. Cambridge: Cambridge University Press, pp. 438–69.

Ó hAdhmaill, S. (2005), 'Ar son an saineolais agus i gcoinne an aineolais', *Indymedia*, 16.11.05. (available online at www.indymedia.ie/article/73018, accessed 02.11.06).

O'Halloran, K. L. (2004), *Multimodal Discourse Analysis: Systemic Functional Perspectives*. London: Continuum.

Ó hIfearnaín, T. (2001), 'Irish language broadcast media: the interaction of State language policy, broadcasters and their audiences', in H. Kelly-Holmes (ed.), *Minority Language Broadcasting: Breton and Irish*. Clevedon: Multilingual Matters, pp. 31–48.

Ó Laoire, M. (1995), 'An historical perspective on the revival of Irish outside the Gaeltacht, 1880–1930, with reference to the revitalization of Hebrew'. *Current Issues in Language and Society*, 2(3), 223–35.

Ó Laoire, M. (2001), 'Language policy and the broadcast media: a response', in H. Kelly-Holmes (ed.), *Minority Language Broadcasting: Breton and Irish*. Clevedon: Multilingual Matters, pp. 63–8.

Olshtain, E. (1989), 'Apologies across languages', in S. Blum-Kulka, J. House and G. Kasper (eds), *Cross-cultural Pragmatics: Requests and Apologies*. Norwood, NJ: Ablex, pp. 155–73.

Olshtain, E. and Cohen, A. (1983), 'Apology: a speech-act set', in N. Wolfson and E. Judd (eds), *Sociolinguistics and Acquisition*. Rowley, MA: Newbury House, pp. 18–36.

O'Neill, E. (2005), 'Controversy as Irish opposition leader Enda Kenny calls for Irish to be made an optional subject', *Eurolang*, 15 November, (available online at www.eurolang.net, accessed 02.11.06).

Ó Riagáin D. (1991), 'State broadcasting and minority languages: the case of Irish in Ireland', *Educational Media International*, 28, 113–18.

Ó Riagáin, P. (1997), *Language Policy and Social Reproduction: Ireland 1893–1993*. Oxford: Clarendon Press.

Palfreyman, D. and al Khalil, M. (2003), ' "A funky language for teenzz to use": representing Gulf Arabic in instant messaging'. *Journal of Computer-Mediated Communication*, 9(1), article 2 (available online at http://.jcmc.indiana.edu/vol9/issue1/palfreyman.html, accessed 02.11.06).

Pardoe, S. (2000), 'Respect and the pursuit of "symmetry" in researching literacy and student writing', in D. Barton, M. Hamilton and R. Ivanič (eds), *Situated Literacies: Reading and Writing in Context*. London: Routledge, pp. 149–66.

Peirce, C. S. (1931–1958), *Collected Papers* (8 volumes). Cambridge, MA: Harvard University Press.

Pennycook, A. (2003), 'Global Englishes, Rip Slyme, and performativity', *Journal of Sociolinguistics*, 7(4), 513–33.

Pennycook, A. (2004), 'Performativity and language studies'. *Critical Inquiry in Language Studies: An International Journal*, 1(1), 1–19.

Peterson, L. C. (1997) 'Tuning in to Navajo: the role of radio in native language maintenance', in J. Reyhner (ed.), *Teaching Indigenous Languages*. Flagstaff, AZ: Northern Arizona University, pp. 214–21.

Pfalzgraf, F. (2006), *Neopurismus in Deutschland nach der Wende*. Frankfurt/M.: Peter Lang.

Philips, S. (2004), 'The organization of ideological diversity in discourse: modern and neotraditional visions of the Tongan state'. *American Ethnologist*, 31(2), 231–50.

Pietikänen S. and Dufva, H. (2006), 'Voices in discourses: dialogism, Critical Discourse Analysis and ethnic identity'. *Journal of Sociolinguistics*, 10(2), 205–24.

Piette, A. (2002), 'Translation on screen. The economic, multicultural, and pedagogical challenges of subtitling and dubbing'. *Benjamins Translation Library*, 42, 189–96.

Piller, I. (2001), 'Naturalization language testing and its basis in ideologies of national identity and citizenship'. *International Journal of Bilingualism*, 5, 259–77.

Piller, I. (2006), 'When life and policy intersect: language testing in the life of a multiple migrant'. Paper presented at *Sociolinguistics Symposium 16*, Limerick – Ireland, 6–8 July 2006.

Pinker, S. (1994), *The Language Instinct*. Harmondsworth: Penguin.

Postman, N. (1994), *The Disappearance of Childhood*. New York: Vintage Books.

Pragglejaz Group (2007) 'MIP: a method for identifying metaphorically used words in discourse'. *Metaphor and Symbol*, 22 (1), 1–39.

Preston, D. R. (2004), 'Folk metalanguage', in A. Jaworski, N. Coupland and D. Galasiński (eds), *Metalanguage: Social and Ideological Perspectives*. Berlin: de Gruyter, pp. 75–101.

Pugh, S. (2005), *The Democratic Genre: Fanfiction in a Literary Context*. Bridgend: Seren Books.

Pusch, L. F. (1984), *Das Deutsche als Männersprache*. Frankfurt/M.: Suhrkamp.

Rampton, B. (1999), 'Displacing the "native speaker": expertise, affiliation, and inheritance'. *ELT Journal*, 44(2), 97–101.

Rampton, B. (1995), *Crossing: Language and Ethnicity Among Adolescents*. London: Longman.

Rampton, B. (2001), 'Language crossing, cross-talk, and cross-disciplinarity in sociolinguistics', in N. Coupland, S. Sarangi and C. N. Candlin (eds), *Sociolinguistics and Social Theory*. London: Longman, pp. 261–96.

Rampton, B. (2006), *Language in Late Modernity: Interaction in an Urban School*. Cambridge: Cambridge University Press.

Reddy, M. J. (1993), 'The conduit metaphor: a case of frame conflict in our language about language', in A. Ortony (ed.), *Metaphor and Thought* (2nd edn). Cambridge: Cambridge University Press, pp. 164–201.

Ricento, T. (2000), 'Historical and theoretical perspectives in language policy and planning', in T. Ricento (ed.), *Ideology, Politics and Language Policies: Focus on English*. Amsterdam: John Benjamins, pp. 9–24.

Richardson, K. (2004), 'Retroshopping: sentiment, sensation and symbolism on the high street', in A. Jaworski, N. Coupland and D. Galasiński (eds), *Metalanguage: Social and Ideological Perspectives*. Berlin: Mouton de Gruyter, pp. 289–308.

Richardson, K. (2006), 'The dark arts of good people: how popular culture negotiates "spin" in NBC's *The West Wing*'. *Journal of Sociolinguistics*, 6(1), 52–69.

Rickford, J. (1999), 'The Ebonics controversy in my backyard: a sociolinguist's experiences and reflections'. *Journal of Sociolinguistics*, 3(2), 267–75.

Riggins, S. H. (1997), 'The rhetoric of othering.' In S. H. Riggins (ed.), *The Language and Politics of Exclusion: Others in Discourse*. Thousand Oaks, California: Sage, pp. 1–30.

Ritchie, D. (2003), ' "ARGUMENT IS WAR" – or is it a game of chess? Multiple meanings in the analysis of implicit metaphors'. *Metaphor and Symbol*, 18(2), 125–46.

Romaine, S. (1982), *Socio-historical Linguistics: Its Status and Methodology*. Cambridge: Cambridge University Press.

Ronkin, M. and Karn, H. E. (1999), 'Mock Ebonics: linguistic racism in parodies of Ebonics on the internet'. *Journal of Sociolinguistics*, 3(3), 360–80.

Rosaldo, M. Z. (1982), 'The things we do with words: Ilongot speech acts and speech act theory in philosophy'. *Language in Society*, 11, 203–38.

Ros-I-Garcia, M. (1984), 'Speech attitudes to speakers of language varieties in a bilingual situation'. *International Journal of the Sociology of Language*, 47, 73–90.

Rumsey, A. (1990), 'Wording, meaning, and linguistic ideology'. *American Anthropologist*, 92, 346–61.

Ryan, E. B. and Giles, H. (1982) (eds), *Attitudes Towards Language Variation*. London: Edward Arnold.

Ryan, M. L. (2004), *Narrative across Media: The Languages of Storytelling*. Lincoln, NE: University of Nebraska Press.

Said, E. (1978), *Orientalism*. Harmondsworth: Penguin.

Scannell, P. (1991), *Broadcast Talk*. London: Sage.

Schieffelin, B. B., Woolard, K. A. and Kroskrity, P. V. (1998) (eds), *Language Ideologies: Practice and Theory*. New York: Oxford University Press.

Schmitz, U. (2004), *Sprache in modernen Medien: Einführung in Tatsachen und Theorien, Themen und Thesen*. Berlin: Erich Schmidt.

Scollon, R. (1998), *Mediated Discourse as Social Interaction: A Study of News Discourse*. London: Longman.

Scott, M. (1999), *Wordsmith Tools*, Version 3. Oxford: Oxford University Press.

Searle, J. R. (1969), *Speech Acts: An Essay in the Philosophy of Language*. London: Cambridge University Press.

Sebba, M. (2007), *Orthography and Society: The Cultural Politics of Spelling around the World*. Cambridge: Cambridge University Press.

Semino, E. (2005), 'The metaphorical construction of complex domains: the case of speech activity in English'. *Metaphor and Symbol*, 20(1), 35–70.

Semino, E. and Masci, M. (1996), 'Politics is football: metaphor in the discourse of Silvio Berlusconi in Italy'. *Discourse and Society*, 7(2), 243–69.

Semino, E. and Short, M. (2004), *Corpus Stylistics: Speech, Writing and Thought Presentation in a Corpus of English Writing*. London: Routledge.

Sesonske, A. (1965), 'Performatives'. *Journal of Philosophy*, 62(17), 459–68.

Shannon, C. E. (1948), 'A mathematical theory of communication'. *Bell System Technical Journal*, 27, 379–423; 623–56.

Shohamy, E. (2001), *The Power of Tests: A Critical Perspective on the Uses of Language Tests*. New York: Longman.

Shohamy, E. (2006a), *Language Policy: Hidden Agendas and New Approaches*. London: Routledge.

Shohamy, E. (2006b), 'Language testing citizenship regime: why language? Why tests? Why citizenship? Why immigrants? What are the consequences?'. Paper presented at *Sociolinguistics Symposium 16*, Limerick, Ireland, 6–8 July 2006.

Shortis, T. (2001), *The Language of ICT – Information and Communication Technology*. London: Routledge.

Siemann, W. (1998), *The German Revolution of 1848–49*. London: St Martin's Press.

Siemann, W. (2001), 'The revolutions of 1848–1849 and the persistence of the old regime in Germany (1848–1850)', in J. Breuilly (ed.), *Nineteenth-Century Germany: Politics, Culture and Society, 1780–1918*. London: Arnold, pp. 117–37.

Silverstein, M. (1979), 'Language structure and linguistic ideology', in P. R. Clyne, W. F. Hanks and C. L. Hofbauer (eds), *The Elements: A Parasession on Linguistic Units and Levels*. Chicago: Chicago Linguistic Society, pp. 193–247.

Silverstein, M. and Urban, G. (1996) (eds), *Natural Histories of Discourse*. Chicago: University of Chicago Press.

Simanowski, R. (2002), 'Zeitgenossen: "Yatoo": Audiovisueller Hypertext als Roll-over-Lovepoem'. *Dichtung-digital* (available online at www.dichtung-digital.com/2002/01-21-Simanowski.htm, accessed 02.11.06).

Sperber, D. and Wilson, D. (1986), *Relevance: Communication and Cognition*. Oxford: Blackwell.

Spitulnik, D. (1996), 'The social circulation of media discourse and the mediation of communities'. *Journal of Linguistic Anthropology*, 6, 161–87.

Spitulnik, D. (1998), 'Mediating unity and diversity: the production of language ideologies in Zambian broadcasting', in B. B. Schieffelin, K. A. Woolard and P. V. Kroskrity (eds), *Language Ideologies: Practice and Theory*. New York: Oxford University Press, pp. 163–88.

Spitzmüller, J. (2005), *Metasprachdiskurse: Einstellungen zu Anglizismen und ihre wissenschaftliche Rezeption*. Berlin: de Gruyter.

Spolsky, B. (1997), 'The ethics of gatekeeping tests: what have we learned in a hundred years?'. *Language Testing*, 14, 242–7.

Standage, T. (1999) *The Victorian Internet: The Remarkable Story of the Telegraph and the Nineteenth-century's On-line Pioneers*, New York: Walker Company.

Stenschke, O. (2005), *Rechtschreiben, Recht sprechen, recht haben – Der Diskurs über die Rechtschreibreform. Eine linguistische Analyse des Streits in der Presse*. Tübingen: Niemeyer.

Sterne, J. (1999), 'Television under construction: American television and the problem of distribution, 1926–62'. *Media, Culture & Society*, 21, 503–30.

Stevenson, P. (2005), 'Once an *Ossi*, always an *Ossi*: language ideologies and social division in contemporary Germany', in N. Langer and W. V. Davies (eds), *Linguistic Purism in the Germanic Languages*. Berlin: Mouton de Gruyter, pp. 221–37.

Stevenson, P. (2006), 'National languages in transnational contexts: language, migration and citizenship in Europe', in C. Mar-Molinero and P. Stevenson (eds), *Language Ideologies, Policies and Practices: Language and the Future of Europe*. Basingstoke, UK: Palgrave Macmillan, pp. 147–61.

Storrer, A. (2002), 'Coherence in text and hypertext'. *Document Design*, 3(2), 156–68.

Stroud, C. and Heugh, K. (2004), 'Language rights and linguistic citizenship', in J. Freeland and D. Patrick (eds), *Language Rights and Language Survival: Sociolinguistic and Sociocultural Perspectives*. Manchester: St Jerome, pp. 191–218.

Suszczynska, M. (1999), 'Apologizing in English, Polish and Hungarian: different languages, different strategies'. *Journal of Pragmatics*, 31, 1053–65.

Sweetser, E. (1987), 'The definition of *lie*: an examination of the folk models underlying a linguistic prototype', in D. Holland and N. Quinn (eds), *Cultural Models in Language and Thought*. Cambridge: Cambridge University Press, pp. 43–66.

Tannen, D. (1990), *You Just Don't Understand: Women and Men in Conversation*. New York: Morrow.

Tannen, D. (1996), 'I'm sorry I won't apologize'. *The New York Times Magazine*, 21 July, 34–5.

Tattersall, A. (2003), 'The internet and the French language', *Centre for Language in Education: Occasional Paper No. 56*. Research & Graduate School of Education, University of Southhampton (available online at http://eric.ed.gov/ERICDocs/data/ericdocs2/content_storage_01/0000000b/80/22/0c/84.pdf, accessed 02.11.06).

Taylor, C. (2002), 'The subtitling of documentary films'. *Rassegna Italiana di Linguistica Applicata*, 34(1/2), 143–60.

Thomas, J. (1995), *Meaning in Interaction*. London: Longman.

Thompson, G. (1996) 'Voices in the text: discourse perspectives on language reports'. *Applied Linguistics*, 17(4), 501–30.

Thompson, J. B. (1984), *Studies in the Theory of Ideology*. Oxford: Polity Press.

Thornborrow, J. and van Leeuwen, T. (2001) (eds), 'Authenticity in media discourse'. *Discourse Studies*, 3(4), 391–498.

Thurlow, C. (2001a), 'Talkin' 'bout my communication: communication awareness in early adolescence'. *Language Awareness*, 10(2/3), 213–31.

Thurlow, C. (2001b), 'Language and the internet', in R. Mesthrie and R. Asher (eds), *The Concise Encyclopedia of Sociolinguistics*. London: Pergamon, pp. 287–9.

Thurlow, C. (2003), 'Generation Txt? The sociolinguistics of young people's text-messaging'. *Discourse Analysis Online*, 1(1) (available online at www.shu.ac.uk/daol/, accessed 02.11.06).

Thurlow, C. (2005), 'Deconstructing adolescent communication', in A. Williams and C. Thurlow (eds), *Talking Adolescence: Perspectives on Communication in the Teenage Years*. New York: Peter Lang, pp. 1–20.

Thurlow, C. (2006), 'From statistical panic to moral panic: the metadiscursive construction and popular exaggeration of new-media language in the print media'. *Journal of Computer-Mediated Communication*, 11(3), article 1 (available online at http://.jcmc.indiana.edu/vol11/issue3/thurlow.html#introduction, accessed 02.11.06).

Thurlow, C. and Jaworski, A. (2003), 'Communicating a global reach: inflight magazines as a globalizing genre in tourism'. *Journal of Sociolinguistics*, 7(4), 579–606.

Thurlow, C. and McKay, S. (2003), 'Profiling "new" communication technologies in adolescence'. *Journal of Language and Social Psychology*, 22(1), 94–103.

Thurlow, C., Lengel, L. and Tomic, A. (2004), *Computer-Mediated Communication: Social Interaction and the Internet*. London: Sage.

Truss, L. (2003), *Eats, Shoots and Leaves. The Zero Tolerance Approach to Punctuation*. London: Profile Books.

Urla, J. (2001), 'Outlaw language: creating alternative public spheres in Basque free radio', in S. Gal and K. Woolard (eds), *Languages and Publics: The Making of Authority*. Manchester: St Jerome, pp. 140–63.

Urban, G. (1996), 'Entextualization, replication, and power.' In M. Silverstein and G.Urban (eds) *Natural Histories of Discourse*. Chicago: University of Chicago Press, pp. 21–44.

van Dijk, T. (1991), *Racism and the Press*. London: Routledge.

van Dijk, T. (1993), 'Principles of critical discourse analysis'. *Discourse and Society*, 4, (2), 249–83.

van Leeuwen, T. (1993), 'Language and representation: The recontextualisation of participants, activities and reactions'. Unpublished PhD thesis, University of Sydney.

van Leeuwen, T. (1999), *Speech, Music, Sound*. London: Palgrave.

van Leeuwen, T. (2001), 'What is authenticity?' *Discourse Studies*, 3, 392–6.

van Leeuwen, T. (2004a), *Introducing Social Semiotics*. London: Routledge.

van Leeuwen, T. (2004b), 'Metalanguage in social life'. In A. Jaworski, N. Coupland and D. Galasiński (eds) *Metalanguage: Social and Ideological Perspectives*. Berlin: Mouton de Gruyter, pp. 107–30.

Vanparys, J. (1995), 'A survey of metalinguistic metaphors', in L. Goosens, P. Pauwels, B. Rudzka-Ostyn, A.-M. Simon-Vandenbergen and J. Vanparys (eds), *By Word of Mouth: Metaphor, Metonymy and Linguistic Action in a Cognitive Perspective*. Amsterdam: John Benjamins, pp. 1–34.

Verschueren, J. (2004), 'Notes on the role of metapragmatic awareness in language use', in A. Jaworski, N. Coupland and D. Galasiński (eds), *Metalanguage: Social and Ideological Perspectives*. Berlin: Mouton de Gruyter, pp. 53–74.

Voloshinov, V. N. (1973), *Marxism and the Philosophy of Language*. London: Seminar Press.

Wallerstein, I. (1983), *Historical Capitalism*. London: Verso.

Wallerstein, I. ([1991] 2001), *Unthinking Social Science: The Limits of Nineteenth-Century Paradigms*. Philadelphia: Temple University Press.

Walther, J. B. and Parks, M. R. (2002), 'Cues filtered out, cues filtered in: computer-mediated communication and relationships', in M. L. Knapp and J. A. Daly (eds), *The Handbook of Interpersonal Communication*. Thousand Oaks, CA: Sage, pp. 529–63.

Watson, I. (2003), *Broadcasting in Irish: Minority Languages, Radio, Television and Identity*. Dublin: Four Courts Press.

Watts, R. J. (1999), 'The ideology of dialect in Switzerland', in J. Blommaert (ed.), *Language Ideological Debates*. Berlin: Mouton de Gruyter, pp. 67–103.

Wee, L. (2002), 'The semiotics of metaphor: the conduit metaphor in Singapore's language policy'. *Journal of Language and Politics*, 1, 199–220.

Wee, L. (2004), '"Extreme communicative acts" and the boosting of illocutionary force'. *Journal of Pragmatics*, 36, 2161–78.

Wiener, N. ([1948] 1961), *Cybernetics: Or, Control and Communication in the Animal and the Machine*. New York: MIT Press.

Wierzbicka, A. (1985), 'Different cultures, different languages, different speech acts'. *Journal of Pragmatics*, 7(9), 145–78.

Wierzbicka, A. (1991), *Cross-cultural Pragmatics: The Semantics of Human Interaction*. Berlin: Mouton de Gruyter.

Wierzbicka, A. (1996), 'Contrastive sociolinguistics and the theory of "cultural scripts": Chinese vs. English', in M. Hellinger and U. Ammon (eds), *Contrastive Sociolinguistics*. Berlin: Mouton de Gruyter, pp. 313–44.

Williams, R. (1977), *Marxism and Literature*. New York: Oxford University Press.

Wolfram, W. (1998), 'Scrutinizing linguistic gratuity: issues from the field'. *Journal of Sociolinguistics*, 2(2), 271–9.

Woolard, K. (1987), 'Codeswitching and comedy in Catalonia'. *IPrA Papers in Pragmatics*, 1(1), 106–22.

Woolard, K. (1992), 'Language ideology: issues and approaches'. *Pragmatics*, 2(3), 235–50.

Woolard, K. (1998a), 'Introduction: language ideology as a field of inquiry', in B. Schieffelin, K. Woolard and P. Kroskrity (eds), *Language Ideologies: Practice and Theory*. New York: Oxford University Press, pp. 3–47.

Woolard, K. (1998b), 'Simultaneity and bivalency as strategies in bilingualism'. *Journal of Linguistic Anthropology*, 8, 3–29.

Woolard, K. and Gahng, T.-J. (1990), 'Changing language policies and attitudes in autonomous Catalonia'. *Language in Society*, 9(3), 311–30.

Woolard, K. and B. B. Schieffelin (1994), 'Language ideology.' *Annual Review of Anthropology*, 23, 55–82.

Wyn, J. (2005), 'Youth in the media: adult stereotypes of young people', in A. Williams and C. Thurlow (eds), *Talking Adolescence: Perspectives on Communication in the Teenage Years*. New York: Peter Lang, pp. 53–71.

Wyn, J. and White, R. (1997) *Rethinking Youth*. London: Sage.

Wynne, M., Short, M. and Semino, E. (1998), 'A corpus-based investigation of speech, thought and writing presentation in English narrative texts', in A. Renouf (ed.), *Explorations in Corpus Linguistics*. Amsterdam: Rodopi, pp. 231–45.

Zabel, H. (1997), *Widerworte. 'Lieber Herr Grass, Ihre Aufregung ist unbegründet.' Antworten an Gegner und Kritiker der Rechtschreibreform*. Aachen: Shaker Verlag/ AOL Verlag.

Index